Forging a Total Force

FORGING
A TOTAL FORCE
The Evolution of the Guard and Reserve

Col. Forrest L. Marion, USAFR (ret.)
Col. Jon T. Hoffman, USMCR (ret.)

Historical Office • Office of the Secretary of Defense • 2018

This volume is cleared for public release. The views expressed or implied within are solely those of the authors and do not necessarily represent the views of the Department of Defense, the Office of the Secretary of Defense, or any other agency of the federal government. Portions of this work may be quoted or reprinted without permission, provided that a standard source credit line is included. The Historical Office of the Office of the Secretary of Defense would appreciate a courtesy copy of reprints or reviews.

Use of ISBN

 This is the official U.S. Government edition of this publication and is herein identified to certify its authenticity. Use of 978-0-16-094388-1 is for the U.S. Government Publishing Office editions only. The Superintendent of Documents of the U.S. Government Publishing Office requests that any reprinted edition clearly be labeled a copy of the authentic work with a new ISBN.

Library of Congress Cataloging-in-Publication Data

Names: Marion, Forrest L., author. | Hoffman, Jon T., 1955– author.
Title: Forging a total force : the evolution of the Guard and Reserve / Forrest L. Marion, Jon T. Hoffman.
Other titles: Evolution of the Guard and Reserve
Description: Washington, DC : Historical Office, Office of the Secretary of Defense, 2018. | Includes bibliographical references and index.
Identifiers: LCCN 2017059869 | ISBN 9780160943881 (alk. paper)
Subjects: LCSH: United States—National Guard—History. | United States—Armed Forces—Reserves—History. | United States. Army—Reserves—History.
Classification: LCC UA42 .M35 2018 | DDC 355.3/70973—dc23

LC record available at https://lccn.loc.gov/2017059869

Cover Photo: National Guard soldiers talking about procedures during a training exercise at the Joint Multinational Readiness Center. (*Army photo by SFC Tyrone Walker. Source: Official DoD Photo Library.*)

♾ *The paper used in this publication meets the requirements for permanence established by the American National Standard for Information Sciences "Permanence of Paper for Printed Library Materials" (ANSI Z39.48-1984).*

For sale by the Superintendent of Documents, U.S. Government Publishing Office
Internet: bookstore.gpo.gov   Phone: toll free (866) 512-1800;   DC area (202) 512-1800
Fax: (202) 512-2104 Mail: Stop IDCC, Washington, DC 20402-0001

ISBN 978-0-16-094388-1

Contents

Foreword

This book is different from the one I encouraged and authorized in 2011—different, but better. While serving as assistant secretary of defense for reserve affairs, preceded by service in the Marine Corps and its reserve, I had a keen awareness of the contributions the men and women of the National Guard and reserve had made since our country was attacked in September of 2001. I believed those contributions needed to be analyzed and recorded by trained historians. I worried that if they were not well preserved, they would not be adequately appreciated in the future.

Taking that charter to heart, Jon Hoffman and Erin Mahan from the Historical Office of the Office of the Secretary of Defense found Forrest Marion to collaborate with Jon on the writing effort. This team has fought through many challenges to produce a work that not only describes the post-9/11 contributions of the reserve and Guard, but puts those contributions into the context to which they properly belong.

Dr. Marion and Mr. Hoffman trace philosophical and political disagreements, challenges met and missed, opportunities seized and lost. They show us history that is complicated in some ways, but very simple in others. It is a story of cyclical repetition of attitudes and prejudices that have sometimes prevented the United States from taking maximum advantage of the potential of its force of citizen-warriors. I would describe this cycle as an example of a phenomenon called "lessons frequently observed, but seldom learned."

But the authors also show us a history of periodic but important success—times at which the friction inherent in our multi-service, full time-part time, state-federal defense structure has been overcome, leading to success on the battlefield. Too often, however, that friction is overcome only at great cost of blood, treasure, and time.

In successive chapters, the authors take us on a methodical march through centuries and decades, recording the ebb and flow of national readiness. They demonstrate that the overall readiness of the armed forces is closely linked, if not directly proportional, to the readiness and capability of the National Guard and reserve. The commentary accompanying this review also shows that the proportional relationship between active and reserve readiness has often been ignored by senior defense leaders until they find themselves unhappily surprised by crises requiring rapid expansion and employment of military and naval forces.

The analysis by Marion and Hoffman provides an interesting review of the mobilization of reserve component forces for Operations Desert Shield and

Storm in 1990–1991. They allude to a congressional concern "that there was an "anti-reserve bias at work" that started with the administration's decision to use the most limited mobilization authority available, followed by a complaint from the defense secretary that limits on the service of reserve units made their employment difficult. Having been personally involved as a serving officer in both the mobilization and its aftermath, and given the long history of active-reserve relations, I believe the authors may be understating the reluctance of all the services in 1990–1991 to employ their reserve components and the support of that reluctant attitude by civilian defense leaders.[1]

The authors do, however, capture the extent of Guard and reserve contributions during the first Gulf War and highlight some of the challenges they faced—challenges that would be addressed, if not completely resolved, in the succeeding decade.

In reviewing the aftermath of Desert Storm, Hoffman and Marion point out many of the major policy issues that informed, but did not perfect, the planning for the next major mobilization. The services began to focus on the importance of family readiness and support during and after mobilization. The negative effects of demobilization uncertainty on individual service members, their families, and employers were at least recognized, as were problems with premobilization and predeployment medical and dental care. Gaps in employer support, and the potential of ESGR (Employer Support of the Guard and Reserve) volunteers, gained new prominence, setting the stage for a stronger ESGR program after 9/11. Despite improvements, we are shown how these issues and others would continue to challenge both service members and Defense policymakers during the extended mobilization of the next two decades.

In the years following the first Gulf War, the Air Force Reserve and Air National Guard remained continuously involved in the day-to-day missions of the Air Force. The Marine Corps Reserve retained reasonably close connections with active component formations. The Navy Reserve dramatically changed its structure and fought the "TAR wars." But the Army National Guard and Army Reserve continued to struggle to find a modus operandi with the active component and with each other.

As the authors point out, hard feelings continued to exist on all sides of the active-reserve component divide, and were certainly not limited to the Army.

---

1. While serving as assistant secretary of defense, I had the good fortune to hear someone who was present in the room describe the interaction between the president, his secretary of defense, and the chairman of the Joint Chiefs of Staff as they discussed—among other things—the mobilization of the Guard and reserves. Based on that "oral history" I believe the authors have correctly captured that attitude, but I now know it was not shared by President Bush (41).

The enforced interdependence of combat in 1991 had not lasted long enough to create much of an increase in familiarity and mutual confidence. The next decades would change that to a significant degree.

The three words that dominate the discussion of the National Guard and reserves following 9/11 are combat, mobilization, and integration. Combat was the necessary end state for many reserve units, and was the reason for their mobilization. The result was integration of the active and reserve components to an extent that had not existed since World War II. The mobilization-combat-integration continuum was not always pretty, as Dr. Marion and Mr. Hoffman well describe. Structural defects compounded long-standing attitudinal issues, but many defects and issues were overcome, and most were at least addressed in some way, making possible the closest thing to wartime mobilization many of us "seasoned observers" ever expected to see or experience.

That extended mobilization continued as combat operations in Afghanistan and Iraq evolved, continuing to create both practical and political challenges. We see the impact Secretary of Defense Rumsfeld had on several of the key policy issues related to unexpectedly sustaining a call to active duty that was spread over the whole of the reserve and National Guard. Mr. Rumsfeld spoke publicly about the need to be "respectful" of reservist's commitments, but he began those remarks by saying, "I was once a weekend warrior too." It is hard to believe he really grasped what the men and women of Guard and reserve had become or appreciated their potential. Many of Secretary Rumsfeld's subsequent decisions on reserve component policy verified both his own lack of understanding and the fact that he frequently ignored or rejected the advice of both uniformed and civilian officials.

The authors describe the way Department of Defense and uniformed service leaders dealt with issues like unit cross-leveling, the disparate impacts of predeployment training, recognition for new approaches to family health care and for postdeployment and ongoing care after reservists returned to their communities.[2]

Lest anyone think that a description of the post-9/11 service of the National Guard and reserves is all about combat, the authors provide an excellent—albeit abbreviated—account of the response to Hurricane Katrina in 2005. Again, there were issues of knowledge, culture, and organizational and command relationships. But the bottom line was that the National Guard led the way with valuable support from active component and Federal Reserve forces to serve the people of the Gulf Coast region. Friction existed, but was largely overcome.

---

2. I mean to take nothing away from Dr. Marion and Mr. Hoffman when I say we still need a book that provides more insight into what the troops have to say about those same issues.

The authors' description of Robert Gates' tenure as Secretary of Defense provides many insights. Describing the fact that two Army National Guard "chiefs" (Steve Blum and Clyde Vaughn) convinced him to make a significant change in mobilization policy is telling. On many issues, Secretary Gates listened—a welcome change.

But on some other issues, his mind was made up. When I interviewed with him in 2009 he told me he thought, "We [DoD] have played a 'bait and switch' on the Guard and reserve—we are asking them to do things they never signed up for." Recklessly for a job seeker, I responded: "I disagree, sir. Everyone serving today in the Guard or reserves either enlisted or re-enlisted since 9/11. They knew exactly what they were signing on for." He said something to the effect that he hadn't thought about it that way, and I thought I had hit a home run. Several weeks later, however, he gave a major speech that included the "bait and switch" observation. Years later, when I read his memoir, *Duty*, I learned that he had made that same "bait and switch" comment to President George W. Bush when interviewing with the president to be SecDef. Deeply held beliefs are hard to change.

The evolution of counterinsurgency doctrine and its increasing application in both Iraq and Afghanistan opened additional opportunities for the reserve and Guard to contribute, sometimes in unique ways. Civilian-acquired skills— agriculture, law enforcement, municipal operations—were embedded in many reserve component units. All services found ways to make some use of those skills, creating another waypoint on the journey from being exclusively an "emergency—break glass in time of war" force to a reliable partner for the active component in the full spectrum of military operations.

Homeland defense and consequence management missions continued to evolve and force structure was revised, particularly by the Air National Guard in response to combined pressure from BRAC closures, aircraft modernization, and the emergence of remotely piloted air vehicles (RPV, drone, UAS).

The review of various studies of reserve component policy since 9/11 points out the unresolved existence of structural barriers that impede the integration of the active and reserve components, and limit the opportunities to take full advantage of the capabilities of both.

But the authors conclude with a review of the case for making the National Guard and reserves a full partner with the active component that should be considered a continuously available resource, dependable and valuable in both peace and war. It appears this case is gaining traction in some quarters, but is unfortunately being ignored in others.

An enduring issue adversely affecting both the active and reserve compo-nents has been their general lack of mutual understanding and respect. Peri-odically, efforts are made to bridge that gap. For example, in 1984 Congress overruled DoD objections and insisted that there be an assistant secretary of defense exclusively focused on "Reserve Affairs" with a broad mandate of oversight and advice to the secretary of defense. Later, again over DoD and service opposition, Congress mandated that three-star officers oversee each of the seven components of the National Guard and reserves. But as the authors also point out, such efforts are difficult to sustain.

Although not described by the authors, Congress was convinced several years ago to revert to a former organizational construct by eliminating the office of ASD(RA), and recently the Senate has proposed the elimination of the three-star reserve and Guard leaders. It remains to be seen how these actions will work out, but at least we have this book to describe the antecedents and precedents for those actions, and to provide insight into the historical highs and lows of Guard and reserve capability. I am not certain we would have that insight if there had not been an ASD(RA) in 2011.

On a purely personal note, throughout this work I read the names and recalled with great admiration the contributions of many colleagues—my predecessors as ASD(RA), my contemporaries and successors as "reserve chiefs," many adjutants general, and others with whom I have had the pleasure of serving. Each of these trailblazers overcame headwinds and adversity in helping to make possible the contributions of the nation's citizen warriors. I take pleasure in knowing them.

As with any work of historical analysis, not everyone will agree with all that Forrest Marion and Jon Hoffman have written. Much scholarship remains undone in the realms of active-reserve component relations, maximizing the impact of defense spending, the role of the citizen-warrior, and many other related issues. This work creates a framework for such scholarship and will, I hope, inspire others to explore where we are, where we should go, and how to get there.

Dennis M. McCarthy
Columbus, Ohio

Preface

In September 1995 Air Force Chief of Staff Ronald R. Fogleman addressed the annual convention of the National Guard Association of the United States. He spoke of what he viewed as "America's return to the militia nation concept." He recounted his own experience three decades earlier flying fighter aircraft in Southeast Asia alongside air guardsmen, including one who made the ultimate sacrifice. During a later assignment with the reserves, the future chief of staff gained further appreciation for the particular issues faced by citizen-soldiers from all the services. General Fogleman emphasized to the guardsmen in attendance: "Certainly a fundamental precept of our American military tradition is that the United States of America is a militia nation." To underscore the point, he repeated: "It is a militia nation."[1]

Broadly addressing the nation's military experience in the remainder of his speech, Fogleman noted the Cold War-era reliance on large standing forces, which he termed "an aberration in our history," the result of a dangerous threat from the Soviet Union. The 1970s' Total Force policy led, by the end of the following decade, to "some of the highest states of readiness [of the reserve component] in the peacetime history of our nation." From the perspective of the middle of the 1990s General Fogleman viewed the ongoing drawdown as closer to a demobilization, one "taking us back toward our traditional reliance on Guard and Reserve forces."[2]

Nearly two decades later, Fogleman returned to his earlier theme. In 2012 the nation had just withdrawn its forces from Iraq. The former chief of staff addressed the current manpower dilemma affecting the nation's armed forces, stating: "In its current form, the force has become unaffordable. Total personnel costs are consuming more than half of the DoD budget. Nonetheless, our nation deserves a modern, balanced and ready defense." His answer remained what it had been in 1995: "We should return to our historic roots as a militia nation . . . the constitutional construct for our military." Summarizing, Fogleman wrote that senior leaders both military and civilian needed "to recognize there is a way back to a smaller active military and a larger militia posture. The fiscal environment and emerging threats demand it."[3]

While General Fogleman suggested the time had come for a reevaluation of the nation's force structure vis-à-vis the regular and reserve components, in spring 2011 the assistant secretary of defense for reserve affairs, Dennis M. McCarthy, conceived the project that evolved into the present volume. A retired lieutenant general who had commanded the Marine Forces Reserve from 2001 to 2005, he wanted to highlight the transition of the reserve component from the Cold War era's strategic force to the post-9/11 era's operational role. McCarthy also wanted to call attention to the major issues that the reserve component was still dealing with despite those "historic roots as a militia nation." While the policy areas addressed in the following chapters—especially the activation or mobilization of the reserves—are primarily related to manpower and personnel rather than equipment, logistics, and infrastructure, that focus does not minimize the significance of industrial mobilization issues. Rather, it recognizes that the manpower mobilization concerns of the reserve component generally differ greatly from the active force and have dominated the attention of political and military policymakers for more than two hundred years.[4]

The original plan called for a single background chapter covering the years prior to 1990. As the research progressed it became clear that a number of issues—for example, training, volunteerism, unit integrity, friction and cultural differences between the components, and the question of who gets called in a limited conflict—were long-term concerns for the reserves, the Pentagon, and Congress. That history required more detailed treatment to understand how the reserve component got to where it was in 1990, resulting in an expansion from one chapter to three.

Chapter One (1790–1918) sketches the unsteady path from colonial times, when every able-bodied male was considered a citizen-soldier capable of taking the field with little or no training, to the modern era requiring much better preparation for combat. Policy changes never kept up with that changing necessity. Chapter Two (1919–1953) outlines the reserves' role from the interwar period through World War Two and the Korean conflict. The Armed Forces Reserve Act of 1952 became the first—and is still the only—comprehensive legislation specifically for the reserve component. Despite the shock of no-notice mobilization for Korea, the law still did not fully address the need for more and better peacetime training, resulting in continuing over-reliance on veterans as the source of ready citizen-soldiers. Chapter Three (1954–1989) brings the narrative to the Cold War's close. The advent of the Selected Reserve, coupled with the Reagan-era defense buildup, produced a reserve component that was better-trained, better-equipped, and more combat-ready than it had ever been during any peaceful era in U.S. history. For the first time since the minutemen of the Revolutionary War era, the reserves approached realistic mobilization timelines not merely in rhetoric but in practice.

The core of this study is focused on the period from 1990 to 2011, with particular emphasis on the decade after 9/11. Chapter Four (1990–2000) highlights the Persian Gulf conflict and the defense reviews and military drawdown of the 1990s. That decade brought increasing reliance upon the reserve component, as the Total Force policy of the 1970s had envisioned. In the wake of the Cold War, a smaller active component became more dependent upon the reserves than it had been since the early days of the republic. Chapter Five (2001–June 2003) focuses on the mobilization and activation of reservists from 9/11 through the middle of 2003, at which point the initial objectives in Afghanistan and Iraq appeared to have been achieved. Despite all the progress made over the previous two decades, serious problems arose as the nation drew heavily on its reserve forces for two major campaigns. Chapter Six (July 2003–December 2006) covers the struggles of the services with Defense Department mobilization policies and practices that were more restrictive than the law required, and seemed to threaten long-term access to reserve ground forces. Meanwhile, various initiatives affecting reservists' health care and family readiness brought incremental improvement and helped sustain the force during a period of high operational tempo.

Chapter Seven (2007–2011) addresses a new defense secretary's revision of mobilization policy in January 2007 that instituted periodic—and predictable—12-month call-ups (primarily for the Army National Guard and Army Reserve, since the other reserve components generally already relied on shorter periods of active duty). Chapter Eight suggests that the nation's increased reliance upon the reserve component in recent years is not so much a new paradigm as a return to its original mission, in consonance with General Fogleman's apt reference to the United States as a "militia nation." It summarizes the primary issues, many of them recurring throughout the history of the reserve component, which policymakers will need to grapple with as they forge the way ahead, especially if the nation's citizen-soldiers continue to serve as an operational force.

Acknowledgments

As with any such effort, we have accrued numerous debts since November 2011, when work began on this project. While we cannot hope to mention every individual who provided timely assistance or encouragement, we would be remiss not to name several.

Special thanks go to Ms. Betty Kennedy, former director of historical services at Air Force Reserve Command, who encouraged Dr. Marion to apply for the project just after he returned from Afghanistan in 2011, and to Dr. Charlie O'Connell, director of the Air Force Historical Research Agency (AFHRA), who allowed Dr. Marion to put his name in the hat and then to work out of AFHRA while detailed to the Office of the Secretary of Defense (OSD) Historical Office. Retired MSgt. Craig Mackey, also of AFHRA, performed the indispensable work of transcribing fully one-half of the 30 interviews for this project. Retired Brig. Gen. David McGinnis, the acting assistant secretary of defense for reserve affairs in 2011, selected Dr. Marion and later sat for an interview. Cdr. Ruby Collins, Rear Adm. Steven Day, and retired Master Chief Petty Officer, Coast Guard Reserve Forces, Jeff D. Smith at U.S. Coast Guard headquarters offered invaluable assistance in researching the smallest of the armed forces (Day and Smith sat for interviews). Retired Capt. Jim Grover, in the Office of the Chief of Navy Reserve, provided timely Navy Reserve documents and introduced several key personnel who agreed to interviews. Dr. Joe Gross, former director of the Air National Guard history program, wrote several books that were quite helpful in the research effort. Retired Chief Warrant Officer 3 Robin Porche of the G-1 office, Marine Forces Reserve, sat for an interview and was always available to check draft paragraphs as the manuscript progressed. Lt. Col. Jeff Larrabee, chief of historical services at the National Guard Bureau, coordinated interviews with Guard personnel and provided fact-checking assistance. Dr. Kathryn Coker and Dr. John Boyd, Office of Army Reserve History, provided copies of published Army Reserve histories, valuable feedback, and fact-checking. Numerous other historians, archivists, and specialists at various history offices, archives, and libraries—including the historic Navy Department Library (Washington Navy Yard, Washington, DC), the Alfred M. Gray Marine Corps Research Center (Quantico, Virginia) and the Fairchild

Information Research Center (formerly Air University Library) at Maxwell Air Force Base, Alabama—also assisted us.

Thanks to the several chiefs of staff at the Office of the Assistant Secretary of Defense for Reserve Affairs and their professional staffs, who supported the project across the years. The members of the manuscript review panel hosted by the OSD Historical Office in September 2014 gave their valuable time and insights, which resulted in a better manuscript: Dr. Jeffrey Barlow, Naval History and Heritage Command; Dr. David Chu, president, Institute for Defense Analysis (and former under secretary of defense for personnel and readiness); Col. Nicholas Gentile, U.S. Air Force, operations officer, Air National Guard Staff, National Guard Bureau; Lt. Col. Jeffrey Larrabee, U.S. Army, chief, Historical Services, National Guard Bureau; Dr. Jim Malachowski, director, Air Force Reserve Command Historical Services; Lt. Gen. Dennis McCarthy, USMC (ret.), CEO, Military Experts (former commander, Marine Forces Reserve and assistant secretary of defense for reserve affairs); Charles Melson, chief historian, Marine Corps History Division; Dr. John Smith, senior historian, Air Force History and Museums Program; and Mr. Tom Welke, deputy director, Operations, Mobilization and Readiness, U.S. Army Reserve Command. Dr. Erin Mahan, chief historian of the OSD Historical Office, supported the project in myriad ways and saw it through to completion, supported by Carolyn Thorne, who coordinated many administrative issues. A number of historians at the OSD Historical Office provided research support, including Dr. Joseph Arena, Dr. Ryan Carpenter, Dr. Anthony Crain, Michael Fasulo, David Hadley, Rachel Levandoski, Dr. Shannon Mohan, and Dr. Corbin Williamson. Dr. Allen Mikaelian did yeoman's work as the primary editor, and Sandra Doyle shepherded the manuscript through final editing and production.

Last but not least, we want to thank our families—Jon's wife, Mary; and Forrest's wife, April, and their children, Nathan, Timothy, Bethany, and Hannah—for their love and support. Nathan and Timothy are both now junior Marine Corps officers and carrying on the tradition of service to our nation.

— CHAPTER 1 —

The Long Road from "Every Citizen a Soldier," 1790–1918

The proto-democracies of ancient Greece and the early Roman Republic equated citizenship with military responsibility—every male who had a right to vote was automatically a soldier, required to maintain his own arms, and subject to the call to duty whenever his nation needed him. From the early Anglo-Saxon days, England also required citizens to provide their own weapons and serve in the militia—a part-time army available for local defense. In the 18th century authorities continued to extol the traditional militia system, but in fact Great Britain had shifted to a professional army. Its colonists in America, however, were too poor to support a permanent armed force and had no immediate threats from nearby nations, so they came to see a standing military as wasteful, undemocratic, and a threat to liberty. Hence they reverted to reliance on a universal militia, with every free male citizen obliged to keep himself armed and available for service. A training manual printed in Boston in 1758 emphasized that a free government required every man to "think it his truest honor to be a citizen soldier." While Americans would hold, in theory, to that view for many years to come, in practice the emerging nation would adapt over time to a more professional and selective military force. The battle between the citizen-soldier ideal and the changing practical requirements of national defense set the stage for many of the policy challenges that the reserve component of the United States faced throughout its history and still faces today.[1]

The Colonial Period

Another well-established tradition in British North America in the 1700s was the common belief that militia forces were equal, if not superior, to a regular army. In several 18th-century joint operations with British forces, the militia learned to mistrust the regulars. In 1711 a British expedition to capture Quebec failed when the commander lost heart and turned back. The militia, now unsupported, also had to withdraw. In 1740–1741 a British naval expedition including militias from nine colonies failed to take Cartagena in the

Spanish Caribbean, strengthening the colonists' low view of British regulars. On the other hand, in 1745, British regular and New England militia forces captured the French fortress at Louisbourg. The admirable performance of the militia in that battle furthered the belief of citizen-soldiers that they were as capable as regulars.[2]

The type and composition of colonial militias took several forms, basically distinguished as either volunteer or standing (also known as common or enrolled) militia. Under colonial law the military-aged, able-bodied, free males in a community comprised the standing militia. Normally, they were organized into company-size units, provided their own arms, and elected their officers. Today's National Guard traces its lineage to the first three militia regiments formed in Massachusetts in 1636. When it came to operational employment, however, in most cases standing militia units served as manpower pools that colonial governments drew from to form volunteer units. This practice, foreshadowing to a degree the contemporary theme of reserve component volunteerism, enabled some militia members from each locale to stay at home to tend farms and businesses while remaining available for local defense.[3]

The colonies also resorted to volunteer units because their laws generally restricted the standing militia to service within defined geographical boundaries, making it largely a force for local operations. Offensive expeditions such as Cartagena and Louisbourg thus could only be carried out by volunteers. For these missions, volunteer units often fleshed out their ranks by recruiting males who were not obligated to serve in the militia, including "farm boys, apprentices, and village loafers," according to one historian. As a consequence of this overreliance on ill-trained and poorly equipped recruits, and lack of unit cohesion, ad hoc volunteer units earned the contempt of British regulars who fought alongside them and assumed that all militias suffered from the same shortcomings. The geographic limitation on the employment of standing militia was one of the first instances of government policy having a significant impact on reserve component mission performance. There would be many more to come.[4]

During the American War of Independence (1775–1783) the Continental Congress authorized a national military force, the Continental Army, but also partly relied on state militias. Throughout the conflict these two types of units served together in a relationship at once competitive and complementary. As Continental Army units improved their training and discipline, they gradually earned a reputation for steadiness in battle, but the militias' performance against the British varied considerably. In the northern theater, militia units proved themselves in several major engagements, including Bunker Hill (1775) and the critical victory at Saratoga (1777). But at Kips Bay (1776) the "greenest of green American troops" fled, as historian David McCullough wrote, "in pell-mell panic" despite General George Washington's enraged attempts to rally them. In the South the militia broke and fled at Camden (1780) but fought with skill and valor at King's Mountain (1780) and Cowpens (1781), key battles leading to Cornwallis' surrender at Yorktown.[5]

The Early National Period

With the war's end, the new nation's military policies were caught up in the larger political debate over the powers of the central government. Those in favor of a strong national government wanted a standing army. Their opponents wanted to retain more authority in the states and argued that militias could meet security needs. Ultimately the U.S. Constitution authorized a national army, known today as the regular component, and state militias, which became the basis of the modern reserve component. The powers granted to Congress, in Article I, Section 8, included the following:

> To raise and support Armies, but no Appropriation of Money to that Use shall be for a longer Term than two Years;

> To provide and maintain a Navy;

> To make Rules for the Government and Regulation of the land and naval Forces;

> To provide for calling forth the Militia to execute the Laws of the Union, suppress Insurrections and repel Invasions;

> To provide for organizing, arming, and disciplining the Militia, and for governing such Part of them as may be employed in the Service of the United States, reserving to the States respectively, the Appointment of the Officers, and the Authority of training the Militia according to the discipline prescribed by Congress.[6]

The Founders chose their words carefully. The distinction between "*raise and support* Armies" and "*provide and maintain* a Navy" was not inconsequential. It reflected the traditional fear of standing armies, brought from Europe and reinforced by colonial experience. In the late 18th century more than a few Americans expected their armies to be short-term entities, established as needed for emergencies. A navy, on the other hand, was essential, even in peacetime, to commerce on the high seas and was not deemed a threat to civil liberty. Likewise the missions of the militia were all inside the nation's borders and maintained the standing militia's emphasis on strategic defense.[7]

In May 1792, stirred by a proposal from President George Washington in conjunction with recent military failures against the Indians in the Northwest Territory, Congress enacted legislation to better implement the Constitution's militia clauses. The Calling Forth Act of 1792 specified the manner in which the militia could be used in federal service to fulfill constitutional roles "to execute the Laws of the Union, suppress Insurrections and repel Invasions." Because both the Federalists and their Republican opponents feared foreign incursions, Congress allowed the president considerable freedom in mobilizing the militia to repel invading armies—a policy that would continue into the modern era under various statutes. But Republican-inspired wariness regarding the militia's use in domestic disturbances resulted in certain restrictions. When enforcing the laws of the land, Congress required a federal judge to notify the president that local authorities were incapable of doing so prior to calling on the militia. The affected state legislature or its governor also had to request federal assistance.[8]

One week after passing the Calling Forth Act, Congress approved the Militia Act of 1792. The law required free, white, able-bodied males between the ages of 18 and 45, with some exceptions, to enroll in their state's militia, provide their own arms and accoutrements, and muster for training. While those forces were available for federal duty, states were not required to coordinate their militia plans or create standardized units that could be quickly integrated into a national military campaign. Because the act left it to the states to enforce compliance by citizen-soldiers, the law represented "the triumph of the Republicans over the Federalists in militia affairs." A post–World War II U.S. Army mobilization study opined, "It was a delusion to suppose that the male population would comply with this requirement when there was no penalty . . . for failure to do so." A 1795 modification to the legislation clarified that a militiaman would not have to perform more than three months of federal service per year "after his arrival at the place of rendezvous." That short duration, potentially harmful during a longer war, would not be repealed until 1861. Despite all these shortcomings, the act would remain the nation's fundamental guiding legislation concerning the militia until 1903.[9]

In keeping with the Republican viewpoint, President Thomas Jefferson took the frugal approach of relying on the militia as the first line of national defense to buy time for the federal government to expand its meager regular forces. A popular saying of the day claimed the militia was the "shield of the Republic" and the regular force its sword. Reality did not match this rhetoric—the standing militia system was already in decline by the opening decade of the 19th century. Some states failed to submit the required annual militia reports. The burden of militia service also fell mainly on the poor. Lastly, the War of 1812 highlighted the fact that there was still no legal basis to require the standing militia to serve in an offensive role on foreign soil.[10]

While the focus had been land forces in the first years of the Republic, Jefferson also was concerned with naval forces. In December 1805 he submitted a bill to Congress to establish a naval militia. The proposed law applied to able-bodied white male citizens between ages 18 and 45, but only those "whose principal occupation is on the high sea or on the tide-waters within the U.S." Once enrolled by their state, these men would be exempt from service in the land militia, but would be required to train six days per year in ship handling and naval artillery and be liable for service up to one year out of every two. Jefferson believed this would provide up to 50,000 men for the Navy. Congress never acted on the proposal. The nation had relied on privateers— commercial ships with civilian crews authorized to seize enemy merchantmen and share in profits therefrom—to supplement the navy in the Revolutionary War and would do so again in the War of 1812.[11]

During the War of 1812 the performance of the militia varied widely, but in the defensive victory at New Orleans in January 1815, under Maj. Gen. Andrew Jackson's leadership, militia soldiers contributed substantially to a lopsided victory. That final battle of the war, as explained by two historians of the militia, "glorified the militia ideal at a time when the militia system was virtually dead." What some militia advocates missed was the role of leadership. When militiamen were led by extremely capable commanders—epitomized by two future presidents, William H. Harrison in 1813 and Jackson two years later—their performance could, indeed, approximate that of well-trained regulars.[12]

Between 1816 and 1835 several presidents offered some 30 recommendations to Congress designed to fix the deteriorating standing militia, but legislators failed to act. While reliance upon the state militias was seen as befitting a republic (especially one protected by vast oceans from foreign powers), was thrifty, and precluded concern for a standing army's threat to liberty, it was weakening the nation's defenses.[13]

One development during this period partially offset the shortcomings of the standing militia. A peacetime, company-level, permanent volunteer militia system arose and grew increasingly popular, especially in northern urban centers. Generally, middle- or upper-class men volunteered for specialized, expensive units comprised of cavalry, artillery, or elite infantry. In addition to their military value, such units conferred social status upon their members. But non-elite infantry units found a place as well, as many immigrants sought

BATTLE OF NEW ORLEANS.

At the Battle of New Orleans in January 1815, under Maj. Gen. Andrew Jackson's leadership, militia soldiers contributed substantially to victory in the war's final campaign, facilitating the myth of militia superiority over regulars. (Source: Library of Congress)

service in a volunteer militia company as a means of demonstrating patriotism for their adopted country. During this long period of relative peace, volunteer units responded to local crises, enforced the laws, guarded prisoners, and dispersed mobs. In the South the militia effectively buttressed the slave patrol system designed to discourage runaways and maintain order on plantations. Overall, the permanent volunteer units partly filled the role that the largely moribund standing militia was supposed to perform.[14]

The most significant potential change to the militia system came from Secretary of War John C. Calhoun's plan for an expansible army, introduced in 1820 in an attempt to place primary reliance upon the regulars rather than the militia. The Battle of New Orleans notwithstanding, Calhoun realized that the few training days per year required by the standing militia were insufficient to prepare its forces to match Europe's professional armies. He envisioned a peacetime army fully manned in terms of its officers but with only half of its enlisted soldiers. In the event of war, new recruits would fill out the ranks of the army's cadre-like units, doubling their size. Unlike previous mobilization plans, the militia played only a limited role. Although Congress rejected the expansible army, the proposal set a precedent. As one historian noted, a secretary of war "had put forth a defense plan that repudiated the militia tradition and acknowledged the primacy of Regulars." Other scholars have referred to Calhoun's proposal as "a permanent legacy" and "one of the most important military papers in American history."[15]

The Mexican-American War and American Civil War

In 1846 the admission of Texas to the Union precipitated a conflict between the United States and Mexico. Concerned about the possibility of a simultaneous war with Great Britain (over Oregon), the James K. Polk administration laid the groundwork for the mobilization of the regular Army augmented by 50,000 U.S. Volunteers prepared to serve for one year. The volunteers, however, would not be called unless and until Mexico initiated hostilities. Given the problems experienced during the War of 1812, the U.S. Army's senior leaders opposed calling the state militias. In any case, the obsolescent standing militia system, already abolished in several states by the mid-1840s, provided a source of volunteers. More than 12,000 militiamen served either as U.S. Volunteers or U.S. Army regulars during the war.[16]

Ulysses S. Grant, a lieutenant during the war, later described the force led by Maj. Gen. Zachary Taylor as being "under the best of drill and discipline," and probably the best army ever to face an enemy. Even allowing for poetic license, Taylor's experienced regulars were led mostly by West Point–educated officers, but they comprised only 30 percent of American soldiers in the war. The statistics could deceive, however, as there was much overlap between the different soldier categories. About one-half of the 30,000 regulars began the war as volunteers, their change in status merely the result of an oath administered in Mexico. A number of states looked first to their volunteer militia companies in order to form federal volunteer regiments, and raised a total of 58. In Georgia, for example, nine volunteer militia companies combined to form the 1st Georgia Regiment. The volunteers, sharing in the wealth of West Point–trained leaders available by that time, normally fought as resolutely as regulars. One of the war's outstanding volunteer regiments, commanded by Col. Jefferson Davis, was the Mississippi Rifles, the antecedent of today's 155th Armored Brigade Combat Team, Mississippi Army National Guard.[17]

In his annual address to Congress in 1854, President Franklin Pierce acknowledged "the valuable services . . . rendered by the Army and its inestimable importance as the nucleus around which the volunteer force of the nation can gather in the hour of danger." Pierce thereby made clear that the nation's defense policy had become wedded to a regular army, albeit one heavily supported by volunteers. Seemingly, even the traditional rhetorical reliance on the militia had passed from the American political scene. Yet the next great conflict drew upon what remained of the old militia system.[18]

When the Civil War erupted in 1861, the militia system of most states had changed little since the Mexican-American War. Likewise, the regular Army was relatively unchanged, epitomized by its general in chief, brevet Lt. Gen. Winfield Scott, then 74, who had served in that capacity since 1841. One month prior to the start of hostilities, the Confederacy's provisional congress took the first step toward mobilization when it authorized President Jefferson Davis to call out the militia for six months and to accept 100,000 volunteers for one year. Following the South's occupation of Fort Sumter, President Abraham Lincoln called for 75,000 militiamen for three months' service in accordance with the Calling Forth Act of 1792. At that time the size of the U.S. Army was a mere 16,000. By the time hostilities ended in 1865 at least 2.5 million men had served in the Union's armies and about 1 million had served under the Confederacy.[19]

Despite the dramatic, unprecedented increase in the size of the U.S. Army, it never had more than 20,000 regulars present for duty. In both North and South, the regular armies were dwarfed by volunteer regiments formed initially from the rosters of the traditional militia companies. Once again, in the 1860s, the state militia rolls became the manpower pools for recruiting volunteers. And, again, the militia proved to be a mixed bag in battle. While many units performed badly, the 69th New York State Militia (also known as the 2nd Regiment of Irish Volunteers and the lineal predecessor of today's 69th Infantry, New York Army National Guard) was one of the exceptions that fought well.

The militia's three-month service limit expired soon after the first major battle in the East, at Bull Run. Lincoln avoided relying on the militia for the rest of the conflict by calling for 500,000 U.S. Volunteers for three-year terms and depending primarily on that manpower source thereafter. Although militia units did not fight as such in large engagements after the summer of 1861, at the war's outset they at least bought time for the North to expand the small regular army with the volunteers.[20]

During the Civil War both belligerents established a new principle that a citizen's military obligation was due not to individual states, but to the nation. That important distinction resulted from desperation on both sides, especially the South, to replace combat losses sustained at rates previously unknown to Americans. Ironically, the Confederacy, while claiming it was founded to protect states' rights, began conscription after the Battle of Shiloh in 1862.

Several months later the Union followed suit with similar legislation known as the Militia Act of 1862. Although the U.S. law never went into effect, it spurred recruiting among volunteer regiments not then in federal service.[21]

In March 1863, following the horrific casualties at Antietam and Fredericksburg in late 1862, the U.S. Congress passed the Enrollment Act. Similar to the old militia laws, the act established the principle of universal military obligation and the machinery to carry it out, though it omitted the traditional militia requirement for a male citizen to equip himself and periodically train. However, Congress intended the law not to conscript directly but rather to encourage voluntary enlistment. In the final tally, only 6 percent of Northern military manpower was secured directly by the draft. Rather, the threat of the draft served as a primary catalyst for otherwise reluctant citizens to volunteer or to pay a substitute to enlist in their stead. The same basic phenomenon took place in the South but to a lesser degree, where 20 percent of Confederate manpower was drafted. Significantly, the conscription procedures of both sides were based on the obligation of military service to the nation, not the states.[22]

The draft did not apply to the Navy and it had no militia to call upon, so it relied entirely on voluntary enlistment throughout the war. The 1864 reauthorization of the draft did allow up to ten thousand soldiers with maritime experience to transfer to the Navy, and for those mariners who were drafted to elect enlistment in the Navy instead. Recent immigrants, often unemployed and clustered around the ports where the Navy recruited, provided a major source. Free blacks, initially prohibited from serving in the Army, volunteered in substantial numbers for the Navy, which had routinely accepted blacks throughout its history. Escaped slaves provided another manpower source, especially to vessels operating on southern rivers or blockade duty. At the height of the conflict, blacks constituted 23 percent of the Navy's enlisted strength, while immigrants (some of whom were black) accounted for 45 percent.[23]

The Advent of the National Guard

In 1865 the Union disbanded its volunteer units, and the small regular Army soon returned to its antebellum role as a constabulary force primarily dealing with Indians in the West. Meanwhile, the National Guard began to develop in almost all of the states. Increasingly, states employed the term National Guard instead of militia, although the new title belied the primary role of this component as a state, not national, instrument. In many cases the volunteer militia companies, more so than the standing militia, formed the core of the states' National Guard units.[24]

The formation of the National Guard Association (NGA, later the National Guard Association of the United States) in the 1870s contributed to the Guard's ascent in part by emphasizing its role as a reserve force to supplement the regular Army. National Guard leaders did not wish their units to be identified with quelling labor disputes on behalf of the business community—although this was a mission they performed often—so the organization consistently emphasized the Guard's role as a "natural component of the nation's military force." The NGA's first president was Brig. Gen. George W. Wingate, who was also instrumental in founding the National Rifle Association. He seized the opportunity to emphasize marksmanship for guardsmen while at the same time promoting rifle competitions that enhanced rapport between part-timers and Army regulars. His initiative represented an early attempt to reduce the barriers between regulars and citizen-soldiers, an issue that would continue to bedevil later generations.[25]

By 1880 Pennsylvania had highlighted the National Guard's maturation by becoming the first state to reorganize its militia during peacetime into a tactical division consisting of a headquarters and three brigades. Thus, the 28th Infantry Division, Pennsylvania Army National Guard, is considered the Army's "oldest, permanently organized combat division." The state's citizen-soldiers drilled one night a week, participated in inspections, and attended a six-day training encampment each summer, a training regimen typical for the period.[26]

Paradoxically, the rise of the National Guard occurred at the same time the regular Army grew increasingly opposed to reliance on state-based part-time soldiery. One of the Army's leading intellectuals in the late 19th century, Maj. Gen. Emory Upton, had become convinced of the limited value of militia unless it was kept under the close supervision of, and subordinate to, Army regulars. The most influential of his several books was *The Military Policy of the United States*, in which he failed to distinguish between the American Civil War's organized militia (largely volunteer units) and the manpower rosters of the old standing militia. He also underestimated the power of the traditional American belief in the militia concept and the fear of large standing armies, which had an outsize impact on practical military matters. The German model that Upton had observed and admired was based on a large, professionally led army of two-year conscripts who spent long years in the reserve after their regular service. Although Upton had a significant impact on Army doctrine for several decades after his death, his desire to replicate the German model in the American military system went unrealized; the United States continued with its "traditional dual military institutions."[27]

At the end of the 19th century the United States fought a war that resulted in overseas colonial gains and world power status, and also demonstrated the ongoing dilemma of manpower mobilization policy. In 1898 the U.S. Congress declared war against Spain for the purpose of securing Cuban independence. War Department leaders wanted to rely primarily on a rapidly expanded regular Army—a basically Uptonian approach—while Congress, traditional allies of the state-affiliated Guard, authorized only a small regular Army increase and turned to the familiar practice of requesting volunteers. President William McKinley called for a total of 200,000 volunteers for up to two years of federal service to be drawn from the existing, partially trained National Guard. In authorizing the states to raise new units of volunteers, Congress provided for a system largely insulated from regular Army influence. Only a single regular officer, for example, could be appointed to a volunteer regiment. The war was extremely popular, and the Army quickly secured the requested volunteers.[28]

Mindful of the constitutional issue of whether militia could be used for purposes other than homeland defense and maintaining civil order, the law required guardsmen to volunteer individually for the Cuban and—after George Dewey's naval victory at Manila Bay—Philippine campaigns. Any unit whose individual members collectively volunteered for overseas service, however, would be accepted as a U.S. Volunteer regiment with its existing organization and officers. In many cases the individual members of National Guard units were sworn into federal service en masse and the former units reconstituted as U.S. regiments with new designations. For example, the 1st Regiment, New York National Guard, was redesignated the 1st Regiment, Infantry, New York Volunteers. Those relatively few individuals who chose not to volunteer were discharged from their former units, their places filled by eager recruits. Nearly 200 National Guard units served during the period as volunteer units.[29]

The raising of volunteer regiments notwithstanding, the Cuban expedition was mainly a regular Army affair. Due to the limited shipping available, most

After the Civil War, Maj. Gen. Emory Upton desired to replicate the German professional model in the American military system. His writings had a significant impact on Army doctrine for decades after his death in 1881. (Source: Library of Congress)

volunteer units were left in the States. The reputation of one of the few volunteer regiments in Cuba, the 71st New York (a redesignated Guard formation), suffered as a result of muddled performance in the Battle of San Juan Hill, while the 1st U.S. Volunteer Cavalry (raised from scratch and known as the Rough Riders) fought admirably in the same engagement. In the prolonged, extremely difficult, and unpleasant operations against Filipino insurgents, the secretary of war later commended the guardsmen/volunteers for their "exhibition of sturdy patriotism which it seems to me has never been fully appreciated." Military historian Brian M. Linn wrote of the Battle of Manila in February 1899: "Much to the surprise of Regular officers, the Volunteers proved themselves courageous and efficient fighters . . . a good case can be made that the Volunteers were the more effective."[30]

The 1898 mobilization had encountered major problems, from a too-small army to a lack of professionalism. Perceiving the Army's shortcomings, the new secretary of war, Elihu Root, implemented important changes during his five years in office. Borrowing heavily from the writings of Emory Upton, Root essentially led the transition of the U.S. Army from the late 19th-century constabulary era into the age of professionally led mass armies. Among Root's major accomplishments, his support of the Militia Act of 1903 helped pass the most significant law in more than a century affecting the reserve component.[31]

The Growing Role of the National Guard

The Militia Act of 1903 was known as the Dick Act in honor of Charles W. Dick, the House Committee on Militia Affairs chairman, NGA president, and an Ohio National Guard major general. Taking advantage of a climate friendly to militia reform, Dick worked closely with Root's War Department to craft the legislation. The Dick Act's major impact was establishment of the principle of providing federal funds and equipment in return for greater control over Guard training and organization, a trend that would continue in the long term. The National Guard's funding became dependent on the degree to which it met federal standards in commissioning officers, recruiting enlisted men, organizing units, and participating in field training. Units that performed at least 24 drill sessions, each normally 1½ to 2 hours long, and summer field training received federal funds. Guard personnel who joined in maneuvers with the Army received federal pay and subsistence. Guard officers became eligible to attend regular Army schools, including the War College.[32]

Five years later modifications to the Dick Act resolved several concerns. The Militia Act of 1908 clarified that the National Guard could be federalized for duty "either within or without the Territory of the United States," eliminated the Dick Act's nine-month limit on length of federalized service, and required the president to mobilize the Guard prior to calling for volunteers or a volunteer force. Those important provisions made the National Guard the preferred source of military forces to augment the regular Army, a status NGA leaders had long sought.[33]

Despite the legislative improvements, by 1910 a new U.S. Army chief of staff grappled with how to raise a wartime army that would be effective on the modern battlefield. Maj. Gen. Leonard Wood, along with other senior Army leaders, believed that citizen-soldiers required a lengthy training period under the supervision of professional officers to prepare them for combat. Unlike Emory Upton, however, Wood understood that he would have to respect traditional American distrust of a large standing army. Whereas Uptonians, following the German army's example, believed it took two years to produce effective soldiers, Wood believed he could do it in six months—if he could ensure a modicum of training for the citizen-soldiery during peacetime. Given the protection of two oceans, he deemed that enough time to raise an army to confront likely foreign enemies. Although the 120,000-strong National Guard potentially provided that partially trained force for rapid mobilization, Wood opposed in principle all state-affiliated military forces and was wary of possible limits on the

The main author of the Militia Act of 1903, Senator Charles Dick—also an Ohio National Guard major general—established the principle of providing federal dollars in return for increased Army control of the Guard. (Source: Library of Congress)

ability to deploy them overseas. The ensuing political battle over mobilization policy between 1912 and 1916 brought U.S. Army–National Guard relations to one of their lowest points. The result was a compromise that included both the National Guard and federal-only reserve components.[34]

Although the United States was concerned about the war that enveloped Europe in 1914, it was subsequent trouble on the U.S.-Mexican border that facilitated the passage of the National Defense Act of 1916. The law not only called for the regular Army to increase over a five-year period to 175,000, expansible to 286,000 in wartime, but also advanced the reserve component's training, standards, and status. The National Guard would rise gradually to more than 400,000 and receive federal funding for an increase in the number of armory drills for guardsmen to 48 per year. In return for greater financial support, National Guard units and officers became subject to federal standards. Henceforth, officers and enlisted men also took oaths to both their state and the nation, swearing to protect the U.S. Constitution and obey the orders of the president, which ensured the legality of overseas federal service. Guardsmen were thereafter subject to overseas duty of unlimited duration, but were assured of serving as National Guard units, not as individual replacements in regular Army outfits (the reality would differ from these promises in later years). These provisions reinforced the Guard's status as the nation's preferred reserve force.[35]

In addition, the law formalized the summer training programs for officer-candidates Wood had initiated, as well as the Officers' Reserve Corps (ORC) and Reserve Officers' Training Corps (ROTC). The legislation also created an Enlisted Reserve Corps, comprised of men who had served on active duty in various technical specialties. Unlike the National Guard, the Officers' Reserve Corps and Enlisted Reserve Corps contained only individuals; there were no units. Finally, the act reaffirmed the obligation of able-bodied men, 18 to 45 years old, to serve in the military if needed.[36]

The Birth of the Federal-Only Reserve Components

Dating back to the adoption of the U.S. Constitution, the nation had viewed a standing navy more favorably than a standing army. Merchant sailors also provided a ready source of trained personnel, and consequently there had been less need for state naval militias. The first tentative attempts to form naval militia or reserve units dated from 1873 when a group of former naval officers met in New York. By the early 1890s several Atlantic seaboard states and California had established their own naval militias, generally designated as naval battalions. By 1899, 18 states and the District of Columbia had naval militias. The year prior, President McKinley had called the naval militias into federal service for the war against Spain; the Illinois and New York naval militias subsequently distinguished themselves in the Battle of Santiago de Cuba.[37]

The 1898 war, along with a growing awareness of problems with the organization and training policies of the naval militias, stirred greater advocacy for a naval reserve, leading to the introduction of several bills after 1901. At the time, congressional interest seemed to favor the states' naval militias in lieu of a federal-only reserve, but in 1912 Congress passed an act forming the Medical Reserve Corps for the Navy and one year after that it followed with legislation establishing the Navy's Dental Reserve Corps. Several months later, Assistant Secretary of the Navy Franklin D. Roosevelt reported that the Navy supported the creation of a national naval reserve. By 1914 Roosevelt and Secretary of the Navy Josephus Daniels oversaw the development of a plan for a 50,000-man naval reserve. The Naval Appropriations Act of 1916 (enacted in March 1915) established the U.S. Naval Reserve (USNR) while providing for continuation of the Naval Militia and National Naval Volunteers. The next year Congress authorized the Naval Reserve Flying Corps. Marines had long served with the Naval Militia, but the August 1916 legislation also marked the official creation of the U.S. Marine Corps Reserve (USMCR).[38]

Attempts to improve the naval militias took place concurrently with Naval Reserve efforts. Although earlier legislative attempts had failed, the Naval Militia Act of February 1914 largely brought the states' naval militias under the secretary of the Navy and henceforth they were to be paid for training days. The president could call the naval militia to active duty in wartime or a national emergency. In the aftermath of the 1915 sinking of the British liner SS *Lusitania* by a German U-boat, which claimed over 100 American lives, the U.S. Navy furthered its practice of dealing with the Naval Militia as a part of the Naval Reserve.[39]

Meanwhile, the Army Reserve had its beginnings in the 1908 establishment of a medical officer reserve corps. By 1916 the number of reserve physicians outnumbered regular Army doctors by four to one. That year, the National Defense Act disestablished the medical officer reserve corps, whose members were then commissioned into the newly designated Officers' Reserve Corps, which later comprised the bulk of the U.S. Army Reserve (USAR). The genesis of the Army Reserve—as well as the Navy's Dental Reserve Corps—suggested the importance of the specialized skills readily available in the reserve components, one of the inherent advantages of the reserves then and now.[40]

World War I

In April 1917 the United States declared war against Germany. At that moment, American military preparedness in relation to the task at hand probably was at one of its lowest points in history. President Woodrow Wilson had directed Secretary of War Newton D. Baker to have a conscription bill ready in the event of war, and in May 1917 Congress passed the Selective Service

Act. It authorized the president to raise the regular Army and National Guard to full war strength, to federalize the Guard, and to conduct a federal draft of 500,000 men. Subsequent legislation increased the number of conscripts and expanded the draft pool to include males between 18 and 45 years. Draftees would account for two-thirds of the U.S. military forces that participated in the war, in contrast with only 6 percent of the Union Army some 50 years earlier.[41]

The extreme unpreparedness of the nation notwithstanding, the manpower mobilizations of 1917–1918 were carried out with considerably greater astuteness, flexibility, and efficiency than those of any previous conflict. Even the War Department's term, *selective service*, helped soften the reality for an American public traditionally opposed to coerced military duty. Of the nearly 24 million men who registered for selective service, an average of only 1 in 8 was actually inducted. Still, nearly 2.8 million men were drafted, while another 1 million enlisted voluntarily.[42]

The War Department filled the ranks of the regular Army and the mobilized National Guard largely with volunteers, while directing most draftees to the newly formed divisions called the National Army. In the summer of 1917 the United States' 1st Division, recently arrived in France, became the first of many faced with the task described by George C. Marshall biographer Forrest C. Pogue as: "to make soldiers of the recruits and military units out of the collections of men." Those processes required months of hard training, but by early 1918 the Americans were in the front lines and began to prove their worth. By July 1918, 250,000 fresh U.S. soldiers were arriving in Europe every month. And in the war's final months the Americans tipped the balance in favor of the Allies at such places as the Marne, Saint-Mihiel, and the Meuse-Argonne. By the time of the armistice of 11 November 1918, 4.8 million American men had served in the armed forces during the war, 3.7 million of them in the Army. Two million men, comprising 43 divisions, served in France with the American Expeditionary Forces. Of those divisions, 18 were National Guard (at least originally), 17 National Army (conscripts), and 8 regular Army. Guardsmen with civilian experience in aviation also served in the Army's fledgling air component, though they had to transfer to the Signal Corps Reserve to do so— the Guard would not establish its first aviation unit until 1921.[43]

The Army was not the only service to mobilize, however. Immediately upon the declaration of war, the Navy called into service both Naval Militia and Naval Reserve personnel. By July 1918 the number of naval reservists and militia on active duty roughly equaled the number of regular Navy personnel. The following month, Secretary Daniels ordered the elimination of distinctions in uniforms and titles of rank between regular Navy and Naval Reserve members. By the time of the armistice, the Marine Corps Reserve—miniscule when America declared war against Germany—boasted a considerable number of veterans of the Aisne defensive and the Aisne-Marne, Saint-Mihiel, and Meuse-Argonne offensives in 1918.[44]

Women provided another source of manpower during the war. Since the legislation establishing the Naval and Marine Corps Reserves referred to persons rather than males, Secretary of the Navy Josephus Daniels opted to interpret that widely and authorized the recruitment of women as early as March 1917. The Navy made immediate use of the option, recruiting some 12,500 women by the end of the war. The Marine Corps demurred until August 1918, and ended up taking in only 305. Officially designated respectively as Yeoman (F) (after the Navy's clerical rating) and Marine Reserve (F), they were colloquially dubbed Yeomanettes and Marinettes. They underwent no basic training after enlistment and generally performed administrative duties stateside to relieve men for combat service. When the conflict ended, the Navy Department began closing down these programs, but they paved the way for greater reliance on women in the military in the future.[45]

Before the war, John McAuley Palmer, the Army's foremost thinker on manpower mobilization issues, stated that the "most important military problem is to devise means of preparing great armies of citizen soldiers to meet the emergency of modern war." The American mobilization of manpower in 1917 and 1918, though far from perfect, succeeded; in so doing, it validated Palmer's thesis. In the process, both the state-affiliated and federal-only reserve components gained legitimacy in the era of modern warfare.[46]

One unresolved issue concerned the difficult relationship between the regular Army and the National Guard. After the war General John J. Pershing testified before Congress that the "National Guard never received the whole-hearted support of the regular Army during the World War. There was always more or less a prejudice against them." Guardsmen felt certain that the regular Army sought to diminish opportunities for National Guard leaders. Only one Guard officer, Maj. Gen. John F. O'Ryan of the New York 27th Division, served for the duration of the war as a division commander. Among divisional commanders in France by November 1918, O'Ryan was the youngest. Guardsmen complained that a number of National Guard general officers considered fit for duty on the Mexican border in 1916 were replaced only one year later by regular Army officers because of alleged physical unfitness. But despite an appearance of discrimination, it was a certainty that combat on the Western Front would be more rigorous than security duty along the U.S.-Mexico border. In Pershing's view, physical fitness and youthfulness generally were key ingredients of effective battlefield leadership, and that explained his tendency to replace older National Guard general officers. O'Ryan, the youngest divisional commander to serve in France, not only met Pershing's criteria, he also had been the first guardsman to graduate from the Army War College.[47]

———— Conclusion ————

In terms of what the nation expected of its citizen-soldiers, World War I offered lessons with policy implications in two major areas: training and the composition of the reserve component. Regarding training, for decades Emory Upton's influence over the Army was such that planners took it for granted that a lengthy period would always be required to prepare citizen-soldiers for the battlefield. Army Chief of Staff Leonard Wood questioned that assumption, but even he envisioned no less than six months' training to turn civilians into soldiers.[48]

But in the middle of 1918, as long-awaited American divisions were beginning to turn the tide in favor of the Allies, Secretary of War Newton Baker concluded otherwise. He stated that given the "inspiration from an existing struggle, it takes no such length of time" as the previously assumed "nine months or a year to train raw recruits into soldiers in peace time." Baker asserted that "men who have had four months' training . . . are pretty nearly ready for use in association with . . . veterans and experienced troops." While the secretary's conclusion may have been valid with respect to turning civilians into competent individual soldiers, and perhaps inserting them as replacements into a veteran division, Baker did not address the intangibles of unit cohesion and the higher-level tactical skills required of ground combat units. Developing an effective unit from scratch, after its soldiers had been trained to individual standards, took additional months.[49]

The experience of the Army's 1st Division suggested as much. Although it arrived in France in the summer of 1917, it was "not a combat division at all, but only the raw material for one sent over for assembly in France instead of at home." In his memoirs Pershing acknowledged that his divisions were but "partially trained," even while lauding their spirit and accomplishments in the Meuse-Argonne offensive of 1918. Pershing's First Army commander, Maj. Gen. Hunter Liggett, wrote that the strain of command during 1917–1918 was "intensified here by the knowledge that they were leading troops only partially trained against the best organized and most skillful man-killing machine ever set going." One lesson, therefore, was that even though individual raw recruits probably could be trained in less time than previously assumed, the training required—and the time spent together—for effective and cohesive combat units was considerably longer than six months. The point argued strongly against a defense policy of waiting until a conflict arose to bring in recruits and form them into trained units while a small standing army backed up by a partially trained, larger—but still not large enough—National Guard bought time for the new divisions to take the field.[50]

Moreover, the war signaled the end of the old paradigm of "every citizen a soldier." From colonial times, Americans had assumed that an army could be put into the field on short notice by calling its male citizens to arms. The reality had been far different. Initially, geographic restrictions had hindered the utility of the standing militia for anything beyond local service. By the early to mid-19th century the states generally neglected their standing militias in favor of much smaller but somewhat better-prepared permanent volunteer militias. By the turn of the 20th century advances in military technology and professionalism rendered wildly impractical the very notion that every citizen could keep himself armed, equipped, and trained to engage in combat. While the draft meant that most male citizens were at least subject to the call to military service, such raw manpower required considerable time and effort to produce effective combat units. Given the experiences of the 1910s, which included watershed legislation, mobilization, and combat operations, it became clear that reservists would have to undergo more, and more intense, training during peacetime to maintain readiness for the modern battlefield.

The issue of the composition of the reserve components was closely related to the lesson regarding training. Shortly after World War I Congress repudiated the nation's historic reliance on volunteer units—not infrequently raised from scratch—that had served from colonial times through the Philippine Insurrection. In addition to the added time required to prepare an army for battle, the oceans no longer afforded the buffer that they had in an earlier era. That vise spelled the end of "the Volunteer Army," which disappeared from the Army's authorized land forces in 1920. Over the next several decades, the nation would increasingly rely on a larger standing army and a larger and increasingly better-trained National Guard and reserve. After more than a century marked by halting steps, the nation's defenses now rested upon trained professionals and partially trained citizen-soldiers formed into permanent units with either state-federal or federal-only affiliation. The era of the traditional, potentially untrained and ill-equipped "every citizen" soldier was firmly laid to rest.[51]

—— CHAPTER 2 ——

Adapting to Global Threats and Global Power, 1919–1953

T he rapid demobilization after World War I marked the beginning of a turbulent period for American defense policy and the nation's reserve components. Fiscal retrenchment gave way to global economic depression, followed by another full-scale mobilization, world war, and hurried demobilization, and finally by an emergency call-up to handle an unexpected conflict in Korea. Throughout all this, the United States continued to refine laws and policies governing the reserves, in part to deal with longstanding issues, but also in response to the evolving strategic, social, economic, and political environment. The result would be a stronger and better-prepared reserve force, albeit one that still faced unresolved challenges.

The Interwar Period

The U.S. military's demobilization in 1919–1920 was at least as drastic as the mobilization two years earlier. Weary of a large and expensive army, a devastating European war, and hints of German-style militarism, Congress reduced the regular Army to about 140,000 men by 1922. Indeed, an official mobilization study referred to "the Army disintegrating under the impact of popular pressure to 'bring the boys home.'" The War Department, believing this ongoing retrenchment went too far, in 1919 proposed a peacetime force of 500,000 regulars along the lines of the old expansible army plan. Congress flatly rejected it. Testifying later in the year before the Senate Military Affairs Committee, Col. (later, Brig. Gen.) John McAuley Palmer so impressed the chairman with his grasp of the issues that the committee brought him in to help draft new legislation. Palmer recommended a much smaller regular force than Army leadership desired because he viewed the nation's citizen-soldiery, rather than its regulars, as the bedrock of U.S. land forces, a principle he saw as part of the "national genius and tradition." The recently victorious field commander, General John J. Pershing, whose citizen-soldier divisions helped win the victory on the Western Front, lent Palmer his considerable support.[1]

Brig. Gen. John McAuley Palmer, the Army's leading thinker on manpower mobilization issues, viewed the nation's citizen-soldiery as the bedrock of U.S. land forces under the Constitution, and a part of the national genius and tradition. (Source: Library of Congress)

The result was the National Defense Act of 1920, officially an amendment to the 1916 defense law but in fact largely new. It designated the several land forces that comprised the Army as follows: "the Regular Army, the National Guard while in the service of the United States, and the organized Reserves, including the Officers' Reserve Corps and the Enlisted Reserve Corps." The recent conflict had convinced planners that volunteer units such as those raised in 1898 were no longer viable in modern warfare, so the 1920 law omitted that option. The act also institutionalized the Reserve Officers' Training Corps system as a peacetime program to provide trained junior officers for future mobilizations.[2]

Reflecting Palmer's influence and congressional desires, the law provided for a small regular Army backed up by a larger National Guard and a smaller Army Reserve. Congress authorized a regular Army of 280,000 soldiers and affirmed the National Guard's standing units as the preferred reserve component, followed by the trained individuals of the Organized Reserve. Due to lack of funding, however, the regular Army hovered near 140,000 men until 1936; the Guard's strength was only roughly 180,000 throughout the 1920s; and the 33 Organized Reserve divisions remained units in name only.[3]

Reflecting the Guard's elevated status and increasing influence with Congress, the 1920 act took control of the Militia Bureau (after 1933, the National Guard Bureau) away from the regular Army and required that a National Guard major general serve as the bureau chief. The new chief also reported to an assistant secretary of war, not the Army chief of staff, thereby minimizing opportunities for regular Army generals to derail Guard initiatives. The measure was the first major step toward the elevation of the bureau chief to four-star rank, achieved nearly 90 years later. Also, Congress increased the number of Guard officers authorized to serve in the Militia Bureau and provided for their assignment to the General Staff.[4]

One key issue was not resolved satisfactorily from the Guard's perspective, however. Although legislators "had sold the bill to their fellows" with the assurance that National Guard outfits would maintain unit integrity during federal service, the law's wording, according to one historian, "did not amount to a firm prohibition against changes following mobilization." Despite attempts to rectify this, including language in the act of June 1933 stating that Guard units would be "maintained intact insofar as practicable" following mobilization, unit integrity was never guaranteed. The National Defense Act of 1920, nevertheless, greatly clarified the respective roles of the Army's components, increased the importance of the National Guard, and improved the foundation of U.S. military policy.[5]

The 1920 legislation also enhanced the position of the Organized Reserve, but fiscal austerity limited the practical impact. There were 72,000 officers on the rolls by 1926, but only 5,000 enlisted men. Throughout the interwar period there were few training opportunities; officers considered themselves fortunate to receive a two-week tour of active duty every four or five years. The lowest point came in 1934, when only one in seven ORC officers secured a spot in the traditional summer camp. The Army, not excited with the task assigned in 1933 to administer the Roosevelt administration's Civilian Conservation Corps (CCC), which put young men to work on parks and other outdoor projects, turned to ORC officers to run the corps' camps. The War Department billed CCC duty as "valuable training" especially in "practical leadership" for young officers. It was not tactical training, however, though the paid CCC duty likely motivated more than a few officers to remain in the ORC during the resource-starved interwar era. Reservists in all the services generally received pay only for two-week training sessions, if they could get one, and not for weekly drill periods.[6]

In implementing the 1920 law, the Army's leadership envisioned that each of the nine regular Army divisions, manned at full strength, would train two National Guard and three Organized Reserve divisions in its region. When the regular Army's budget dipped even lower than anticipated, Palmer recommended abandoning some of the planned regular divisions in order to keep those that remained at full strength. Instead, in a reversion to the expansible army plan, the War Department maintained all of them in a skeletonized form, planning to fill them with draftees. That decision adversely affected the training of its reservists, as the regulars remained at home station, fully occupied by tasks in their understrength units. It also meant that even the regular divisions were woefully unprepared for combat, since they accomplished little more than individual and small-unit training, and would have to build full-scale units from scratch when the next war came.[7]

The ground forces were not alone in facing draconian postwar measures. By 1922 the U.S. Navy's reserve forces consisted of just 6,500 officers and enlisted men in a paid status, with the rest transferred into the nonpaying Volunteer Naval Reserve or disenrolled. The Marine Corps Reserve had likewise dwindled to less than 600 personnel. The Naval Reserve Act of 1925 at least offered legitimacy when it established the redesignated Naval Reserve as a part of the Navy, and the Marine Corps Reserve as "a component part" of the Marine Corps. Moreover, a month later Congress amended the 1916 defense act to establish the Naval Reserve Officers' Training Corps (NROTC) as a counterpart to the Army program. But the Department of the Navy largely cancelled the two-week summer training sessions in 1932 and 1933 and temporarily halted all pay for reservists in 1933.[8]

Despite the lack of funds, the Marine Corps Reserve made some strides in the mid-1930s. In 1934 the Marine Corps began to commission a small number of NROTC graduates. It also implemented a new system of summer training, known as Platoon Leaders Class, to procure second lieutenants for the Volunteer Marine Corps Reserve. Another significant initiative was the Inspector-Instructor (I-I) program, which placed a small cadre of regular Marine officers and noncommissioned officers (NCOs) with each reserve unit to assist in training and in maintaining equipment. A key feature of the program was "the careful choice of Inspector-Instructor personnel and their resultant high caliber," including the ability to "guide and instruct without assuming command." Seventy years later a congressionally mandated commission would laud the ongoing I-I program.[9]

In 1920 the Militia Bureau and the Army Air Service forged a plan for National Guard aviation units, and a year later the Minnesota National Guard's 109th Observation Squadron received federal recognition. In a pattern that continued for decades, however, the active air components typically sought to relegate those functions they considered less important—such as aerial observation in the 1930s—to the National Guard (and later the Air Force Reserve). Nevertheless, the fledgling Air Guard quickly made a name for itself. Charles A. Lindbergh, a captain in the Missouri National Guard's 110th Observation Squadron, stirred interest in aviation with his historic nonstop transatlantic flight in 1927. Other less spectacular but important uses of airpower included the Arkansas National Guard's 154th Observation Squadron air-dropping food, supplies, and medicine to inaccessible flood-ravaged areas on the Mississippi

River that same year. Such civil support missions, repeated often in coming years, cemented the importance of the aerial reserve component to state and local communities.[10]

Naval reserve elements also began to develop an aviation capability. The Naval Aviation Act of 1935 established an aviation cadet program that offered pilot training for qualified college graduates and then a commission in the Naval Reserve or Marine Corps Reserve. Since many reserve aviators worked as commercial pilots, their readiness suffered less than that of their counterparts in other military specialties who had minimal opportunities to hone their skills.[11]

While tight funding throughout much of the interwar period negatively impacted the size and readiness of the reserve component, changes in law and policy improved the prospects for the future.

World War II

When the German blitzkrieg overran Poland in September 1939, President Franklin D. Roosevelt announced a "limited national emergency" and issued an executive order increasing the size of the regular Army and the National Guard. The majority of the Guard's expansion went to bolster its 18 infantry divisions. To boost further the Guard's preparedness for war, the president also increased drills from 48 to 60 per year and extended the annual field training from 15 to 21 days. By the summer of 1940 the National Guard had reached a peacetime high of more than 240,000, while the regular Army, adding 80,000 soldiers in a single year, topped 260,000. Meanwhile, in 1939 the number of ORC officers increased to more than 100,000, nearly one-half of whom would be serving on active duty by May 1941.[12]

Despite the outbreak of war in Europe, Roosevelt—concerned about isolationist sentiment—did not initially advocate conscription or mobilization of the reserve component. This changed in the late summer of 1940 in light of Germany's rapid conquest of France. In August Congress passed a joint resolution authorizing the president to mobilize the National Guard and other reserves for one year of active duty. Three weeks later legislators passed the first peacetime draft in the nation's history, authorizing selective service of males between 21 and 35 years old for 12 months. Both measures limited duty to the Western Hemisphere except for U.S. possessions such as the Philippines. On the day the president signed the selective service bill into law, he also mobilized the first four National Guard divisions, which required conscripts to fill their ranks.[13]

Army Chief of Staff George Marshall, faced with the need to reinforce forward-deployed forces in the Philippines and Panama, realized that the immediate result of the Guard's mobilization in 1940 was *decreased* readiness.

During the resource-starved 1930s, the Civilian Conservation Corps offered practical leadership experience for many Army Reserve officers. George C. Marshall (center), later the Army chief of staff, viewed the CCC favorably and acknowledged its leadership benefits. (Courtesy of the George C. Marshall Foundation)

Regulars, who were badly needed in their own understrength units, now had to train the guardsmen. Within the next year a series of incremental mobilizations brought the remainder of the National Guard into federal service, but no division came onto active duty with more than two-thirds of its required manpower. The crisis of 1940 passed without the United States having to go to war, and by the summer of 1941 the Army's strength reached 1.2 million. Of the 29 divisions on active duty in early 1942, 18 were National Guard. Ultimately the Guard had made an enormous contribution to the Army's rapid expansion prior to the United States joining the conflict, providing immediately available, partially trained, organized divisions to supplement the regular Army. That bought time for divisions constituted from scratch to become combat ready. The availability of a large number of ROTC-trained junior officers in the Organized Reserve played an important role in filling out regular, Guard, and conscript divisions. In 1941 General Marshall applauded the high quality of Army Reserve officers as "probably our greatest asset during this present expansion."[14]

The integration of the Guard into the Army was not without problems. "Haunted by recollections of the droves of unfit commanders" that Pershing had reassigned in World War I, during this mobilization Marshall was quick to relieve senior commanders who appeared to lack what was required to succeed. In 1940 he told the House Military Affairs Committee: "Leadership in the field depends to an important extent on one's legs, and stomach, and nervous system, and on one's ability to withstand hardships, and lack of sleep, and still be disposed energetically and aggressively to command men, to dominate men on the battlefield." Despite cries of discrimination against the nonregulars, according to a Marshall biographer, "the percentage of field-grade officers retired in the National Guard was somewhat less than in the Regular Army." Only one Guard division commander remained in command throughout the war: Maj. Gen. Robert S. Beightler, who led Ohio's 37th Infantry Division in the Pacific theater. Lt. Gen. Raymond S. McLain, the only guardsman promoted to three-star rank, took command of the U.S. XIX Corps in October 1944, marking the first time a nonregular had become a corps commander since the Civil War.[15]

Although Guard divisions remained intact after mobilization, as envisioned in the 1920 National Defense Act, there was a perception, as reported by later historians, that subordinate units were "ruthlessly reorganized or broken up," while others underwent "wholesale reshuffling to break up local officer cliques." Some of this was likely due to the ongoing reorganization of all Army divisions from the prewar square configuration (two brigades of two regiments each) to the new triangular structure (three regiments with no intervening brigade headquarters). The shuffling of Guard personnel to cross-level experience between units being filled with new conscripts also might have contributed to a feeling of dislocation after mobilization.[16]

Of the first 14 Army divisions to deploy overseas, 8 originated in the Guard. The first Army regiment to take the offensive in the Pacific, the 164th Infantry (North Dakota), part of the Guard-heavy Americal Division, fought on Guadalcanal beginning in October 1942 and won praise from a veteran Marine battalion it reinforced in the midst of a night battle. The first Guard division in the European theater, the 34th (Iowa, Minnesota, North Dakota, South Dakota), entered combat in North Africa in November 1942. The second American division to arrive in the United Kingdom, the 29th (Maryland, Virginia, DC), was 60 percent conscripts but still retained what one historian called "a distinctive Guard flavor." It formed part of the assault waves at Normandy on 6 June 1944, the only National Guard division to do so.[17]

In contrast to the outstanding performance of some Guard units, one operation in the Pacific theater illustrated the potential for unhealthy regular-reserve relationships. During June–July 1944, U.S. forces took the heavily defended Central Pacific island of Saipan from the Japanese at high cost. Marine Corps Lt. Gen. Holland M. Smith commanded all U.S. forces on the island, comprised of the 2nd Marine Division, 4th Marine Division, and the Army's 27th Infantry Division, a Guard outfit. In a move that sparked an acrimonious Marine-Army dispute and garnered national attention, Holland Smith relieved the 27th Division's commander, (regular) Army Maj. Gen. Ralph C. Smith, for a perceived lack of aggressiveness. The Marine general's rancorous postwar memoir provided an underlying rationale for his decision:

> The trouble with the Twenty-seventh Division was, if I may coin a word, "militia-itis." As originally mobilized, the division had come entirely from the New York National Guard, with a good record and tradition from World War I. Much of its leadership . . . stemmed from a gentlemen's club known as the Seventh Regiment, traditionally New York's "silk stocking" outfit, and likewise a worthy unit, *per se*, with an impeccable reputation for annual balls, banquets and shipshape summer camps. . . . Any division, however, springing from such sources and maintained intact after mobilization, contains the entangled roots of home town loyalties, ambitions and intrigues. . .and behind all there was Albany, where the State Adjutant General's office allocated peacetime plums.[18]

Perhaps drawing on Marine Corps practice regarding its own reserve forces, General Smith argued that it would have been better "to disband the division after mobilization." Smith's conviction that "home town loyalties" acted like "barnacles on the hull" to decrease combat effectiveness may have had some merit, but it also flew in the face of the widespread view that unit cohesiveness, resulting from personnel serving together for extended periods, made units stronger and more effective.[19]

The Marine Corps Reserve, in contrast, did not have a state-centered component, was proportionately much smaller in numbers relative to the regulars, and was broken up upon mobilization and used to fill out existing active units. According to one Marine brigadier general, those reservists mobilized in 1940 "quickly lost their . . . identities as Reserves, becoming indistinguishable from the career Marines with whom they trained side by side." Although 68 percent of the half million men and women who ultimately joined the Corps during the war were officially designated as reservists, this status had no practical meaning. A wartime reservist went through the same training as someone who joined with a regular designation. That explained why, according to a reserve history, regular Marine Corps senior officers later indicated "that they never really bothered to inquire whether an officer or an enlisted man was a reservist or a Regular." While draftees filled out the National Guard divisions, the units maintained their Guard identity (for better or worse, as the 164th Infantry Regiment and the 27th Infantry Division showed).[20]

The experience of the Naval Reserve was much like that of the Marine Corps, with mobilized reservists largely subsumed as individuals into existing regular squadrons and ships, and many of those joining during wartime receiving a largely meaningless reserve designation. At the opening of 1944, the Navy secretary observed that "nine out of ten line officers with the fleet were Reserves procured and trained since the outbreak of the war." Unlike the Corps, however, regular Navy officers maintained a definite disdain for their reserve counterparts. A 1944 board reported that relationships between the two components were "marred by unfavorable factors that militate against the most effective and efficient operation of the Navy."[21]

The Coast Guard made a small step toward acquiring a reserve component in 1939, when Congress enacted legislation creating the Coast Guard Reserve, though this actually was a nonmilitary entity described by one author as "comprised of volunteer boat owners and yachtsmen tasked with promoting seamanship and boating safety." Two years later Congress passed an act that redesignated this organization as the Coast Guard Auxiliary and established a true Coast Guard Reserve. The entire Coast Guard fell under operational control of the Navy on 1 November 1941, and it remained in that status for the duration of the conflict. In a fashion similar to the other sea services, by the end of the war more than 80 percent of Coast Guard personnel were officially reservists, but indistinguishable from regulars in practice.[22]

World War II also marked the first widespread recruitment of female military personnel, all of them brought onto duty as reservists, and generally as part of newly created female-only components: Women's Army Corps (WAC), Women Accepted for Volunteer Emergency Service (WAVES) for the Navy, and Semper Paratus Always Ready (SPARs) for the Coast Guard. The Marine Corps was the sole service to treat its female reservists as a more or less integral component. The commandant, General Thomas Holcomb, told a national news magazine in 1944: "They are *Marines*. They don't have a nickname and they don't need one. They get their basic training in a Marine atmosphere at a Marine post. They inherit the traditions of the Marines. They *are* Marines."[23]

In 1940–1941 the nation's reserve components fulfilled their role, providing readily available, partially trained units and personnel to augment the regular forces. The president's increase in annual training and drilling requirements in the year prior had furthered that process, but his decision was a tacit acknowledgment that guardsmen and reservists in the modern era required more training before they could be expected to go to war. The effective service of thousands of reserve junior officers, mostly ROTC, validated officer acquisition policies put in place from 1916 to 1920. The need to flesh out mobilized units with large numbers of conscripts and the debate over maintaining cohesiveness versus breaking up units to avoid hometown loyalties made clear that the nation had yet to determine how best to handle the makeup of citizen-soldier units. Later generations would continue to grapple with these issues.

Postwar Challenges

When the conflict ended, President Harry S. Truman presided over the demobilization of nearly 12 million uniformed personnel. In his memoirs, he opined, "Once hostilities are over, Americans are . . . spontaneous and . . . headlong in their eagerness to return to civilian life. No people in history have been known to disengage themselves so quickly from the ways of war." At a press conference in April 1946 he noted that seven million soldiers had already been discharged, calling it "the most remarkable demobilization in the history of the world, or 'disintegration,' if you want to call it that."[24]

Amidst the demobilization, Truman recognized the need to maintain military capability as tensions ratcheted up with the Soviets, and he saw the reserve component as an inexpensive way to accomplish that. Ever since his experience in the National Guard during World War I, he saw "a prepared soldier-citizenry" as an alternative to a large standing army. In August 1945 the president proposed "a system of universal training during peacetime which would provide this country with a well-trained and effectively organized citizen reserve to reinforce the professional armed forces in times of danger." As an added benefit, he wanted a program that included "self-improvement" features that would foster "the moral and spiritual welfare of our young people."[25]

Truman's plan envisioned a small professional Army, Navy, and Marine Corps; a larger National Guard and reserve of trained units; and "a General Reserve composed of all the male citizens of the United States who had received training." In effect, it was a return to the nation's early reliance on the "every citizen a soldier" ideal. His plan also harked back a generation earlier to John McAuley Palmer. In fact, Marshall had recalled Palmer to active duty at the start of World War II to plan the postwar military. By 1944 Palmer favored a program of universal military training (UMT), which he thought was the only means of supplying adequate numbers of partially trained citizen-soldiers to meet future national emergencies. In contrast to a more militaristic system dominated by professional officers, he believed there should be opportunities for citizen-soldiers to "rise by successive steps to any rank for which they can definitely qualify."[26]

While Palmer's plan—both in 1919 and 25 years later—at first blush seemed to presage a bigger role for the Guard, guardsmen had reason to be skeptical based on their experience during World War II. During mobilization the Army publicly portrayed the National Guard in a poor light. Likewise, the regulars had removed senior Guard leaders for unfitness and placed restrictive age brackets on officer grades that appeared to many a contrivance to make room for younger regular officers at the Guard's expense. Moreover, the Army relegated the National Guard Bureau (NGB) to an inconsequential wartime role despite the 1920 statutory requirement that the Guard participate in the development of War Department policies affecting its component.[27]

Concerned that the War Department was planning to reduce the Guard to insignificance, the National Guard Association president, Maj. Gen. Ellard A. Walsh, held a series of meetings in 1944 between the NGA and the department. George Marshall, who had served in the mid-1930s as a senior instructor with the Illinois National Guard, understood both the Guard's merits and its challenges. Perhaps recalling the understrength Guard divisions mobilized after the fall of France and the small size of the enlisted Organized Reserve, he believed that only with UMT "can full vigor and life be instilled into the Reserve system." Walsh and the NGA told the War Department that the price of their support for a UMT plan was a renewed commitment to the NGA's historic goals—that the Guard remain the preferred reserve component and maintain its dual state-federal status. The NGA's persistence paid off when the War Department, unwilling to risk its preferred postwar plan should the Guard fuel a congressional battle, officially supported retaining the National Guard as "an integral part and a first line Reserve component" of the armed forces. Once again the Guard emerged with the upper hand in a political wrestling match with the regular Army.[28]

The National Guard proved equally adept in protecting and enhancing its role in the aviation realm. The Army Air Forces (AAF) argued that future conflicts would likely be destructive, short-lived affairs settled by aviation—a position reinforced by the use of atomic weapons against Japan—and therefore the AAF should become an independent service. Army aviation leaders believed that a million-member active-duty air component would be the primary guarantor of national security, and they relegated the Guard contribution to antiaircraft artillery units. Walsh and the NGA's political pressure led a reluctant AAF to change its plans considerably, however. In October 1945 Secretary of War Henry L. Stimson committed to both a federal entity (which would become the Air Force Reserve, or AFRES, as part of the creation of the Air Force in 1947) and the state-federal Air National Guard (ANG). Moreover, the ANG would be the main source of reserve combat-ready air units, giving it a greater role than the AFRES, initially characterized by one Air Force general as "a stew-pot, composed of leftovers not included in either the Regulars or Air National Guard." The Air Guard would have a defensive orientation, though, in keeping with the militia tradition, and consist mainly of fighter, aircraft control and warning, and antiaircraft artillery units. By mid-1949 all the authorized ANG units had attained federal recognition, and most were fully manned.[29]

Like the Guard, the AFRES faced the old question of reserve unit integrity during mobilization. While the AFRES was organized into units for training and administrative control, the Air Force intended that mobilized reservists would become individual replacements for Air Force and Air National Guard units. Acknowledging that this policy might negatively impact recruiting and retention, Air Force leaders concealed these plans from reservists. When mobilization came in 1950, many reservists were outraged when their units were broken up and they were reassigned. In the meantime, the Air Force placed a low priority on funding the traditional 15-day summer training since they had no intention of employing the units as such.[30]

Meanwhile, larger changes in defense policy took place, manifested initially in the National Security Act of 1947. Following nearly two years of political controversy surrounding defense reorganization, the law created a National Military Establishment (soon to be reorganized as the Department of Defense), headed by a secretary of defense. The new entity took control of the Navy Department and the former War Department, now separated into Army and Air Force Departments. Although this consolidation did not immediately impact the reserves, it laid the ground work for greater centralization of policy for the disparate reserve components.

The president and Congress allowed the wartime Selective Training and Service Act to expire in March 1947, a time when postwar manning appeared adequate to peacetime needs. One year later the intensifying Cold War propelled passage of the Selective Service Act of 1948. The president signed it on 24 June 1948, the day the Soviet Union closed Berlin's ground transportation routes to the West. The law required male citizens between 18 and 26 years to register for the draft, with induction beginning at age 19. Those picked would serve on active duty for 21 months, followed by five years in a nondrilling reserve component or three years in a drilling unit of either the National Guard or Organized Reserve. The legislation encouraged enlistment in the Guard by those younger than 18½ years by offering them deferment from induction in some situations as long as they satisfactorily participated in unit training. Furthermore, the act facilitated the president's access to the reserves, authorizing him to order reservists to active duty without their consent for up to 21 months without a declaration of war or national emergency. Thus, the 1948 law provided an early instance of presidential call-up authority that presaged by three decades the option later known as the presidential reserve call-up (PRC).[31]

In opting for a new selective service act, Congress rejected the universal training system championed by the president and the Army. Despite losing out on universal military training, the Army did improve its reserve system by merging the separate officer and enlisted reserve pools into a single Organized Reserve Corps. With a massive number of wartime veterans available, the Army planned for 25 divisions in the Organized Reserve, but funding was so scarce that there was no unit training until fiscal year (FY) 1949. Nearly simultaneously, legislation in 1948 authorized members of all reserve components to earn retirement points by participating in peacetime training. Personnel who accrued the minimum number of points for 20 or more years would be eligible for retirement pay at the age of 60, thus providing an additional incentive for recruitment and retention in the reserve components. Finally, congressional action authorized peacetime career opportunities for women, mainly as nurses and medical and administration specialists in the regular Army and the Organized Reserve.[32]

The postwar policy changes that spurred recruiting and retention, coupled with the large number of wartime veterans maintained on the rolls of the reserves, provided an apparent strength in numbers that the reserve component badly needed. The Army National Guard, for instance, experienced unprecedented growth in 1948. But that masked an ongoing problem. In a continuation of prewar practice, new reservists and guardsmen joined their units without any initial training, such as boot camp or an advanced-skill program, relying instead upon on-the-job training at the local unit. Since that training came at the rate of one evening a week and two weeks each summer, it was a long, slow process to acquire basic military skills. Meanwhile most of the veterans did not affiliate with a unit and therefore participated in little or no training, so their hard-won skills slowly perished as time passed. The long lead-up to World War II had enabled the reserve components to mobilize and prepare well before they had to go into combat. The next conflict would not provide the same luxury.

The Gray Board

In late 1947 Secretary of Defense James V. Forrestal, frustrated by the "open schism between the National Guard and the Organized Reserve" and the fact that "the reserve forces and the regular services were continually engaged in the criticism of one another" formed the Committee on Civilian Components (as reserve forces were then known). Chaired by Assistant Secretary of the Army Gordon Gray, it conducted "a comprehensive, objective and impartial study" of the role of reserve components in the newly unified military. The postwar reserve programs had many critics, including the reservists themselves, who saw limited opportunities, uncertainty about their place in the new defense establishment, and a lack of information. The Gray Board reviewed appropriate missions and functions; size, composition, and organization; standardization of policies and practices; and the joint use of facilities (such as armories). The panel completed its report in June 1948.[33]

The board's most significant and sweeping conclusion fell under the heading: "National Security Requires That All Services Each Have One Federal Reserve Force." It called for the National Guard and the Organized Reserve Corps to be merged under the designation "The National Guard of the United States," which the board thought would assuage Guard concerns about the merger. Because Air National Guard units lacked the lengthy history and traditions of the Army Guard, the ANG was much smaller relative to the Air Force Reserve, and modern aircraft

Named for Assistant Secretary of the Army Gordon Gray (left), the 1948 Gray Board produced a comprehensive review of the role of the reserve components in the National Military Establishment, foreshadowing the policy of periodic operational deployments of Guard and reserve forces. (Source: National Archives)

were generally unsuitable for state missions, the board recommended the Air National Guard and the Air Reserve be combined under the designation "The United States Air Force Reserve."[34]

To an impressive degree the Gray Board achieved its desired scope, objectivity, and impartiality, and its results deserved careful consideration. Its perspective was clearly Palmerian rather than Uptonian, since it accepted that even if it was "financially feasible for us to maintain in peacetime a regular establishment adequate by itself to defend the nation—and it is not—American tradition would forbid it." The board viewed the nation's reliance upon citizen-soldiers not as a necessary evil but as a positive aspect of American culture. At the same time the board took a realistic position concerning the state of military preparedness in 1948: "The impression that these [reserve] forces now contain elements which are ready for combat is a dangerous illusion." The board acknowledged that the Guard had been "extremely valuable for mobilization purposes" but pointed out that oceans and allies could no longer provide a cushion of several months or more to prepare for combat operations. This led directly to two recommendations: federal control of the National Guard to ensure it could perform as a "modern Federal striking force" and provision for "pretrained personnel" in the reserve forces.[35]

The board concluded that direct federal control of the Guard was the only way to properly "combine authority with responsibility." As the law plainly stated, the National Guard was unavailable for a federal mission unless Congress declared a state of national emergency. Even then, the transfer of "property and equipment from the States to the Federal Government" would consume valuable time in a mobilization scenario. The board believed these delays were contrary to the rapid mobilization that modern warfare required. The board included a letter from John McAuley Palmer arguing that in order to be "fully effective," any Army reserve component must be organized under the Constitution's clause "to raise and support armies." The militia clauses, in contrast, assigned states the responsibility for organizing and training such forces and for selecting their officers, thereby denying the "national war-making power" the requisite authority to prepare reserve forces to meet national security missions. Palmer therefore viewed the National Guard's status as "fundamentally unsound." The Air Force, displeased with maintaining separate state and federal reserve components, agreed with Gray and Palmer.[36]

With regard to pretrained personnel, the board reminded its audience that the nation had always relied upon a small professional force backed up by a partially trained citizen-soldiery. However, "the supply of *trained citizens* has never been assured," the board stated with candor. In the postwar era only a "continuous flow of pretrained personnel" would ensure reserve forces were ready to carry out their missions. The Gray Board was skeptical about the 1948 selective service law allowing "untrained young men to join the National Guard," since they had little military value. Worse, their presence inflated numbers and produced an illusion of greater defense preparedness than was in fact the case. A better option was to rotate reserve units and personnel on active duty "for substantial periods of time." Thus, the board advocated an early version of the reserve rotational policy embodied in the Army Force Generation plan some 50 years later.[37]

One of the board's most insightful conclusions was that federal control of the Guard would not detract from the local nature of Guard units, nor from local support, loyalty, and pride. It perceived that reserve units were inherently local and therefore would not be damaged in terms of support and loyalty by federal instead of state affiliation. Preserving that local identity constituted "a matter of great concern to the federal authority," because of the important values such as cohesion and morale "inherent in this identity." But board members believed that most guardsmen were primarily motivated to serve the nation, rather than their home states, dating back at least to the late 19th century when NGA leaders sought to ensure the Guard's primary role in national security. The guardsman's "pride in service attaches to the position and prestige which that service gives him in his home community rather than to his military relation to the State." Thus, "the deep roots of the Guard units . . . and the spirit and pride which come of these things" would continue even with a shift from state to federal control.[38]

The Gray Board's most far-reaching suggestion—merging the National Guard into a federal-only Army reserve force—struck at the heart of the Guard's affiliations and its source of political power in the states. President Truman, well aware that the report was "filled with political dynamite and during a Presidential campaign can defeat its own purpose," did not support the recommendation. Guard leaders also appealed to Congress, which rejected the proposed merger. While the board did not change the status quo, it had identified and judiciously addressed the basic manpower problem faced by the United States. For too long the nation had relied on a small regular military establishment supplemented by partially trained reservists, but national policy had never ensured that the reserve was large enough or well enough trained. The nearly concurrent 1948 Selective Service Act highlighted the problem, as the incentives it put into place did not lead to as large a surge in reserve enlistments as expected. A combination of war-weariness, confidence in the U.S. atomic monopoly, the Truman administration's commitment to balanced budgets and small defense outlays, and the resulting low odds of a young man being drafted all conspired to render the nation's reserve forces undermanned and underprepared. The fate of the Gray Board's recommendations only served to illustrate that any significant change in policy had to pass muster with the Guard and its allies in Congress if it was to have any hope of becoming reality.[39]

The anemic state of the reserve forces led President Truman to issue an executive order on 15 October 1948 that required the secretary of defense to "proceed without delay" in bringing the reserve components to full strength and to "establish vigorous and progressive programs of appropriate instruction and training." He required a report of progress from the secretary within 60 days and urged every citizen to do their "utmost in aiding the development of effective reserve components." The need for action and further policy review led in September 1949 to Secretary of Defense Louis A. Johnson establishing a standing Civilian Components Policy Board to advise him on reserve issues. Chaired by a civilian from outside the government and composed of an under or assistant secretary, a regular officer from each military department, and two reserve officers from each reserve component, its purpose was to provide advice to the secretary of defense, develop unified policy, and coordinate the activities of the various reserve elements. Each military department in turn established a similar board to assist the service secretaries in overseeing their reserve components. The Gray Board's report served as the starting point for the new board. In May 1950 the first chairman summarized the state of the reserve forces: "Despite the fact that the civilian components are at their greatest peacetime strength in history, it is obvious from the many problems to which I have alluded that much remains to be done to bring them to the minimum strength and state of readiness essential to meet their assigned mobilization missions."[40]

The Korean Conflict

In late June 1950 North Korea invaded its southern neighbor and provided a catalyst for American rearmament. After the start of World War II in 1939 the United States had more than two years to prepare for its entry into combat, but the Korean conflict took the United States completely by surprise. The president quickly committed a woefully unprepared U.S. force to defend the Republic of Korea and to repel the North's Soviet-equipped forces. On 19 July 1950 Truman announced a partial mobilization of the National Guard and Organized Reserve for a period up to 21 months. In the next few weeks the Pentagon federalized four National Guard infantry divisions: the 40th (California), 45th (Oklahoma), 28th (Pennsylvania), and 43rd (Connecticut, Rhode Island, Vermont). The 40th and 45th divisions had no more than half their authorized strength, which required a large infusion of conscripts and considerable training to achieve combat readiness. That was emblematic of the overall unpreparedness of the reserves. The first Guard unit to join the fight, the Arkansas National Guard's 936th Field Artillery Battalion, did not arrive in Korea until February 1951. By the time the 40th and 45th divisions joined the fighting in early 1952, the guardsmen who had come onto active duty with those organizations were already nearing the end of their 21-month commitment, leading to personnel turbulence and a loss of unit cohesion. In late 1951 the 28th and 43rd divisions deployed to Germany to defend against any potential Soviet incursion and suffered a similar loss of mobilized personnel.[41]

Following a series of setbacks for the UN forces early in the war, the September 1950 Inchon landing and follow-on operations into North Korea offered hope for a quick victory and eased concerns about the state of U.S. preparedness. But after communist China entered the war in November and gravely threatened allied forces, Truman declared a state of national emergency and announced an increase in the armed forces from 1.5 million to 3.5 million. This buildup also addressed the recognized need to strengthen the American commitment to defend Western Europe against a potential Soviet invasion. Although the United States relied heavily on draftees to meet manpower needs, in January 1952 it federalized four more National Guard divisions. They remained stateside for training, providing a source of replacements for units overseas and serving as part of the strategic reserve.[42]

At the start of fighting in Korea, the Army's Organized Reserve Corps consisted of nearly 510,000 officers and enlisted, but fewer than 190,000 participated in paid drills. In the immediate crisis of 1950, the Army called a significant portion of the Organized Reserve to active duty, including 400 units that reported by the end of August. Many of those recalled as individuals were World War II veterans who had not received training, pay, or other benefits since 1945; many of them felt it was unfair that they were being activated when many units did not receive orders. Such inequities aside, more than 200,000 Organized Reserve personnel served on active duty, most of them in 1950 and 1951. Even some of those not recalled were affected, as employers were wary of hiring men who might suddenly receive orders. In late 1950 a member of the Civilian Components Policy Board declared that reservists found themselves "unduly penalized [financially] in time of limited mobilization," an issue that would continue to resurface in the future.[43]

The Naval Reserve was in the same boat as the Army. In June 1950 it had a paper strength of 1.1 million, but only one in six drilled with a unit. By the end of August 53,000 naval reservists were on active duty. By June 1951 the total was 182,000, but a majority of them came from a nondrilling reserve status. Not surprisingly, in November 1950 the commander of Fleet Air Japan reported: "Almost without exception, Reserves proved to be conscientious and properly motivated, but lacking in technical skill and knowledge which only continuous naval duty can give." The Marine Corps Reserve fared only somewhat better. While the Corps strongly supported the reserve program with high-quality regulars in key positions and an emphasis on regular assistance to reserve summer training, and while the reserve had a very high proportion of World War II veterans, young men who joined units in the late 1940s still did not undergo any training other than that gained on the job during drills and two weeks each summer. In July, when General Douglas MacArthur requested a Marine division in Korea, the Corps relied heavily on activated reservists to bring the 1st Marine Division to fighting strength. In a matter of days the Corps segregated out those who had less than a year in the reserves and had not attended summer training and assigned the remaining individuals to fill out regular units. But even so, that meant some reservists with as little as two weeks of active duty and less than a hundred hours of drill time were heading off to combat. At the time of the Inchon landing in September 1950 reservists made up 20 percent of the division, a proportion that rose to 50 percent during the first half of 1951, as reservists initially constituted the lion's share of combat replacements. By that time also, Navy and Marine Corps reserve pilots were flying up to one-third of the combat sorties over Korea.[44]

The war in Korea did not require a total mobilization, which raised the issue of which reserve component units and individuals would bear the cost of combat duty. From the Pentagon's standpoint it made sense to call up large numbers of nondrilling reservists, mostly World War II veterans, to flesh out regular units for early deployment to the conflict, while simultaneously leaving untouched numerous reserve component units, supposedly the most-ready elements, to serve as a strategic reserve in case a wider conflict erupted with the Soviet Union. While the result was not equitable for those who already had fought one war for their country, Secretary of Defense George Marshall believed that "there was no alternative to this procedure." By the time an armistice halted the Korean War in July 1953, the U.S. Army had brought more than 2.8 million personnel onto active duty. But due to the administration's decision to rely heavily on draftees, only one-third of Army guardsmen had been activated and they accounted for only about 5 percent of that total.[45]

In contrast to the Army Guard, approximately 80 percent of the Air National Guard was federalized for Korea. Prior to the war, the ANG, in the words of Lt. Col. Thomas G. Lanphier Jr., was arguably "little more than a flying club," in large part a consequence of the U.S. Air Force's (USAF's) inability to deal successfully with the state-controlled nature of the ANG during peacetime, an issue the Gray Board had highlighted. Given the Air Guard's problems, it was no surprise when the regular Air Force found most of the earliest mobilized units were, according to one officer, "not in a position to do what is expected." Most units were broken up and their personnel used to fill out regular outfits, leading the NGA's Walsh to accuse the Air Force of "cannibalizing" the Air Guard. But the conflict forced a reversal of the steadily deteriorating relationship between the Air Guard and the Air Force, and the former's capabilities steadily increased. Thus, the Korean War represented a watershed for the dual-status air reserve component, especially in terms of manpower strength and appropriations.[46]

As for the Air Force Reserve, nearly all its combat and support units were mobilized during the Korean conflict, about three-fourths during the first year. Although the National Defense Act of 1916 required the National Guard to be the first-called reserve component when a crisis required the expansion of the armed forces, in 1950 the AFRES was mobilized prior to the ANG. In addition to the Air Guard's lack of combat readiness, two other factors played a part. The Far East Air Forces primarily needed specific capabilities such as troop carrier and bombardment aircrews that were generally resident in the Air Force Reserve. In addition, the Pentagon wanted to maintain Guard units in strategic reserve for a European contingency. In the end, the requirements of the situation overrode the dictates of law.[47]

In response to considerable disgruntlement with the initial calls to active duty, in October 1950 Secretary Marshall appointed a board "to recommend policies to eliminate any uncertainties and inequities that have arisen under [the] present system." In the interim, he directed the service secretaries to publish policies for their respective components that would, "insofar as military conditions permit," give a reservist at least 30 days from notification until his reporting date. In addition, the services should determine their manpower requirements six months in advance, to provide even greater notification to reservists than the minimum 30 days.[48]

Since 1945 the president and defense leaders had favored universal military training as the only economical means to maintain adequate military preparedness. But the hostilities in Korea and consequent mobilization convinced President Truman it was inadvisable to pursue the measure at that time. The services, in particular the Army, were already fully engaged in training draftees and activated reservists and guardsmen while establishing new units for an expanding force. Training, housing, and equipping an even larger pool of recruits brought in under a UMT program, only to send them back to civilian life after six months, was more than the nation could afford in the midst of fighting a war. Still, Truman favored the policy in the long term even if the ongoing conflict made its implementation untimely, and he submitted a bill reflecting that thinking in January 1951. Congress passed the Universal Military Training and Service Act in June, but it was universal in name only. By authorizing a commission to develop the details of a National Security Training Corps and submit implementing legislation to Congress, it essentially called for a plan for UMT that Congress would decide on later. In practice, the act amended the 1948 selective service law to extend the service of draftees (still only a portion of all males ages 18 to 26) to two years on active duty and an additional six years in a reserve component. It also set the permanent ceiling of the armed forces at just over two million but allowed a waiver for the ongoing conflict for up to five million members. The actual wartime peak in manpower came in April 1952 with nearly 3.7 million personnel in uniform.[49]

The mobilizations, mainly in the first year of the Korean conflict, included about 640,000 World War II veterans, many of them drawn from unpaid, non-drilling status. As Secretary Marshall noted in September 1951, "providing as quickly as possible combat-ready reinforcements for the forces fighting in the Far East . . . could be accomplished only by extensive calls for additional service from the veterans of World War II." Their availability considerably ameliorated the consequences of the nation's inadequate reserve system in 1950. While many had not had any military training in five years, the weapons and tactics used in Korea varied little from those they had employed in the previous war. Their proven combat experience offset the lack of recent training and allowed them to assimilate quickly into units heading off to war. As a result, the nation's reserve system appeared better than it was. But the United States could not depend on having a similar large pool of recent veterans available for the next conflict.[50]

The Armed Forces Reserve Act of 1952

The early employment of reservists in combat in Korea highlighted the concerns raised by the Gray Board. In January 1951 Representative Carl Vinson, chairman of the House Armed Services Committee, directed the Department of Defense (DoD) to draft a bill that would replace the myriad laws that governed the reserve components with a single act that would "assure the maintenance of a strong and vigorous Reserve force." The task of writing the legislation fell to the newly renamed Reserve Forces Policy Board, or RFPB (formerly the Civilian Components Policy Board). Congress took up the proposal in June 1951, greatly amended it based on extensive input from guardsmen, reservists, and other interested parties, and finally passed it as the Armed Forces Reserve Act of 1952. President Truman signed it into law in July 1952.[51]

Following the Armed Forces Reserve Act of 1952, Anna M. Rosenberg became the Pentagon official with principal responsibility for all reserve affairs; she was concerned that veterans continued to bear the burden of reserve component mobilizations. (Source: OSD/HO)

The act achieved several worthwhile goals. It consolidated the various statutes and regulations affecting the reserve components and provided increased standardization respecting the composition, duties, and regulation of the reserves. It recognized seven reserve components: the National Guard of the United States, Army Reserve, Naval Reserve, Marine Corps Reserve, Air National Guard of the United States, Air Force Reserve, and Coast Guard Reserve. Most important, it enhanced the role and influence of the reserves in defense planning in three ways. It codified the Reserve Forces Policy Board, making it "the principal policy adviser to the Secretary of Defense on matters pertaining to the reserve components." It directed that an assistant secretary of defense would have "principal responsibility for all Reserve affairs," with that portfolio initially going to Anna M. Rosenberg, the assistant secretary of defense for manpower and personnel. It required that each service assign a general or flag officer responsible for reserve affairs, with direct access to the service chief, and that reserve officers on active duty be assigned to the service staff "to assist and participate in the preparation and administration of all policies and regulations affecting their reserve component."[52]

The act also provided individual reservists with assurances and benefits they had sought for years. Primary among these was a more equitable promotion system, so that reservists would be promoted at roughly the same time as their regular counterparts. The law made reserve officer appointments indefinite, thereby removing what one historian called "the stigma of probationary scrutiny of reservists." Reservists agreeing to extended active duty would now receive written contracts that guaranteed separation pay if they were released from duty earlier than expected. For a host of reasons, then, the Armed Forces Reserve Act of 1952—the most comprehensive legislation ever enacted for the reserve component—has been considered the reserves' Magna Carta.[53]

Despite the act's substantial improvements, it fell short in terms of mobilization policy, both in the critical matter of providing greater fairness for veterans during future recalls, and in providing sufficient and immediately available combat power. Assistant Secretary Rosenberg had testified before the Senate Armed Services Committee that the eventual adoption of UMT would prevent "the recurrence of past inequities where veterans were called back to service to meet an emergency while there were still young men in the community who had never served at all." But, she noted, "It has been virtually impossible to get enough men—trained or untrained—to fill out our Guard and Reserve units. The lack of previous training in military skills and military habits has proved an almost insuperable handicap." The NGA's Walsh thought the failure to implement meaningful universal military training rendered the law "a delusion" from which "the awakening would be bitter indeed." Supporters of UMT argued that it alone would provide the trained manpower needed to fill the reserve establishment. Without it, the nation would be forced to repeatedly call veterans back to the colors as it had for Korea and to draft others to fill the remaining need, with a consequent bulge in the training establishment at a time when a regular force rushing off to war was least able to handle it. Moreover, as leaders and mobilization planners had realized increasingly since 1900, it took considerable time to turn raw manpower into an integral part of units that could fight on the modern battlefield. Nevertheless, for the time being the nation would continue to rely on a reserve force that had too little trained manpower and relied too heavily on veterans as its source of immediately employable combat power.[54]

The 1952 act did provide at least limited protection for veterans by establishing three categories of reservists: Ready, Retired, and Standby. The Ready Reserve's authorized ceiling was 1.5 million and consisted of "those units or members of the reserve components, or both, who are liable for active duty either in time of war, in time of national emergency declared by the Congress or proclaimed by the President, or when otherwise authorized by law." The language governing the Standby Reserve omitted the phrase "or proclaimed by the President," thus requiring congressional action to place those personnel on active duty against their will. In addition, to access the Standby Reserve for active duty the secretary of defense had to certify that the needed capability was not available in the Ready Reserve. Thus a veteran could elect to serve his time in the Standby Reserve, where the odds of being activated were somewhat lower. The Retired Reserve was made up of personnel under age 60 who had retired from reserve duty but who could be recalled under limited circumstances (such as a declaration of war or a national emergency) and only by an act of Congress.[55]

—— Conclusion ——

Between the end of World War I and the armistice in Korea, the nation continued to rely upon a small regular military establishment backed up by a partially trained National Guard and federal-only reserve that was expected to hold the line in an emergency before large numbers of draftees could be formed into new units and take the field. Although hindered by extremely limited funding during most peacetime years, the reserves gradually improved in terms of training and professionalism. The Armed Forces Reserve Act of 1952 offered for the first time a comprehensive approach to planning, administration, management, and regulation of the reserve component. But despite the wake-up call sounded by the hasty mobilization for Korea, the perennial concerns over reserve unit integrity and the need for better-trained manpower in a national emergency remained unresolved. Faced with the choice of returning to the historic ideal of every male citizen being a soldier, a solution that would have at least provided sufficient numbers in the reserve components, Congress balked. That idea, long discarded in practice, would never again resurface for serious consideration.

—— CHAPTER 3 ——

Toward a War-Ready Reserve Component, 1954–1989

The Armed Forces Reserve Act of 1952 had failed to settle a number of lingering questions, and the role of the reserves continued to be defined more by circumstance than by broad vision. President Lyndon B. Johnson's decision not to mobilize the reserves for Vietnam struck an unintended but devastating blow, though the establishment in 1967 of the Selected Reserve laid the groundwork for a better future. The end of the draft and transition to an all-volunteer force in the 1970s wrought further havoc upon the reserves. The defense buildup in the 1980s finally placed the Selected Reserve on solid footing in terms of manpower, pay, benefits, family and employer issues, training, and equipping—improvements that came just in time as the new presidential selected reserve call-up (PSRC) authority made it far more likely than before that the reserves would be activated for frequent operational commitments.

The New Look and New Initiatives

President Dwight D. Eisenhower came to office in 1953 with the goal of balancing the nation's security and economic health. To reduce the cost of the Cold War, he advanced the New Look strategy—a heavy reliance on air-delivered nuclear weapons to deter war and on allies to defend themselves, backed by much smaller and less expensive American active-duty conventional forces and even cheaper but larger reserve elements. In early 1953 Eisenhower's defense secretary, Charles E. Wilson, declared that "the Reserve forces must become more than ever an integral component of national defense to supplement the Armed Forces on short notice."[1]

The difficulty was that the reserve components were not appreciably more ready than they had been in 1950. While they had proven sufficient to augment the regulars in a limited war, primarily due to the availability of World War II veterans, they were ill-prepared to meet the demands of a global conflict that would require mobilization of the entire reserve—a problem that would grow worse over time as the proportion of combat veterans began to decline. The 1952 law had not provided an enforcement mechanism or higher drill pay to ensure active participation in the units of the Ready Reserve. Consequently, in the two years following its enactment few young men leaving active duty with reserve obligations chose drill-pay status. In mid-1955 there were 2.8 million ready reservists on the rolls, but only about 28 percent participated in paid drills; most of the remainder were inactive members deemed of limited military value. In the Army Reserve, of 1.53 million in the Ready Reserve, barely 10 percent served in a drilling unit. A congressional report noted that "the Ready Reserve, while increasing in size, has not attained the degree of organization or training required for its mobilization role." Another report concluded that the number of personnel on the rolls "was in nowise a measure of the military strength of the Ready Reserve." Simply put, the reserves were not ready for war.[2]

The significant mobilization problems during the Korean War and the increasing importance of the reserve in defense strategy galvanized Washington to undertake studies that would lead to additional legislation. Arthur S. Flemming, the director of the Office of Defense Mobilization, led one review and reported his findings to President Eisenhower in January 1954. Flemming acknowledged that the United States lacked "reserve forces adequately organized and trained" to meet its security needs. He noted the need for an "immediately callable reserve" and a "selectively callable reserve," which equated to the 1952 law's Ready and Standby categories. But he emphasized that the Ready Reserve had to be "instantly available" and capable of high "military competence." While personnel leaving active duty with reserve obligations provided the level of experience needed, if the number of such men continued to fall short of requirements, he proposed drafting men for service in the reserves, beginning with a period of active duty so they could "be given initial intensive training for reserve service."[3]

In January 1954 the president directed Flemming to brief the National Security Council, which, along with the Defense Mobilization Office and the Defense Department, developed a plan outlining the nation's reserve requirements. They agreed with Flemming's position that the reserves should form around "a substantial proportion of prior-service personnel" who had the requisite level of training. To achieve that goal, they believed that the requirement for draftees to serve six years in the reserves after their initial two years of active duty should include *forced* participation in a unit of the Ready Reserve. Equally important, they concluded that "Service prescribed initial training is necessary for all nonprior service personnel entering" the reserves. That would solve the problem of direct enlistees in the reserves receiving only on-the-job training. To spur such enlistments, they recommended exempting reservists from being drafted as long as they participated satisfactorily. The reserves needed to bring in young men directly, since relying too heavily on the prior-service pipeline resulted in an older force; less than 17 percent of the men in the Army Reserve were younger than 24. Army Chief of Staff General Matthew B. Ridgway thought that the combination of increasing prior-service participation in the Ready Reserve and requiring initial entry training for direct enlistees would shorten the time needed to get activated reserve units into combat from 10 months to 5.[4]

In January 1955 Eisenhower asked Congress to pass legislation incorporating much of the work of Flemming's task force. The president pointed out the nation's recurring failure to maintain in peacetime a "proper military posture," with the cost of the resulting lack of readiness "manifold—in treasure, in blood, in the heartbreak of a mighty nation buying time with the lives of men." In keeping with the New Look, he argued that "active military forces are only the cutting edge of our nation's full strength. A vigorous economy, a strong mobilization base and trained citizens are the invincible elements in our military striking power." Congress ultimately agreed in part, and incorporated many of the administration's proposals in the Reserve Forces Act of 1955. The law authorized the enlistment of men between 17 and 18½ years old directly into the reserves for a period of eight years, with a required period of initial active duty for training of between three and six months (in practice generally the latter). It also extended the draft to 1959 and made reservists who failed to participate satisfactorily in unit training subject to induction. Finally, it increased the authorized strength of the Ready Reserve (all services) from 1.5 million to 2.9 million and authorized the president to call as many as one million ready reservists to active duty whenever he declared a national emergency. With the extension of the draft, many leaders anticipated significantly increased enlistments to follow, but such hopes went unrealized.[5]

As with previous reserve legislation, the 1955 law fell short of what many proponents had envisioned. Eisenhower was disappointed particularly in the law's failure to ensure "a hard core of prior service personnel to the National Guard" by not making available the same incentives for men leaving active duty to join the Guard as they had to join a federal Ready Reserve component. In addition, direct enlistees in the Guard had no obligation to undergo basic training beyond that conducted by their unit. The failure to include the Guard in major provisions of the law largely resulted from a dispute over a proposal to require racial desegregation of the state forces. There was a spur for new Guard enlistees to volunteer for basic training, as they would not be drafted if they completed at least three months of active-duty training. The positive impact of that provision was limited, however, because the training could occur at any point during the enlistment, though it was most needed and effective at the start. Conversely, Eisenhower felt that the pay provided to those enlisting in the federal reserves under initial entry training programs, just two-thirds of what they would receive if they joined the Guard and went to the same training, provided an unfair advantage to the Guard.[6]

The debate over the requirement for, and the length of, basic training for guardsmen brought renewed rancor between the Army and Guard. Secretary Wilson did not help matters when he accused the Guard of being a "draft dodging" haven. The House Armed Services Committee worked out a compromise, implemented via Army regulation, which permitted the Guard to continue its recently adopted 11-week training period through 1957, with Guard enlistees thereafter undergoing the same six months of basic training as federal reservists.[7]

Another piece of 1950s legislation, the Reserve Officer Personnel Act of 1954, established a long-overdue system governing the promotion of reserve officers. One official study declared that the act "was of tremendous importance to officers in the Army Reserve, because it gave to them and other Reservists a statutory basis for promotion and service" similar to that of regulars. The law also materially improved reserve officers' opportunity for seniority vis-à-vis their regular counterparts by crediting their inactive duty for training in determining date of rank. Another critical congressional action, in 1955, amended the law known colloquially as the Veterans' Reemployment Rights Act. Originally enacted in 1940 to give those who were drafted or mobilized the right to reemployment in their civilian jobs (federal government or private sector), the new amendment extended that protection to reservists for initial active-duty training, active duty for training, and inactive-duty training—the kinds of duty typically performed by reserve component members. Five years later Congress and the president expanded it to cover the Guard in the same circumstances. Finally, in 1956, Congress passed legislation allowing women to serve in the National Guard for the first time, albeit only at the officer rank in medical specialties.[8]

The roots of another key development in the training and administration of reserve units went back to 1916, when the government first hired full-time civilian personnel to tend to the National Guard's federally owned horses. The program expanded over the years to encompass training, maintenance, property accountability, and administration. The Army Reserve adopted its version in 1950, and a decade later required the civilian technicians to also be reservists in the units they supported. The Naval Reserve established a somewhat similar program in 1953, dubbed Training and Administration of the Reserves (TAR), which brought reservists on full-time active duty to maintain the readiness of their units. The Air Force followed the lead of the Army in 1957, establishing the Air Reserve Technician program to increase Air Force Reserve and Air National Guard combat readiness. Like the Army, the Air Force employed reservists and guardsmen as civilian technicians during the normal work week and then integrated them into the unit in their role as military personnel on training weekends or during active duty periods. The work of the technicians and TARs ensured that units and their personnel obtained the maximum benefit from the limited training time available.[9]

Among the reserve components, the Air National Guard, the newest and the least married to tradition, experienced the most dramatic improvements during the post-Korea period. From 1953 through the remainder of the decade, according to an ANG historian, the Air Guard experienced "enormous growth, modernization, and increasing [integration] with the active duty Air Force." The ANG doubled its budget and its strength, while its flying wings gained definite and diversified missions, standardized aircraft types, improved training regimens, and mobilization assignments. By 1960 the ANG was an all-jet-fighter force. That year the Air Force chief of staff, General Thomas D. White, wrote that the importance of the air reserves "in terms of *total force* can be gained from the fact that two-thirds of the tactical reconnaissance units, nearly half of the tactical fighter units, and more than three-fourths of the troop carrier units available to the Tactical Air Command in an emergency" were contained in the ANG and Air Force Reserve. Significantly, the Air Guard folded its training into the routine operations of the Air Force and the air reserve forces increased their peacetime support of regular Air Force missions, marking an early effort to integrate the regular and reserve components into a single force—an effort that would become known as Total Force policy. In parlance that would appear decades later, the ANG already was becoming part of the operational force.[10]

By the end of the 1950s, the reserve component had grown dramatically in size, especially in the critical cohort of enlisted strength in Army Reserve units, which doubled. The total number of drill-pay reservists among all services in 1960 approached one million, up more than 200,000 in five years. By making nonparticipants subject to the draft, the 1955 reserve act put teeth into the requirement to participate in a drilling unit. Other measures required direct enlistees in the Guard and reserves to undergo six months of active duty to complete entry-level individual training. Taken together, these changes in policy vastly improved combat readiness. The Ready Reserve was much better prepared than it had been, though not yet fully prepared, to fulfill its role as a force that could mobilize and quickly support the regular components in active operations.[11]

Flexible Response and Cold War Crises

In 1961 the incoming John F. Kennedy administration brought with it a new defense policy known as Flexible Response. Contrasting their approach with Eisenhower's New Look, Kennedy and his secretary of defense, Robert S. McNamara, wanted the United States to have more options than "humiliation or all-out nuclear action." That required an increase in the nation's conventional capabilities, as well as its strategic nuclear weapons, where the Soviets had been steadily gaining ground. McNamara, cost-conscious and committed to efficient management of defense resources, closed unneeded military bases and inactivated units—including reserve elements—even as he built up the capability of the nation's forces. Like Eisenhower, he saw the reserve component as an inexpensive way to increase capability.[12]

Following a summit in June 1961 between Kennedy and Soviet Premier Nikita Khrushchev, in which the president appeared to lack resolve, the Soviets took measures intended to force the Western powers out of West Berlin. On 25 July 1961 President Kennedy pledged to defend "our rights in West Berlin and our commitments to its people," and sped up defense initiatives announced earlier in the year. He also requested that Congress authorize him to order selected Ready Reserve units and individual reservists to active duty, indicating his intent to call AFRES air transport and ANG tactical air units to ensure "the airlift capacity and protection that we need." One week later, Congress responded, granting authority to mobilize 250,000 reservists for 12 months. Soon after, Secretary McNamara ordered thousands of air reserve members to active duty by 1 October. Seven ANG squadrons totaling 216 single-seat fighters quickly deployed to Central Europe, a feat that a House committee called perhaps "the outstanding accomplishment" of the mobilization. In fact, the U.S. Air Force had never in its history deployed a larger number of jet fighters. Air guardsmen accounted for four-fifths of the air reservists who served on active duty during the crisis.[13]

The standoff did not escalate into a "hot" war, so no Army National Guard (ARNG) units deployed overseas, though some were activated and underwent intensive training at installations in the continental United States to serve as a strategic reserve. Mobilization for that role, as opposed to a shooting war, was something neither the members nor their families and employers had anticipated. It created turmoil in personal and family lives, schools, and businesses, and led to considerable resentment because it seemed unnecessary. Kennedy justified his action: "We called them—in order to prevent war, not to fight a war." While it served that purpose and also improved combat readiness in the bargain, it raised fears that similar call-ups might happen any time U.S.-Soviet tensions increased. By March of 1962, however, McNamara's thinking had shifted. He no longer viewed it practical to call the reserves to meet repeated Cold War crises and adopted the policy of "relying on the reserve forces for augmentation only when armed conflict is imminent," although he did credit the rapid force buildup the reserves made possible with helping to demonstrate U.S. resolve and stabilize the Berlin situation. As a result, during August 1962 the Pentagon demobilized those who had been activated. When the Cuban Missile Crisis arose in October 1962, President Kennedy mobilized just over 14,000 Air Force reservists, primarily in troop carrier wings and aerial port squadrons—necessary building blocks to prepare for an invasion of the island. They were demobilized the following month.[14]

The Berlin mobilization was a strategic success, but it had revealed serious deficiencies in policies and practices, prompting the House Armed Services Committee to open an inquiry into reserve component readiness. In August 1962 Representative F. Edward Hébert's (D–LA) subcommittee published its report. The review found that the Pentagon sometimes improperly notified reservists of their recall, with word getting out via the news media rather than official channels. Congress also received numerous complaints from reservists who had not been given the expected 30 days to prepare their personal affairs prior to reporting for active duty. Far more concerning was the problem of fillers. In a replay of prior mobilizations, "many units had less than 50 percent of their assigned drilling strength when recalled." The Army, in particular, lacked the documentation it needed to rationally select units for activation, and "every Army Reserve unit recalled to active duty required a considerable number of fillers to bring them up to required active duty strength." The issue went beyond a unit's shortage of personnel at the time of mobilization. The prevalence of untrained, inexperienced personnel in the units increased the need for fillers. A clerk typist filling a helicopter mechanic billet, for instance, had the same impact as an empty slot. Of the 30,000 drilling Army reservists mobilized in 1961, fully one-third occupied "spaces for which they were not qualified." The "generally low experience level of drilling personnel assigned to Reserve units" necessitated the recall of nondrilling reservists with the needed skills. The subcommittee realized that unless drilling units could attract and retain experienced reservists, particularly in the noncommissioned officer grades, future mobilizations "will again require the automatic recall of veterans not assigned to drilling units."[15]

The Berlin mobilization, coming after a decade of changes designed to rectify the shortcomings exposed by Korea, suggested an inherent problem in the nation's geographically based reserve system. When personnel separated from active duty with obligated reserve service, they ideally joined a unit where they lived that had a need for their occupational specialty. But instances of mismatch frequently arose. An artilleryman, for instance, might end up in an area where there were no artillery units. Or his unit might be repurposed from artillery to another mission, such as logistics, as the needs of the service changed. Even those who enlisted directly in their hometown reserve unit might move to a new location and thus have to join a new unit. Often a reservist in this situation would not be able to go back on active duty to acquire a new skill. The alternative was learning on the job, but that took time, and meanwhile the individual would be unqualified or marginally qualified. The challenge of ensuring that reservists' skills matched those required by their units only increased in scope as American society became more mobile. And absent a shift away from geographical organization, there was no easy solution.[16]

Following the Berlin and Cuba crises, McNamara looked for ways to improve reserve component combat readiness. Between 1962 and 1967 he increased efficiency by reorganizing and reducing the size of the Army reserves, including deactivation of the six newest infantry divisions. He also attempted to implement one of the key recommendations of the Truman-era Gray Board by creating a single ground-reserve entity, though he planned to merge the Army Reserve into the National Guard. While that idea would not run into the same strong opposition from the National Guard Association that had tabled the Gray Board's proposal, the reserves enjoyed the support of their own professional organization, the Reserve Officers Association, established in 1922, which counted 170 congressmen as members. By 1965 McNamara realized that he could not implement any major reserve component reorganization because there was no congressional support to drastically reorder the status quo.[17]

The Vietnam War

The American military commitment in Vietnam had increased during the Kennedy administration, but rose dramatically in 1965 with the introduction of U.S. combat troops and the aerial bombing of North Vietnam. Despite the large-scale deployment of forces, President Johnson overruled McNamara and resisted calling up the reserves. Instead, Johnson doubled the monthly draft calls and increased the regular forces in piecemeal fashion. As units departed for Vietnam, the strategic reserve in the United States dwindled. To address that problem and achieve some improvement in reserve combat readiness, in 1965 McNamara announced the formation of a 150,000-strong Selected Reserve Force. His goal was a fully manned, highly trained, and well-equipped element within the Ready Reserve that would be ready to deploy rapidly in a national emergency—the ground forces within weeks and aviation units within days. One of the primary changes in training for the new force was an expansion of the then-standard two-hour drill period to four hours.[18]

In early 1968, in response to the North Korean seizure of the USS *Pueblo* and the Tet Offensive in South Vietnam, President Johnson finally called up a limited number of Ready Reserve units. But by that time, reserve units had become known as "havens for those who wanted to avoid active military duty and Vietnam," to use James T. Currie's echo of Secretary Wilson's barb. Johnson's long delay thus had the unintended consequence of helping create widespread negative impressions about the reserves. Popular notions notwithstanding, many reservists were veterans and a number had been in their units for years prior to the war. Many thousands also had served on active duty, mostly as volunteers. Air Force Reserve C–124 (Globemaster II heavy-lift transport) groups, as an example, flew missions into Southeast Asia on inactive duty status between 1966 and 1972 in support of the Military Airlift Command. Their largest effort came in early 1968, when reserve C–124s airlifted the 82nd Airborne Division and more than 3,000 U.S. Marines to Korea and South Vietnam.[19]

In the end, not all of those recalled served overseas, and the reserves constituted a very small portion of the more than 500,000 U.S. personnel deployed in Southeast Asia at that time. At least the rapid mobilization and excellent performance of a number of Selected Reserve Force units, particularly ANG tactical fighter units, demonstrated the effectiveness of McNamara's initiative. The air reserves, in particular, played key roles. In response to the *Pueblo*'s seizure, the ANG activated several tactical fighter and tactical reconnaissance groups. When the crisis did not escalate into open hostilities, some units went to Vietnam instead. By June 1968 four ANG F–100 Super Sabre units deployed to the war zone and for the next 10 months flew combat missions. The January 1968 mobilization, however, encountered major problems associated, to some degree, with the fact that there was no 30-day alert period as called for in Air Force plans. Not surprisingly, some reservists learned of their recall via the media rather than through official channels (as in 1961). Those reservists recalled in May, however, enjoyed the 30-day warning and experienced a smoother mobilization.[20]

Acknowledging the growing importance of the reserves, the Reserve Forces Bill of Rights and Vitalization Act of 1967 established the position of deputy assistant secretary of defense for reserve affairs (RA), who served under the assistant secretary of defense for manpower and reserve affairs. In an affirmation of McNamara's initiative two years earlier, the law also authorized a Selected Reserve within the Ready Reserve of each service, with a strength set annually by Congress. Although McNamara's wartime policies earned strong criticism, his initiative in establishing the Selected Reserve was both significant and enduring.[21]

The 1967 law also established the positions of the chief of Army Reserve and chief of Air Force Reserve to advise their respective service chiefs of staff on reserve matters. The House of Representatives' version of the bill had the chief of Army Reserve as commander of the Army Reserve, but that stipulation did not survive the legislative process. For the time being, command and control of the Army Reserve remained with the Continental Army Command. For the Air Force, the reserve chief's office placed AFRES's top-level policymaker on an equal footing with his Air Guard counterpart. In 1968 the Headquarters Air Force Reserve was activated at Robins Air Force Base (AFB), Georgia. But following serious disagreements between the Office of Air Force Reserve and Headquarters AFRES over their respective management responsibilities, in 1972 the Air Force gave the chief of Air Force Reserve a second hat as the commander of AFRES.[22]

Although the seaborne reserve forces did not play a major role in the conflicts and crises of the 1960s, they learned from the experiences of the mobilized components. The Naval Reserve discovered after the Berlin crisis that, much like the Army Reserve and Guard, only 50 percent of its personnel were qualified for their mobilization billets, a problem it took steps to correct as much as possible, in part by increasing the proportion of full-time reservists. In a 1962 effort to enhance readiness, Marine ground reservists, for the first time, conducted annual field training outside the continental United States. The next year the Marine Corps began requiring reservists to complete the same annual physical readiness test as regulars. The Coast Guard, following its transfer from the Treasury Department to the new Department of Transportation in 1967, joined the military services in using new authority in the Military Selective Service Act of 1967 to call ready reservists to active duty involuntarily if they failed to perform obligated service.[23]

Transition to the All-Volunteer Total Force

In the late 1960s opposition to the Vietnam War and the draft fueled a protest movement that reduced political support for both policies. As Russell F. Weigley wrote in his history of the U.S. Army, "Eliminating the draft was inevitably a part of the nation's disentangling itself from the war and allowing the wounds of the war to heal." In 1968 Richard Nixon promised that he would end the draft and the war if elected. Once in office, he took a gradual approach to both issues. In 1969 he implemented a more equitable lottery system and appointed former Defense Secretary Thomas S. Gates Jr. to lead a committee charged with developing a plan to transition to an all-volunteer force. The Gates Commission unanimously agreed that "the nation's interests will be better served by an all-volunteer force, supported by an effective standby draft, than by a mixed force of volunteers and conscripts." To spur enlistments, its 1970 report called for significant pay increases, better training and educational opportunities, and improved living conditions for military personnel. As American participation in the war dwindled, so did draft calls, and in January 1973 Secretary of Defense Melvin R. Laird announced the termination of conscription.[24]

As the Gates Commission had recommended, the Selective Service System survived in a standby status for a future emergency. But the reservoir of ill will toward conscription made that an unlikely source of manpower to augment regular forces and ensured that in the next crisis the reserve component, not hastily inducted draftees, would be the first source of reinforcements. Likewise, stung by growing antipathy toward the military among a wide swath of the population, policymakers and defense leaders wanted to ensure that U.S. forces would not be committed again to a conflict without overwhelming public support. They believed that one means to guarantee that was to make the reserve component indispensable to fighting a war. As the Army's chief of staff, General Creighton W. Abrams, is supposed to have put it: "They're not taking us to war again without calling up the reserves."[25]

The Vietnam War also led Congress to attempt to preclude presidents from taking the country into conflicts without securing national support. The War Powers Act, passed in 1973, required the president to obtain congressional approval for deployment of military forces within 60 days of committing them to combat. Three years later, to ensure that the act did not unduly limit executive decision making in a crisis, Congress provided for reserve forces call-up authority, which permitted the president to call 50,000 Selected Reserve members for 90 days without a presidential declaration of national emergency. At the end of 1980 President Jimmy Carter signed a law increasing the number of reservists to 100,000. In 1987 Congress increased the number to 200,000 and provided for another 90 days (for a total of 180) with congressional notification. In the future this presidential selected reserve call-up authority would play a significant role in several small-scale post–Cold War contingencies.[26]

In August 1970 Secretary Laird announced the new Total Force concept, which emphasized the role of reserve forces "as the initial and primary source of augmentation of the active forces in any future emergency requiring a rapid and substantial expansion of the active forces." Testifying before the House Armed Services Committee in February 1972, he stated that "we are placing increased emphasis on our National Guard and Reserve components so that we may obtain maximum defense capabilities from the limited resources available. The strengthening of the National Guard and Reserve Forces . . . is an integral part of the Total Force planning approach." In August 1973 the new secretary of defense, James R. Schlesinger, upgraded the concept to "a Total Force policy which integrates the active, Guard, and reserve forces into a homogeneous whole."[27]

The Army took the idea to the ultimate level in 1970, initiating the Roundout concept, which integrated designated Guard or reserve combat units into regular brigades or divisions to bring them to full strength upon mobilization. Thus a regular division might have two regular brigades and one Guard brigade. The Army pushed the concept in part to field more regular divisions under its limited manpower cap, but also to further the goal of making it difficult to go to war without resort to reserve mobilization. By 1978 every stateside active Army division had an Army Reserve or National Guard roundout unit assigned. By 1980 ARNG units deployed annually to West Germany for realistic combat training in exercises based on war plans for the defense of Western Europe. The reserve component roundout units received a resource priority equal to their gaining command, which theoretically meant newer equipment, more supplies, and other benefits, though the practical effect was limited due to constrained Defense budgets. The Army also pegged some reserve component units as augmentation to regular commands, meaning that they added combat power beyond the standard table of organization and would deploy with them or soon after them. As part of that process, the designated wartime parent organizations began overseeing the training and readiness of their assigned reserve units.[28]

The air reserves did not establish a formal program of integration into regular commands, but they established a reputation, and were—according to a National Defense University study in 1985—a "text book case of success for the total-force policy." Among several factors contributing to their performance were close affiliation between the reserve units and their gaining commands; a low proportion of personnel with no prior service; the high level of experience of those with prior service; and the tendency of Air Force leaders to support additional flying training for the air reserves. The ANG historian wrote that in the 1970s air guardsmen "dominated 'William Tell,'" the Air Force's air-to-air gunnery competition, tangible evidence of air reservists' higher experience levels in comparison with regulars.[29]

Increased opportunities for overseas training and operational support also played a role. In 1977 the AFRES deployed a fighter unit to Germany for a NATO (North Atlantic Treaty Organization) exercise—its first overseas deployment. The Creek Party operation, a 10-year effort that had Air Guard tankers refuel tactical fighters over Europe, demonstrated that part-time airmen—generally performing two-week tours of active duty—were equal to the task of participating in complex air operations and maintaining a long-term commitment. The real-world experience boosted the ANG's recruiting and retention and was another early example of serving as part of the operational force. During the same period both the Air Guard and Air Force Reserve provided ongoing airlift support to the U.S. Southern Command. Typically, aircrews on two-week tours performed missions such as embassy support, cargo movement, paratroop drops with the Army, and humanitarian work in response to hurricanes and earthquakes.[30]

In a similar fashion the Marine Corps Reserve began training extensively with regular Marine units, other services, and NATO allies. From 1978 to 1980 alone, 16 such major exercises occurred, including 3 in Germany, Denmark, and Norway. For the Coast Guard, the 1970s marked a major shift from traditional classroom training to operations-oriented augmentation training, which entailed reservists performing actual Coast Guard missions. Within two years, augmentation expanded from about one-sixth of reservists' training time to account for nearly two-thirds. The more meaningful regimen increased retention and encouraged many members of the Individual Ready Reserve (IRR) to transfer into the Selected Reserve. It proved operationally valuable in 1980, when Coast Guard reservists responded to the Cuban refugee operation, only the second time reservists had been mobilized under the 1972 law that authorized the involuntary recall of Coast Guard ready reservists for major natural or man-made disasters.[31]

Although the reserve components grew ever more critical to national defense after Vietnam, the 1970s marked a low point for the nation's readiness and mobilization capabilities. The diversion of money from research, development, and acquisition to carry on the Vietnam War; budget cuts following the conflict; the prevalence of problems such as racial discord and illegal drug use; and the transition to an all-volunteer force produced a significant decline in the nation's defense posture. Active-duty strength decreased from 3.5 million during the war to 2.1 million by 1976, while the quality of personnel recruited initially was lower than that brought in by the draft. Neither the regulars nor the reserves were ready. During the 1973 Yom Kippur War, when U.S. forces assumed increased alert status, the 82nd Airborne Division was the only U.S. Army division rated as combat ready, and even it had major deficiencies.[32]

In 1976 the Pentagon conducted its first major mobilization exercise since 1961. While one historian called it a "disaster," defense leaders reported: "Solutions to problems uncovered are currently being effected." But two years later, despite some improvements, the next such exercise likewise demonstrated major difficulties. The "hodgepodge of old and unconnected Presidential emergency orders, policies, regulations and procedures" was partly to blame, according to the Army Reserves' official history, but also at play was what a later study called "serene skepticism" among Pentagon officials, many of whom believed that any conflict with the Soviets would be so short as to preclude a big call-up. The 1980 mobility exercise, Proud Spirit, demonstrated that the shortcomings continued, but they were overshadowed by the failed hostage rescue attempt in Iran.[33]

The reserve ground components faced large personnel shortfalls in the 1970s. The postwar decrease in the size of the active forces, coupled with longer voluntary enlistments in place of the two-year term for draftees, resulted in a much smaller stream of personnel departing active duty with a reserve commitment. Lingering antiwar sentiment and the failure of military pay and benefits to keep pace with the civilian economy, especially for junior enlisted, also contributed. The Army was hit particularly hard. Over the course of the decade the ARNG's rolls fell 15 percent from 409,000 to 347,000, while the Army Reserve suffered an even more precipitous 30 percent decline, from a drilling strength of 263,000 in 1971 to about 185,000 in 1978. The Army's nondrilling IRR melted away at an astounding rate—from more than one million in June 1972 to only 144,000 six years later. The decimation of the IRR, the primary source of pretrained fillers for both regular and reserve units, was a major problem for planners who envisioned a pool of 400,000 IRR personnel available within 90 days of a general mobilization. An official study observed that "the net effect of ending the draft was increased [reserve] responsibilities, and hence greater numerical strength requirements, while the capability to fill the [reserve] ranks was decreased." In 1980 the Reserve Forces Policy Board noted that the shift to the All-Volunteer Force had a "dysfunctional influence on both the numbers and type of personnel affiliating with the Reserves during the 1970s."[34]

The Army Reserve also fell short in another personnel area. A 1978 Pentagon study concluded that it had "the least effective full-time support (technician) force of the seven Selected Reserve Components." Full-time support personnel accounted for only 4 percent of Army Reserve strength, compared with 22 percent in the Air Force Reserve. While that difference to some degree reflected the greater technological requirements of air as opposed to ground units, the Pentagon recognized that full-time support personnel were "one of the key elements—and may be the key element—in achieving the readiness standards essential to meeting our national defense strategy requirements." Both the Army and Air Force Reserve, however, suffered from a growing problem: over time some technicians lost their reserve status, often through no fault of their own. Unlike the Guard, the two federal reserve components allowed these now purely civilian personnel to continue as technicians even though they no longer constituted mobilization assets. The dual civilian-military status of all technicians, Guard and reserve, also raised issues such as stagnation, since technicians might remain in the same unit and billet for many years instead of broadening their experience and advancing in authority consistent with a normal career progression. In 1977 the House Appropriations Committee lambasted the technician program and advocated that the services fill full-time support billets with active-duty personnel.[35]

The all-volunteer era forced the services to dramatically increase recruiting efforts and change their methods. In 1978 the Army Reserve partially addressed the personnel shortfall by recruiting more women. In 1972 it had fewer than 500 women, but a decade later there were 64,000. The Army achieved this in part by signing up women to the same six-year (active and reserve) military obligation that applied to men. Women, however, were restricted from combat jobs and so could not fill the critical gaps in fields such as infantry. In 1980 the Navy similarly opened its TAR program to women. To make reserve duty more attractive, the Navy led the services in seeking enhanced benefits for reservists such as tuition assistance and group life insurance. In 1974 the Coast Guard Reserve initiated an innovative program that allowed reservists to fulfill their active-duty training requirements in two nonconsecutive stints. This particularly benefitted students, who could complete the requirements over two summers and therefore enlist without disrupting their education. The Coast Guard found that the option not only boosted enlistments but also educational levels in the reserve. The Army Reserve followed suit in 1978 and the other services soon after. It was in effect a partial reversion to the 11-week initial-entry training program offered by the National Guard in the 1950s and rejected by the Army as too short to be effective. It had taken nearly two decades, but U.S. defense policy finally split the difference by spreading the required six months over two summers. It was a simple but long-overdue solution. Those efforts notwithstanding, in 1981 the Reserve Forces Policy Board expressed "its grave concern to finding solutions to Reserve manpower problems, especially the IRR."[36]

The Reagan Defense Buildup

During the 1980 presidential campaign, Ronald W. Reagan promised to "rearm America." Once in office, he dramatically boosted spending—for higher pay and benefits, increased personnel strength, enhanced training, and

In 1982 President Ronald W. Reagan's secretary of defense, Caspar W. Weinberger (left), championed the First to Fight, First to Equip policy. It marked a sea change for the reserves, facilitating the reserve component's increased readiness by the late 1980s. (Source: National Archives)

more and better equipment—resulting in the largest peacetime defense buildup in U.S. history. All of these initiatives benefitted the reserve components. But Congress also emphasized its views on the growing importance of the reserve establishment. One key aspect of this was creation of the dedicated position of assistant secretary of defense for reserve affairs, or ASD(RA), in September 1983; no longer would it be an adjunct mission of an assistant secretary with a broader portfolio. Although the Pentagon opposed the idea, Senator Roger W. Jepsen (R–IA), a former Army paratrooper and reservist, believed it was the only way to focus "attention to Reserve and National Guard issues at the highest level within the Department of Defense." The first incumbent, who took office on 3 May 1984, was James H. Webb Jr., a decorated Marine veteran of the Vietnam War. He reported directly to Secretary of Defense Caspar Weinberger, who took note of his "high-level support, oversight, and advocacy for the reserves in the resource allocation and budgeting processes."[37]

In the equipment arena, in June 1982 Secretary Weinberger announced that "units that fight first shall be equipped first regardless of component." This policy marked a sea change for the reserves, which had relied heavily in the past on aging weapons and gear handed down from the regular forces. Those items were not only more expensive to maintain, they also lacked commonality with the upgraded equipment of regular forces, making it difficult for reserves and regulars to train and fight together. Senator John C. Stennis (D–MS) spearheaded the legislative effort to give the reserves "equipment that still has the factory paint on it." Congress began putting significant money behind the policy in the fiscal year 1982 Defense appropriation act, providing for purchases above the levels the Pentagon requested. This translated into, for example, nearly 70 new C–130 Hercules military transport aircraft for the ANG by 1991. The Army's roundout units finally began receiving the same equipment as their parent combat divisions, including major items such as M1 Abrams tanks and M2 Bradley fighting vehicles. The Marines pursued the same goal for their ground reserve units, gradually transitioning to their reserves being equipped the same as the regulars. In 1982 Secretary of the Navy John F. Lehman announced that Naval Air Reserve squadrons would receive new aircraft at the same time the regulars did, beginning with the F/A–18 Hornet. The Navy, which funded Marine aviation, initially did not do the same for the Marine Reserve air wing. In 1985 the Reserve Forces Policy Board recommended that the Navy's air integration policy "be applied equitably among all Marine Corps assets." While the board recognized in the same year that "equipment shortages are the most serious limiting factor affecting readiness in the Army Guard and Reserve," by the end of the decade, the board concluded that—although shortages remained—the reserves' warfighting capability had "increased significantly."[38]

The defense buildup, coupled with an improving public attitude toward military service, dramatically reversed the pattern of decline in reserve end strength. In 1983 the Selected Reserve exceeded one million personnel for the first time, and continued to grow. The Naval Reserve saw the most dramatic increase, climbing more than 50 percent, from 97,000 personnel in 1980 to over 148,000 in 1987. The Air Force Reserve went from 155,000 to 195,000 in the same period. Over the course of the 1980s the Army National Guard expanded by nearly one-third, from a post-Vietnam low of 347,000 to 457,000, a peacetime high. By 1988 the Army's Selected Reserve components (National Guard at 452,000 and Reserve at 310,000) nearly equaled the regular force (772,300) in strength.[39]

In a change that affected both manpower and training, Congress took steps to vastly increase the number of reserve component personnel serving on extended active duty. While this initially was designed to mitigate the services' misuse of active duty for training to provide full-time recruiters for reserve components, it also began to solve the ongoing problems with the Military Technician (MT) programs of the Army and Air Force. By establishing a separate budget authorization for full-time active duty for the purpose of organizing, administering, recruiting, instructing, or training the reserve forces, Congress ensured that the services would not skimp on these vital components of reserve readiness. This new category became enshrined in the Army and Air Force as the Active Guard and Reserve (AGR) program. It experienced "phenomenal growth" from 1980 to 1984, according to U.S. Army staff judge advocate Thomas Frank England, who studied the new program. Full-time support personnel—AGRs and military technicians—accounted for 24 percent of the ANG Selected Reserve in 1980, 26 percent in 1983, and 27 percent by 1988. The number of TARs on active duty rose to comprise one-seventh of the Navy's Selected Reserve by 1984. The Marine Corps continued to rely on regulars for its Inspector-Instructor program, but it brought reservists on to active duty in other capacities that supported reserve training. In the reserve component overall, in 1983, full-time support personnel filled 13 percent of the Selected Reserve's ranks; by 1989 it was almost 15 percent. The RFPB observed that the services found full-time support "at the unit level to be especially important to assure that unit personnel optimize their training time rather than spend their time performing day to day functions during training drills."[40]

The services expanded or initiated other programs to enhance reserve training. The Army's Key Personnel Upgrade program provided selected guardsmen in leadership billets a chance to shadow an active-duty counterpart during field exercises. By the end of the decade thousands of guardsmen and reservists were participating in major exercises overseas and at the Army's National Training Center at Fort Irwin, California. Between 1981 and 1986 the number who trained abroad increased more than fourfold, but this was not without controversy. Several governors who opposed U.S. aid to the anti-Sandinista movement in Nicaragua attempted to use a decades-old statute to prevent their National Guard units from training in neighboring Honduras. In 1986, when more than 5,000 guardsmen from some 18 states were scheduled for training in Honduras, at least a dozen governors expressed concern about sending personnel to a nation on the edge of a war zone. Seeking to resolve matters, ASD(RA) James Webb addressed a Senate armed services subcommittee, noting that all Guard units were federalized when deployed overseas for training or other duty. Ultimately, Congress settled the controversy with the passage of the Montgomery Amendment in 1986, which stripped governors of the authority to withhold consent for their Guard units to train outside the United States unless those units were required for domestic emergencies.[41]

The fruits of the quickening pace toward a true Total Force were most readily apparent in the Air Force, which held annual competitions mixing regulars and reservists. In 1983 an AFRES wing won the Tactical Air Command's Gunsmoke award for best A–10 Thunderbolt II maintenance. The next year the AFRES took top honors in two competitions: best C–141 Starlifter aircrew and maintenance team. From 1985 to 1989, the AFRES won several more honors at Gunsmoke, Military Airlift Command, and Strategic Air Command competitions. But the Total Force policy had a major impact across all services. In 1982 the commander of the new Rapid Deployment Joint Task Force referred to himself as one of the reserve component's "foremost 'customers,'" especially for support capabilities such as civil affairs and psychological operations, which in the U.S. Army resided almost exclusively in the Army Reserve. Similarly, the Marine Corps Reserve provided all of the Corps' civil affairs groups, nearly two-thirds of its bulk fuel companies, and one-half of its force reconnaissance and air/

As part of the reserve component's increased importance to the nation's combat readiness in the 1980s, James H. Webb Jr. became the first assistant secretary of defense for reserve affairs in 1984. He reported directly to Defense Secretary Weinberger. (Source: National Archives)

naval gunfire liaison companies. The following year the Reserve Forces Policy Board rightly declared that "today's Reserve Component Force is not a force 'in Reserve,' but rather an integral part of the Total Force performing 'real world,' everyday missions together with the Active Components—indeed, 'a force in being.'" Congress fully agreed that same year: "The integral role of the reserves in our Nation's security is often misunderstood. . . . In many instances, the active forces would be unable to deploy and accomplish their mission without reserve augmentation."[42]

Despite the progress toward implementing Total Force, the Pentagon remained anxious regarding the size and status of the IRR. Webb characterized the Army's IRR as comprised of "people who had been discharged for other than good reasons," and in many cases the Army did not even have current addresses for them. The assistant secretary pushed the idea of a one-day recall as a way to provide at least address verification and a physical exam for IRR personnel. The Joint Chiefs of Staff (JCS) and the Army opposed the idea, but in late 1985 and early 1986, the Army Reserve conducted several small, voluntary musters of IRR personnel. A Pentagon spokesman observed that the actual numbers and results were not as important as changing "the mind-set of the individual ready reservist. We want him to know he's still in the Army."[43]

Congress added funding to the FY 1987 Defense budget for a much larger one-day call-up. The same legislation contained a provision, subsequently known as Section 673b authority, permitting a president to call up to 200,000 reservists involuntarily for up to 180 days. Stephen M. Duncan, the new ASD(RA), viewed the option as "technically *not* a form of mobilization" because it could be used for "any operational mission not involving a war or national emergency." He primarily designed the 1987 "limited-notice, partial call-up" to test notification and reporting procedures under the new authority, so it largely affected units rather than the IRR. The services succeeded in contacting nearly 94 percent of the more than 15,000 participants, including members from 120 units, as well as individual reservists, all within 72 hours.[44]

With the growing use of the reserve components in overseas training deployments and high-profile exercises far from home, a new issue came to the fore. The Reserve Forces Policy Board virtually ignored the topic until its 1986 report highlighted family readiness for the first time. The RFPB acknowledged that year that "preparing family members for mobilization, their roles, and responsibilities is an integral part of the mobilization process." The board recommended that units develop mobilization orientation programs for families and asked the Pentagon to produce a mobilization handbook for spouses and dependents. In the same year the Pentagon conducted its first comprehensive survey of reserve component spouses. The 1987 board commended the establishment of the U.S. Army Family Action Plan, the Naval Reserve's premobilization guide and guide to family readiness, the Marine Corps Reserve's Casualty/Family Assistance Team concept, the National Guard's family program, and the Air Force's family support centers. In 1989, for the first time, the report included a section on "Single Parents and Military Couples."[45]

The increasing demands of reserve component training caused employer issues to rival family concerns in their detrimental effects on retention. The Pentagon had begun to address that problem through the National Committee for Employer Support of the Guard and Reserve (ESGR), which was established in 1972 to ease the transition to an all-volunteer force. In 1985 the Reserve Forces Policy Board acknowledged the effectiveness of ESGR programs, but it believed the committee required additional resources to handle the growing burden. In 1988 the board highlighted the Veterans' Reemployment Rights Act, which allowed reserve component members time off from civilian jobs to perform military training. The board noted approvingly that fewer reservists were contacting ESGR and more employers were doing so themselves, presumably an indication that employers were more fully grasping their obligations and fewer reservists were encountering problems. By 1989 the ESGR gained several thousand trained volunteers under a new program to ensure that every reserve training site would have someone available to resolve reservist-employer issues. Despite some notable progress, many employers still made it difficult for reservists to continue their service. In a 1989 statement to Congress, Assistant Secretary Duncan noted that "approximately one-third of the National Guardsmen and reservists who leave the Selected Reserve before completing their first five years of Reserve service will leave because of employer pressures." Oddly enough, the U.S. Postal Service appeared to be the leading offender of reservists' job rights.[46]

—— Conclusion ——

The 1980s proved pivotal for reserve component readiness. In 1978 a study conducted for the Pentagon had stated in stark terms: "A truly mission-ready Selected Reserve is not one of several alternatives to assure our country of an adequate defense—*it is the only alternative.*" The emphasis on every aspect of the force—personnel, training, and equipment—contributed to the creation of reserve forces that demonstrated a higher degree of peacetime readiness than ever before. Brief IRR recalls, enactment of Section 673b authority, and family and employer programs reminded reservists, their families, and their employers that the Selected Reserve would be called upon when needed. At the close of the decade, Assistant Secretary Duncan spoke to the House Appropriations Committee: "Since 1980, the strength of the Ready Reserve Forces has increased by more than 350,000 personnel, an increase of 29 percent. The bulk of that growth has taken place in the Selected Reserve, which has increased some 32 percent. Today, the Ready Reserve Forces of the United States total more than 1.64 million personnel." Of those, 1.18 million were selected reservists. Most important, the reservists and guardsmen of 1989 were better trained, better equipped, better paid, and perhaps even more motivated than they had been 10 years earlier.[47]

It had taken three and a half decades, with ups and downs that included conflicts hot and cold, enactment of various imperfect but nonetheless helpful laws, the end of the draft and the transition to an all-volunteer force, the emergence and acceptance of the Total Force policy, creation of a leadership position in the department devoted to reserve affairs, implementation of First to Fight, First to Equip, and an unparalleled peacetime defense buildup. But by the end of this era it was clear that the reserve component was finally, as Secretary of Defense Charles Wilson had declared in 1953, "an integral component of national defense."[48]

—— CHAPTER 4 ——

Growing Reliance on the Reserve Component, 1990–2000

A t the close of the 1980s the Total Force policy was nearly 20 years old, the Selected Reserve was well above one million strong, and its personnel were better trained, better equipped, and better compensated than ever before. The unexpected Iraqi invasion of Kuwait in 1990 tested that policy and the reserve components, with mixed results. The end of the Cold War also brought a significant force drawdown and multiple defense reviews that impacted the reserve components and drove further integration with their active counterparts. As the 1990s proceeded, the increase in contingency operations, coupled with the decrease in the size of regular forces, resulted in a growing reliance on reserve elements to perform operational missions.

Desert Shield and Desert Storm, 1990–1991

On 2 August 1990 Iraqi dictator President Saddam Hussein launched an invasion of Kuwait. Within two days his forces controlled the entire country and appeared poised to continue the attack. On 4 August, President George H. W. Bush met with his top advisers, including the head of the U.S. Central Command, General H. Norman Schwarzkopf, and decided to commit the United States to the defense of Saudi Arabia. The gears of a massive deployment, known as Operation Desert Shield, began to turn.[1]

On 22 August President Bush ordered the first call-up of the reserves since 1970, declaring the decision "essential to completing our mission." The next day Secretary of Defense Richard B. Cheney authorized the service secretaries to activate nearly 49,000 Selected Reserve members, half of them from the Army Guard and Army Reserve. They were the initial wave of 230,000 reservists from all services who would eventually come on active duty in response to the crisis. This early resort to the reserve components proved prescient; ultimately, they provided one of every four U.S. military members deployed to the Persian Gulf. But in late August, it was unclear whether U.S. forces would be required strictly for deterrence and defense or, eventually, for offense. Whether

In response to Iraq's invasion of Kuwait and its threat to Saudi Arabia, in August 1990 President Bush called up selected reservists under PSRC authority (Title 10, Section 673b). In January 1991, he implemented partial mobilization authority. (Source: George H. W. Bush Presidential Library and Museum)

or not this uncertainty influenced Bush's decision to use presidential selected reserve call-up authority, under Title 10, Section 673b, rather than his partial mobilization authority, the choice was both consequential and difficult to fathom. While PSRC could serve as a step toward partial mobilization, by itself it granted only 90 days of active duty, which the president could extend by an additional 90 days with congressional notification. Active duty beyond 180 days, however, required congressional approval. The other significant limitation with PSRC was that it did not provide access to the Individual Ready Reserve, the pool of individual fillers, many of whom had skills in high demand.[2]

The decision to use 673b authority led to a debate with some members of Congress who wanted the administration to rely more heavily on reserve forces and thereby test the validity of the Total Force policy. Secretary Cheney argued that the time limits inherent in 673b authority made it difficult to employ the reserves. But that was a constraint the administration had self-imposed by opting for 673b in the first place. It could have invoked partial mobilization based on the national emergency the president had declared on 3 August, which would have allowed mobilization of up to a million reservists for two years. Concerned that there was an anti-reserve bias at work, Congress removed any impediment by passing legislation granting a one-time extension of 673b authority to a total of 360 days of active duty. An Air National Guard historian noted: "The stakes were enormous, for the specter of Vietnam had to be exorcised and the Total Force policy validated."[3]

By the end of October 1990, with no indication that Saddam Hussein intended to withdraw, President Bush decided to double the size of the U.S. force in Southwest Asia in preparation for an offensive to drive the Iraqis out of Kuwait. On 5 November he signed the 673b waiver into law and eight days later approved an extension of the active duty of affected Selected Reserve units and individuals to 360 days. By December, Secretary Cheney authorized the services to activate up to 188,000 from the Selected Reserve. In the early morning hours of 17 January 1991 the war began with an air campaign. The next day President Bush finally declared a partial mobilization and authorized activation of units and individuals in the Ready Reserve for up to two years.[4]

Partial mobilization also provided access to the Individual Ready Reserve, a critical source for the battlefield replacements that everyone anticipated would be needed in large numbers, especially by the Army and Marine Corps. But the initial resort to 673b already had imposed adverse consequences on the mobilization process. The president's decision to delay partial mobilization until after hostilities had begun had made it especially difficult to fill empty billets in already mobilized reserve units or replace those who did not have the proper skills. The services were forced to activate individuals from other Selected Reserve units, thereby disrupting organizations that might themselves be called to active duty later. Congress subsequently addressed this problem in the fiscal year 1998 Defense authorization act by allowing the president to call up 30,000 IRR members to fill vacancies in units preparing to deploy under PSRC. That provision would prove its worth in the next major conflict.[5]

In spite of the limitations imposed by the use of 673b authority, the reserve components still played an important role in the war. The air reserve elements, consistent with their high proportion of full-time personnel and their program of affiliating reserve aircrews with regular squadrons, faced the fewest challenges when it came to rapid deployment. After the Iraqi invasion on 2 August, and well before receiving authority to involuntarily activate reservists, the Air Force called for volunteers (as did the other services, though they did not call for as many). Within 72 hours, more than twice the required number came forward. About one week after the invasion, the first Air National Guard and Air Force Reserve C–141 Starlifters began ferrying American troops and equipment to Saudi Arabia. Two days later KC–135 Stratotankers crewed by Kansas air guardsmen arrived in Saudi Arabia to support the U.S. buildup. Air Force Reserve associate airlift units, whose reserve crews shared C–141 and C–5 Galaxy aircraft with active crews, volunteered in large numbers. By 22 August, when President Bush announced the Section 673b augmentation, there were already thousands of Air Guard and reserve volunteers on active duty (and 10,000 total volunteers across all the services). During that month they carried out more than 40 percent of strategic airlift and one-third of aerial refueling missions. A number of those who volunteered were later involuntarily activated under Section 673b or the partial mobilization of 18 January 1991.[6]

In 1992 the Air Force Reserve activated its first C–17 airlifter associate squadron, one of several post–Cold War initiatives that deepened the integration of the reserve and regular components in furtherance of the Total Force policy. (Source: National Archives)

For the first time in ANG history the majority of guardsmen activated for a contingency came from nonflying units, with support specialists such as medical, aeromedical evacuation, security police, and firefighters slightly outnumbering airlift, tanker, and fighter unit personnel. In particular, the ANG and AFRES activated large numbers of medical personnel to handle expected high casualties. By February 1991 the AFRES had called up all of its medical units, which comprised nearly 45 percent of AFRES personnel on active duty. Many support personnel backfilled at stateside and European installations for regulars who deployed to the combat theater. In some cases partially qualified regular medics went to Saudi Arabia while fully qualified ANG medics replaced them in stateside hospitals. Reminiscent of the Berlin mobilization in 1961, reservists were chagrined to be pulled away from families and civilian careers only to serve in a nonoperational role.[7]

The war repeated at least one historical precedent. During the Korean conflict the reserves had been used largely as a replacement pool, a morale-killing practice that reserve component leaders vowed never to repeat. During Desert Shield and Desert Storm, however, Air National Guard and Air Force Reserve leaders often accepted the activation of individuals and tailored small elements in place of their parent units. Saudi-imposed limits on the number of U.S. personnel that could be based in its territory, along with the logistical difficulty of transporting and sustaining an already large force far from the United States, required that deployments remain limited to mission-essential personnel.

The AFRES's only aviation combat unit to be activated, the 706th Tactical Fighter Squadron, an A–10A ground-attack unit from New Orleans, mobilized in late December. Within 10 days it departed for Saudi Arabia, the first AFRES fighter unit in history to be deployed for combat. The 706th had the critical mission of taking out Iraqi air defense radar and early warning systems at the war's outset. Later, it took on the task of hunting Scuds, participating in the destruction of mobile launchers and missiles. The unit completed its wartime service without losing a single aircraft or suffering any casualties. In a dramatic engagement, a 706th pilot shot down an Iraqi helicopter, making history with the first A–10 air-to-air kill. By proving their readiness for a short-notice deployment and combat, the unit was a successful product of the Total Force policy.[8]

The Navy called up its first units and individual reservists, primarily in the areas of medical, port security, and minesweeping, on 25 August. In mid-December, following the president's decision to prepare for offensive operations, the Navy activated additional reservists, including its only two combat search and rescue helicopter squadrons. As in the air reserves, naval reservists in the medical specialties accounted for many of those activated during January and February, and by mid-March medical personnel accounted for one-half of all U.S. Naval Reserve personnel on active duty. Like their counterparts in air reserve medical elements, many backfilled at stateside facilities for deployed regular personnel. Stephen Duncan, the assistant secretary of defense for reserve affairs, disliked the policy because it required "two personnel moves instead of one" and damaged reservists' morale.[9]

In its first major call-up since 1950, the Marine Corps Reserve activated 54 percent of its Selected Reserve, a significantly higher rate than that of the Army, Navy, and Air Force. They constituted 15 percent of all Marines in the combat theater, and took on other missions such as filling in for regular battalions in the unit rotation to Okinawa. In terms of equipment, the reserves and regulars enjoyed a marked improvement in interchangeability from a decade earlier. But the Marine reserves had their share of problems as well. Unlike in Korea, this time the Corps kept infantry battalions and regiments intact and deployed them as units, which revealed shortcomings in the peacetime training regimen. Because each Marine reserve battalion was scattered in company-size or smaller elements over several states, the vast majority of monthly weekend drills focused largely on small-unit and company-level training. Combined with the recent active-duty experience of many younger reservists, particularly among junior officers who had to serve a minimum of two years on initial active duty, there was a high degree of competence at the company level. The battalions seldom trained together except during their annual two weeks of active duty, and often only for a few days at best. A regiment almost never came together as a unit for training. Compounding the challenge of developing higher-level unit skills was the fact that the more-senior reserve officers and noncommissioned officers—those expected to lead the battalions and regiments—had been off active duty the longest and had never served on extended active duty at that level, and so were the most in need of opportunities to train at their jobs. A senior Marine officer offered his perspective after Desert Storm: "Companies were great, battalions were marginal, regiments were useless." An example of a "great" Marine unit was Company B, 4th Tank Battalion. Activated in late November, it traded in its old M60A1 tanks for modern M1s and underwent an abbreviated 18-day training program on the new Abrams model. Arriving in Saudi Arabia on 19 February, it went into battle 5 days later (less than 90 days after its mobilization) and ultimately destroyed 59 Iraqi tanks and numerous other armored vehicles without losing any of its own.[10]

Although the Marine Corps, particularly through its long-successful Inspector-Instructor program, promoted the mindset that being a Marine was more important than whether one was a regular or a reservist, the Desert Storm battle assessment team noted that many reservists suspected that regulars did not regard them as full teammates. Even if some of the regulars were dismissive of the reservists as a whole and more senior reservists in particular, according to historian Mark F. Cancian, many active-duty Marine commanders felt that the younger "reservists were, Marine-for-Marine, *better* than regulars, even as good as regulars are today. As one regular officer observed, 'In the regulars . . . you're not going to have squad leaders in their third year of chemical engineering.'" Despite policies designed to integrate the two components, there remained a certain amount of tension and mistrust between them.[11]

In fall 1990 the Coast Guard Reserve marked its 50th year while responding to an involuntary overseas mobilization for the first time in its history. Three port security units (PSUs), found only in the reserve, deployed to Saudi Arabia and Bahrain in the Persian Gulf, where they operated modified Boston Whaler boats equipped with machine guns to ensure the safe transit of military and civilian cargo.[12]

Mobilization of the Army Reserve brought an unusual challenge. Beginning in late 1989 the Army initiated Project Quicksilver, a downsizing of its forces in response to the thawing of the Cold War. During the massive U.S. deployment in the fall of 1990, transportation units were in high demand. One heavy equipment truck company (the 660th Transportation Company) had inactivated in October. Two weeks later the Army decided it needed the unit. Its personnel had been reassigned and its equipment dispersed, but the company was miraculously reconstituted, mobilized, and deployed. Similar cases "occurred numerous times," an Army Reserve historian observed.[13]

During Desert Shield and Desert Storm, the Army Reserve activated a total of some 84,000 soldiers, including nearly 650 units and elements and 14,000 individual reservists who served in a wide variety of combat support (CS) and combat service support (CSS) roles (CS refers to combat engineer, military police, chemical, and signal units, while CSS includes logistical units such as medical, transportation, supply, and ordnance). Tragically, on 25 February 1991, an Iraqi Scud missile hit a barracks in Dhahran, Saudi Arabia, that housed units including the 14th Quartermaster Detachment, an Army Reserve water purification outfit from Greensburg, Pennsylvania. The missile killed a total of 28. Thirteen of the dead, plus another 43 wounded, were members of the detachment, resulting in an 80 percent casualty rate, the highest for any American or coalition unit in the conflict and the highest in a U.S. Army unit since Vietnam. The episode highlighted another negative aspect of the geographically rooted reserve system: one locale might bear the brunt of the suffering from a single incident.[14]

In 1990, 42 percent of the Army's combat divisions resided in the Guard, as did 55 percent of the Army's nondivisional combat units. Of the seven round-out brigades, six were in the Army National Guard. Ultimately about 63,000 Army guardsmen in nearly 400 units served on active duty during Desert Shield and Desert Storm, and roughly 45 percent deployed to the Persian Gulf region or Europe (mainly Germany). As it was in the other services, many activated personnel who wanted to play their part in the conflict instead backfilled for regulars who went off to war. While many CS and CSS units served in the Persian Gulf, the only major Guard combat units to fight were two field artillery brigades.[15]

The no-notice nature of the crisis and the initial decision to rely on 673b authority wreaked the greatest havoc on the Army. The first problem arose in the logistics field, where the 377th Theater Army Area Command, a reserve unit, was the organization designated in war plans to oversee Army logistics in a Persian Gulf contingency. It had devoted all its training to that scenario and had well-developed relationships with the Third Army, the Army component command under Central Command. With no authority to mobilize reservists in early August, the Third Army hastily created a logistics headquarters from scratch in Saudi Arabia. When access to the reserves came on 22 August, Army leaders in the United States were ready to activate the 377th. But Central Command opposed that option. It already had pulled together regulars to accomplish the task and was reluctant to try to meld the 377th into that ad hoc organization, and also viewed the 90-day active-duty limit as a show-stopper in a crisis likely to exceed that time frame.[16]

The problem that garnered the most attention from Congress and the public involved the roundout brigades. Two of the major ground units that headed to Saudi Arabia early in Desert Shield were the 24th Infantry Division and the 1st Cavalry Division. Both had National Guard roundouts: the 48th Infantry Brigade (Georgia) and the 155th Armored Brigade (Mississippi), respectively. But both regular forces deployed without their Guard brigades. Instead, the Army filled out the 24th Division with Fort Benning's school brigade, the 197th Infantry, which had never trained with its new parent outfit. The 1st Brigade of the 2nd Armored Division fleshed out the 1st Cavalry Division. Although three Guard roundout brigades—the 48th, the 155th, and the 256th Infantry Brigade (Louisiana)—eventually were activated in December, none of them went to the Persian Gulf.

Assistant Secretary Duncan believed that "the strong working presumption had always been that the roundout brigades would deploy as scheduled after the deployment of the remainder of their parent divisions." But he later felt "there is more than a little reason to believe that Schwarzkopf had never supported the roundout concept." Schwarzkopf acknowledged that disagreements over employing Guard brigades generated "heated discussions" with the Army staff in Washington, in part due to the duration of 673b activation. Schwarzkopf recalled: "The roundout brigades made no sense for the 180-day call-up. . . . These troops would need months of training to be ready for combat; by the time we sent them to the Middle East, I'd have to worry about bringing them home." It was a plausible argument.[17]

The decision to not deploy these roundout brigades became one of the thorniest issues of the conflict. The nation's Total Force policy, the Army's Roundout concept, Weinberger's First-to-Fight, First-to-Equip program, and the heightened emphasis on training and readiness associated with those initiatives had created an expectation in some quarters, as National Guard historian Michael Doubler later noted, that the "Roundout brigades should be ready for immediate deployment with their parent divisions and require little or no training after mobilization." Even some senior officials, including Representative G. V. "Sonny" Montgomery (D–MS), a retired National Guard major general, assumed that the roundouts were ready to deploy on extremely short notice. In the excitement of August 1990, after President Bush announced the initial call-up, Montgomery declared that the nation's reservists "are well prepared right now, and could be on the job alongside the active forces in a matter of days." While his statement might have applied to certain types of units, it most certainly was not accurate with regard to the roundout brigades in a combat role, although his words were understood to include them. Other members of Congress believed that it was important to test the Total Force policy as the nation contemplated force reductions and restructuring in the aftermath of the Cold War.[18]

Army Chief of Staff General Carl E. Vuono and other senior leaders held a different view: roundout brigades, however well prepared, would need further training before deployment, and it was never the intention for them to ship out with their divisions. Army plans in July 1990 provided that a regular brigade would fill out regular divisions that needed to deploy soon after a crisis arose, due to the training requirements the reserve component roundout brigades would have to meet. Only in certain circumstances, including a partial mobilization that allowed up to 24 months of active duty, would the roundout brigades actually deploy and fight as part of their divisions. In late 1991 a congressional report agreed:

> Roundout brigades were never intended to deploy without some postmobilization training, and it was never envisioned that they could deploy immediately in response to a no-notice crisis. Unfortunately, a combination of excessive optimism, overreliance on numerical readiness ratings, and high-level inattention to the actual readiness levels of the roundout brigades before Desert Shield/Storm led many to assume that they were as ready as similar active Army brigades.[19]

The report clarified that the postmobilization training should last "at least several weeks." Based on the Army's readiness ratings of the 48th, 155th, and 256th, the brigades should have required between 15 to 28 days or 29 to 42 days of training, depending on circumstances, prior to deployment. That was sufficient when war clouds on the horizon allowed time to prepare, as had occurred in World War II. But even if the roundout brigades had been ready to deploy on short notice, timing would have played a significant role. The 24th Division began loading on ships on 10 August, nearly two weeks before the call-up of reserves began. The 1st Cavalry Division started its movement overseas on 4 September, which would have allowed very little time to issue mobilization orders, process personnel onto active duty, and marshal equipment for transportation.[20]

The Army National Guard's role in the Persian Gulf conflict became inextricably linked to the roundout brigade program, a cornerstone of Total Force policy. Once the 48th, 155th, and 256th brigades were on active duty in December, they began an intensive predeployment training period that lasted into February 1991. That process brought several readiness issues to light.

A General Accounting Office (GAO) study concluded the Army had "not adequately prepared" its Guard roundout brigades "to be fully ready to deploy quickly." Maintenance skills and gunnery training were key deficiencies. In a repeat of past mobilization experiences, too many soldiers in certain critical jobs, such as turret mechanics, were untrained, contributing to unacceptably low maintenance rates for M1 Abrams tanks and M2 Bradley infantry fighting vehicles. The GAO also noted deficiencies among roundout brigade NCOs and officers, including lack of leadership training and lapses in standards and discipline, which had led to the removal of the 48th's commander.[21]

Dental health proved to be another major problem. Because access to dental care is very limited during operational deployments, longstanding policy required that soldiers meet certain dental criteria to be eligible for overseas duty. Upon activation, one-third of the 48th Infantry's personnel were deemed nondeployable for dental reasons. There was room to argue over whether guardsmen or the leadership of the Guard brigades or the Army bore primary responsibility for dental health, but the GAO found that there was, inexplicably, no requirement "for the Army to provide routine dental treatment to National Guard soldiers during peacetime . . . [and] no requirement for the soldiers to maintain healthy teeth as a condition of continued participation in the unit." Thus the root issue was the lack of policies that would ensure dental readiness in the reserve component.[22]

Other factors added to the delay in achieving readiness. The Army had each combat brigade go through a 30-day period of training and evaluation at the National Training Center, which required travel to and from Fort Irwin, California, but only one brigade could cycle through the center at a time. The Guard outfits also underwent Iraq-specific training that many other units conducted after deploying to the theater. In addition, the 256th was still gaining experience with the newly acquired Bradley fighting vehicles. Some other Guard units, in contrast, did not have to go to Fort Irwin, and the 142nd Field Artillery Brigade arrived in Saudi Arabia just one month after its activation.[23]

After the cease-fire, in spring 1991 discussions turned to how much time the Army needed to prepare a reserve brigade for combat. Although six months earlier Secretary Cheney had told the House Armed Services Committee that 60 days was sufficient, by the end of Desert Storm he had revised his thinking: "The planning would take into account not that they deploy the first day of the war but rather that they get 90 days, 120 days of work-up before you send them." The Army chief of staff, General Gordon R. Sullivan, declared to the same committee that 90 days was his best estimate. Ultimately the Army had validated the 48th Infantry as combat ready 90 days after mobilization, which a congressional report viewed as "an unprecedented achievement compared with past callups of similar reserve component units." (In the next war with Iraq, the Army and the Marine Corps would devote that amount of time to predeployment training of their reserve combat units.) The experience in the first Gulf War, however, sounded the death knell of the Roundout concept. One senior colonel at Army National Guard headquarters aptly considered the program to be "an anachronism—a Cold War construct that was simply not relevant to the circumstances following the 1990 Iraqi invasion of Kuwait."[24]

The demobilization of the reserves proved nearly as controversial as the roundout issue. During spring and summer 1991, the Pentagon demobilized nearly one-quarter million Guard and reserve members, a process it had not performed since Vietnam and not on this scale since Korea. The same tendency of the American people that President Truman had noticed after World War II—rushing to demobilize as energetically as they had mobilized—was still operative. After the fighting ended on 28 February 1991, this pattern played out again, with reservists anxious to return to families and civilian jobs. Shortly after the cease-fire, General Schwarzkopf established a command redeployment policy of "first-in, first-out." As long as units were not required for operational purposes, those that had arrived in the theater first would be the first to be released.[25]

Duncan viewed Schwarzkopf's decision as consistent with Total Force policy, treating active and reserve units alike. At the same time, the assistant secretary was sensitive to the financial hardships many reservists suffered when foregoing salaries higher than their military pay grades. Duncan also observed that, even in cases "where the first-in, first-out principle was being fairly applied," commanders had a hard time setting and then adhering to release dates. A complicating factor was the large number of reserve units that performed logistics and maintenance functions, which needed to continue after the end of hostilities. And more than 60 percent of such Army units resided in its reserve components. By mid-June, when three-fourths of activated reservists had been released, most of those still on duty were in service units.[26]

Considering that it took five months to complete the buildup of forces in the region, the demobilization compared favorably. For most reservists, it was the uncertainty rather than the actual time frame that proved most disconcerting. As Senator John Glenn (D–OH) noted: "The main complaint we get . . . is people do not know what to plan on. They do not know whether they are going back to school, they do not know whether they are going back to their business." Duncan agreed. In April 1991, when about one-fifth of activated reservists had been released, he claimed that even a distant return date "would be far more welcome to reservists and their civilian employers and families than no information at all." Not surprisingly, demobilization concerns would surface again in the decade after 2001.[27]

The transition to an all-volunteer force had heightened the importance of family and civilian employer issues, but in the first large-scale mobilization under the new system, existing policies were found wanting in many cases. Once activations began in late 1990, each service developed or enhanced its own family support programs. In general, programs included briefings or seminars for deploying members and their dependents, publications, hotlines, and support groups. In some cases, support groups sprung to life on an ad hoc basis when the spouses of deployed members or local retirees took the initiative to assist reserve families. But few observers judged these laudable efforts sufficient to the broader need. A Guard historian acknowledged the need for comprehensive family support, particularly including childcare, and an Air Force Reserve historian noted how disconcerting it was for some mobilized personnel to realize there were no family support centers at their reserve installations, and therefore no place where their families could go for assistance. Shortly after the conclusion of Desert Storm, the Reserve Forces Policy Board declared: "Family support, together with employer support, are perhaps the two most important elements of concern." The board advocated service funding of family support programs that would continue even "well after the cessation of hostilities, the return of the mobilized personnel, and demobilization."[28]

All the services made strides to improve in this area. A new Army policy designated the National Guard the lead agent for family support and required National Guard and Army Reserve commanders to operate family assistance programs. Following the Navy's example, the Army developed a family reunion program for redeploying personnel. In 1991, for the first time, the Army made nonappropriated funds available for reserve family support activities. In 1994 the U.S. Army Reserve Command (USARC) established its first family action program advisory council as a means of promoting family well-being. The next year the Army Reserve implemented a policy whereby key unit personnel and volunteers underwent training at newly established regional family program academies. By 1996 the Army Reserve had gone, according to one historian, "from nearly zero family support to an extensive system and network." In 1992 the Air Force established a reserve family support program and called for family support centers at all 15 of its reserve bases. The AFRES created command billets for family support program personnel and authorized specialists for its groups and wings at all active and reserve bases.[29]

Policies that addressed civilian job security were somewhat more effective. In 1972 Congress established the National Committee for Employer Support of the Guard and Reserve to assist both reserve component members and civilian employers in managing the process of reservists temporarily leaving civilian jobs for active duty. Nearly two decades later, the committee fulfilled its intended role during Desert Shield and Desert Storm. Committee members and volunteers wrote articles for hometown newspapers and conducted interviews for local media, and the Advertising Council launched a massive pro bono campaign to highlight employer issues. Most employers supported their reservists and many went beyond their legal obligations. One survey found that one-third of companies paid the full civilian salaries and benefits of activated employees for at least some portion of their Persian Gulf–connected service.[30]

Despite the nationwide effort to inform both employers and reservists about their obligations, there were problems. And, embarrassingly, a few federal agencies, including the Postal Service, accounted for an inordinate share of employer-related problems. An Air Force-sponsored conference in 1992 at Robins AFB, Georgia, highlighted challenges faced by both large and small companies, and the hardships placed on activated reservists who worked in civilian medical practices. Air Force Reserve leaders learned that in a number of cases, reservists had failed to identify themselves as part-time military members to their employers—a problem that resurfaced after 2001. Another discovery was that some employers had no knowledge of the existence of the National Committee for Employer Support of the Guard and Reserve. Likewise, an air reserve historian wrote, "Few reservists knew what their job rights were. DESERT STORM rapidly changed that."[31]

The Iraq war experience was the first real test of the nation's Total Force policy. The roundout brigade controversy unfortunately brought back old conflicts between the regular Army and the Army Guard. Nevertheless, the Selected Reserve had responded well overall to the first Total Force call-up. And the valuable lessons gained through actual experience would drive changes in law and policy to make the reserve components better prepared for future mobilizations.

The Base Force, 1990–1992

The Persian Gulf conflict coincided with dramatic changes in U.S. national security concerns. For more than 40 years the Soviet Union had represented the primary strategic threat, so the reserve component was mainly structured to participate in a global war against another superpower. As the Soviets grew less threatening in the late 1980s the focus slowly began to turn to more likely regional conflicts. The fall of the Berlin Wall in late 1989 and the beginning of the Warsaw Pact's disintegration (followed by that of the Soviet Union itself) accelerated the shift in U.S. defense policy, leading to the first of four major defense reviews in the 1990s. On 2 August 1990, hours after the beginning of the Iraqi invasion of Kuwait, President Bush announced the Base

Force concept, which would reduce the U.S. armed forces by as much as 25 percent within five years. He envisioned the regular component decreasing from roughly 2.1 million to 1.6 million in strength, while the reserve component dropped even more, from over 1.6 million to 906,000. General Colin L. Powell, chairman of the Joint Chiefs of Staff, viewed the Base Force as "a shift from a solely *threat-based* force to a *threat- and capability-based* force" that would "maintain certain fundamental capabilities." He anticipated shifting "certain units or functions into the reserves to avoid the costs associated with keeping them in the active force structure." Assistant Secretary Duncan added that "major reliance will continue to be placed upon reserve forces, as well as upon active forces."[32]

The Iraqi invasion of Kuwait and the U.S. response to Saddam Hussein's aggression postponed much of the congressional and public discussion and debate surrounding the president's plan. In fall 1990 the brewing Persian Gulf conflict took defense cuts proposed for FY 1991 off the table. Following Operation Desert Storm, in August 1991 President Bush again highlighted the shift in U.S. security priorities:

> In a world less driven by an immediate, massive threat to Europe or the danger of global war, the need to support a smaller but still crucial forward presence and to deal with regional contingencies . . . will shape how we organize, equip, train, deploy and employ our active and reserve forces. Today, we must reshape our Guard and Reserve forces so that they can continue their important contributions in new circumstances.[33]

Members of Congress, however, ever sensitive to the Guard and reserve presence in their districts, refused to approve the Bush administration's desired cuts to the reserve component. In November 1991 the House Armed Services Committee led the way in rejecting "the administration's plan to eliminate hundreds of thousands of Guard and Reserve personnel and force structure over five years."[34]

Four months later Defense Secretary Cheney and General Powell attempted to influence a reluctant Congress, albeit indirectly, in a news briefing on the reserves' balanced drawdown. Explaining that the more likely threat now came from regional conflicts, which required a new strategy and a smaller military, Cheney affirmed the Guard and reserve would play "an absolutely vital part of that new base force that we designed to implement that strategy." He envisioned a Selected Reserve of 920,000 by 1997, including 6 National Guard divisions, 2 cadre divisions, and 11 tactical fighter wings. Attempting to relieve congressional anxiety, the secretary pointed out that although the reserves stood to lose 270,000 personnel, reserve strength by 1997 actually would be 50,000 higher than it had been in 1980. Whereas the reserves had accounted for 30 percent of the total force that year, under Bush's plan, the figure would be 36 percent by the time the cuts were completed in 1997.[35]

Powell explained the rationale for placing more of certain capabilities in the reserves:

> Where you have units that have readily transferable civilian skills associated with those units—stevedore units, transportation units—where it's not difficult to bring them up on active duty and then send them somewhere, and you don't need that kind of capability during normal peacetime activities, that's a prime candidate to put in the reserve force.[36]

The chairman did not overlook the need for some combat units in the reserve components, but, harkening to the Desert Storm roundout controversy, he acknowledged they needed "enough time to get ready after mobilization. . . . You just can't call them up on Day 1 and expect them to reach the proficiency of the units that you have in the active force." (Of course, this was a bit of a straw man; no plan suggested that they could be ready to fight on the first day.) Focusing on the most controversial aspect of the drawdown, Powell observed that for the last two years Congress had forbidden reductions "to bring the Army Reserve down to its base force level so that it matches the rest of the force." Cheney stated that the plan, which would eliminate 830 Guard and reserve units, had been well thought out, coordinated throughout the Pentagon, and enjoyed the support of the service chiefs as well as the unified commanders. The majority of reductions affected units originally designed to support active Army divisions fighting the Soviets. Cheney and Powell hoped for congressional approval, but in vain.[37]

A month later Duncan addressed a subcommittee of the House Armed Services Committee regarding the reserves' capabilities and future needs. He emphasized that a key principle of the new strategy was to avoid involuntarily bringing "large numbers of reservists to active duty in the initial stages of every contingency," which he thought would cause retention problems if it became the norm. Duncan had to admit, however, that following Desert Storm, the retention rate among those mobilized was "as high or higher than the rate for those members who were not activated." (This phenomenon reappeared after 2001.) The Gulf conflict had enjoyed the support of the American public, so reservists felt proud of and rewarded by their service.[38]

Another major issue for reservists was turbulence, the shift to new locations or new missions, often the result of closing installations or dissolving units.

Secretary Duncan pointed out that 93 percent of reserve enlisted members and 82 percent of officers resided within a two-hour commute of their units. "Unlike active component personnel who can immediately be reassigned to other units where their military skills are needed," reservists were more geographically connected. They were less likely to stay with the service if reassigned to distant units or new missions requiring extensive initial training that involved considerable time away from home and a civilian job.[39]

In October 1992 Congress took action to enhance reserve component readiness in response to the roundout brigade experience of Desert Storm. The Army National Guard Combat Readiness Reform Act expanded on and gave formal sanction to ongoing Army initiatives known as Bold Shift and Standard Bearer. The efforts focused on improving the quality and preparation of officers and NCOs, medical readiness, premobilization unit training levels, readiness reporting, active component support to the Guard, and equipment compatibility. Some steps, particularly in the equipment realm, would take years to fully implement, but progress was immediate and significant.[40]

The Bottom-Up Review, 1993

By the time President William J. Clinton took office in January 1993, the work of defining a post–Cold War strategy remained largely incomplete. His secretary of defense, Les Aspin, quickly initiated another major re-evaluation of national defense. In September 1993 Aspin announced the conclusions of the Bottom-Up Review (BUR), so named because the Cold War's end called for a reassessment of the military from the bottom up. It concentrated on conventional force structure, addressing the basic question: "How much defense is enough in the post–Cold War era?" With the Pentagon focused on North Korea and Iraq as the most likely adversaries, the BUR based its analysis on the requirement for the United States "to win two major regional conflicts that occur nearly simultaneously." Planners determined that even under that scenario, a large reduction in force was appropriate. The Air Force would go from 22 general-purpose fighter wings to 13; the air reserves would go from 12 to 7 wings. The regular Army would shrink from 18 combat divisions to 10, and reserve divisions from 10 to 8. The BUR set the strength of the Army Reserve at 208,000. With the disappearance of the Soviet blue-water navy, the U.S. Naval Reserve's ship augmentation units were unnecessary, leaving the USNR smaller and more specialized. The Marine Corps Reserve's performance in Desert Storm—it activated more than half of its Selected Reserve and two-thirds of its reserve combat structure with minimal train-up time—along with the

The Bottom-Up Review was the second of four major defense reviews in the 1990s as the U.S. defense establishment attempted to reorient following the end of the Cold War. Secretary of Defense Les Aspin Jr. (right) and Chairman of the Joint Chiefs of Staff General Colin L. Powell (left) discuss the review before the House Armed Services Committee. (Source: National Archives)

Corps' traditional focus on missions unrelated to the Cold War, spared it from major changes.[41]

In terms of reserve policy, two of the most important BUR decisions focused on the Army. The first clarified the Pentagon's intent to expand Army Reserve CS and CSS capabilities to support the regular Army's combat units and other U.S. forces. The second posited that Guard combat brigades, if mobilized early in a crisis, "could provide extra security and flexibility if a second conflict arose while the first was still going on." Furthermore, in the case of prolonged operations, "additional Army National Guard combat units will provide the basis for the *rotational forces*." Thus the BUR declared a policy, albeit without fanfare, of the periodic rotation of Army reserve units, especially Army Guard combat units, as a part of the operational force. It was not until after 2001 that the policy and its implications became obvious, both within and outside of the Pentagon. To achieve this goal, the BUR replaced the roundout brigades with enhanced readiness brigades or simply, enhanced brigades, with existing roundout brigades becoming the first of 15 enhanced brigades. Planners expected that by 1999 these brigades, given high priority for personnel and equipment, could deploy within 90 days after mobilization—but not to fill out a regular combat division as the roundouts had been designed to do. This apparent demotion in status, following close on the heels of the acrimonious debate over the roundouts during the Gulf conflict, increased the distrust that many guardsmen felt toward the regular Army.[42]

In a move that undoubtedly contributed to congressional acceptance of the Bottom-Up Review's widespread realignment of reserve forces, for the first time senior regular Army leaders and the chiefs of the Army Reserve and Army National Guard reached a coordinated decision on major restructuring matters. Their 1993 meeting crafted what became known as the Army's Off-Site Agreement, which led to a large-scale swap of capabilities, with most CS and CSS structure at the corps level and above residing in the Army Reserve and most combat and division-level support forces in the National Guard. The regular Army benefitted by maintaining a higher proportion of combat units in its structure, while retaining fuller control over the logistical structure, residing in the Army Reserve, needed to support those forces in a contingency. The Army Guard would maintain the combat structure and associated logistical units that were generally not needed short of a major war. The Army Reserve retained a few combat units, such as the 100th Battalion, 442nd Infantry Regiment—the most highly decorated battalion of World War II, with 8 Presidential Unit Citations and 21 Medals of Honor.[43]

In conjunction with the Bottom Up Review, Secretary Aspin reintroduced a 1992 proposal, first offered by Assistant Secretary Duncan, to increase access to the reserve components under Title 10, Section 673b (presidential selected reserve call-up authority) by expanding its two periods of 90 days of active duty to 180 each. That would allow the president to activate selected reserve components without declaring a national emergency for a total of 360 days without congressional approval. Congress passed a compromise in the FY 1995 Defense authorization act that granted 270 days, which provided enough time for predeployment training (likely three months) followed by six months of availability for operational commitment. One year later, in late 1995, President Clinton employed the 270-day option for the Balkans.[44]

Ever since the creation of the assistant secretary of defense for reserve affairs, the officeholder had, as one RAND study observed, "operated with relative autonomy." But in 1994 a broad defense reorganization put that position, along with the assistant secretaries for force management policy and health affairs, under the control of the newly created under secretary of defense (USD) for personnel and readiness (P&R). This interposition of a new layer of management limited the access of the assistant secretary to the secretary of defense. After 2001 that issue came to the fore, with some claiming that the change had hobbled the person in charge of reserve affairs at a time when the reserves were more important than ever.[45]

Congress also tried to solve an acute problem with employment protection that arose during and after the Desert Shield/Desert Storm mobilization. Under the Veterans' Reemployment Rights Act of 1968, the burden of proof to obtain relief was high. In 1994 Congress passed the Uniformed Services Employment and Reemployment Rights Act (USERRA) to address the increasing strains on employer-employee relationships arising from the expanding use of the reserve component in an operational role. The revised law applied to voluntary and in-voluntary service, in peacetime and wartime, within the nation's borders and overseas, and to almost all employers in the United States, including federal, state, and local governments and private employers regardless of size. Taking note that many federal employees had faced mobilization-related challenges, Congress for the first time applied an enforcement mechanism specifically to the federal government and also urged that it become a "model employer." The law also authorized double damages for willful employer violations, the right to a jury trial, and reimbursement of attorney fees for successful plaintiffs. The Supreme Court subsequently placed additional limitations on employer defenses typically available in employment discrimination cases.[46]

The Commission on Roles and Missions, 1994–1995

Concerned about service redundancies and wastefulness, in 1994 Congress created the Commission on Roles and Missions of the Armed Forces, which reported on possible changes "in the allocation of roles and missions . . . to ensure that the Nation will have properly prepared military forces." With regard to the reserve components, the commission's 1995 report recommended sizing and shaping the reserves to meet new national security needs, furthering integration with the regular component, improving training and evaluation, and eliminating unnecessary forces.[47]

The commission called for reorganizing or doing away with some of the National Guard combat divisions—at that time there were eight, with a total of 110,000 personnel—which a leading Guard historian termed "Cold War relics." Since the regular Army reported a shortfall of 60,000 CS and CSS soldiers, the Guard divisions seemed to provide a ready answer. Although it was painful due to long traditions, ARNG leaders agreed to convert the equivalent of four combat divisions to CS/CSS units. The commissioners believed that the remaining combat divisions and their 50,000 personnel should be eliminated. While the enhanced brigades would remain, the commissioners concluded that they had to include active-duty advisers and full-time military technicians if the Army wanted them to deploy within 90 days, as the Bottom-Up Review had recommended.[48]

To enhance integration, the report argued that reserve units should be assigned to missions they could accomplish within approved mobilization and deployment timelines. The commission observed that the "most effective Reserve units have strong, recurring association and cooperation" with regular counterparts through assignment to specific unified commands and from training with active units. It acknowledged that reserve units might not be able to perform as many or as varied tasks as regular units, but recommended they should train "to perform specific tasks to the same standards" as regulars. In 1996 Army Chief of Staff General Dennis J. Reimer affirmed an integrated role for the reserves in the service's long-term strategy, *Army Vision 2010*:

> Reductions in the active force have made the reserve component even more essential to meeting the Nation's needs across the full spectrum of operations, from disaster relief to war. They are equal partners in meeting the challenges of the 21st Century and must be trained and equipped with modern, compatible equipment to perform assigned missions with their active duty counterparts and coalition partners.[49]

Reimer's reference to "assigned missions" indicated an emphasis on accomplishing a particular task rather than achieving broader capabilities, in line with the commission's viewpoint.

The Quadrennial Defense Review, 1996–1997

One of the recommendations of the Commission on Roles and Missions was that the nation should comprehensively reevaluate its strategy every four years. The Clinton administration conducted the first Quadrennial Defense Review (QDR)—and the fourth defense reassessment since the end of the Cold War—between November 1996 and May 1997. The QDR attempted to balance the requirements of strategy with available resources, looking ahead from 1997 to 2015. In addition to maintaining the recent focus on the ability to fight two nearly simultaneous regional conflicts, the updated strategy emphasized promoting regional stability, deterring regional aggressors, and being ready to respond across the spectrum of conflict, including what it termed smaller-scale contingency operations. The latter recognized that U.S. forces were increasingly engaging in operations short of major wars—the Army counted 25 such deployments from 1990 to 1997. While the QDR stressed the need to upgrade weapon systems, exploit the revolutions in military and business affairs, and remain prepared for unexpected threats, General Charles C. Krulak, the Marine Corps commandant, considered the exercise "simply a continuation of the national 'demobilization' planning" since the end of the Cold War.[50]

Consistent with the 1993 Bottom-Up Review and the 1995 commission, the QDR concluded that, with the Soviet Union dissolved, a large strategic reserve was no longer required. It recommended cuts of 45,000 Army Guard/ Army Reserve personnel and an acceleration of the planned conversion of four of the Guard's eight combat divisions to CS/CSS roles. But neither ARNG nor U.S. Army Reserve senior leaders had been involved in the final decisions, and the QDR announcement generated, in the words of Representative Stephen E. Buyer (R–IN), an "explosion of criticism," especially from the National Guard. In July 1997 witnesses before his House subcommittee made clear that although the Army considered that the Guard's 15 enhanced brigades had a legitimate role in fulfilling national security requirements (and could meet the 90-day mobilization timeline), the Army's greatest need was for increased Army Guard CS/CSS assets. Ultimately another meeting of Army leaders in June 1997 delayed the bulk of the proposed ARNG/USAR manpower cuts to 2001 and beyond, but confirmed that the Army Reserve would continue to restructure itself to provide CS/CSS to the Army and other U.S. forces.[51]

Further Steps toward Regular-Reserve Integration

During the 1980s several of the reserve components began a de facto transition from a strategic toward an operational reserve—later termed *a part of the operational force*—but that evolution became increasingly evident in the 1990s. This was especially true for aviation units due to the air-centric nature of many operations following Desert Storm. In their 1997 written testimony to Representative Buyer's House subcommittee, Pentagon officials claimed that the "Air Force has the most integrated total force on a day-to-day basis." The air reserves were in high demand, typified by their participation in humanitarian missions, such as support to the Kurds in Iraq beginning in 1991, and, later in the decade, the combat operations over Iraq known as Northern Watch and Southern Watch. Air reserve forces conducted operations in the Balkans, Somalia, Rwanda, and Haiti and supported domestic relief efforts following Hurricane Andrew in 1992.[52]

From 1991 to 2001 the regular Air Force drew down from 510,000 to 353,000 personnel. During the same period the ANG sustained only modest reductions, from 117,000 to 108,000 personnel. Moreover, the Air Guard increased its full-time support program—already the highest among the reserve components—from 28 percent in 1991 to nearly 31 percent a decade later. The ANG already had a history of providing volunteers on short operational tours to help meet U.S. Air Force commitments. In the 1990s the Guard did even more, in locales ranging from Iraq to Africa to the Balkans, typically deploying part-time guardsmen for 15 to 30 days while full-time support personnel often served longer tours. In most of these cases, real-world deployments took the place of the standard 15-day annual training period. Often, Guard aircraft and personnel from multiple units deployed as a package that formed a "rainbow" unit, such as the amalgamation of parts from four ANG F–16C Falcon squadrons that went to Turkey in late 1993 to deter Saddam Hussein. In perhaps the Air Guard's most significant integrative development of the decade, between 1993 and 1997 the ANG assumed the entire fighter-interceptor continental air defense mission and took command, from Air Combat Command, of the First Air Force headquartered at Tyndall AFB, Florida. In 1991 the AFRES accepted full responsibility for the Air Force's weather reconnaissance mission. A year later the command activated its first C–17 Globemaster III airlifter associate squadron. At the start of 1993 the AFRES activated its first space operations squadron, and in fall 1994 the associate mission expanded to include KC–135 tanker aircraft. At about that time, the Air Force stopped using the term *associate* in the official designation of AFRES units, an indication of the program's maturity.[53]

In the half-decade following Desert Storm, the U.S. Navy improved the integration of its regular and reserve components. Rear Adm. Thomas F. Hall, who later became the longest-serving assistant secretary of defense for reserve affairs (2002–2009), saw this process as going hand-in-hand with his component's forward-looking study, *Vision 2000*. During his tenure as Naval Reserve chief, his component's strength declined by one-third, from about 133,000 to 96,000, but it also deployed ten Naval Reserve guided missile frigates overseas during FY 1995. The ability to prepare for lengthy deployments that were typically the purview of full-time sailors largely resulted from a policy that authorized reservists to combine required drill periods for longer, but less frequent, duty. The Navy also saw reservists' civilian skills as an increasingly valuable resource and in the mid-1990s established a database with that information, a precursor to a broader initiative throughout the reserve components after 2001. Integration was not always a smooth process. The proportion of the Naval Reserve's full-time Training and Administration of the Reserves personnel remained steady at 17 percent, but Admiral Hall recalled the "TAR Wars," an "acid-like" reaction from regulars and part-time reservists to a system that gave prime positions, such as command of units and ships and flag rank promotions, to TARs while not subjecting them to unwanted deployments like other personnel.[54]

Over the course of the 1990s the active Marine Corps went down from 190,000 to 174,000. The Marine Reserve Forces commander, Maj. Gen. James E. Livingston, reasoned that if half of the Marine Corps Selected Reserve had been activated during the Persian Gulf War, then a regular Corps reduced by 16,000 personnel could not expect to fulfill the nation's two-major-regional-conflict strategy without mobilizing an even greater percentage. He envisioned that "reservists will have to commit to activation in scenarios that fall far short of 'the big one.'" Furthermore, Livingston advocated an end to the skepticism of many regulars regarding reserve readiness and capabilities. Seconding the suggestion of the Marine Corps commandant, General Carl E. Mundy Jr., Livingston endorsed the idea of erasing "the 'R' from the designation of Marines" in the reserve: "All Marines would then be 'USMC.'"[55]

Livingston did not believe the 4th Marine Division's battalions and the 4th Marine Aircraft Wing's squadrons were "as prepared as their regular counterparts to assault a hostile shore tomorrow. Nevertheless, the current structure of the Marine Reserve component—together with enhanced training opportunities—will enable the Marine Corps to realistically rely upon its reserve for prompt introduction into hostilities." He listed several recommendations to enhance combat readiness, including lengthening the traditional two-week annual training period to four weeks, which might be split into two active-duty periods of two weeks each, approximately six months apart. In 1994 the Corps renamed its Full-Time Support program as the Active Reserve (AR) and made changes to provide better professional development and promotion opportunities for those full-time reserve Marines. But Brig. Gen. Ronald D. Richard, the assistant deputy chief of staff for manpower and reserve affairs at Headquarters Marine Corps, assured everyone that the system of active component inspector-instructors "is a proven method of training Reserve units and will remain in place."[56]

In the mid-1990s the Coast Guard took regular-reserve integration to its logical conclusion, largely merging the two components into one and eliminating reserve units. The post–Cold War drawdown, which reduced the service's drilling reserve billets by a third, motivated changes to ensure the Coast Guard could meet its responsibilities. An experiment at San Diego offered a promising new approach, with reserve units collocating with regular counterparts. A combined administrative office handled such functions (which typically consumed up to 25 percent of reservists' duty time), while innovative training initiatives ensured mobilization readiness. During 1994–1995 the

Coast Guard expanded the San Diego experiment across the service, despite the policy's one significant drawback: integration eliminated the traditional reserve command structure, depriving most reserve officers of command opportunities and calling into question the roles of senior enlisted reservists.[57]

In 1994 Rear Adm. Robert E. Sloncen became the first Coast Guard reservist to be appointed chief of the Office of Readiness and Reserve. Later in the year the Coast Guard commandant, Admiral Robert E. Kramek, formally introduced service-wide integration under a moniker coined by reservists in 1992—"Team Coast Guard"—which consisted of "one set of missions, one command structure, and one administrative structure." Rear Adm. Steven E. Day, U.S. Coast Guard Reserve (USCGR), believed "there were some pockets of successes with integration and there were some pockets of not such good success." Reservists sometimes felt that active-duty units only reluctantly embraced them, or did not fully understand their different requirements. Coast Guard Reserve Rear Adm. Richard W. Schneider suggested going even further, with legislative changes that "would allow active duty personnel to swing in and out of reserve status based on individual personal circumstances such as maternity leave, post-graduate opportunities, etc. Likewise, reservists need easier ways to go on active duty." Schneider's recommendations anticipated those of later studies, including the 2005–2008 congressionally mandated Commission on the National Guard and Reserves (CNGR).[58]

Depending on context and reserve component, views differed on the timing of the reserve components' transition from a strategic to an operational reserve. But in November 1999 Rear Adm. Carlton D. Moore, USCGR, the Pacific Area's reserve chief, already considered the Coast Guard Reserve to be an operational reserve: "With few exceptions, field commanders openly state that they could not carry out their missions today without their reservists." Lending credence to his conclusion: reservists comprised nearly 100 percent of the Coast Guard's expeditionary warfare forces: harbor defense, naval coastal warfare, and port security units.[59]

Both civilian and uniformed leaders in the Defense Department appreciated the importance of eliminating barriers to active-reserve integration. To mark the 25th anniversary of the Total Force policy, highlight accomplishments to date, and encourage further improvements, Secretary of Defense William S. Cohen called on the Pentagon's leadership to remove "all residual barriers structural and cultural" that stood in the way of integration and create a "seamless Total Force." Cohen's memorandum, prepared by the office of Assistant Secretary of Defense for Reserve Affairs Deborah R. Lee and released in September 1997, was arguably one of his most significant directives. He believed integration must be founded on the "conditions of readiness and trust needed for the leadership of all levels to have well-justified confidence that Reserve component units are trained and equipped to serve as an effective part of the joint and combined force within whatever timelines are set for the unit—in peace and war." He emphasized it was the responsibility of senior leaders throughout the active and reserve components "to create the necessary environment for effective integration." Even prior to the Cohen memorandum, Admiral Jeremy M. Boorda, in one of his first decisions as chief of naval operations, directed the merger of the Navy's regular and reserve flag officer lists—an example of removing the structural barriers to which Cohen alluded. In 1998 the implementation of the green ID card for both active and reserve personnel represented another symbolic step in keeping with Cohen's directive.[60]

The significant advances towards integration and the increasing reliance on the reserves as an operational force grew ever more apparent during the Balkans deployments. As communist regimes unraveled in Europe after the fall of the Berlin Wall, so too did the ethnically diverse state of Yugoslavia. When the country broke apart and conflicts arose, the United States joined several peacekeeping efforts and combat operations. Reserve component units and personnel participated, with most of those called up under presidential selected reserve call-up authority coming from the Army Reserve and ARNG. The other components generally met their much smaller requirements largely through volunteers. The operations included peacekeeping in Bosnia (Joint Endeavor, 1995–1996), stabilization in Bosnia and Herzegovina (Joint Guard, 1996–1998), an air campaign against Serbia (Allied Force, 1999), and peace enforcement in Kosovo (Joint Guardian, 1999–2013). Although these operations were much smaller in scale than Desert Shield/Desert Storm, reserve components played a significant role due to the high concentration of some capabilities, such as civil affairs and psychological operations, in the reserves, and due to the high operational tempo experienced by shrinking regular forces. During 1997, for instance, about one-fourth of the U.S. Army's personnel in Bosnia were from the reserve components. The new paradigm went a step further in the long-running Joint Guardian operation, in which ARNG divisions from Pennsylvania, Indiana, California, Texas, and Virginia contributed units for six-month tours of duty, spelling regular brigades in the rotation. The once-moribund IRR also played a significant role: between 1990 and 1997, more than 37,000 of its members participated as volunteers in various Balkan contingencies. At the time, the IRR could be involuntarily called only by use of mobilization authority or a declaration of national emergency. Congress finally changed the law in the FY 1998 Defense authorization act to permit IRR call-up under presidential selected reserve call-up authority. PSRC soon changed to presidential reserve call-up to reflect the expansion beyond the Selected Reserve.[61]

In spring 1999 the ANG and Air Force Reserve (now widely referred to as the AFR rather than the AFRES) participated in Operation Allied Force, the air campaign undertaken to protect ethnic Kosovars from the Serbian army and the most intense U.S. action in the Balkans during the 1990s. On 27 April, one month after the start of the operation, Defense Secretary Cohen announced an involuntary call-up of air reservists, with a first increment of 2,000 personnel and 47 aircraft from nine air refueling units. Five of these units were ANG, four were AFR; Cohen underscored the necessary reliance on these units when he noted that 55 percent of U.S. air-refueling assets were in the reserves. Air reservists also conducted airlift and special operations missions, in addition to support functions like logistics and communications. Beginning on the night of 21 May, air guardsmen conducted strikes against Serb forces as part of the 104th Expeditionary Operations Group, a rainbow unit including guardsmen from A–10 units in Massachusetts, Michigan, and Idaho. The air reserves' role had become indispensable even in a limited operation such as Allied Force.[62]

—— Conclusion ——

Beginning with the Persian Gulf conflict, the United States became more dependent on the reserve component, as the Total Force policy had envisioned two decades earlier. Driven initially in part by the desire to ensure the nation would be fully behind any commitment of the military to war, the shift gathered steam due to the fiscal savings that accrued from moving missions and structure to the reserves. The integration of the active and reserve forces advanced measurably in all services, but unsurprisingly, the Army, the largest service, experienced the greatest challenges and most dramatic changes. The transition of the Army Guard's primary role to one of providing combat units to be deployed 90 days after activation—sooner than ever before—and of the Army Reserve's role of providing indispensable CS/CSS units facilitated the service of both in the Balkans as a part of the operational force. Congress assisted this evolution with legislation in 1995 that authorized 270-day PSRC activations and the 1998 law that provided access to the Individual Ready Reserve without a partial mobilization. The effectiveness of these initiatives and the readiness of the reserve components to play a vital role in a lengthy major war would be tested much sooner than anyone anticipated.

——— CHAPTER 5 ———

Mobilizing for the Global War on Terrorism, 2001–June 2003

The attacks of 11 September 2001 hastened the transition that had been underway for years, making the reserve components an even more integral part of the nation's operational force. Citizen-soldiers responded to new and extensive operational requirements in Afghanistan (Enduring Freedom) and Iraq (Iraqi Freedom) and to protecting lives and critical infrastructure at home (Noble Eagle). In each case, reservists were among the operation's earliest participants. Furthermore, the attacks highlighted the mission of homeland security and led to increased roles for the National Guard and Coast Guard. With this heightened use, perennial issues—such as mobilization/demobilization, active-reserve integration, medical/dental/family readiness, and civilian employer support—assumed a new urgency.

Homeland Security and the 9/11 Attacks

Around the turn of the millennium, homeland security and homeland defense became household terms as the threat of terrorist activities on U.S. soil increased. In 1999 and 2000, Michèle A. Flournoy, a former principal deputy assistant secretary (and future under secretary of defense for policy), led a study preparing for the statutorily required 2001 Quadrennial Defense Review. In a far-reaching assessment, her group recommended that the National Guard assume a leading role in responding to terrorist attacks in the continental United States. The new requirement, termed consequence management, would become the primary responsibility of the forces assigned, with deployment in support of theater contingency plans only a secondary mission.[1]

Some thought that Flournoy's assessment called into question the National Guard's traditional standing as part of the nation's first line of defense. The QDR study group admitted that the transformation of a portion of the Guard's force to focus on the homeland consequence management mission held "the greatest potential domestic political volatility, as well as significant fiscal impact" of any of their recommendations. Acknowledging the "huge

In preparation for the 2001 Quadrennial Defense Review, Michèle A. Flournoy, a former principal deputy assistant secretary of defense, led a study that recommended the National Guard assume the mission of responding to domestic terrorist attacks. (DoD photo by Scott Davis)

change in thinking on the part of the National Guard" that her ideas required, Flournoy still believed that the reserve component "is the one part of the force structure, particularly the National Guard's ground forces, that I feel needs to be considered for major restructuring." Her group's work, released in April 2001, mirrored the George W. Bush administration's independently developed restructuring initiative that was part of the 2001 QDR. Although many defense observers anticipated the QDR would initiate major changes, even a transformation within the Pentagon, its release on 30 September was overshadowed by events. Nonetheless, the report's call for the department to "institutionalize definitions of homeland security, homeland defense, and civil support" helped clarify domestic security challenges facing the nation.[2]

Congress underscored the growing importance of the reserve component in the fiscal year 2000 Defense authorization act by elevating the reserve chiefs to three-star rank. Lt. Gen. Thomas J. Plewes, the U.S. Army Reserve Command commanding general, noted that the new rank gave the Army Reserve chief "a comparable voice" at the resources table and brought "a great deal more respect to the position." Vice Adm. John B. Totushek, the Naval Reserve Force commander from 1998 to 2003, viewed the decision as proof of "the value of the Reserve Component to the active force." His successor, Vice Adm. John G. Cotton, said the change put him "at the table where the money decisions are made." The first three-star Air National Guard director, Lt. Gen. Daniel James III, felt that the promotion "levels the playing field rank wise. . . . There are a lot of generals in Washington, but the decision makers . . . wear three stars." The additional clout proved advantageous in the mobilizations to come.[3]

The terrorist attacks launched by al-Qaeda on the morning of 11 September 2001 killed nearly 3,000 people and shocked the nation and the world. Within hours, citizen-soldiers responded in force. In the District of Columbia, officials sent out in small groups more than 600 local Army National Guard personnel to help police provide security. In New York, Governor George E. Pataki brought into state active duty more than 4,200 traditional guardsmen, in addition to the nearly 2,000 who already served in full-time support billets. By mid-afternoon on the 11th, guardsmen set up a medical triage center and electrical generators one block east of Ground Zero, while others established a casualty collection point at a nearby sports complex. That evening, an ARNG/Air Guard civil support team arrived and began collecting air samples, which calmed fears that the airliners might have carried chemical or biological agents. Guard field artillery and infantry units established a security cordon across lower Manhattan. The next day four military police companies mobilized to secure the Pentagon and other key facilities in the Washington area. Army guardsmen in New York, New Jersey, and Pennsylvania worked from New York City armories to provide logistics support, security, and transportation.[4]

Army Reserve members responded as well. In Flushing, New York, the 77th Regional Support Command reacted quickly, delivering support items to

Three days after the 11 September 2001 attacks, President George W. Bush implemented partial mobilization, authorizing the involuntary call-up of Ready Reserve members for up to two years. (Source: National Archives, photo by Eric Draper)

assist in the effort at the World Trade Center. Other U.S. Army Reserve personnel, including emergency preparedness liaison officers, crisis action teams, and military police units, went into action in New York City and Washington or readied themselves at home unit installations. On 14 September, President Bush announced a partial mobilization of the reserves. Three days later soldiers from the Army Reserve's 311th Quartermaster Company (Mortuary Affairs) from Puerto Rico were on duty at the north parking lot of the Pentagon. By 26 September nearly two hundred 311th personnel were serving, all of them on mobilization orders.[5]

On 9/11 the U.S. Coast Guard (USCG) suddenly became responsible for tightening security at some 350 U.S. ports, a mission made even more daunting by the fact that maritime and port security had been neglected during the 1990s. The Coast Guard recalled upwards of 3,000 reservists, its largest mobilization since World War II. Many of them served in the port security units, almost entirely manned by reservists; the first of these deployed to New York City by 14 September, where it remained on duty for six weeks patrolling the Hudson River and adjoining bay areas.[6]

The Air Force Reserve Command (AFRC) commander and chief of the Air Force Reserve, Lt. Gen. James E. Sherrard III, noted that his command pro-

On the afternoon of 14 September 2001 Craig Duehring, principal deputy assistant secretary of defense for reserve affairs, conducted a DoD news briefing on the president's decision to implement partial mobilization for the first time since 1991. (Source: Defense Imagery Management Operations Center, photo by R. R. Ward)

vided nearly half of the aeromedical evacuation assets and the vast majority of mortuary affairs support that arrived immediately after the attacks. Reserve airlift crews delivered critical supplies, equipment, and personnel including federal emergency response teams, excavators, search dogs, and fire trucks. Under Operation Noble Eagle, AFR F–16 fighters flew combat air patrols over major U.S. cities or stood ready on ground alert, with reserve airborne warning and control system aircraft, tanker aircraft (KC–135s), and tactical airlifters (C–130s) providing support for the new air defense mission. ANG fighters (F–15 Eagles and F–16 Fighting Falcons) also conducted combat air patrols over 30 major U.S. cities and maintained alert at locations around the nation, furnishing the bulk of the greatly expanded contintental air defense effort. In addition, ANG airlift, security forces, civil engineering, and communications assets either responded directly or went on alert.[7]

The air patrols over major U.S. cities required some 265 aircraft and 12,000 airmen (the vast majority from the ANG and AFR), a commitment that the U.S. Air Force chief of staff, General John P. Jumper, viewed as unsustainable. By comparison, Operation Enduring Freedom (OEF) required the support of some 14,000 airmen. As a sense of security gradually returned, in the spring of 2002 the Air Force transitioned from daily air patrols to random ones and implemented a tiered alert program that provided more flexibility. Between 11 September 2001 and June 2004, U.S.-based jet fighters intercepted roughly 1,500 airplanes due to security concerns.[8]

The 11 September attacks brought homeland security to the forefront of defense department priorities. The nearly completed 2001 QDR already en-visioned the reserve component (in particular the National Guard) playing a significant role, with its presence in about 5,000 communities nationwide making it a natural fit for many homeland security tasks. The Guard had long prized its combat role, however, and found an ally in Secretary of the Army Thomas E. White. In early 2002 the retired brigadier general expressed his view that homeland security should be "*a* mission for the Guard, but not *the* mission for the Guard." The reliance of the regular forces on the Guard to meet other needs was highlighted by the 29th Infantry Division (Light). In October 2001 it carried out the largest reserve overseas deployment since the Persian Gulf conflict when it took over the U.S. operation in Bosnia for six months.[9]

Within a week of President Bush's late September request, about 7,000 guardsmen (mostly ARNG) began providing security at some 440 U.S. airports, a role that continued until May 2002 (in Title 32 status). That duty heightened public awareness of the Guard, and the ARNG chief of staff, Col. Charles P. Baldwin, considered the mission to have been "incredibly successful." In early 2002 President Bush declared the Winter Olympics in Salt Lake City, Utah, a

National Special Security Event that warranted heightened ground and air security measures. At the peak of the games more than 5,000 guardsmen served at ground checkpoints, airports, and other stations. And in the Olympic competition itself, three bobsledding guardsmen contributed to two U.S. medals, one gold and the other bronze.[10]

After 9/11 guardsmen served in full state status, federally funded state status under the governor's control (Title 32, U.S. Code), or full federal status (Title 10, U.S. Code). The fact that thousands mobilized under state authorities rather than federal authority limited the benefits they would receive for service. Because Title 32 did not subject personnel to worldwide deployment, guardsmen earned no credit toward veteran status, which conveyed benefits such as home loans and hiring preference for jobs. Nonetheless, Guard leaders urged President Bush to keep guardsmen in Title 32 status for most homeland security missions, as it allowed governors to fulfill their traditional role of maintaining security within their borders. Moreover, federalizing the Guard for this mission would have run afoul of the Posse Comitatus Act of 1878, a statute that prohibited the use of federal troops for domestic law enforcement. Finally, as the Adjutant General Association president, Maj. Gen. John Kane of Idaho, stated, "Routinely federalizing the Guard for homeland security missions erodes the control of the governor over our soldiers and airmen. It also degrades our training and readiness for other state emergencies and for overseas missions in support of the Army and Air Force."[11]

By now it was clear that "other state emergencies" could include the unthinkable. In 2002 President Bush authorized an increase, from 32 to 55, in the number of Guard civil support teams, organized to respond to the use of weapons of mass destruction. Each team consisted of 22 ARNG and ANG members trained in 14 specialties and prepared to test for nuclear, biological, or chemical agents in the air, soil, and water that could prove harmful to emergency responders or the public. Upon certification, a team was prepared to conduct operations within and outside its state under the Guard's national response plan.[12]

Homeland security responsibilities were intrinsic to the Coast Guard, but it had greatly neglected that mission as a result of budget cuts in the 1990s. After 9/11, however, the USCG experienced the most dramatic proportional increases in manpower and money of any of the armed forces. On 9/11, the Coast Guard Reserve had one-third fewer reservists than it did a decade earlier. Moreover, unlike the Defense Department services, the Coast Guard's active component was fully committed during peacetime with environmental, humanitarian, and other duties on a day-to-day basis. As a result, it lacked the surge capability of its sister services. Realizing the Coast Guard was not sufficiently funded to carry out its post-9/11 mission, Congress boosted its budget 20 percent to $6 billion. One year later Coast Guard Selected Reserve strength had increased 50 percent, from 5,200 to 7,800.[13]

Operation Enduring Freedom

In response to the 9/11 attacks, the United States took aim at the Taliban regime in Afghanistan, which provided a safe haven to al-Qaeda. On 14 September, President Bush authorized the partial mobilization of up to 50,000 ready reservists for up to 24 months (under Title 10, U.S. Code Section 12302). The initial service calls were 10,000 Army, 13,000 Air Force, 3,000 Navy, 7,500 Marine Corps, and 2,000 Coast Guard. On 7 October 2001 the United States launched air and missile attacks to initiate Operation Enduring Freedom—the U.S.-coalition campaign against al-Qaeda and the Taliban in Afghanistan. Ground forces joined the campaign 12 days later, and Secretary of Defense Donald H. Rumsfeld increased the mobilization caps for the Army to 34,000; Air Force to 40,600; and Navy to 14,400. Those mobilizations were in addition to ongoing presidential reserve call-up, or PRC, activations for operations in Bosnia-Herzegovina, Southwest Asia, and Kosovo. The ARNG, for example, during FY 2002 deployed 6,700 personnel to Bosnia, Kosovo, Macedonia, Kuwait, and Saudi Arabia.[14]

By the end of October 2001, ARNG elements mobilized for OEF included linguists and intelligence specialists from Utah's 142nd Military Intelligence Battalion. In December, Utah's 19th Special Forces Group entered active service, and only a month later it began arriving in Uzbekistan. In April 2002 detachments from the 19th searched caves in eastern Afghanistan for enemy combatants. In January, Alabama's 20th Special Forces Group entered active duty and provided security for government officials and supply convoys in Afghanistan. In spring 2002 the United States transferred more than 500 captured enemy combatants to detainee facilities at Guantanamo Bay, Cuba. A detachment from Maryland's 115th Military Police Battalion became the first guardsmen assigned to the joint task force there. One-third of them had significant experience as corrections or police officers, and since 9/11 personnel from that unit had guarded the Pentagon and backfilled for active-duty soldiers at Fort Stewart, Georgia.[15]

The air reserves participated in OEF from the outset, with AFR-crewed C–17s conducting combat airdrops and humanitarian missions and C–5 airlifters and KC–10 Extender tankers contributing heavily to the air bridge from the continental United States to Europe and Southwest Asia. Two weeks into the operation, AFR fighters conducted the first F–16 combat sorties of OEF. By late October EC–130E aircraft of the Pennsylvania Air Guard's 193rd Special Operations Wing were broadcasting music and information to many Afghans. In January 2002 South Carolina's 169th Fighter Wing deployed six F–16CJ aircraft and more than 200 personnel to Qatar, conducting air-to-ground operations against Taliban and al-Qaeda elements and returning home in early April. Given the long distances from Southwest Asia bases to Afghanistan, air refueling was indispensable for U.S. and coalition fighter operations. By April 2003 the ANG had flown nearly one-quarter of OEF fighter sorties over Afghanistan and one-fifth of the tanker sorties. Meanwhile the AFR and ANG were still participating in Operations Northern Watch and Southern Watch (both over Iraq) and Bosnia/Kosovo missions, as well as Noble Eagle at home. By July 2002 the number of federalized air reservists (ANG and AFR) exceeded 30,000, and nearly 8,000 volunteers served. While some reservists demobilized, in September 2002 the Air Force announced the extension of more than 14,000 mobilized ANG and AFR personnel into their second year due to ongoing operational requirements at home and abroad. Fully two-thirds of the extended reservists filled security forces billets, many of whom went on to serve during Operation Iraqi Freedom (OIF) in 2003.[16]

Operation Iraqi Freedom

In October 2002, following congressional approval of the use of force to topple the Saddam Hussein regime in Iraq, the United States began preparing for offensive action. Operation Iraqi Freedom began on 19 March 2003 with air and missile strikes, followed soon after by a ground invasion. The coalition assault consisted primarily of U.S. and British forces, with smaller contributions from 40 other nations. The force was roughly half the size of that employed in Desert Storm, but it succeeded in capturing Baghdad and ousting Hussein from power on 9 April. Despite the much smaller numbers of troops involved, the operation relied heavily on reserve support. The contribution of citizen-soldiers grew even larger as the lightning conventional campaign gave way to a struggle against a stubborn insurgency that would persist for years.

In late 2002 and early 2003 the Army National Guard mobilized nearly 32,000 soldiers in connection with OIF, mainly infantry, military police, engineering, ordnance, and logistics units. One of the Guard's most unusual missions was protecting sealift assets, a task that arose as a result of the Marine Corps' heavy wartime assignments. An ARNG infantry brigade from Puerto Rico took up this unique role. Elements of eight infantry battalions—with the largest contingents coming from Florida, Indiana, and Oregon—performed missions such as providing security at special forces compounds and guarding enemy prisoners of war. The ARNG also contributed aviation and linguistic support to the task force that searched for weapons of mass destruction in Iraq. By late March the National Guard had mobilized and deployed 95,000 personnel for Noble Eagle, Enduring Freedom, and Iraqi Freedom—as many as had deployed for the Korean conflict 50 years earlier. And in Iraq, for the first time since the Korean War, a Guard infantry battalion (1st Battalion, 293rd Infantry from Indiana) went into combat as a unit. In early April an Arizona truck company became one of the first U.S. Army transportation companies to be based in Iraq and was among the first ARNG units to reach Baghdad.[17]

The Army Reserve mobilized various combat support and combat service support units for Iraq. Deploying in January 2003, the 362nd Quartermaster Battalion (Petroleum Supply) hauled millions of gallons of fuel and water in support of the Army's V Corps. The 459th Engineer Company (Multi-Role Bridge), in support of the Marines' advance on Baghdad, threw up hasty bridges across the Diyala and Euphrates Rivers under enemy fire. The 323rd Engineer Detachment (Fire Fighting) deployed to Iraq in April 2003 and put out oil pipeline and other fires, inspected structures, and provided base fire department and aircraft crash-rescue services. In February the 445th Medical Detachment (Veterinary Services) mobilized, arriving in Kuwait in May. The detachment, which had an area of operations spanning ten countries from Kuwait to Kyrgyzstan, cared for military working dogs and handled food inspection quality assurance for more than 18 million meals over the next nine months. Military police units established an enemy prisoner-of-war camp and provided security for an air base.[18]

The ANG and AFR were equally committed to the fight in Iraq. In the opening weeks of OIF highly experienced ANG A–10 and F–16 pilots operating over the western Iraqi desert provided close air support to special operations forces. Of the 60 A–10s in combat operations during OIF's opening phase, 48 belonged to the Air Guard. Most significant, Air Guard A–10s accounted for 60 percent of the Iraqi targets destroyed by all USAF fighter aircraft. In addition, 72 of 124 Air Force C–130 transports belonged to the ANG. Guard C–130 aircrews flew the first airlift of humanitarian supplies into Baghdad International Airport. The ANG accounted for one-third of all Air Force tanker aircraft deployed for OIF while continuing to support Noble Eagle requirements at home. Moreover, the Air Force deployed the 116th Air Control Wing—its only "blended wing," manned by active component and ANG personnel—sending 9 of its 11 E–8C intelligence collection aircraft to the Central Command theater. In addition, the ANG provided 3,500 combat support personnel for OIF beginning in March 2003, accounting for 27 percent of total USAF civil engineering assets in Iraq.[19]

Air Force Reserve airlifters—as they had done earlier for Afghanistan—contributed heavily to the air bridge from the continental United States to Europe and Southwest Asia. In fact, the AFR provided nearly 50 percent of the Air Force's C–17 and C–5 aircrews. In the initial phase of Iraqi Freedom, Air Force Reserve special operations MC–130s refueled USAF MH–53M helicopters that inserted special mission teams at strategic locations in Iraq, and six Air Force Reserve F–16s conducted missions over western Iraq, including the search for Iraqi Scud missiles. Meanwhile, an AFR aeromedical liaison team, embedded with the Marines near the al-Rumaila oil fields, coordinated the aerial evacuation of casualties.[20]

The Navy relied on widespread volunteerism for overseas duty and had reservists handling some stateside logistics work during their regular training periods, which meant that only one reserve logistics squadron needed to be mobilized. In another success story, a reserve F/A–18A squadron—VFA–201 from Fort Worth, Texas—was "basically mobilized over a weekend," according to Admiral Totushek, and quickly demonstrated its readiness at training sites in Nevada and California. Deployed to the Mediterranean Sea from March to May 2003, VFA–201 conducted combat operations as part of OIF.[21]

In some cases, all the specialized assets in a reserve component served in operations. Between February 2002 and November 2003 all of the Marine Forces Reserve (MarForRes) intelligence units were employed in stateside or overseas missions. The Marine Corps had no civil affairs units outside of the reserves, and by late 2002, prior to OIF, elements of its two civil affairs groups had been mobilized for duty either in Afghanistan, Kosovo, or both. The Marine Forces Reserve commander, Lt. Gen. Dennis M. McCarthy, reinforced the commandant's priorities and maintained the reserve's focus on combat operations. In late 2002 McCarthy reminded his reservists, "our reserve force is a combat force and we [are] not going to activate reserves for 'other' missions." Within a year the Marine Corps commandant, General Michael W. Hagee, reported that 21,000 reserve Marines had been mobilized in support of OEF and OIF, and roughly 70 percent were within Iraq's borders at the peak of OIF.[22]

There were early cases of back-to-back deployments of reserve units, a foretaste of future challenges. The 2nd Battalion, 25th Marines, returned home to New York in late 2002 after a lengthy deployment to Camp Lejeune, North Carolina. While there the battalion had deployed some of its companies to the Balkans and otherwise provided relief to over-committed 2nd Marine Division units. Just one month after its return home, however, the battalion received notice of its impending mobilization for Iraq. In March 2003 the 2nd Battalion conducted three weeks' predeployment training in North Carolina; in early April it began combat operations at a captured Iraqi army base. By May the battalion—which included many with civilian law enforcement experience—began creating a new Iraqi police force in the southern city of An Nasiriyah. By the end of July the 2nd Battalion returned stateside, completing its second deployment in about 18 months.[23]

Ongoing Challenges to an Operational Reserve

The nation's civilian and military leadership had made efforts to resolve the challenges and problems that the reserve component had experienced during Desert Shield and Desert Storm. The frequent resort to reserve forces for contingency operations during the remainder of the 1990s had provided opportunities to test those initiatives. Nevertheless, many of the same issues cropped up during the early 2000s, revealing that the fixes were inadequate and much remained to be done.

Individual reservists not assigned to units played an increasing role in the reserve response to the crises of 9/11 and after. These included both individual mobilization augmentees (IMAs, who trained regularly and drew drill pay) and members of the Individual Ready Reserve (IRRs, who did not train or receive pay). In the first six months of Enduring Freedom, IMAs constituted one-fourth of all activated Air Force reservists. In spring 2002 some 3,300 IMAs served in a wide variety of specialties, an unprecedented participation rate. During 2001 the Naval Reserve had primarily activated individuals, rather than units, especially in the law enforcement/force protection, medical, supply, and intelligence fields. For the first time since 1990–1991, IRRs were used in large numbers to fill out units or to find people with very specific skills. In late 2001 Marine Forces Reserve Commander Lieutenant General McCarthy emphasized the importance of IRRs when he noted that they "keep units together by eliminating the need to take key personnel from units to fill individual requirements."[24]

The mobilization of the Individual Ready Reserve presented special concerns. In some cases members appeared "only *dimly aware* of their IRR status and its obligation," even expressing surprise at their call-up, according to Dr. David S. C. Chu, the under secretary of defense for personnel and readiness. Partly as a result of that lack of awareness, the services could not locate thousands of individual reservists who had failed to update their contact information. Part of the problem was also institutional, as exemplified by the Marine Corps. Until the end of 2002, the annual muster of Marine IRRs consisted of mailing postcards. If the postcard did not come back marked undeliverable, the Corps considered the addressee to be officially accounted for. Given the decade since the last mobilization of the Marine Corps IRR and the lack of a rigorous muster process, challenges after 9/11 were no surprise. Yet another issue involved the process for identifying individual augmentees for activation. The MarForRes personnel chief, Col. J. J. Garcia, identified another problem. In 2002–2003 some activated individuals were relieved for poor performance because the requesting unit had not properly specified the skills and experience required, resulting in reservists being assigned to jobs for which they were unqualified.[25]

Mobilizing IRRs at the same time some regulars were leaving active duty as their obligated time expired created additional headaches. In 2002 Army Reserve Chief Lieutenant General Plewes acknowledged:

> IRR has been very difficult from day one. . . . The leadership of the Army was very concerned about . . . the equity of calling up the IRR. . . . Why call them up when you are . . . letting active Army people go out the other door? . . . So, the first issue was, well, if you are going to call up the IRR, you need to have a stop-loss. The stop-loss was not a very pretty sight. Somehow, the Army Reserve and National Guard got left out of the first stop-loss order [and the second]. . . . Third stop-loss order, we were in it, finally.

Plewes further observed that the offices responsible for implementing stop-loss were unaccustomed to applying it to the reserve component, so "it was a comedy of errors."[26]

In 2003 the Reserve Forces Policy Board stated that "the IRR is a valuable pool of Reservists." The change in law in FY 1998 that authorized IRR involuntary activations under presidential reserve call-up had increased the IRR's value. But in the context of the Global War on Terrorism, the PRC option was not required because the partial mobilization authorization included the IRR. The RFPB advocated that drawing from the IRR "should be done with the consent of the member being called to full time duty, if possible; or if involuntarily activated, preferably using IRR not previously called." Although that policy worked well initially for OEF and OIF, a number of IRRs went on to serve multiple tours.[27]

Between fall 2001 and spring 2003 the Pentagon oversaw the mobilization of some 280,000 reservists, compared with nearly 230,000 during Desert Shield/Desert Storm a decade earlier. There was a much greater disparity in the number of mobilization orders used, however. For the first war against Iraq, according to a General Accounting Office study, it took fewer than ten deployment orders to bring nearly a quarter million personnel onto active duty, but after 9/11, it took 246 orders to mobilize the force. Part of that was due to the time span from the original terrorist attacks through the start of OIF. But that trend was exacerbated by Secretary Rumsfeld's desire to demonstrate the transformation of the Department of Defense, to minimize boots on the ground in Afghanistan and Iraq, and to send signals of growing resolve to Saddam Hussein. He also questioned the manner in which total force policy had been carried out in recent years. In particular, he was concerned about the Army's Offsite Agreement, which placed a disproportionate percentage of logistical capability in reserve components: "My instinct is that it doesn't make sense to have the people who are required very early in a conflict in the reserves." As a result, he closely scrutinized all mobilization requests, forcing the services to justify each unit and to call up many

As the under secretary of defense for personnel and readiness, Dr. David S. C. Chu promoted the "continuum of service" concept within the Defense Department and sought new ways to attract cutting-edge professionals for reserve component wartime service. (DoD photo by Helene C. Stikkel)

smaller force packages rather than entire divisions, wings, or other large commands. While that more tailored approach fit the secretary's policy objectives, the incremental mobilization played havoc with longstanding plans for the movement of forces overseas. The GAO further observed that the Pentagon lacked the ability to closely track and process the mobilization of the many small units and individuals being called up. In addition, there were difficulties in activating reservists once they were identified for duty. Along with the many IRRs who could not be located, another 70,000 reservists turned out to be ineligible for mobilization due to incomplete training or fitness, medical, or dental issues.[28]

The basic task of generating orders proved difficult. In June 2001 the Air Force implemented a new system known as the Military Personnel Database System, but among other issues it lacked the ability to produce the necessary orders for operational contingencies. As the need for IMAs accelerated after

9/11, the deficiencies of the system became obvious, and the Air Reserve Personnel Center turned to older methods. To accomplish the task of activating more than 2,000 individuals, personnel specialists returned to the 1950s era and set aside regular duties to establish an assembly line, of sorts, for orders production. Furthermore, the personnel database did not interact well with the pay system. If the pay system rejected the data pertaining to the activated individual, the personnel center did not find out about the error until the reservist got in touch to ask why he or she hadn't been paid. A working group eventually resolved most of the pay system's problems.[29]

By the end of 2001 the Marine Corps Reserve had implemented the Reserve Order Writing System (ROWS). Manpower expert and retired Chief Warrant Officer 3 Robin C. Porche of the MarForRes personnel office stated ROWS initially had limited integration with the Marines' pay and personnel software, the Marine Corps Total Force System. One report observed that ROWS was—like the Air Force's system—designed for peacetime fiscal accountability and suggested modifications to support activated reservists. After these changes, which included switching to a web-based system, ROWS became a model for others. In 2013 Porche commented on its influence: "After seeing what ROWS could do, the Navy contracted . . . to build a version of ROWS. . . . They made their system web-based, added . . . functionality and called it the Navy Reserve Order Writing System." Most of the other services went on to develop their own versions of an order-writing system. Accordingly, by 2003 the Naval Reserve's John Totushek reported that both his reservists and the fleet were pleased with the new system, which replaced no fewer than "three legacy systems that were later shut down." In the same year the Army Reserve's new automated permanent order system began to cut in half the time required to create its orders.[30]

Administrative systems presented another set of challenges related to the tracking of individual training and readiness. In 2002 the new USARC commanding general, Lt. Gen. James R. Helmly, directed the establishment of a Transients-Trainees-Holdees-Students account, a method for tracking individuals who might normally be counted as part of a unit but who were not able to deploy because they were transferring between units, were not yet fully trained, or had some other issue (such as medical or legal) that precluded full participation. The Army's active component had employed the transient account beginning in 1981, but incompatible personnel accounting systems precluded its use by the Army Reserve. By Helmly's time, the USARC's adoption of transient accounts appeared feasible because of the much-anticipated common personnel systems database known as the Defense Integrated Manpower Human Resources System. Adoption of transient accounts promised to ensure timely completion of initial occupational specialty training, enhance unit readiness by keeping nondeployable personnel off official unit rolls, and permit units to spend less time managing these individuals, who accounted for roughly 12 percent of the Army Reserve's strength. At the direction of the U.S. Army chief of staff, between 2003 and 2006 the ARNG established a transient account.[31]

The Naval Reserve also maintained transient accounts. In 2003 Vice Admiral Totushek estimated roughly 10 percent of his reservists were in a status that limited their utility. He acknowledged the U.S. Naval Reserve needed to do a better job of managing and training those personnel in order to maximize their usefulness. To achieve that, the Naval Reserve chief pursued a single regular/reserve pay and personnel system, though a decade later it remained unfinished. By the end of 2001 the Navy had implemented a new web-based pay and personnel system dubbed the Navy Standard Integrated Personnel System. Totushek viewed it as an improvement and a step toward a truly integrated system for the Navy's active and reserve accounts but realized its introduction to the force was his "greatest challenge." Maximizing the number of reservists who could be employed was especially critical after 9/11. In FYs 2000 and 2001 the Navy had failed to attain its authorized enlisted strength in the Selected Reserve, and Operation Enduring Freedom only made it more difficult for the Naval Reserve to attract sailors who were finishing their regular service obligations. As Totushek noted, those who "wanted to be involved in the war on terrorism, they stayed on active duty." But those who reached the end of their active service and no longer wanted to deploy "didn't want to come into the Reserve Force, for fear that they would be recalled. . . . So we hit a rock."[32]

The challenge of filling Selected Reserve units was not confined to the Navy. By FY 2003 the ARNG was concerned with its growing reliance on cross-leveling—the transferring of trained personnel and functioning equipment from a nondeploying unit to fill gaps in another that was getting ready to deploy. From September 2001 through June 2004, the Army Guard transferred 74,000 personnel (more than 20 percent of its entire strength) and 35,000 pieces of equipment into deploying units. In the first year alone after 9/11, equipment readiness (measured on a peacetime basis that was already lower than required for combat) dropped from 87 percent to 71 percent. Colonel Baldwin observed that cross-leveling was acceptable for one or two rotations but over time evolved into "death-spirals" as each successive wave of mobilizing units had fewer and fewer qualified personnel eligible to deploy. The ARNG got by in part with an ad hoc solution, relying heavily on soldiers who repeatedly volunteered—"deployment junkies" in Baldwin's parlance—because they either lacked civilian jobs or preferred being deployed as much as possible. A significant negative effect of cross-leveling was the impact on unit cohesion across the force due to the added churn of personnel.[33]

In the 15 months after September 2001, the Pentagon enacted six stop-loss measures that prevented reservists eligible to retire from doing so. The last of these measures, at the end of 2002, applied to entire units, while the previous ones had been applied to individuals with specific types of skills. All were intended to help preserve the readiness of mobilizing reserve units and avoid the use of cross-leveling. Regardless, cross-leveling continued as a major issue at least through 2008, when the Commission on the National Guard and Reserves stated the practice "does significant harm." However, according to retired Col. Paul E. Pratt, formerly the MarForRes operations/plans chief, some Guard and reserve colonels who dealt with mobilization simply considered it "a fact of life" or "a reality."[34]

The Air Force experienced its own difficulties managing its deployable reserve forces, initially due to the belief that the response to 9/11 would be short term. In 2008 the AFRC assistant vice commander, Brig. Gen. Richard R. Severson, reflected on his perspective as an airlift wing commander seven years earlier: "I'm not sure early on we had a real good feel for the requirement, so we burned up crews rapidly at the time" by mobilizing them and thus starting their 24-month clock. Two years later, Maj. Gen. John A. Bradley, the assistant for reserve matters to the Joint Chiefs of Staff chairman, judged that a long-range view to meeting operational requirements was the better approach. But for Operation Iraqi Freedom, the Air Mobility Command insisted on mobilizing airlift personnel because, recalled Bradley, "they didn't think the war would last long." The future AFRC commander added that the staff said, "We're just going to mobilize for a short time to make sure we have the capability we need, and then we're going to be done." Bradley acknowledged that mobilization held advantages as well as disadvantages but emphasized the benefits of using volunteers for reasonable tour lengths, usually not exceeding 120 days. Significantly, AFRC retention and recruiting figures remained high, and the command enjoyed a surplus of volunteers to meet its Air Expeditionary Force requirements.[35]

There were also misunderstandings regarding who was responsible for assigning reserve units and people to meet contingency requirements. Totushek recalled that in 2001, when reserve activations began, a question arose: "Who owned the mobilization process?" He noted, "I don't think it was evident to a lot of people, including very senior people in the Navy, that it *wasn't* the Naval Reserve Force. . . . It's pretty clear that N3/5 [the Navy staff] owns the process." The recognition that the regular Navy was responsible eventually led to improvements, including establishment of a special mobilization cell in Millington, Tennessee.[36]

Vice Admiral Totushek also referred to the mistaken perception that the USNR was slow to act regarding mobilization/activation. Usually by the time the Naval Reserve received official notification of a validated billet requirement, weeks had passed—a reality shared by other reserve components. The process was slowed in part because the Navy staff had "no tools" to validate requirements, other than saying, in Totushek's words, "Gee, I think that's a real requirement, or, gee, I don't think that's a real requirement." By 2003 the process was much improved. For the first time "the Reserve Force got 'read into' the war plan," thereby enabling it to advise on units and individual skills that might be needed and available. But the outgoing Naval Reserve Force commander surmised that "if we don't do another mobilization for awhile . . . we're going to have the same kind of situation happen again." In late 2002 Secretary Rumsfeld believed that the entire mobilization process had to be revamped and centralized: "I think we are going to have to find a way to take all of the responsibility for activating the guard and reserve from the services, the joint forces command and the combatant commanders and put them in one place so that the flow of forces, whether it is active duty or reserves, is all in one location. We can't do anything skillfully the way it is currently arrayed."[37]

Medical, dental, and physical fitness qualification issues continued to be a problem area. At the time, reserve component personnel were required to have physical exams every five years, plenty of time for health problems that could interfere with readiness to develop undetected. Regulations also still prohibited citizen-soldiers from receiving dental care at government expense unless they were on active duty for longer than 30 days, or during the 75 days prior to mobilization (though advance notifications of call-up, often as short as 3 to 10 days, limited the usefulness of that option). Under Secretary of Defense David Chu also cited the tendency of Americans to "chintz" on dental care as a significant factor in reservists' dental unreadiness. But the fact remained that it was the military's mission to ensure readiness; regulars received free dental care to keep them ready, and reserve personnel did not, rendering them less ready.[38]

In 2003 Brig. Gen. Robert V. Taylor, the National Guard Association of the United States' Army vice chair, noted that 30 percent of recently mobilized Guard and reserve soldiers initially were nondeployable due to dental problems (though many of those ultimately did deploy after they became eligible for care and had their issues corrected). To address the problem, he proposed a policy change to authorize Guard dentists to provide services to soldiers in nonemergency situations. He also sought a better dental insurance program "that soldiers can opt out of if they have sufficient civilian dental coverage." The ARNG's Charles Baldwin recalled that dental readiness for the OIF mobilization "was a disaster." He related an anecdote that Army Chief of Staff

General Eric K. Shinseki frequently shared concerning one citizen-soldier who, after being mobilized for OIF, volunteered to have several teeth pulled so he could deploy with his unit. Within months the ARNG took steps to make dental resources available to soldiers prior to the tightly packed predeployment period. In time, earlier official notification of call-up also enabled soldiers to obtain more timely dental services. Even the Naval Reserve, which had the best record, still had 19 percent of its personnel show up for active duty in 2003 with dental issues that prevented immediate deployment.[39]

By 2003 the services were having many reservists undergo annual medical and dental checks. Dr. William Winkenwerder, the assistant secretary of defense for health affairs, soon established an individual medical readiness policy that required regular health assessments to supplement the more thorough and less frequent physical examinations. Nevertheless, several years later a military health care task force concluded that dental readiness continued as "the greatest obstacle to medical readiness" for most of the reserve component.[40]

Health *after* deployment arose as a new concern, largely due to increasing awareness following the first Gulf War of the health risks (physical and psychological) associated with wartime service. In spring 2003 Winkenwerder implemented a three-step process to improve the tracking of service members' health upon their return from overseas. They first had to complete a new post-deployment health assessment form with more detailed questions than prior versions. Second, they underwent a mandatory face-to-face health assessment with a military health care provider. And third, they provided a blood sample that would become part of the member's permanent medical record. Medical care after demobilization remained an issue despite a 2002 law that extended health care coverage to many activated members for 120 days after their tours ended. A significant number of reservists were unable to use these benefits and blamed the TRICARE system. Often the period expired before personnel could obtain the official documentation of their active duty (Department of Defense Form 214) needed to access medical services; in other instances, reservists were simply unfamiliar with the health-care program and how to use it. In addition, a survey of reserve personnel indicated problems frequently occurred when they and their family members dropped civilian insurance and switched to TRICARE. In 2003 Congress extended reservists' eligibility for TRICARE upon completion of active duty to 180 days.[41]

Family issues had risen to the fore during the first war with Iraq, but for the next ten years fell into some neglect in the absence of mass mobilizations. In spring 2001, however, during the Army's biannual review of its programs, the Army Reserve raised the subject of emergency financial relief for mobilized soldiers. In the spirit of cooperation, the USAR and U.S. Air Force Reserve also conducted a joint program in which each service alternated hosting an annual workshop focused on various topics of interest to families. But the mobilizations after 9/11 showed that improvements were still needed in the preparation of reserve and Guard families for the activation of their military members.[42]

The National Military Family Association adopted the term "the suddenly military" to describe the families of citizen-soldiers facing mobilization or activation, particularly for the first time. Despite extensive reserve component participation in numerous contingencies in the 1990s, prior to 9/11 most families of ARNG and USAR soldiers had not given much thought to a prolonged mobilization or deployment, let alone one that involved combat. Naturally, families that never anticipated a deployment tended to be unprepared for mobilization. In fact, in a 2002 survey 40 percent of Guard families described themselves as "unprepared" for mobilization. Nevertheless, Guard spouses reported receiving more assistance—in the form of newsletters, support groups, and social events—from their soldiers' units, when compared with USAR families. Volunteers, mostly "from the Guard culture," were the key difference, according to Colonel Baldwin of ARNG headquarters.[43]

In FY 2002 the Army/Air Guard touted a nationwide force of more than 20,000 trained volunteers—mainly retirees, spouses, or parents—which the National Guard Bureau considered its "greatest asset" in supporting families. Even so, the ARNG viewed the geographical dispersion of its 350,000 members' families as among its "greatest challenges" in family support matters, despite some 3,000 readiness centers (formerly armories). Perhaps equally challenging was the lack of an ongoing commitment to family support among many ARNG/USAR units, as they tended to establish programs after notification for mobilization and to disband them upon demobilization.[44]

Recognizing the problems with this ad hoc approach, the National Guard established a new paradigm for families. Rather than the family *support* of the Desert Storm era, family *readiness* became the watchword. As the chief of NGB's family program office observed, "Support has a different connotation than readiness. . . . In the past, families might come out to the unit once a year for a family picnic. Today the focus is different . . . benefits, entitlements, budgeting, child-rearing . . . empowering families to quickly handle situations on their own." The Internet became the preferred vehicle for disseminating information. The chief of California's family programs explained, "[The web] is one place where they can get just about anything they need." In FY 2003 the ARNG operated 390 family assistance centers (including some in U.S. territories) from which volunteers performed outreach and follow-up, provided information, and guided families to additional resources. Some states had as many as 20 such centers.[45]

To enhance its programs, the Army Reserve established a billet for a family readiness coordinator who reported to the deputy chief of staff (personnel). In 2003 the USAR family program office sponsored the first family readiness rear detachment commanders' courses. The mobilization of more than 1,700 Army Reserve IMA and IRR personnel in late 2001, and 1,500 the next year (including retirees), presented a special problem. Since they did not belong to a unit, the usual structure of unit-based programs did not work for their families, so the personnel directorate created a dedicated office to manage an IRR/IMA family program to help close that gap. More than a few IRR members, however, resided too far from military facilities to take advantage of the available services.[46]

In April 2003 the Naval Reserve highlighted the inextricable link between family readiness and mission readiness in its monthly publication, describing in detail the *Family Readiness Program's Tool Kit*, a predeployment and mobilization handbook. In addition, the article promoted the *Guide to Reserve Family Member Benefits,* which was available in hard copy or online, and the Naval Reserve Assistance Center, available to reservists and their families 13 hours daily, 7 days a week. Harvey C. Barnum Jr., the deputy assistant secretary of the Navy for reserve affairs, viewed the "biggest challenge as getting the information into the hands of our Reserve families and ensuring that they are comfortable with and understand the mobilization process."[47]

A relatively new vehicle for disseminating information to reservists and their families was Military One Source, a 24-hour hotline that promised confidentiality. As one Tennessee guardsman testified before a congressional subcommittee, the system enabled "somebody from Buck Snort, Tennessee . . . to call One Source and within 20 seconds have someone answering the phone and talking to a real person. . . ." By the end of 2002, Marine reservists had access to Marine Corps Community Services One Source, billed as a "'virtual' family service center for the Marine Corps" and reportedly especially helpful for those living far from an installation.[48]

Employment readiness presented a similar picture of partial success and unresolved issues. In 2003 Bob G. Hollingsworth, the executive director of the National Committee for Employer Support of the Guard and Reserve and a retired Marine major general, reported that the work of his organization's 4,200 volunteers nationwide was a remarkable "good news story." Hollingsworth observed that the reserve component was 46 percent of DoD's military manpower and was "shared with America's employers, large and small, public and private. This inextricably links America's employers to our national defense." He cited examples of employers that exceeded the requirements of the Uniformed Services Employment and Reemployment Rights Act of 1994, including Home Depot, Sears, Verizon, General Motors, and Boeing.

Some companies provided pay differential, extended insurance benefits, and family support to their activated employees and families. Hollingsworth touted ESGR's 540-plus trained ombudsmen who provided information and guidance to employers seeking to comply with USERRA.[49]

Even with those efforts, there was an increased flow of telephone calls and emails precipitated by the war on terrorism, so the ESGR co-located some of its workers with the Navy call center in Millington, Tennessee. The ESGR group handled some 2,000 cases monthly, resolving more than 95 percent in-house, with the remainder requiring formal involvement of the Department of Labor. One long-running issue concerned voluntary versus involuntary active duty under Title 10, U.S. Code. Although the law prescribed that voluntarily activated reservists enjoyed the same civilian job protections as those who served under Title 10 involuntarily (i.e., resulting from mobilization), a strong perception to the contrary was widespread among the reserve component and employers. The ESGR worked to rectify the misperception.[50]

Defense leaders had long touted the fact that many reservists' civilian jobs gave them highly valuable, sometimes unique, skills, but DoD had done little to establish an inventory of reservists' civilian skills, according to the RFPB. In 2001 the Defense Department asked reservists to voluntarily provide their employment information. By early 2002 the Navy administered a mandatory skills database system known as Naval Reserve Skills On-Line, a web-based system that made it easier for reservists to provide and update information about their skills, and easier for commands to learn what skills were available. At about the same time, in U.S. Senate testimony, Under Secretary Chu expressed his interest in finding new ways to attract "cutting edge professionals in key areas such as biometrics and information technology." One possibility, he surmised, involved "creating new 'critical specialty' categories of reserves that are incubators for new and emerging talent pools." Attesting to the presence of unique skills among his reservists, Vice Admiral Cotton stated the Navy had "identified 800 civilian skills among reservists that don't exist in the active duty service."[51]

Examples abounded of reservists applying their civilian expertise in post-9/11 operations, such as Maryland ARNG's 115th Military Police Battalion, which drew one-third of its soldiers from civilian law enforcement. Many reserve component aviators were commercial pilots and therefore had more experience in some areas that carried over to military aviation. The Marines' reserve combat assessment team noted that among two reserve aerial refueler transport squadrons, crews averaged 800 flight hours more than their regular component counterparts deployed with them in Iraq. In an outstanding example of a reservist uniquely qualified for an unforeseen mission, Marine

Corps Col. Matthew Bagdanos, a Manhattan assistant district attorney with a master's degree in classical studies, deployed in 2003 to lead the investigation into the looting of artifacts from the National Museum of Iraq in Baghdad.[52]

But civilian employment could be a double-edged sword. Given the increased concern for homeland security, the Pentagon was reluctant to call up reservists who worked as civilian emergency responders—the same individuals required for an overseas crisis might be needed for one at home. To address the issue, in March 2003 Under Secretary Chu directed the services to implement a mandatory program that required disclosure of civilian employers, addresses, job titles, and years of experience. This information would alert defense officials to reservists who might be needed for a homeland emergency, which they could then factor into their mobilization decisions. In August 2004 the Defense Department implemented regulations for the new program. The downside, of course, would be a loss of unit cohesion when individuals were not mobilized with their unit and had to be replaced by an IRR or a cross-leveled individual from another unit.[53]

By summer 2002, with al-Qaeda and its Taliban supporters seemingly neutralized in Afghanistan and Iraq still primarily a diplomatic issue, the subject of demobilization garnered increased attention at the Pentagon. In June, General Jumper and the air staff were trying to "determine which Air Force specialties can be demobilized as soon as possible," while shifting from crisis response "to our 'new steady state,'" which would utilize volunteer Guardsmen and Reservists to help meet our mission taskings." Lt. Gen. Daniel James III, the ANG director, asked about beginning demobilizations in a timely manner: "Will [air guardsmen] be able to take their leave, outprocess and be off the books and headed back to their families and jobs before we hit that one-year point?" He worried that retention might be hurt by mobilizations extending beyond one year without a clearly identifiable requirement. At the time James spoke, there were some 23,000 air guardsmen involved in the war on terrorism, nearly 7,000 of them volunteers. The Air Guard director remained attuned to the relevance of his part-time force, acknowledging that the homeland security mission "fits well within the National Guard" but affirming the need to "maintain our relevance across the full spectrum of missions," which included combat operations, not just the Noble Eagle air defense mission.[54]

One demobilization issue that affected morale in the air reserves concerned postdeployment downtime, a chance to spend time with families while remaining in a present-for-duty status. With the beginning of OEF redeployments, the potential for inequity between returning regular and reserve component personnel in this area became apparent. Air Force commands were authorizing redeploying members a set number of days of time off, not counted against normal leave, based on length of deployment. Air Force leadership intended for the time "to be compensatory in nature and provide time for the member to take care of quality of life issues that resulted from long periods of deployed time away from home and family." Members were considered "'present for duty' with the duty location being '*at home*.'" But whereas almost all regular personnel resided within the area of their unit, many Air Force reserve component members lived far from the base their unit returned to prior to demobilization. In April 2002 Air Force Reserve officials argued that the policy "has the potential to create an inequitable situation" between active component and reserve personnel. Over the following decade, however, various attempts to rectify the inequity ended in vain.[55]

Pressing Ahead with Regular-Reserve Integration

The series of contingencies and large-scale mobilizations beginning on 9/11 gave added impetus to ongoing efforts to better integrate the regular and reserve components. In 2002 Chu explained the Pentagon's new continuum of service concept within the context of Secretary Rumsfeld's transformation initiative. Chu asserted the transformation challenge required a continuum ranging from the traditional two-week annual tour plus 48 drill periods per year to lengthier mobilization options. He referred to "a continuum that may be as little as a few days in the case of an information technologist, whose services we . . . [may not] need this year, to perhaps as much as nearly full-time as we have indeed done with so many volunteers during the current mobilization." Chu expected the continuum of service to become DoD's new norm. In 2003 the Army Reserve, according to Lt. Gen. James Helmly, envisioned the continuum offering an easier transition between active duty and reserve status "dictated not only by the needs of the Army, but also by what is best for the Soldier developmentally and educationally."[56]

The naval services, significantly smaller than the army components, appeared better situated for progress. In 2003 Vice Admiral Totushek promoted continuum of service "to expand sailor opportunities and optimize recruiting, retention, and assignment practices." His successor, Vice Admiral Cotton, viewed the continuum concept as providing "off-ramps and on-ramps" with respect to an individual's service over perhaps a 40- or 50-year time period. Age should not matter, he stated in a 2013 interview. Cotton lauded the Marine Corps as setting the institutional standard for a mindset consistent with the service continuum: "They never stop being Marines."[57]

Continuum of service sought to eliminate unhelpful differences between the regular and reserve components. To that end, congressional policy changes enacted in post-2001 national Defense authorization acts implemented more equal treatment. The FY 2002 act authorized new reservists to use commissaries "immediately upon entering service, instead of waiting until they have attended unit drills for one year." It also authorized a Survivor Benefit Plan annuity to the spouse of any reservist who died "in the line of duty while serving on active duty." The FY 2004 defense act provided reservists with unlimited use of commissaries and amended the survivor benefit plan such that the spouses of reservists not eligible for retirement who died "from injury/disease incurred in the line of duty during inactive duty training" henceforth received benefits. An Army Reserve historian considered the change in survivor benefits significant because previous law did not authorize benefits until a reservist qualified for retirement.[58]

Administrative systems were a key component of any strategy to improve the flow of personnel between active and reserve duty. The Marine Corps and Coast Guard led the way in this area thanks to their integrated pay and personnel systems developed in the 1990s. Personnel expert Robin Porche noted that the Marine Corps Total Force System provided all Marines with a "cradle-to-grave" personnel system from boot camp to retirement. Unlike the other services (except the Coast Guard), the Marine Corps system did not require the member to be removed from one personnel system and then accessioned into another—a process that could take months. Rather, with two simple data entries, a Marine transferred seamlessly from reserve to active-duty status, and his or her active-duty pay would begin in a timely manner.[59]

Between 2000 and 2003 the vice chief of naval operations, Admiral William J. Fallon, in the words of John Totushek, sought "to make the Naval Reserve much more responsive to the active force," a theme Vice Admiral Cotton immediately took up. In June 2002 Admiral Fallon and William A. Navas Jr., the assistant secretary of the Navy for manpower and reserve affairs, cosponsored a study intended to redesign the Naval Reserve, with the goal of increasing active-reserve integration. In terms of personnel management and organizational structure, the study claimed that the USNR lacked "visibility to the Active Force." The "single-most agreed upon issue" among participants in the study was "Active Force ignorance of the Reserve Force in terms of both capabilities and limitations," an assessment shared by Deputy Assistant Navy Secretary Harvey Barnum. To improve that situation, the Navy's new roadmap for programs, plans, and operations, *Sea Power 21*, pushed the idea of "ONE Navy to fulfill the Nation's missions."[60]

The Coast Guard had led the way in the 1990s in formally integrating its active and reserve components. But in the process the reserve support structure that tracked individuals' requirements—including physical exams, security clearances, training requirements, and mobilization codes—suddenly disappeared. The retired master chief petty officer of the Coast Guard Reserve Forces, Jeffrey D. Smith, likened the situation to taking a "basket of kids . . . to the front porch in the middle of the night at the local commands," turning around, and running the other way. When the Coast Guard activated large numbers of reservists after 9/11, there were cases of boatswain mates who had not "been on a boat for five years because of the other things [they had] been doing." No one had been tracking their requirements or providing "clear direction about what people should be doing" to meet mobilization needs, Smith observed. While Rear Adm. John C. Acton bluntly called this "a failure of personal leadership within the Reserve force," it was also an institutional failure to maintain a process to oversee reserve readiness.[61]

Those challenges served as a catalyst to form the Reserve Strategic Assessment Team, which, according to Rear Adm. Steven E. Day, USCGR, facilitated the "full integration" the service achieved after 2003. Led by Rear Adm. Robert J. Papp Jr., a future commandant, the review identified the gaps—84 in the reserve program —"that hinder readiness and the things we have to do to fix them." Nearly all were in the administrative arena. In response, the Coast Guard began shifting many full-time support billets down the operational chain to the command level where two-thirds of reservists actually worked, so those full-time personnel could manage reservists' administrative and equipment readiness issues. In fairness, then, the Coast Guard's *full* integration occurred only after 2003, a decade later than its nominal date. A bigger change for the Coast Guard came in May 2002, when the Bush administration proposed the reassignment of the Coast Guard from the Department of Transportation to the new Department of Homeland Security (created in November 2002).[62]

A key aspect of making the reserves a stronger part of the Total Force involved the integration of citizen-soldiers on active duty or in full-time civilian slots into the reserve structure. Even before 9/11, Lieutenant General Plewes considered the number of soldiers filling this role in his component to be "insufficient . . . to support over 2,300 Army Reserve units in day-to-day operations." With traditionally one of the lowest percentages of such personnel, he believed that expanding these programs in the USAR was one of his biggest challenges. That year Congress agreed and responded by giving him 950 additional full-time authorizations. In 2002 the Army Reserve was able to fill its more than 13,400 Active Guard and Reserve billets, but it needed even more.[63]

The Army Guard's problem was almost as great. In FY 2002 Congress provided funding for some 23,600 Active Guard and Reserve and 25,200 military technicians, but that was just 58 percent of its validated billets. The follow-ing year, Congress authorized an additional 1,500 billets, taking the Guard to about 61 percent. The National Guard Bureau considered this issue "a top priority." The Army programmed annual funding increases beginning in FY 2004 to provide the 59,700 AGR and MT personnel needed to meet minimum readiness standards by FY 2012. But Guard leaders sought a more rapid ex-pansion, with the National Guard Association's chairman, Maj. Gen. Gus L. Hargett, pushing to reach the goal by FY 2008.[64]

The Air Force Reserve's authorized AGR strength had increased from 400 to 1,400 between 1990 and 2001, but no one element of the staff "exercised overall control" of the program. The AFR chief, Lieutenant General Sherrard, established a new office in 2002 to provide "a single point of contact of all AGR matters."[65]

The Marines continued their successful Inspector-Instructor program as the backbone of their full-time support effort for reserve units. Colonel Pratt viewed the inspector-instructors as providing important "linkages" and "per-sonal ties" between the reserve and regular components. Pratt considered the I-I force—which was 4,000–4,500 strong for most of the decade following 9/11—essential because they brought regular expertise to the reserves and then cycled back to active units, carrying with them fresh insights from the reserve component. A 2004 Marine Corps study agreed, adding that the prac-tice of board-selected battalion inspector-instructors made the program "even stronger now than during [Operation Desert Storm]." Pratt largely credited the Marines' ability to mobilize more than 20,000 and deploy more than 13,000 reservists by early 2003 for Iraqi Freedom to the inspector-instructors, who maintained relationships with their fellow regulars in the active force that helped smooth the process.[66]

The Marine Corps had the Active Reserve program of reservists on full-time active duty, but it was about two-thirds the size of the I-I program and gener-ally functioned in a different capacity. While I-Is almost exclusively resided at the unit level in direct support of unit training and readiness, a significant portion of ARs filled reserve recruiting billets, staff billets in the command echelons of Marine Forces Reserve, or reserve-related planning and liaison billets at headquarters outside the reserve (such as Headquarters Marine Corps, Marine bases, and other active component commands). Following 9/11 some ARs ended up deploying, either as part of the units they supported, or as indi-vidual augmentees (leaving their normal billet vacant). As the war continued, however, the AR program refocused on supporting the reserve establishment rather than getting into the fight, and more AR billets also migrated to reserve units to assist the I-Is in preparing units for the more active role they were playing in ongoing contingency operations.[67]

——— Conclusion ———

As the Total Force policy envisioned, and as most civilian and military leaders had declared for years, the mobilizations between fall 2001 and spring 2003 demonstrated that the reserve component had become indispensable to the conduct of U.S. military operations of any significant size and duration. The reserves were indeed a part of the operational force. But in the implementation of the partial mobilization President Bush authorized in September 2001, the Defense Department encountered serious problems. As a result, officials turned their attention to fixing a host of systemic issues, from health and dental care to administrative systems that did not mesh with each other to family and employer programs. Though the processes were more painful than they needed to be, in the end some 280,000 reservists were mobilized for Operations Noble Eagle, Enduring Freedom, and Iraqi Freedom. And, in general, the larger mobilization for OIF in 2003 proceeded somewhat more smoothly than did the 2001 OEF mobilization. Much work remained to be done, however, to make the total force a seamless system that could respond to the fast-moving crises of the modern era. Although the major operations in Afghanistan and Iraq appeared to be largely complete in summer 2003, events would soon bring additional serious concerns to the attention of senior leadership within the Pentagon and beyond.[68]

CHAPTER 6

Part-Time Warriors, Full-Time Stress, July 2003–December 2006

The length and scale of ongoing combat operations in Iraq and Afghanistan, exacerbated by changes in mobilization policies, placed the reserve component under new levels of stress and challenged the viability of the Total Force concept. By 2004 the Army National Guard and the U.S. Army Reserve were struggling with major retention concerns, leading to the Army Reserve chief's "broken force" memorandum warning that administration policies could have crippling effects on the part-time force. Other reserve components faced similar challenges, albeit to a lesser degree. It would take policy changes, an institutionalized Army rotation system, increased benefits for reservists and their families, improvements in family readiness/support, and better health-care programs to turn things around.[1]

A Challenging Long War

Many thought Operation Iraqi Freedom would be a replay of the first Gulf War, with U.S. forces rapidly returning home after a successful conventional campaign. Although President George W. Bush landed on the carrier USS *Abraham Lincoln* under a banner that read "Mission Accomplished" and thanked American troops for "a job well done," his qualification—"We have difficult work to do in Iraq"—was lost in the euphoria. A growing insurgency surprised many U.S. leaders and led to a lengthy commitment that lasted until a full, if short-lived, withdrawal in December 2011. Well into 2010, American troop levels in and near Iraq remained well above the 150,000 of the initial invasion. Meanwhile, Operation Enduring Freedom continued in Afghanistan; U.S. forces remained committed to the Global War on Terrorism in places such as Djibouti, the Philippines, and Guantanamo; and other troops fulfilled operational commitments in the Balkans, the Sinai, and elsewhere around the world.[2]

The Global War on Terrorism, or the Long War, as it became known for a time, was unprecedented in the nature of its demands on the reserve component. In some previous conflicts (such as the world wars), the entire reserve establishment and the nation mobilized for the duration, with a draft providing additional manpower. The first year of the Korean War placed heavy demands on the reserves, but thereafter regular forces and conscripts carried almost the entire load. President Johnson largely kept the reserves out of Vietnam. Desert Shield and Desert Storm were over in a matter of months, freeing citizen-soldiers to return quickly to their civilian lives. Other contingencies in the 1990s, such as the Balkans, impacted only a small percentage of the reserve component. In the two years after September 2001, few planners expected that those called up for Noble Eagle, OEF, or OIF might be mobilized a second time. Many, like Robert H. Smiley, the principal director for readiness, training, and mobilization in the assistant secretary of defense for reserve affairs' office, believed that "this would be a one-time deal" for reservists. But as the conflicts in Afghanistan and Iraq dragged into 2004 with no end in sight, and the nation decided not to significantly increase the size of its regular forces, the true import of Total Force policy and an operational reserve became apparent—citizen-soldiers, like their regular counterparts, would have to deploy repeatedly as part of an indefinite rotation of forces.[3]

General Peter J. Schoomaker, the Army chief of staff from 2003 through 2007, realized that the high operational tempo "was muddying the distinction between service in the active and reserve components. Soldiers . . . found themselves continually on call." By October 2003 the USAR had mobilized or activated 35 percent of its manpower including nearly half of its deployable units, proportionally "the largest mobilization we've had since World War II," according to its chief, Lt. Gen. James Helmly. By the end of 2005 Army Reserve soldiers had filled 144,000 mobilization billets since 9/11—a significant number given the USAR's strength of 200,000, though some soldiers, including volunteers, served more than once. The issue had been exacerbated by the mobilization of large numbers of reserve component personnel in the immediate aftermath of 9/11 for homeland security missions. Jet fighters in the skies and guardsmen in the airports reassured the American public, but also made it more difficult to use those same units again for later combat missions.[4]

As Schoomaker noted, this increased use of the reserve component challenged the very nature of being a citizen-soldier. Most joined with the expectation that they would only be mobilized for a major conflict, or perhaps for a smaller contingency for a short period, which might happen only once in their career, if at all. Being involuntarily called to serve repeatedly was a major disruption to civilian careers, and was something few reservists had anticipated. Moreover, repeated tours of active duty came as an equal shock to families and employers. Even the length of the deployments proved an unwelcome surprise in the Army, which required 12 months in-theater for all its units—active, reserve, or Guard—a major change for personnel accustomed to the six-month standard for the Balkans and Sinai deployments. While the average period of active duty for all reserve personnel had been 156 days during Desert Shield/Desert Storm, it was exceeding 300 days in the current conflict. This new paradigm came amid other changes that placed added stress on the force.[5]

The first additional source of strain arose out of Secretary Rumsfeld's ongoing effort to transform the U.S. military to make it more responsive, lethal, and agile. One element of this wide-ranging set of initiatives, set out in a July 2003 memorandum, sought to "promote judicious and prudent use of the Reserve components" to "reduce strain," a matter he considered "of the utmost urgency." He wanted to achieve several goals: to allow U.S. forces to respond more rapidly without waiting for reserve

Donald H. Rumsfeld, the secretary of defense from 2001 to December 2006, sought to limit over-reliance on the reserve component during the Long War and favored volunteerism in lieu of partial mobilization authority. (DoD photo by Helene C. Stikkel)

call-ups; to be able to act without telegraphing intentions by mobilization; to reduce the risk that the frequency and/or duration of mobilizations would adversely affect recruiting and retention in the reserve components; and to rely on "volunteers to the greatest extent possible." To achieve those objectives, in January 2004 Under Secretary of Defense for Personnel and Readiness David Chu issued implementing guidance to rebalance forces between the regular and reserve components so as to "reduce the need for *involuntary mobilization* during the initial 15 days of a rapid response operation and limit *involuntary mobilization* to not more than one year in every six." One exercise had indicated that a rapid response scenario would require some 9,000 immediate involuntary mobilizations of reservists in critical specialties, and would subject these personnel, their employers, and their families to woefully short notification.[6]

While the primary thrust of rebalancing was to allow the regular component to respond rapidly in a crisis without waiting for reservists to mobilize, the one-year-in-six ratio for involuntary mobilizations highlighted an even greater potential problem with the Total Force concept. The latter issue most affected those types of units existing entirely or primarily in the reserve components. The Army faced the biggest challenge given the ground-centric nature of the war, but all services were affected. As an example, in January 2004, 69 percent of all reserve law enforcement personnel had already been mobilized at least once since 9/11. In a lengthy conflict those units would be subject to a much higher mobilization rate than units which could be more readily found in the regular component. In accordance with Rumsfeld and Chu's directive to reduce the stress on personnel in these units, the Army planned to convert 5,600 regular billets to high-demand specialties, including chemical, military police, engineering, and medical, by 2006. In the long term, that would reduce the likelihood and/or frequency of reserve component call-ups, but planners estimated rebalancing might ultimately impact up to 12 percent of the total force. The Army experienced turbulence in the short term as units and personnel had to convert to new specialties. And until such time as rebalancing was complete, the types of units residing heavily in the reserve establishment would experience high rates of mobilization.[7]

Rebalancing took place amid a much larger Army effort to reorient itself from a Cold War force centered on forward-stationed troops, such as those in Germany, to one primarily maintained in the States and ready for rapid deployment to a wide range of potential crisis spots around the world. While experimentation and study had been underway in this area since 1991, the process only swung into full implementation in summer 2003. Although no one yet realized the scale and duration of the commitment in Iraq, General Schoomaker viewed the war as "a strategic opportunity to pull the Army into the future." To achieve a more expeditionary capability, the Army began converting from its division-centric structure to a modular one in which the much smaller brigade would serve as the primary element that could deploy as a self-contained unit capable of independent action. Each brigade would be able to add or shed subordinate elements to tailor it for the mission at hand. As part of this transformation, some brigades would convert from heavy armored units to lighter ones built around the Stryker wheeled vehicle, thus making the task of rapidly transporting them overseas much easier. As operations in Iraq intensified in late 2003, the Army took stock and concluded there were not enough combat brigades to meet the needs of the ongoing conflict. To address this shortfall, in early 2004 the defense secretary approved 10 additional active component modular brigades, taking the total to 43.[8]

The Army Guard went through the same transition from divisions to modular brigades, with some of the latter units also undergoing conversion from heavy formations to Stryker units. Initial plans called for the ARNG to have 34 combat brigades, down from 42 equivalent units in 2000 in its old division structure. But in January 2006 Secretary of the Army Francis J. Harvey announced that six of the planned brigades would transition to combat support units, primarily for support of homeland defense requirements. That would leave 28 combat brigades. Although the Army as a whole in 2006 was only halfway through the reorganization, planned for completion in 2011, the emphasis was on sending newer modular units to the war in Iraq. By the end of 2004 every ARNG brigade in Operation Iraqi Freedom was modular. The task of converting units that were also preparing to deploy only heightened the turmoil of the process.[9]

The Marine Corps had always been an expeditionary force, but that created its own set of challenges. For many years prior to the current conflict, every infantry battalion and many aviation squadrons were either in the seven-month rotations for Marine Expeditionary Unit deployments at sea or the Unit Deployment Program in Japan. Those requirements continued even as the Corps became heavily involved in the counterinsurgency phase of OIF. The only way to meet all those obligations was to actively engage reserve units in the rotation for all three. Given the relatively small size of the Selected Marine Reserve (roughly one-quarter of all Marine units), the result was a frequent and repeated use of its citizen-soldiers. While the Navy and Air Force were not initially as greatly affected by the ground-centric operations in Iraq and Afghanistan, as time went on defense leaders looked for ways to utilize those two services more frequently to provide relief to the Army and Marine Corps.

The growing rotation problems, especially in the Army, began to hit home in March 2004. As it became clear that OIF required a high level of forces for longer than anticipated, Department of Defense leaders realized that they had too little time to deploy fresh units to replace those scheduled to rotate home, and too few brigades and support elements ready and available for deployment. As a result, the Pentagon announced the involuntary extension for up to 90 days of some 20,000 soldiers in the Iraqi theater. Roughly one in four was an ARNG or Army Reserve soldier, with 21 Guard units from 14 states represented in the total. Those who were affected received an additional $1,000 for each month beyond their original scheduled date of return. That compensation often did not assuage the disappointment of service members and their families, and certainly provided no relief to employers.[10]

The short-term adverse impact of rebalancing and modularity was soon reinforced and even exceeded by another change that took many planners by surprise. The new policy involved the secretary's interpretation of the primary source of mobilization authority used by the Defense Department for OIF and OEF—Section 12302, Ready Reserve, paragraphs (a) and (b), of Title 10, U.S. Code. Enacted fifty years earlier and known as partial mobilization, it provided:

> In time of national emergency declared by the President after January 1, 1953, or when otherwise authorized by law, an authority designated by the Secretary concerned may, without the consent of the persons concerned, order any unit, and any member not assigned to a unit organized to serve as a unit, in the Ready Reserve . . . to active duty for not more than 24 consecutive months.[11]

Over the past five decades, the nation had never required any part of its reserve component to remain on active duty for up to two years. As a consequence, hardly anyone had parsed the meaning of "not more than 24 consecutive months," although most mobilization planners prior to 2001 probably would have argued that units and members were limited to two years continuous active duty. Presumably then, after some appropriate period off active duty, they would be eligible again for involuntary activation. That also would comport with a standard judicial doctrine of statutory interpretation, which presumes that legislators included words because they had significance. In this case, if Congress had meant to limit involuntary activation under partial mobilization to two years total, the word *consecutive* would have no meaning.[12]

Just days after the 9/11 terror attack, Under Secretary Chu had advanced as policy the view that "the total combined periods of service" could "not exceed 24 months." But military leaders, never expecting the war to last that long, had overlooked or ignored the potential impact of that constraint. His emphasis on cumulative service first came to the fore during the rotation known as OIF-2. Shortly after 9/11, one battalion of Arkansas's 39th Brigade Combat Team had completed a six-month peacekeeping deployment to the Sinai Peninsula (which involved more than six months of active duty, given pre- and postdeployment time). In October 2003 the entire brigade became the second ARNG brigade federalized for OIF, and in March 2004 it deployed to Iraq. It was only when the 39th was serving in-theater that the issue of the 24-month cumulative limitation rose to the attention of Army leaders, as well as senior planners such as Col. Dennis P. Chapman, the mobilization branch chief at Headquarters Army National Guard from 2004 to 2006. Since the brigade already had spent six months on active duty in predeployment preparation and was scheduled for 12 months in Iraq, Chapman and other Guard leaders suddenly realized "there is almost an entire battalion's worth of soldiers in

Iraq who are going to hit 24 months' *cumulative* before the mobilization ends. And that is very disruptive."[13]

At a Pentagon press briefing on 21 July 2004, the Defense Department announced that it would ask those guardsmen to voluntarily extend beyond two years, though an Army spokesman emphasized that "all options are still open right now." Asked specifically about the two-year limit, Rumsfeld noted the distinction between the law's use of consecutive and Chu's policy of cumulative and called it "an interesting question." But the very next day, the secretary of defense decided to disapprove the Joint Staff's request to require the soldiers to complete their tour in Iraq. He was motivated in part by the Army's poor planning and bureaucratic errors, which had caused the problem, but also by the effect it would have on reserve component "retention, recruiting and morale." While not expressly affirming Chu's policy, Rumsfeld's memorandum memorializing his decision employed the "24 months cumulative" language. From this point forward, planners had to assume that the number of months a reservist or guardsman served under one mobilization order based on Section 12302 would be added to the months of any subsequent mobilization order under the same authority, with the total not to exceed 24. A break in time between the two periods would not reset the count to zero.[14]

While the text of the Armed Forces Reserve Act of 1952 did not seem to support the cumulative interpretation, the law's legislative history clearly expressed congressional intent "to at least minimize (since they cannot be eliminated) the inequities inherent in again recalling the veteran for a second period of service, while other physically fit young men have yet to be called for a first time." Of course that sentiment applied to an era when the draft was available, and nonveterans could be readily obtained as needed. In addition, paragraph (b) of Section 12302 gave the secretary of defense the authority to consider "the length and nature of previous service, to assure such sharing of exposure to hazards as the national security and military requirements will reasonably allow." Clearly Rumsfeld's guidance fit within the letter and spirit of that provision, as well as his desire to emphasize volunteerism when mobilizing reserve personnel.[15]

Whatever its legal merits, the policy created significant hurdles for officials responsible for mobilizing forces and accounted for some of the reserve component's greatest challenges during Secretary Rumsfeld's tenure. In July 2004 Chapman noted that he and his ARNG mobilization planners "really had to jump through hoops" to provide incentives, such as special payments, to encourage soldiers to volunteer to complete their deployments. Those inducements proved insufficient, as 75 percent of those eligible decided to return home. The Guard had to draw from other recently mobilized units to fill those vacancies. The result was a loss of valuable experience in mid-deployment, as well as reduced cohesion in both the 39th Brigade and the units that contributed replacements. Since nearly 162,000 of the 190,000 reserve component personnel serving on active duty in February 2004 were ARNG or USAR, Secretary Rumsfeld's policy had its greatest impact on the ground forces.[16]

The genesis of Rumsfeld and Chu's choice of cumulative over consecutive undoubtedly had its roots in a concern for the long-term health of the reserve component. During the 2000 presidential election, George W. Bush made overdeployment of the Guard and reserves in the Balkans and elsewhere a campaign issue against Vice President Al Gore. In a February 2001 speech, President Bush had noted the strains of repeated long stints of active duty: "It's not only a tension for employer to employee. It's tensions often times between husband and wife. And overdeployments, constant deployments really create a severe issue for morale all throughout the military." In December 2002, as the Pentagon prepared for Operation Iraqi Freedom, Bob Hollingsworth, executive director of the Pentagon's Office of Employer Support of the Guard and Reserve, noted: "Our concern is with employers who've just had guys demobilized, and now may have them remobilized if this goes down. How will employers react to this?" A few weeks later Rumsfeld responded to a question at the Reserve Officers Association conference: "If we want to have a total force, if we want that concept to work, we've got to be respectful of the fact that people in the Reserves and the Guard have jobs and they're perfectly willing to be called up, but they only want to be called up when they're needed and for something that's a real job." His off-the-cuff answer drew applause. This Bush administration point of view acknowledged that if reserve duty was too disruptive for employers, families, and citizen-soldiers, that would ultimately impact recruiting and retention, the lifeblood of a volunteer reserve force.[17]

Despite the clarity of the new policy, Rumsfeld understood that reality might intrude upon it. Responding to anxieties felt by many 39th Brigade guardsmen and their families, at a Pentagon news conference in July 2004 he stated that the department had no "plan *at the moment* to extend people beyond the 24 months." That conditional phrase left open the possibility of longer mobilizations. Ultimately, however, no soldier had to serve involuntarily on active duty beyond 24 cumulative months during Rumsfeld's tenure, although many exceeded two years voluntarily.[18]

The way the policy came to pass, with no direct consultation with reserve leadership and without warning, was just another source of frustration for mobilization planners during a very difficult period. Thomas F. Hall, assistant secretary of defense for reserve affairs from 2002 to 2009 and a retired rear admiral, never had a one-on-one meeting with Rumsfeld on a major reserve component issue. Hall's contact with the secretary was limited to attending meetings during which he was rarely called upon for advice or information. It was a frustrating experience for the senior official whose job it was, statutorily, to be the secretary's primary adviser on all matters involving the Guard and Reserve. It also highlighted the impact of the 1994 reorganization that had interposed an undersecretary between the secretary of defense and the assistant secretary. It was much the same for Lt. Gen. Dennis McCarthy, the Marine Forces Reserve commander during most of Rumsfeld's tenure. Despite heading a reserve component that provided a major portion of the ground force for Iraq, he never met with Secretary Rumsfeld and felt he had no opportunity for policy input with him. While an assistant secretary and reserve component leaders would not normally have direct access to the secretary of defense, they were nevertheless frustrated at their inability to directly influence the policies they had to carry out. Lt. Gen. H. Steven "Steve" Blum, the National Guard Bureau chief, for one, believed that the assistant secretary of defense for reserve affairs needed to be "elevated" and have a "straight shot voice, straight to the Secretary." Under Secretary Chu, on the other hand, believed that Secretary Rumsfeld was aware of the concerns of reserve leaders and often listened, specifically in adopting the one-year-in-six mobilization standard.[19]

Secretary Rumsfeld's mobilization decisions had long exasperated planners. Colonel Chapman knew that partial mobilization authority granted the president and the secretary of defense leeway to equitably implement mobilization, taking into account issues such as length and nature of previous service, family obligations, and civilian jobs critical to national interest. The problem, according to Chapman, was that none of the secretary's decisions regarding the application of these factors were put into writing: "You would just learn when you had a mobilization packet arrive on the Secretary's desk that he changed his rule. And it would throw your preparation in disarray and you had to start over again, because a whole bunch of people in the unit would no longer have to go." Air Force Reserve Col. Barbara Y. Lee recalled that planners had to keep track of what the defense secretary "lined out" on the briefing slides during weekly mobilization meetings in order to determine what the policies were, and that verbal policies largely remained the standard throughout Rumsfeld's tenure.[20]

Approaching the Breaking Point

General Helmly, the Army Reserve chief from 2002 to 2006, called 2003 an "absolutely volatile, tumultuous year," and the following year's continuing high operational tempo provided no respite. Seeing no end in sight, in

In December 2004 the chief of the Army Reserve, Lt. Gen. James R. Helmly, warned that current mobilization policies and practices threatened to result in a "broken force." His memorandum facilitated improvements in the total Army's wartime posture. (DoD photo by Scott Davis)

December 2004 Helmly wrote a memorandum to General Schoomaker that arguably marked a watershed moment for the country's Army components in the decade following 11 September 2001. In what became known as the "broken force" memorandum, the Army Reserve chief warned the Army chief of staff that "under current policies, procedures, and practices governing mobilization, training, and reserve component manpower management," the USAR was incapable of meeting both its mission requirements in Iraq and Afghanistan and its need "to reset and regenerate its forces for follow-on and future missions." Helmly's foremost concern was that his forces' "capabilities are limited severely by a successive series of restrictive mobilization policies and controls" that have "failed to encompass a longer range, strategic view of operational requirements and Army capabilities."

Moreover, in his view, those policies were implemented without proper consideration of the long-term effects they would have on retention.[21]

The Army Reserve chief argued that several policies threatened his component's operational effectiveness. These included policies limiting the training of demobilized soldiers (designed to permit them to spend more time with their families after long deployments), outdated retention and personnel management policies, and the requirement to leave most equipment in-theater to save on transportation costs. This last issue the reserves shared with the regular component, but it impacted the reserves more heavily given their greater dispersion; they could not borrow from similar units at home stations. In short, the USAR was "rapidly degenerating into a 'broken' force." At the end of 2004 a Joint Staff report indicated close to 50 percent of USAR personnel (almost 100,000) had been mobilized since 9/11, including 15,000 who had been mobilized twice and 2,000 mobilized three or more times. Helmly recommended serious efforts by the Pentagon and Congress to deal with the question of "how long and how often" reservists should be deployed in contrast with the regular component. The memo endorsed the Army Reserve Expeditionary Force rotational model already being implemented, but that by itself could not solve the larger problems Helmly had highlighted.[22]

Given the projected mobilizations and the 24-month-cumulative limit, by March 2005 the Army Reserve anticipated having only 31,000 soldiers (roughly 15 percent of its strength) with remaining eligibility for future involuntary activation. Moreover, some of those 31,000 were in specialties or grades that were not needed at the moment, so the actual number available to meet expected requirements was even smaller. Secretary of the Army Harvey also pointed out that the Army's stop-loss program and "a strong Active Component retention program"—both of which lowered the number of soldiers separating from regular service—had shrunk the pool of personnel who would normally join the Army Reserve upon completion of their active duty obligation. To help correct the manpower shortages, the Army added some 700 recruiter billets in the USAR in addition to implementing bonus and incentive programs. But it would take time to recruit new personnel, who would then have to undergo at least six months of initial training before they could join a unit and deploy, and they still would lack the level of experience of the prior-service personnel. In short, there was no quick fix.[23]

The pervasiveness of cross-leveling—transfers of personnel and equipment from a nonmobilizing unit to a mobilizing unit—provided strong evidence of the downward spiral in the Army Reserve. Between September 2001 and April 2005, about one in four USAR soldiers (53,000) and more than a quarter million pieces of equipment had been cross-leveled, despite the fact that the Army Reserve acknowledged the practice "broke unit integrity and readiness." While personnel cohesion was the primary concern, the equipment exchanges also could have subtle but pernicious effects, such as reducing the incentive to properly maintain gear and increasing the likelihood of organizations dumping their poorer quality materiel on units preparing for deployment. Schoomaker referred to excessive cross-leveling as "evil," because "military necessity dictates that we deploy organized, trained, equipped, cohesive units; and you don't do that by 'pick-up' teams." A 1995 DoD policy prohibited taking personnel from one unit to fill out another "in numbers that would degrade the readiness standards of their parent Reserve units." But in the post-9/11 crisis, it was routinely ignored.[24]

While Helmly's memorandum specifically addressed the Army Reserve's status, a Guard historian wrote that it "succinctly summarized many of the same challenges citizen-soldiers faced in the other reserve components, including the National Guard." Schoomaker's alarm about cross-leveling, as well Secretary Harvey's concern over the reduction in the flow of prior-service personnel into reserve components, applied equally to the Guard, which was beginning to struggle to maintain its manpower strength. By mid-2004 the Guard had cross-leveled 74,000 soldiers (more than 20 percent of its strength) and 35,000 pieces of equipment. The latter figure had jumped to over 100,000 items a year later. The fact that Guard units typically had less than 75 percent of their required equipment to begin with only exacerbated the situation. A Minnesota combat brigade mobilized in 2005 illustrated the scale of the impact. By the time it deployed to Iraq in 2006, 1,703 of its soldiers (42 percent of its strength) had joined it from other units. Another brigade found that one-quarter of the light machine guns it received from other outfits were defective. These problems coincided with the height of the Army Guard's participation in Operation Iraqi Freedom, with eight of its combat brigades—each with about 4,000 soldiers—forming half of all such units in Iraq in mid-2005. That increased commitment came at a price. In 13 of the 15 months between October 2004 and December 2005, at least 10 Army guardsmen deployed for OIF or OEF died; the worst period was August–October 2005 when 69 soldiers perished.[25]

Maj. Gen. Raymond W. Carpenter, later the acting ARNG director, recalled that many soldiers decided to leave the Guard upon returning home from Iraq in 2004 and 2005. Like those in authority, most guardsmen had expected that conflict "to be a single event, one turn . . . over in six months, not unlike what happened in Desert Storm." When it became clear they were likely to face multiple deployments to Iraq, and possibly Afghanistan as well, some soldiers voted with their feet. Perhaps they were unaware that the secretary's policy did not allow for any involuntary second mobilization that would cause the soldier to exceed 24 months cumulative mobilization time, or perhaps some knew of the policy but did not expect it to last. Whatever the explanation, Carpenter noted that in less than a year Army Guard strength declined from 350,000 to near 330,000 by mid-2005, a growing concern for ARNG leadership. The falloff in Guard strength resulted in new programs designed to boost recruiting and retention, including recruiter assistant programs, much higher bonuses, and, according to Carpenter, "more than anything . . . [telling] . . . the story of the National Guard, service to country." But similar to the Army Reserve, those initiatives could not quickly solve the shortfall.[26]

The pace of deployment affected not only part-time citizen-soldiers, but also the Full-Time Support (FTS) personnel—comprised of Active Guard and Reserve and Military Technician personnel in the Army and Air Force, the Active Reserve in the Marine Corps, and the Training and Administration of the Reserves in the Navy—who formed a key part of the reserve component. In 2003 additional FTS authorizations were the ARNG/USAR leadership's

From 2005 to 2008, the congressionally mandated Commission on the National Guard and Reserves addressed dozens of issues connected with transitioning the reserve component from a strategic reserve to a part of the operational force. (Source: National Archives, photo by MCSN Cale Bentley, USN)

"number one priority," and the Army committed to an increase of 2 percent per year in AGRs and military technicians through fiscal year 2012. The congressionally mandated Commission on the National Guard and Reserves considered FTS programs essential, declaring, "The FTS force is the caretaker element necessary to keep all people and equipment in mission-ready status for training and potential operational missions." But the Army's good intentions foundered for a time on the same shoals that were endangering the overall reserve establishment.[27]

In FY 2005 the entire reserve component averaged an FTS rate of 21 percent of end strength, but the USAR lagged badly at 11 percent, a level the Army considered "insufficient to support an operational Army Reserve." But even that number masked greater problems. In 2006 the USAR reported new FTS taskings above programmed requirements, to include providing more than 700 additional recruiters to the U.S. Army Recruiting Command. Administrative billets of that type could not enhance operational capabilities. In fact, an Army study found that fewer than one in four billets were located "at the company level or below," where they were most needed to ensure readiness. In addition, in early 2006 the U.S. Army Reserve Command deputy commander directed that up to 20 percent of AGRs deploy to fill personnel shortfalls. Using these full-time personnel to fix recruiting problems and fill open billets overseas significantly reduced the ability of the AGR program to accomplish its true mission.[28]

The Army National Guard also struggled with FTS issues. In FY 2004 the National Guard Bureau reported "up to 18% of ARNG Technicians were on leave of absence" due to mobilizations at home or overseas, creating challenges for those units with vacated technician positions. The ARNG chief of staff from 2000 to 2003, Col. Charles P. Baldwin, noted that when units mobilized, their FTS members often deployed with them. But, with an armory to maintain, stay-behind personnel including pre- and post-basic training individuals to manage and train, and equipment that still required servicing, Baldwin stated, "The shell of that unit is still there. . . . The work is still there." In FY 2007 the ARNG's FTS percentage was about 15 percent of end strength, far short of the benchmark set by Lt. Gen. Clyde A. Vaughn, the ARNG director. In March 2006 he told a congressional subcommittee: "Increased full-time resources are necessary to achieve acceptable unit readiness. It is critical we increase full-time support in the near term to a minimum of 90 percent of the total validated requirement." That was considerably higher than the 72 percent goal the ARNG planned to reach by FY 2012. In comparison to the Army numbers, the USMCR, U.S. Naval Reserve, and USAFR stood at 16 to 18 percent of end strength, with the ANG posting an impressive 34 percent. Robert Smiley considered the air reserves "much more ready [than the Army reserves] because they have got so many full-time manning folks." At a time when the Army reserve components were a "broken force," the issues in its FTS programs exacerbated the problems.[29]

The mobilization challenge became even greater late in 2005, when Secretary Rumsfeld verbally expressed his position that any remobilization under the September 2001 presidential declaration of partial mobilization had to be *voluntary*—regardless of how many months remained in the 24-cumulative-months "gas tank." The ARNG's Chapman stated bluntly: "This throws a monkey-wrench in the mix for a brigade that is trying to go out the door." By that time many if not most of the units and personnel in the Army reserve components already were unavailable for a second mobilization due to the 24-cumulative-months policy, but in the other services, which generally employed shorter rotations of seven months or less, the new guidance prohibiting involuntary remobilization had a greater impact. The Marine Corps, the second largest contributor of forces on the ground in Iraq, faced the most significant potential problem.[30]

Rumsfeld's new stance highlighted an issue Helmly had raised in his "broken force" memo. The Army Reserve general pointed out that typically his soldiers wanted to serve, and as a result the USAR was "losing as many Soldiers through no use as we are through the fear of overuse." Alluding perhaps to the defense secretary's well-known concerns regarding over-reliance on reservists, the USAR chief argued, "Demands to use only 'volunteers' from the Reserve Components threaten to distort the very nature of service" in the reserves. Lieutenant General Helmly noted that while soldiers remained protected under the Uniformed Services Employment and Reemployment Rights Act regardless of their volunteer/nonvolunteer status, "the Soldier is seen as having a clear choice by his family and employer." Thus a soldier who wanted to serve might be deterred from volunteering due to pressure, real or imagined, from those quarters, but would willingly respond if ordered. Helmly was convinced that "failure to use the inherent authorities of involuntary mobilization during this threatening period in our Nation's history will set a difficult, dynamic precedent for future involuntary use." Lieutenant General McCarthy shared this view. Later, as ASD(RA) from 2009 to 2011, McCarthy stated, "If you want . . . Marines from a battalion in the 1st Marine Division to serve, you don't tell them to all volunteer. You just send them a set of orders . . . and I guarantee you, they will show up to a man."[31]

Some of the component chiefs, however, favored volunteerism over mobilization. Lt. Gen. John A. Bradley, Air Force Reserve Command commander (and Air Force Reserve chief) from 2004 to 2008, stated: "What we try to do is keep the tours at a reasonable length and not mobilize people. There are benefits to being mobilized. There are also cons to it, too. But, there are benefits to using volunteers, and that's what has made it successful for us. We've not had a shortage of volunteers for our requirements." Recruiting and retention remained strong in the AFR in spite of repeated, albeit generally short, deployments. Aircrews usually served 40–45 days, other personnel 120 days. Bradley viewed mobilizations as "a last resort," but his preference for volunteerism could hardly be divorced from the far shorter duration of deployments and higher quality-of-life standards enjoyed by the air reserves in comparison with their ground force counterparts. Moreover, cohesion was much less of a concern when most elements actually engaged in combat were often as small as two pilots.[32]

By early 2006 the Army felt it was turning the corner on many of its challenges, with the increasing availability of regular component combat brigades and progress on rebalancing reducing the need for reserve component forces to deploy. But in the spring of 2006 sectarian violence began spinning out of control in Iraq, and Secretary Rumsfeld admitted that "al-Qaida had seized the initiative." The increased need for forces for OIF (and to a lesser extent for Afghanistan) brought the Army to a crisis. In one well-publicized case, in August the defense secretary extended the yearlong deployment of a regular unit, the 172nd Stryker Brigade, by several months in an effort to quell the violence around Baghdad. Rumsfeld traveled in person to Alaska to meet with distraught family members who had been expecting the imminent return of their soldiers. Citizen-soldiers were affected as well. The Minnesota National Guard's 34th Infantry Division (mainly its 1st Brigade) was supposed to return from Iraq in spring 2007, but had to remain until July. The families of the Minnesota unit were as upset as those of the 172nd, but in this case civilian employers also had reason to be unhappy with the change in return dates. These long extensions came on the heels of an August 2005 report by the ASD(RA)'s office showing that reserve component tour lengths already had increased to an average of 338 days, up from 312 days at the start of the year. At that time, 45 percent of the entire Selected Reserve was mobilized or had been mobilized since September 2001. Cross-leveling reached its highest levels in 2006, with the average mobilizing unit drawing more than 30 percent of its personnel and 60 percent of its equipment from elsewhere. With the added demands, Major General Carpenter later stated, "It got to the point in about 2006 where the National Guard was not going to be able—and the Army Reserve was not going to be able to meet their mobilization responsibilities." The threat of no

The longest-serving assistant secretary of defense for reserve affairs and a retired rear admiral, Thomas H. Hall (center) initiated the watershed "Utilization of the Total Force" memorandum that Secretary Robert Gates issued in January 2007, offering predictability and 12-month mobilizations to the reserve component. (DoD photo by R. D. Ward)

guaranteed return date on the far end of a deployment became another factor harming retention. ASD(RA) Thomas Hall spoke for many in the Pentagon when he stated, "The most important thing to guardsmen and reservists and families is predictability."[33]

In an effort to maximize the amount of deployed time within the 24-month mobilization window, reserve component leaders had units conduct some required predeployment training and processing during weekend drills and annual active duty. However, as Carpenter—from 2009 to 2011 the acting director, ARNG—recalled, the Army did not count these requirements as completed unless they happened during federalized service:

> And so consequently we saw the situation where people did weapons qualification not one time, not twice, sometimes three times . . . four times. We saw people get the same series of immunizations over and over . . . because . . . if it didn't happen at Title 10 status, it wasn't valid, which made absolutely no sense.[34]

One might argue that repeating a weapons qualification was not a bad thing at all, but immunizations were another matter. The seemingly senseless duplication not only wasted valuable training time, it harmed morale. More than a few soldiers, who were willing to be deployed again, were terribly discouraged with the mobilization process itself. The ARNG boss recalled soldiers saying to Lieutenant General Blum: "I want to be part of what's going on, but don't ever mobilize me again. Don't send me through that process again, because it's broken." Similarly, Lieutenant General Vaughn, ARNG director from 2005 to 2009, remembered soldiers telling him, in effect, "Sir, I'll go for a year downrange, but I'm not going to the MOB [mobilization] station and take that kind of abuse."[35]

As the war dragged on, the Pentagon looked for ways to help pay for it. One method was a new Base Realignment and Closure (BRAC) commission, which ended up causing discontent in the Air Force's reserve components. In 2005 the Air Force attempted to rectify the inefficiencies of maintaining too few aircraft at certain installations with their proposals to the commission, but from the Air Guard's point of view, those plans undermined the recent history of trust and goodwill. The U.S. Air Force sought to reduce the Guard's fleet of 1,106 aircraft by 166, affecting 29 ANG wings. The National Guard Association of the United States (NGAUS) was displeased that the mandated process meant that "BRAC decisions were made without consultation with the governors or the Department of Homeland Security." The states' adjutants general also had no opportunity to provide input. The BRAC commission agreed substantially with the USAF's recommendations, but the following year the Air

Force took steps to mitigate the impact. Eleven of the 17 states that expected to lose ANG flying units were able to keep them through organizational changes, often by further integrating with a regular unit or relocating to an active-duty base. By 2006 ANG leaders had a much less negative view about the shift. The Air Force Reserve also underwent BRAC-induced changes that Lieutenant General Bradley deemed "painful for our people." The command lost six flying wings—which had a major impact—but only one base. In a concurrent initiative, in 2005 the new Air Force chief of staff, General T. Michael Moseley, directed a personnel cut of 40,000 across the USAF. The Air Force Reserve Command was expected to lose 7,700 between FYs 2008 and 2010, though it took the bulk of that reduction in the individual mobilization augmentee category rather than in the traditional unit reserve program.[36]

Repairing a Moving Vehicle

The Army, which faced the most challenging reserve component problems, had been actively trying to solve them even as those issues grew worse from 2003 onward. In addition to devoting far more manpower and financial incentives to recruiting, in 2005 the USAR/ARNG raised the age limit for enlistment from 34 to 39 years. The following year Congress authorized a 30,000-soldier increase in Army end strength, which would ultimately reduce the need for mobilizations. But those solutions addressed symptoms, not root causes; what the system really needed was structural reform. Lt. Gen. Jack C. Stultz, who in 2006 succeeded Helmly as Army Reserve chief, aptly summarized the challenge. He described "two consuming factors" that demanded his attention and energies: one was the need to transform his component, and the other was the need to do this without stopping "what we're doing now, because we still have to supply about 30,000 soldiers every year to the war."[37]

With a realization that the war would not end soon, in the latter part of 2003 Army Reserve leaders conceived the Army Reserve Expeditionary Force (AREF) rotational system, a cyclic approach to training and deployment. Lieutenant General Helmly saw it as the "lynchpin of Army Reserve readiness." It divided the majority of Army Reserve forces—combat support and combat service support units—into 10 packages, with rotation cycles set at five years and 2 packages assigned to each year. As initially envisioned, units counted down the years toward the goal of deployment availability in year one of the cycle. In year five, forces (presumably just returned from deployment) underwent regeneration, resetting, and restructuring, if needed. That meant replacing worn or outdated equipment, recruiting new personnel to bring the unit to full strength again, and focusing on individual training. In year four, attention shifted to collective training at the lowest level, such as the squad. Years three and two emphasized larger element training at the company level and higher, with unit validation/certification expected by the close of year two. In year one, units should be ready to deploy within 120 hours from notification, and were expected to remain in that state of readiness for 12 months. Ideally a unit would deploy at the start of year one, but if mobilization came toward the end, that would push its completion of the AREF cycle to six years.[38]

The first designated AREF packages began filling overseas requirements in 2004 (though they had obviously not gone through a full cycle leading up to deployment). The following year AREF packages provided about 75 percent of the Army Reserve's mobilized units. In 2006 that number declined to 53 percent, as the process of implementation fell short of the need, but it climbed back to 78 percent in 2007. As of February 2007 more than 166,000 Army Reserve soldiers had been mobilized since 9/11, one in four of them more than once without exceeding 24 cumulative months.[39]

In early 2006 the secretary of the Army approved a similar scheme for his entire service, dubbed the Army Force Generation (ARFORGEN) model. The concept featured three groups: a reset/training pool for units recovering from extended operations; a ready pool for units undergoing advanced preparation and training; and an available pool of units fully prepared to deploy, either as part of an ongoing rotation or in response to a new contingency. Unlike AREF, a unit's current state of readiness, not time, determined its pool, although it was obvious that a unit spending an inordinate length of time in other than the available pool would garner special attention from higher up. The model provided, in the words of one historian, "inevitability and stability"—something previously unknown to soldiers, families, and employers—while promoting greater unit cohesion. The Army anticipated trained, ready forces to be the bottom-line result. With the advent of ARFORGEN, the Army Reserve refined its five-year AREF progression plan to match, with units spending the first two years in the reset/training pool, two years in the ready pool, and one year in the available pool. In FY 2006 the Defense authorization act included designated unit pay for non-obligated soldiers with critical skills in ARFORGEN units slated for deployment who were willing to commit to further service. Keeping more of them in the units reduced the need for personnel cross-leveling and enhanced both retention and stability.[40]

Another change, more attitudinal than structural, was DoD's greater reliance on the Individual Ready Reserve. Secretary Rumsfeld had approved mobilization of personnel from that source in December 2003. The issue was a difficult one for the Guard, which did not have a true IRR component at that time. Its equivalent Inactive National Guard was a small pool primarily holding enlistees waiting longer than 120 days to ship to initial training and soldiers who were medically unqualified to continue service in a unit. As a result, the Army National Guard would have to rely on the USAR's IRR, composed almost entirely of inactive Army reservists and former active soldiers serving out remaining obligated service in the reserve. Colonel Chapman recalled that the Army Guard was skeptical at first and its basic perspective on using the nondrilling, no-pay IRR was that "it would be an admission of failure of some kind to the Army that we couldn't fill our own ranks." Deployment officials also had to overcome the reluctance of some if not many of the state adjutants general, who opposed the idea of bringing unknown soldiers, many without recent training, into their units. Nevertheless, Lt. Gen. Roger C. Schultz, the Army National Guard's long-serving director, agreed to give the IRR a try. In summer 2004 approximately 5,600 IRR soldiers received mailgrams ordering them to report to a mobilization site in order to fill the requirements for 4,400 soldiers as part of the rotations dubbed OIF-3 and OEF-6. The excess of 1,200 above the operational requirement provided a margin for the inevitable cases of individuals found to be nondeployable for various reasons. By 2005 Chapman's mobility branch began requesting 200 IRR soldiers for every deploying brigade, because "in the end you will always need them." Given the inactive status of IRRs, planners expected a certain percentage of them either to be no-shows or to be unqualified for active duty. "So we ordered two for every one we needed. . . [and] over time we won acceptance," noted Chapman. Eventually, the ARNG "became the IRR's biggest customer and kept the IRR relevant."[41]

The Marine Corps Reserve also made good use of the IRR, activating nearly 4,000 of them by August 2004. The Marine Corps' assistant commandant, General W. L. Nyland, noted that "the IRR is an integral part of the Marine Corps Reserve," but there still were hiccups along the way. The policy was to activate first those IRRs who volunteered and, when required, to mobilize those not previously called. But in the buildup for Iraq in 2003, the Marine Corps "misused the IRR," according to Lieutenant General McCarthy. As the MarForRes commander, McCarthy wanted to manage the IRR mobilizations, but the active component manpower division insisted on taking over. Instead of looking for available IRRs within the area local to the unit they would join, according to McCarthy, the manpower division simply followed established procedures that in some cases resulted in "sending a set of orders to Corporal Jones who lived in San Diego and sending him to Camp Lejeune [NC] and some kid who lived in Jacksonville, North Carolina, and [sending] him to Camp Pendleton [CA], because they did not have the sophisticated knowledge of what was in the IRR." In such situations, IRR Marines had few opportunities to travel home when off duty. McCarthy likened the Marines' IRR mobilization process to "killing flies with a sledgehammer."[42]

Only once after 9/11 were IRR Marines subject to an involuntary mobilization, and it was, according to one MarForRes official, "a disaster." The Corps sent notices to some 8,000 IRRs, and went through an expensive process of bringing 5,500 who passed initial screening to Kansas City (rather than using 29 regional sites). Of those, only 2,000 met all criteria and ended up serving on active duty. The meager 25 percent success ratio served as a catalyst for a return to the in-person IRR musters of the previous decade, which began towards the end of

Chief of Naval Reserve Force, Vice Adm. John Cotton (right), congratulates Master Chief Petty Officer David Pennington as the new Navy Reserve Force Command Master Chief. Cotton facilitated cultural improvements between the Navy's regular and reserve components, emphasizing "ONE Navy" and a "sailor-for-life" mindset. (Source: U.S. Navy, photo by Photographers Mate 2nd Class Cynthia Z. De Leon)

2006 with scheduled one-day events. Those IRR personnel who showed up received pay for the day, Veterans Affairs (VA) program updates, access to local universities and job fair partners, and an opportunity for personal interaction with the Corps. It also provided a chance to determine the status of an IRR's uniforms and whether the member had medical/dental issues that potentially could affect a mobilization. The IRR-managing entity, later redesignated the Marine Corps Individual Reserve Support Activity, began conducting roughly 10 to 12 such events annually at locations around the country. Typically, up to 600 IRRs attended each event. As time went on, there were few IRRs who had not already been deployed (most during a tour as regulars before going into the reserves). By 2013, 80 percent of Marine IRRs had completed one combat deployment, and more than 50 percent had served more than one. An unresolved concern, however, was that officials lacked the authority to conduct official physical examinations and thus could not administratively separate IRRs with unwaiverable medical conditions. Despite the system's imperfections, the Marine Corps took the IRR seriously. As Vice Adm. John Cotton, chief of Navy Reserve from 2003 to 2008, expressed: "the Marine Corps does the best job of mustering their IRR."[43]

Increased reliance upon the IRR on the part of the Army Guard and the Marine Reserve was consistent with broader initiatives within the Defense Department. In January 2004 the Office of the Deputy Assistant Secretary of Defense for Reserve Affairs (Readiness, Training, and Mobilization) published *Rebalancing Forces: Easing the Stress on the Guard and Reserve*. The report cited the need to increase access to the IRR "to make IRR members a more viable source of military manpower and to provide greater depth of capabilities." The Reserve Affairs secretariat anticipated that greater reliance on this resource would result in less cross-leveling of personnel and could redefine "how the IRR is used in the 21st century." Two new initiatives geared toward IRR were the Defense Wireless Service Initiative (which sought spectrum managers and wireless engineers) and the Army's linguist program (which drew heavily from native speakers in the Arab-American community).[44]

The Army Reserve also sought to more efficiently use its authorized manpower. It had established its Transients-Trainees-Holdees-Students account in 2003 to allow unit commanders to better focus on training and readiness by removing the distraction of personnel who could not fully participate. In 2006 the account target was 12,000 billets, roughly one-half of the traditional 10 percent of USAR's selected reserve strength that was unqualified at a given time. The Army Reserve planned to convert and restructure those saved billets over the next several years into spaces in operational units, thereby increasing capability without adding manpower. As part of that process, in 2005 the USAR had begun eliminating force structure exceeding authorized end strength (205,000) and eliminating some billets in nondeploying units.[45]

Another Pentagon effort to relieve the over-stressed ground reserve components involved increased and sometimes-creative employment of air and Navy elements. Two of the Navy's most resourceful contributions occurred in landlocked Afghanistan. In the first case, USNR personnel augmented provisional reconstruction teams, which previously had been sourced largely from the Army. The teams worked in rural areas to improve the quality of life for local Afghans and thereby increase loyalty to the national government. In winter 2004–2005 a full-time support Navy reservist, Cmdr. Kimberly Evans, commanded one of a dozen provisional reconstruction teams near Herat in western Afghanistan. In another example, EA–6B Prowler electronic warfare crewmembers and other electronic warfare specialists—regular and reserve— deployed to eastern Afghanistan in mid-2006 and augmented U.S. Army elements tasked with countering roadside improvised explosive devices. Before the Navy personnel arrived, some soldiers were not maintaining or even turning on the electronic warfare equipment in their vehicles because they had not been trained in how to use it. Senior Army leaders lauded the Navy personnel for saving lives by enabling soldiers to more effectively deal with the roadside bombs.[46]

As the war dragged on and more reservists were subject to repeated deployments, health care grew in importance both as a key readiness issue and as a retention incentive. In mid-2004 military health-care officials announced that reservists who met certain contingency-connected eligibility requirements could seek reimbursement from TRICARE if they had paid their medical and dental bills and saved their receipts. Not long after, in the FY 2005 Defense authorization act, Congress created an improved health-care plan known as TRICARE Reserve Select (TRS). The plan was nationwide, premium-based, and resembled the active component's TRICARE Standard coverage. In April 2005 TRS became available to all reserve component personnel who had been activated 90 consecutive days or more and agreed to further service. For each additional 90 consecutive days of service and additional one-year commitment, they would receive an additional year of coverage. For example, one who served 360 days of qualifying active duty became eligible for four years of TRS coverage if he signed up for four additional years of service in the reserve component.[47]

Stephen M. Koper, the NGAUS president and a retired brigadier general, considered TRS an improvement, but still "several steps short of what we actually need." Rather than treating health care "as a reward for special service," his organization argued that individual readiness was the primary issue, and from that perspective, TRS should be made available to all selected reservists. Lieutenant General Stultz expressed concern that families not have "to switch health care every time the Soldier gets off active duty." The plan did not result in widespread coverage, as many Selected Reserve personnel either lacked qualifying service or did not wish to extend their service contracts, and so remained ineligible for the program. Congress heard these concerns and responded in the Defense authorization for FY 2006, which extended TRS eligibility to include all Selected Reserve personnel in a three-tier premium system, with coverage available no later than 1 October 2006. The member could purchase individual or family coverage. The revised program also offered IRR members who served a qualifying period of active duty a one-year period following release from active duty to sign up for the Selected Reserve and retain TRS coverage. In addition, all Selected Reserve members with 12 or more months on their service commitment were eligible for the TRICARE Dental Program, which could cover family members as well.[48]

Family readiness had improved after 2001 due to increasing reliance upon trained volunteers and the implementation of the Military One Source program, but experience during OIF in 2003 indicated there was room for further improvement. One strategic study in 2006 advocated "that every unit have one full-time paid staff member," in addition to volunteers, to assist with family issues of deployed personnel. The CNGR felt that volunteers enabled family members of the deployed to "maintain a sense of belonging to the command" but that paid staff was necessary at the unit level to ensure all critical tasks were accomplished. Despite the best of intentions, most volunteers were, according to testimony before the CNGR, "spouses with full-time jobs trying to take care of the home front while the soldier was in theater, and quite frankly, they couldn't do it all." Moreover, a 2006 survey reported that only 18 percent of reserve component respondents had accessed Military One Source, while two-thirds remained unaware of the program's existence.[49]

In the midst of the turbulence and heightened stress experienced after 2003, the Army reserve components in particular sought to demonstrate in tangible ways that they valued soldiers and their families. Major General Carpenter summarized the Army Guard's perspective: "You cannot have a mission-effective soldier without the support of the family. If something is going on at home and the soldier's distracted, that's a detractor from the mission downrange. If you don't have the support of the family and the employers in the community, you find that, over time, the soldier gives up and leaves the National Guard." All the other components would have agreed with that assessment. Carpenter had in mind several truck companies that were extended in-theater—one more than once—with resulting negative impact on retention. Other challenges arose from new technology and capabilities. Carpenter noted cases in which soldiers with satellite phones called home in the middle of an operation: "When you get off the satellite phone, if you don't call back ... the family, for the most part, is going to think the worst." Such problems affected all military families, but reserve component families were far less likely to be clustered on or near a base, and thus had much less opportunity to share these trials and tribulations with others in a similar situation.[50]

In 2004 the USAR implemented the congressionally authorized Welcome Home Warrior-Citizen Award Program to honor those who answered the nation's call, initiated a rear detachment operations training program to help families learn how to use Army and volunteer support programs, and published a financial guide that mobilizing soldiers received during home station processing. Family assistance centers played key roles, and their number increased nationwide from some 390 in FY 2003 to 430 by FY 2005. But even in areas where a center did not exist, help was available. The chief of the National Guard's family program believed that the Guard "is uniquely suited to ensure that military families who don't live on or near military installations don't fall through the cracks," because the Guard was "geographically dispersed . . . centered in every community throughout the nation."[51]

The Bumpy Road to Greater Regular-Reserve Integration

Representative Ike Skelton (D–MO) observed in 2004 that the U.S. military had a reputation for ignoring "the notion of cultural awareness." While he was referring to understanding people in other lands, his comment just as aptly summarized the gulf between regulars and reservists. Although much had been done to eliminate barriers between the two, more work remained. In 2013 former ASD(RA) Thomas Hall distilled the discussion of cultural issues to a simple question: "Why doesn't the active duty like the reserves?" As a regular Navy rear admiral who commanded the USNR in the mid-1990s, he was uniquely qualified to frame the question. Both Hall and Dennis McCarthy, another former component commander who later served as ASD(RA), agreed that ongoing deployed operations since 2001 had increased cultural understanding and appreciation between the active and reserve components. Both leaders viewed this goodwill as a perishable commodity, however, that could quickly evaporate under the pressures of budget cuts and reduced employment of the reserve component as a part of the operational force in the future. McCarthy observed: "People who operate together find ways to reduce the friction, but if they never see each other until it's *in extremis*, then the potential for misunderstandings, for misinterpretations, for different cultures to . . . clash is greatly increased."[52]

The chief of the Navy Reserve, Vice Admiral Cotton, devoted considerable attention to the issue of culture and active-reserve integration. Thinking along the same lines as Lieutenant General McCarthy, Cotton dispersed dozens of his headquarters personnel to active Navy units to establish daily contact and explain the USNR's capabilities as well as its limitations. The Chief of Naval Operations (CNO) from 2000 to 2005, Admiral Vernon E. Clark, had selected Cotton as his reserve chief in no small part for his shared commitment to improving active-reserve integration under a One Navy concept. Examining his service's biggest issues, Cotton concluded the culture was "what had to be fixed most in Navy active and reserve components." Accordingly, he told reservists in a town hall gathering in late 2004: "You're all in the Navy. You're not in the Reserve anymore." Instead of thinking in terms of Naval Reserve requirements, Cotton affirmed "there are only *Navy* requirements."[53]

Vice Admiral Cotton recalled that in the 1990s he logged his duty in the Navy Command Center as "peacetime contributory support," while a regular doing the same job logged it as operational duty. But as he pointed out, reserve activities were clearly operational: "We're lobbing cruise missiles. We're in

Bosnia. We're doing these kinds of things." When he became the USNR boss in 2003, Cotton employed terminology to facilitate culture change, redesignating reserve centers as operational support centers, and retitling reserve liaison officers as operational support officers, as well as relocating them to the more prominent operations section in the command headquarters. But the most visible title change occurred with the redesignation in 2005 of the Naval Reserve to Navy Reserve. Notwithstanding numerous statutes that used the term naval, and the opposition of naval associations and traditionalists, in April 2005 Cotton secured President Bush's signature on a memorandum redesignating his component the U.S. Navy Reserve. Shortly thereafter, the chief of naval operations stated that both regular and reserve personnel were "all U.S. Navy sailors" and, as Cotton observed, "that was the real change in culture, when everyone dropped the 'R'" (from USNR). The retired vice admiral summed up his perspective: "In the new world, there is no reserve. . . . And so it really is the RE-serve Component."[54]

Another avenue toward greater integration was the concept of continuum of service. Since the military was hard-pressed to offer attractive compensation and working conditions to those with advanced skills in fields such as information technology, biometrics, certain foreign languages, and medical specialties, DoD considered ways to provide more variability in service options. The goal was to allow participation to ebb and flow over the years depending on one's personal life and civilian career as well as military needs, with movement from one spot on the continuum to another to be seamless and for benefits to match the member's contributions. Service might range from full-time duty on one end of the spectrum to availability as an IRR (with no requirement for military training or periodic duty) for mobilization when needed.[55]

In 2004 a commercially published collection of essays on the 30-year-old all-volunteer force highlighted "an increased spirit of volunteerism on the part of reservists," a trend that continuum of service advocates used to their advantage. Promoters pointed as supporting evidence to the documented average of 45 days of paid duty on the part of reservists in FY 2000—a modest but nonetheless significant increase above the normal requirement. By expanding part-time service options, continuum advocates also argued, "the connection between the reservist and the community may provide a link to skills, resident within that community, that may be needed to support unique, unusual, or specialized military requirements." A community might be a geographic location, a professional field, or some other grouping of people. A good example was the Army's linguist program, whereby many native speakers, particularly those of Arab extraction, joined as IRRs and were available to serve as translators.[56]

Lieutenant General McCarthy viewed the Cold War era's manpower, personnel, and administrative systems as a "circuit breaker"—one was either on or off active duty. But what was needed for the Long War, he argued, was "a rheostat" that permitted reservists to move "back and forth across the continuum of service" according to the needs of units and the members themselves. McCarthy considered the "artificial barrier that counts personnel on temporary active duty for more than 179 days against active component authorizations" as the foremost obstacle to volunteerism. For the rheostat to work smoothly, however, administrative systems required an overhaul, and regulars needed to be knowledgeable about their reserve partners. McCarthy lamented that it was "still common to hear senior officers and leaders acknowledge that they know little about the Reserve. Worse, there is little desire to learn."[57]

Congress addressed the 179-day active-duty issue in 2004 by establishing a new strength category, designated Active Duty for Operational Support (ADOS), for reserve component members on active duty in support of a contingency. It allowed a reserve member to serve up to three years out of four on ADOS (informally known as the 1,095-rule because three years equaled 1,095 days) without being treated as an active component member for personnel/career management and strength accounting. DoD officials believed this would make it easier to accept the voluntary service of reserve component members in support of contingencies, but not all agreed that it would necessarily increase volunteerism. In January 2008 the Commission on the National Guard and Reserves recommended phasing out the ADOS category. In its place, the commissioners wanted Congress to "designate long-term billets as either active duty or civilian or as part of a program that rotates reserve members on full-time active duty tours." Those options would provide career-broadening opportunities for reservists as well as meeting Defense Department requirements. In short, the CNGR considered ADOS ineffective for force management purposes mainly because it was based on concern for service end strength.[58]

The 2005 Quadrennial Defense Review report recommended other changes to improve access to reserve personnel. It called for an increase in the limit on presidential reserve call-up authority from 270 to 365 days; Congress responded and enacted the new maximum in FY 2007. The QDR also suggested looking into "the creation of all-volunteer reserve units with high-demand capabilities." The Army Reserve soon pursued that initiative under the moniker Ready Response Reserve Units, with a pilot program in place in FY 2008. In accordance with the continuum of service idea, Lieutenant General Stultz, the USAR chief from 2006 to 2012, advocated a "soldier-for-life mentality," a concept the Army chief of staff soon promoted for the total Army.[59]

Despite the efforts to improve regular-reserve integration, disparities remained between the components and sometimes had greater negative impact on citizen-soldiers. A case in point was the recognition and treatment of post-traumatic stress disorder (PTSD). Rapid aeromedical evacuation of battlefield wounded in concert with advancements in medical care were saving many lives, but the full extent of injuries, especially mental injuries, did not always manifest until much later. Due to increasing awareness of the prevalence of PTSD among veterans, in 1989 the Department of Veterans Affairs had established the National Center for Post-Traumatic Stress Disorder. However, it was not until March 2005 that the assistant secretary of defense for health affairs took steps to emphasize mental health issues for military personnel returning from combat. He initiated the Post-Deployment Health Reassessment Program, which provided personnel with information, screening, and evaluation for postdeployment health concerns. The process included a questionnaire to be completed three to six months after redeployment, and provided the member with access to a health-care professional. Further developments by 2006 included a congressionally directed mental health task force focused on the armed forces and a mental health screening website offering assistance to military members and their families.[60]

By then, Long War veterans were increasingly aware of PTSD. For instance, in July 2005 *National Guard* highlighted the issue, citing a recent medical journal report that nearly one in six "who serve in a combat zone return home with PTSD." At the time, Guard policy prevented redeploying soldiers from involuntarily reporting to their units for at least 60 days after their return home. The laudable goal was to maximize their time at home with family, but it also isolated them from fellow veterans and the opportunity to talk about their experiences with others who understood. It had not been so with earlier generations of warriors. Vice Admiral Cotton paraphrased his boss, Assistant Navy Secretary William Navas, noting that from the days of the Roman legions through the two world wars of the 20th century, when soldiers departed the combat theater and headed home, either by foot or by ship, they had time to come "down from the high of battle." Many a doughboy and GI spent his evenings on the boat home playing cards, drinking coffee, and telling war stories, probably with considerable therapeutic effect. Cotton asked rhetorically, "How do we come home from war now? We sit in Kuwait . . . with a table like this . . . and we look at 'em and say, 'Is there anything wrong with you? And if there is, we'll keep you here and we'll fix you.'" Not surprisingly, few chose that option, and it was likely to their detriment. Cotton observed that "the Marines have learned, you get a couple days off, but you get right back with your unit, and you gotta decompress with them over time."[61]

Rarely did redeploying personnel willingly acknowledge their mental concerns, which some viewed as evidence of cowardice or weakness. Further, as Robert Smiley acknowledged: "We didn't spend a lot of time with demobilization which is probably a 'ding' on us. . . . The other side of the coin [was that] the troops didn't want to hear anything about it. They didn't want one extra moment at a demobilization station." In at least one case a U.S. senator requested that a Guard unit return several days earlier than scheduled so he could welcome them home. While soldiers and families alike appreciated the initiative in the short term, the soldiers had not completed their out-processing. Reserve component leadership also appeared, to some, slow to recognize the devastating effects of PTSD and other neurological consequences sustained by some deployed members. And unlike regulars, most reservists, once home, were no longer in daily contact with their units. Lt. Col. Anthony Lanuzo, chief of services division at Air National Guard headquarters, noted: "The reserve side is tougher because . . . we only see the member . . . the guardsman, one weekend of the month. And normally if they are seeking . . . medical help, it is from a civilian provider. And the military may not even know about it." Furthermore, some if not many members avoided informing their units of conditions they perceived could damage their careers.[62]

On some occasions the apparently seamless interaction of regular and reserve forces worked to the detriment of citizen-soldiers, because the reserve components failed to receive credit for their accomplishments. One such instance, the subject of a best-selling book and a movie, occurred on the night of 2 July 2005, when a joint U.S. team including two Air Force Reserve HH–60 Blackhawk helicopters flew through canyons in darkness into northeastern Afghanistan's Taliban-infested Kunar Province. With friendly fighter aircraft dispensing ordnance illuminating the sky, one of the HH–60s landed on a rocky ledge and rescued Navy SEAL Marcus Luttrell, the only survivor of a mission that cost the lives of his 3 teammates and 16 other special operations personnel whose helicopter was shot down. Luttrell's 2007 account, *Lone Survivor*, never mentioned the role of the Air Force Reserve.[63]

A much bigger example of a failure to emphasize the contributions of the reserve component occurred in the response to Hurricane Katrina. Striking in late August 2005, the storm was one of the deadliest and costliest natural disasters in the nation's history, with more than 1,800 killed and an estimated $148 billion in damage. Within two weeks, more than 51,000 citizen-soldiers were on duty as part of one of the largest humanitarian response forces ever formed. Guardsmen from all 54 states and territories (including the District of

Columbia) and members of the federal reserves (Army, Navy, Marine Corps, Air Force) participated during the three-month operation. The humanitarian airlift was one of the largest ever. The National Guard provided the bulk of relief personnel and was credited with the rescue and/or evacuation of some 87,000 people. The vast majority were carried to safety by the ANG, which conducted nearly 75 percent of Katrina airlift sorties. The scale of the response was even more impressive because almost 80,000 other guardsmen were deployed at the time, mostly overseas in support of combat operations in Iraq and Afghanistan. Like the reserve component's participation in the Long War, this large-scale domestic mission in the midst of a major conflict was unprecedented. Ironically, Louisiana's 256th Infantry Brigade was in Iraq when Katrina struck, producing a situation in which guardsmen serving their country were unable to assist their families and neighbors at a time of great need.[64]

The operation, and particularly the absence of the 256th Brigade, highlighted the importance of Emergency Management Assistance Compacts. In use for more than a decade, these agreements between states enabled Guard personnel from one state to lend assistance in another state during a crisis. The compacts proved their value after Katrina. While President Bush had the authority to federalize the entire force under a single commander and discussed that option with the Gulf Coast states' governors, they demurred. An ANG study of the Katrina response concluded that "it would have been easier and quicker if the federal government [had] intervened immediately to manage the relief operation," rather than relying on the compacts, but a serious drawback with that option would have emerged. The troops would have been under Title 10 (federal) control in the operational area and, except in rare cases, the Posse Comitatus Act of 1878 forbade federal (or federalized Guard) troops from performing law enforcement duties. Guardsmen under state control could, and did, enforce the laws—a critically important role especially in the first week of the Katrina crisis. Additionally, keeping the troops in Title 32 (state) status avoided the sometimes-cumbersome federalization process.[65]

Many media accounts appeared to represent Army Lt. Gen. Russel L. Honoré, the "colorful, cigar chomping" head of Joint Task Force Katrina, as the commander of the entire relief effort, but in fact the governors—by virtue of the state-to-state compacts—directly controlled the majority of the relief force. Guard personnel, who actually outnumbered their regular counterparts by more than three to one, were, according to one observer, "dismayed to find that the national media consistently portrayed them as active-duty Soldiers" under Honoré. The misperceptions regarding command arrangements and the source of personnel underscored the importance of clear, accurate, engaging communications to the American people concerning reserve component operational roles and contributions. Citizen-soldiers often appreciated hearing senior leaders note that they saw no difference between regulars and part-time professionals, but this was a missed opportunity to trumpet successful action by the reserve component.[66]

——— Conclusion ———

Between 2003 and 2006 the demands of the Global War on Terrorism placed unprecedented strain on the reserve components, especially the Army Reserve and Guard, and challenged the viability of the Total Force concept and the notion of an operational reserve. New policies, such as the Army's rotational models and the DoD-wide introduction of TRICARE Reserve Select and its subsequent extended eligibility to all Selected Reserve members and their families, slowly began to right the ship. In the midst of a major war, Hurricane Katrina relief efforts confirmed the importance of homeland security as a (but not *the*) mission of the National Guard.

By the fall 2006 election cycle, the American public had become weary of stalemate and increasing casualties in Iraq. Sadly, the U.S. military death toll in Iraq reached 3,000 on the last day of the year. In small communities like Houma, Louisiana, and Paris, Illinois, the concentrated loss of hometown guardsmen had been devastating. In the November congressional elections, the Democratic Party regained control of both the U.S. House and Senate for the first time since 1994. Secretary Rumsfeld had offered his resignation prior to the election, but it was not until after the results came in that President Bush announced he and his defense secretary had agreed to change the leadership at the Pentagon. The president nominated former CIA director Dr. Robert M. Gates, then serving as president of Texas A&M University, to succeed Rumsfeld. The new secretary would continue and even accelerate the effort to ensure that the Total Force—in particular its reserve component—was equal to the demands of the ongoing conflict.[67]

CHAPTER 7

Regularizing Reserve Mobilization for a Long War, January 2007–September 2011

I n 2007 a new defense secretary, Robert Gates, acted quickly to end his predecessor's 24-cumulative-months mobilization policy while affirming the one-in-six ratio. The ground reserves required considerable time to fully implement the change, but the clearly written policy statement, which offered the reasonable hope of predictable deployments to reserve component personnel, their families, and their employers, marked a watershed moment in the post-9/11 era. It came just in time, as the slow withdrawal from Iraq was offset by a substantial increase in troops in Afghanistan. Coupled with fresh domestic missions, the demand for reserve forces remained high through 2011, which marked a full decade of unprecedented operational tempo for the nation's citizen-soldiers. Throughout this period, policies continued to evolve to better adapt the reserve component for its increased role in national defense.[1]

A New Mobilization Policy

By 2006 the Pentagon was increasingly hard-pressed to meet the mobilization and deployment requirements for ground combat units in Iraq. A joint staff briefing on 31 August made the point in stark terms—all 34 Army reserve component brigade combat teams and four of nine Marine Reserve infantry battalions had used their available mobilization time. The five remaining reserve infantry battalions in the Corps and a total of 68,000 Army and Marine individuals had "12 months residual time left on their clock." But the Defense Department's criteria regarding the ratio of time spent with boots on the ground (BOG) compared to time at home—BOG-to-dwell in military shorthand—meant that the Army would not have a single reserve component combat brigade eligible for activation until sometime in 2008, close to 18 months away. The next two eligible Marine Reserve battalions would not become available until 2009. Secretary Rumsfeld's policy of no involuntary remobilizations, more restrictive than the governing law, further constrained options to solve the problem. Moreover, the one-in-six standard applied to individuals, which made it much more complicated for the services, as they primarily managed mobilization in terms of units. While Rumsfeld's focus on volunteerism fit with his emphasis on the long-term sustainability of the reserve components, it played havoc with unit integrity and cohesiveness, especially critical factors for ground units in the midst of combat. To demonstrate the dwindling pool of available manpower, Army charts depicted how many personnel had not yet deployed and when to expect the barrel to be empty. A number of observers felt that unless the Pentagon continued indefinitely to rotate regular ground combat units at an arguably unsustainable BOG-to-dwell ratio of one to two (or less), the department's mobilization policy would soon face a crisis point.[2]

Robert Smiley, the principal director for readiness, training, and mobilization in the Office of the Assistant Secretary of Defense for Reserve Affairs, who had prior mobilization experience in the Army secretariat, recalled the genesis of the new mobilization policy: "In 2005 we were supposed to have three brigades . . . in Iraq." The situation proved to be dramatically worse than expected and the Army needed to deploy significantly more forces, but

could not "go 'back to the well' for the Guard and Reserves" due to Secretary Rumsfeld's decisions on cumulative months and involuntary remobilizations. Smiley credited Lt. Gen. Steve Blum, the National Guard Bureau chief, and Lt. Gen. Clyde A. Vaughn, the Army National Guard director, with suggesting to the new defense secretary that "if you drop the tour length down to one year, we can go a second time. And they convinced Secretary Gates when he came in the door." Smiley summarized Gates' change as simply, "We are going to get rid of cumulative and just use consecutive."[3]

In January 2007 the new defense secretary, Robert M. Gates, issued a utilization memorandum that limited mobilized reservists to "a maximum one year at any one time," and promised predictability to reservists, families, and civilian employers. (Source: National Archives, photo by Monica King)

On 19 January 2007 Gates issued a two-page memorandum, "Utilization of the Total Force," originally developed by ASD(RA) Thomas Hall's office, which spelled out the new policy. It contained three major provisions:

First, from this point forward, involuntary mobilization for members of the Reserve Forces will be for a maximum one year at any one time. At service discretion, this period may exclude individual skill training required for deployment, and post-mobilization leave.

Second, mobilization of ground combat, combat support and combat service support will be managed on a unit basis. This will allow greater cohesion and predictability in how these Reserve units train and deploy. Exceptions will require my approval.

Third, the planning objective for involuntary mobilization of Guard/Reserve units will remain a one year mobilized to five years demobilized ratio. However, today's global demands will require a number of selected Guard/Reserve units to be remobilized sooner than this standard. Our intention is that such exceptions be temporary and that we move to the broad application of the 1:5 goal as soon as possible. Continue to plan your force structure on that basis.[4]

The fundamental improvement of the Gates policy over his predecessor's was the assurance that a single mobilization would no longer extend beyond 12 months. He reinforced Rumsfeld's goal that mobilizations should be no more frequent than one year in six. Taken together, that offered increased predictability to citizen-soldiers, their families, and employers. To help make that possible, he gave the services leeway to conduct some predeployment training prior to mobilization and to avoid setting aside time near the end of the year of service for personnel to use accrued leave. Practically speaking, the new policy primarily affected the Army Guard and Army Reserve because the Marines already relied on 12-month mobilizations that encompassed predeployment training, 7 months overseas, and postdeployment requirements. The Air Force not only featured shorter deployments, its units also generally were more ready to deploy at the time of mobilization due in large measure to their much higher proportion of full-time support personnel, so they required much less training after activation.

The change met with widespread approval among reserve component personnel, families, and employers. The ARNG director from 2005 to 2009, Lieutenant General Vaughn lauded the new policy:

> What Secretary Gates did was historic. . . . we couldn't go
> back in and regenerate this force again, asking soldiers that
> have been away from their employers and their families for 18
> months to go back three or four years later . . . for another 18
> months. [But] if you move it back to 12 months total, and
> then you increase the value of the training, and if you get
> *validation of task* in the year prior to training, you could do
> two mobilizations of 12 months over a period of eight or
> nine years.[5]

The National Guard Bureau's deputy chief of plans and readiness, David Germain, added in late 2007 that under the Rumsfeld policy the ARNG had deployed soldiers "without certainty when they were coming back. Now, we're going to take a soldier and he'll be back in one year." One corollary policy that the ASD(RA)'s office clarified days after Gates issued his memorandum was that individuals could still volunteer for additional active duty beyond what their unit was required to perform, but such duty counted as dwell time— volunteering members still had to "plan to mobilize according to their unit's schedule." A few weeks later the Joint Chiefs of Staff chairman stated before the Senate Armed Services Committee: "Predictability of deployments for all Service members is a key factor to quality of life."[6]

While the memorandum acknowledged that the goal of one year out of six deployed would not always be realized in the near term, it provided a basis for the services to make force structure decisions that supported that rate of employment over the long term. In January 2007 Congress made the goal more achievable by authorizing a temporary increase of 74,200 soldiers: 65,000 (Army), 8,200 (ARNG), and 1,000 (U.S. Army Reserve). Two years later the Army gained an additional temporary increase in end strength of 22,000 soldiers.[7]

Preston M. "Pete" Geren, the secretary of the Army from 2007 to 2009, recalled that the ordeal of Minnesota's 1st Brigade Combat Team, 34th Infantry Division (1/34), "crystallized" the wisdom of Secretary Gates' new policy. Mobilized in October 2005, the unit went to Iraq in early 2006. In January 2007, near the end of its yearlong deployment, President Bush announced his decision to significantly increase the number of troops in an effort to change the course of the war. The surge, as it became known, extended the 1/34 Infantry tour by four months. When the brigade returned home in July/August 2007, it had served 16 consecutive months in Iraq—among the longest of any combat unit in the war. The extension itself had been difficult enough for the guardsmen and their families, but a firestorm of discontent arose when just over half met the qualifying period (730 consecutive days—two full years on active duty) for Montgomery GI Bill educational benefits, while the remainder fell short by a month or so, and some by as little as a single day.[8]

Robert Smiley of the ASD(RA)'s office recalled, "We wrestled with that one and spent a lot of time with [the 1/34 case]" because "some of them were on duty for . . . *725 days* which made them not eligible for the Montgomery GI Bill benefits, and that just caused a huge flap." The soldiers had received individual orders that did not all start on the same day or require the same length of mobilization. Seeking to redress what many perceived as inequitable treatment, Minnesota's adjutant general testified in October 2007 before the House of Representatives. The Army National Guard Readiness Center, the Army Review Boards Agency, and the Office of the Assistant Secretary of the Army for Manpower and Reserve Affairs ultimately joined hands to implement a process to review the individual cases of 1/34 Infantry soldiers, and in the end most of those who appealed were found to qualify for the educational benefits. Col. James E. "Eddie" Porter—who commanded a Guard engineer battalion in Baghdad in 2005–2006—commented that in some cases the "small policies" such as those affecting promotions and entitlements were of even greater consequence to citizen-soldiers than the mobilization policy.[9]

It took time, as the Gates memo had anticipated, to reach the intended ratio of one year deployed to five years dwell. In 2009 the Army chief of staff, General George W. Casey Jr., affirmed the transition would require several years: "The Army will complete transformation of the Reserve Components to an operational force by changing the way we train, equip, resource, and mobilize units by 2012." In the meantime, a command history noted that "units rotated on cycles shorter than the ARFORGEN goals," with many mobilized after less than four years of dwell time due to the operational necessities of Iraq and Afghanistan. Colonel Porter, the long-serving chief of staff of the 11,000-strong and heavily deployed Alabama ARNG, emphasized in 2013 that his units "hadn't seen one-to-five since this thing started." There also were cases of new ARNG units being established and then mobilized some 20 months later.[10]

Despite short-term challenges to full implementation, the new BOG-to-dwell mobilization policy fit well with the Army Force Generation model, the five-year cyclical deployment plan that Secretary of the Army Francis Harvey had approved in 2006. But the change from the prior practice of 18-month mobilizations to 12 months presented a major challenge. Army leaders, including Army Reserve Chief Lt. Gen. Jack Stultz, immediately recognized that six months to get ready and "six months boots on the ground is not going to cut it," in terms of supplementing active component ground units that were still deploying for a full year. Maximizing the time of reserve component units in the war zone meant cutting deeply into the time that had been devoted to predeployment training during the period between mobilization and departure for overseas. It was now critical to reduce that postmobilization training to a minimum, without negatively impacting combat readiness. The only solution, as Stultz explained, was to shift much of the training to the one to two years prior to a mobilization.[11]

Whereas the training requirements (primarily individual) in the first two years of the ARFORGEN model probably could be met with the reservists' traditional 39 training days per year, a greater commitment would be required later in the cycle. Instead of the traditional 15-day annual tour, Stultz estimated up to three weeks in the third year, and for the fourth year "we need at least a 29-day training exercise to get all the warrior tasks done so that when we show up at the mobilization site, we have very little training left to do." The focus of training after mobilization would be on mission rehearsal—preparation for the specific tasks assigned to the unit once it was in theater. The Army Reserve chief anticipated transitioning to a maximum of three months of predeployment training followed by nine months of boots-on-the-ground, "which would give us adequate time, pre- and post-[mobilization], and still be on the same cycle as our active duty counterparts." Secretary Geren felt the Gates mobilization policy's call for force structure planning provided the necessary backing for the Army's full implementation of ARFORGEN.[12]

To help implement the shift in the timing of and responsibility for training, in spring 2008, the Army Reserve opened two regional training centers (RTCs)—at Fort Dix, New Jersey, and Fort McCoy, Wisconsin—to supplement its existing center at Fort Hunter Liggett, California. The new centers provided the wherewithal for USAR/ARNG units to accomplish many of the 130 predeployment tasks identified as suitable for completion prior to mobilization. Those same three installations doubled as combat support training centers, conducting eight-day brigade-level exercises to cut back on postmobilization training while providing more time in-theater. In the Army National Guard, most deploying units conducted the bulk of premobilization training at in-state installations, although some units utilized the Army Reserve's RTCs. The ARNG also designated seven training sites as mobilization platforms. Once mobilized, a Guard unit moved from home to one of six installations—Camp Atterbury, Indiana; Camp Shelby, Mississippi; Fort Bliss, Texas; Fort Dix, New Jersey; Fort Hood, Texas; or Fort Lewis, Washington—while Fort Benning, Georgia, handled Individual Ready Reserve soldiers and contractors.[13]

Lieutenant General Stultz stated that under the new USAR approach to training, "Commanders are now empowered to develop their deployment training plans, determining which tasks will be trained during pre-mobilization and which will be accomplished at the mobilization station." By the end of 2008, in most cases, Army Reserve units had decreased the number of postmobilization training days. The Army Reserve chief noted in 2009 that the improved training regimen increased the "'boot-on-ground' time for combat support hospital units by 45 days, military police battalions by 37 days and combat engineer companies by 31 days." By mid-2008 the ARNG touted that "Guard brigades mobilize for a year . . . [including] approximately 10 months of overseas duty after two months of post-mobilization training."[14]

Robert Smiley, who spent time in the field observing the training ramifications of the Gates mobilization policy, noted that one important aspect was simply making the mobilization stations "much more efficient" at their job: "The theater-required training became much more specific . . . you had less down time." Another part was improving the process of certifying that training was accomplished satisfactorily. The Army's Forces Command was responsible for validating the training required for deployments, and in many cases before 2007, it made Guard units repeat certain training tasks under its watchful eyes. The challenge was convincing officials to accept training they had not actually seen. Smiley believed that one of the biggest mobilization issues solved during Gates' tenure as defense secretary was giving state adjutants general the authority to certify that their units had accomplished predeployment training, a change the Army chief of staff directed in 2007. Another initiative was the adoption of contiguous training, a block of active duty, state-managed but federally funded under Title 32, taking place immediately prior to mobilization under Title 10 orders. This initially was as long as 90 days, but Department of Defense policy soon limited it to no more than 30 days of such training within the 90-day window before the mobilization date (aviation units were authorized 45 days of contiguous training). This large block of training further reduced postmobilization requirements and thus increased deployed time. In March 2011 Secretary Gates effectively ended this program, since it violated the spirit of his 12-month limit on mobilization.[15]

While the number of postmobilization training days was generally lowered, a mission change could undo some of what a unit had accomplished, since it impacted the specifics of mission rehearsal—the primary focus of training at the mobilization station. David L. McGinnis, who served as acting assistant secretary of defense for reserve affairs for part of 2009 and 2011–2012, recalled a visit in 2009 to Camp Shelby, where the 155th Brigade from Mississippi was conducting final preparation just a few weeks before deploying to the combat theater: "They had all kinds of gates, and they were doing well. The day I was there, they got a mission change, [and they] had to completely reorient."[16]

Army Reserve force restructuring, which continued under the leadership of Lieutenant General Stultz, facilitated training and readiness improvements. From 2006 to 2008 the USAR activated from scratch or converted existing nondeployable support organizations to add nearly 400 deployable operational and functional units with some 16,000 deployable billets. This included the establishment of eight modular sustainment brigades and two combat support brigades (maneuver enhancement) from existing units/organizations. One of the most significant actions was replacing the 10 regional readiness commands with 4 regional support commands based at Fort McCoy, Wisconsin; Moffett Field, California; Fort Dix, New Jersey; and Fort Jackson, South Carolina. With the change, command/control and training/readiness oversight shifted to 22 (deployable) operational and functional commands. Stultz observed that the restructuring "enables us to source more operational units from the space savings" from reduced overhead throughout USAR. One of the new organizations, the 316th Expeditionary Sustainment Command went to Iraq in August 2007—where it held its formal activation ceremony one month later. The success of this modular unit, the first of its type to deploy to an operational theater, led the Army to allocate 5 more such commands to the Army Reserve, bringing the total to 10.[17]

The Army National Guard also strove to increase readiness, particularly by reducing the number of soldiers who lacked qualification in a military occupational specialty. The ARNG went from 26,000 awaiting training in 2008 to about 10,000 a year later, and also touted the fact that since 2005, the percentage of skill-qualified soldiers rose from 77 to 91 percent. In late 2009 Guard officials reported "personnel readiness is at the highest levels in history." The Marine Corps Reserve, taxed by equally high deployment rates, began to experience a shortage of junior officers and senior noncommissioned officers in its selected reserve units during this period. One year out from mobilization, many infantry battalions had no more than two officers per company (instead of the usual six). It took creative solutions, such as assigning newly graduated regular infantry officers and pulling seasoned lieutenants from active duty to fill out the battalions during the critical team-building months leading up to mobilization.[18]

A May 2007 briefing by the Office of the ASD for Reserve Affairs emphasized that "a direct relationship exists between the number of full time personnel assigned to a unit and the readiness status of that unit." A year later the Commission on the National Guard and Reserves devoted a dozen pages to full-time support programs and reported that, unlike the four reserve components under the Air Force and Navy departments, the programs in the ARNG/USAR "*do not* promote total force integration and uniform operational standards." Part of the problem was that in 2007 the Army's previously approved plan to increase the ARNG's percentage of full-time positions was derailed at least temporarily. The Guard reported that no new full-time support positions had been added to the 2007 budget, and it disappointingly considered the "just plain gloomy" fiscal year 2008 budget sufficient perhaps for a strategic reserve, but not an operational force. *National Guard* magazine also noted one downside to the Gates 12-month mobilization policy: "Guardsmen will perform more pre-deployment training and post-deployment recovery at home stations, which shifts expenses for those activities from the active component to the Guard." That change exacerbated the ARNG's funding deficiencies. The setback was rectified to some extent by the 2009 budget, which enabled the ARNG to add more than 3,500 full-time personnel, most of them AGRs. The Guard bureau approvingly called it "the greatest increase in 22 years." Tempering the good news was the fact that in some states the Guard remained well below the number of validated full-time support billets even after the increase.[19]

Army Guard officials viewed the lack of full-time personnel as their primary shortfall. In 2008 National Guard Association of the United States Chairman R. Martin Umbarger, when queried by the Army chief of staff, believed that fixing the Army Guard's full-time manning shortage was the "Silver Bullet to accelerate our transformation." A year later an Indiana Guard human resources officer argued that the operational nature of the Guard's service for the last decade required it to be manned as an operational force, and he considered personnel "our center of gravity." Another official noted that in a typical military police company in the South Carolina Guard, five personnel from the Active Guard and Reserve personnel and one technician were required, but at current funding levels only three billets were filled.[20]

In May 2006 George W. Bush presided over the change of command ceremony in which Admiral Thad W. Allen (left) relieved Admiral Thomas H. Collins. This was the first time a sitting president attended a change of the U.S. Coast Guard commandant, signifying that service's increased importance to national security. (DoD photo by Staff Sgt. D. Myles Cullen)

The Coast Guard also addressed its full-time support issues, which had arisen primarily as a result of the loss of reserve program administration billets during the integration with the regular component in the 1990s. Between 2008 and 2010, the Coast Guard made significant headway in realigning about one hundred full-time support billets to staff the U.S. Coast Guard's new Reserve Force Readiness System. This initiative reflected the Coast Guard leadership's commitment to improving reserve readiness and mobilization/demobilization processes, major challenges after 9/11. The USCG commandant, Admiral Robert Papp, credited the realignment of Full-Time Support billets and personnel down to the sector level (where two-thirds of reservists worked) with contributing to the relatively trouble-free mobilization for the Deepwater Horizon disaster in 2010.[21]

New Missions

At the same time that the surge in Iraq was bringing increasing stability to that country, a resurgent Taliban threatened progress in Afghanistan. In May–June 2008, for the first time since Operation Iraqi Freedom had begun five years earlier, U.S. and coalition combat losses in Afghanistan exceeded those in Iraq. Priorities shifted further when President Barack Obama entered office in 2009 with the goal of ending U.S. involvement in Iraq and placing greater focus on "al Qaeda and its allies—the terrorists who planned and supported the 9/11 attacks." In March 2009 and again that December, he ordered U.S. troop surges in Afghanistan that added 51,000. From a strength of 218,500 in September 2007, American forces in OIF declined to 96,200 in September 2010. Over the same period, the U.S. commitment in Afghanistan expanded from 25,240 to 105,900. At the close of 2008, 121,000 reserve component personnel were on active duty supporting the partial mobilization, with the ARNG/USAR accounting for some three-fourths, or 94,000 of the total.[22]

This same period witnessed the expansion of nontraditional missions and programs for reserve components. The Army Guard was particularly well-suited to one of these initiatives, the agricultural development team (ADT) program. The brainchild of Army Secretary Harvey, Clyde Vaughn, and Missouri Farm Bureau President Charles Kruse, ADT sought to improve agricultural productivity and rural communities in Afghanistan by deploying teams of guardsmen with farming, livestock, and agribusiness expertise to assist with matters such as irrigation, soil, seed production, crop yield, and livestock health. Such teams could only be found in the Guard, according to Army Secretary Geren, and they capitalized on the farming and livestock expertise of guardsmen from states such as Missouri and Texas, which established the

The brainchild of Army Secretary Francis J. Harvey, Army National Guard Lt. Gen. Clyde A. Vaughn, and the Missouri Farm Bureau's Charles E. Kruse, Agricultural Development Teams strengthened the Afghan economy and improved rural life by deploying guardsmen with farming, livestock, and agribusiness expertise. (DoD photo by 1st Lt. Lory Stevens, U.S. Army)

initial two teams. The first ADT of about 50 personnel deployed in late 2007 and consisted entirely of Army guardsmen, but the second team included some Air National Guard members as well.[23]

The ADT program capitalized on the civilian work experience of Guard personnel—skills for which there was no equivalent military occupational specialty. One agricultural team from California boasted a horticulturalist (Sgt. Jason Stevens); a team from Indiana included an agronomist (Maj. Larry Temple); and a Kansas team featured a soil scientist (Capt. Jeffrey Mann). ADTs were only an email away from tapping additional experts in academic or government institutions back home, like the Kansas ARNG brigade commander who in civilian life worked in the inspector general's office of the Department of Agriculture. At the start of 2010 there were no fewer than eight teams on the ground in Afghanistan. While their activity was civilian in nature, their real objective was counterinsurgency—if a farmer could provide for his family, he was less likely to support the antigovernment rebels.[24]

It did not always require innovative programs to leverage the civilian skills resident in the reserve component. Lt. Col. Morgan Mann, the executive officer of the 25th Marines, a reserve infantry regiment, quoted the Marine Corps commandant as stating that "in some ways a Reserve battalion is even more effective at COIN [counterinsurgency] than a regular battalion." As of 2011, Marine Reserve battalions had deployed no less than 13 times for Iraqi Freedom alone, representative of the heavy commitment of all reserve components. Mann elaborated that many reservists brought with them civilian expertise in areas critical for counterinsurgency success—"law enforcement, trades, medical skills, agriculture, and business skills"—all of them enablers for reestablishing basic governmental functions and improving the economy and quality of life of local inhabitants.[25]

Navy reservists were also increasingly on the ground in both Afghanistan and Iraq, even as the strength of the Navy's Selected Reserve declined from 88,000 in 2004 to 68,000 in 2008. The Navy Expeditionary Combat Command (NECC), established in 2007, quickly evolved to provide maritime capabilities in the near-coast, inner harbor, and riverine settings. Vice Admiral Cotton referred to the new command as "the 'boots-on-ground' people." By spring 2008 the command managed 40,000 sailors, of which nearly 50 percent were reservists. More than 11,000 NECC sailors were deployed, many of them in traditional functional areas such as naval construction (Seabees), diving and salvage, and explosive ordnance disposal. In the expeditionary logistics support specialty, reservists accounted for more than 90 percent of personnel. The NECC included nontraditional functions such as maritime civil affairs, expeditionary intelligence, and expeditionary training. The Navy activated its first civil affairs unit in 2007, with reservists filling nearly one-half of the billets. A number of NECC civil affairs personnel joined their Army brethren in provincial reconstruction teams in Afghanistan or Iraq.[26]

Civil affairs exemplified the larger issue of high-demand/low-density (HD/LD) capabilities—specialties that were not often used in peacetime, and therefore not usually maintained in the regular component in large numbers if at all, but which were important when the need arose. Former acting ASD(RA) McGinnis believed: "If there's anything that you ought to give to the reserve components . . . it's the HD/LD list. . . . [It] represents the chasm between service culture and the needs of the nation, because the services will not invest their money . . . in these things that they don't think [are] important to their culture." In a move consistent with his analysis, in 2006 the Army realigned its civil affairs and psychological operations functions, shifting them from the U.S. Special Operations Command to the Army Reserve Command. In 2007 the Army owned 96 percent of the military's civil affairs elements, and 93 percent of these were in the Army Reserve. Civil affairs/support teams trained at two Indiana National Guard installations: Camp Atterbury and the Muscatatuck Urban Training Center. The latter base's simulated urban environment included the Muscatatuck "Embassy" staffed with personnel wearing golf shirts featuring the U.S. State Department crest and the name of their faux outpost. McGinnis noted that they trained at these locations because "nobody [in the regular component] would train them. . . . [or] give them any place to train." As the thoughtful, outspoken McGinnis summed it up, "If the Reserves didn't do it, who would?"[27]

As the war continued, the Army increasingly used Guard brigade combat teams to conduct security force missions, which encompassed tasks such as convoy escort, base security, and other force protection measures. From 2007 through 2011, seventeen of 26 mobilized Guard brigades served in a security force role. Another three brigades operated with Task Force Phoenix, which provided adviser and training elements for the Afghan National Army. These nonstandard missions impacted organization, equipment, and the skills required of soldiers. As examples, a Guard infantry brigade assigned a security force mission needed a large increase in vehicles, while soldiers in fields such as artillery might need significant training to serve in a perimeter defense role. The nonstandard missions meant that even a unit manned, trained, and equipped at normal levels (the goal for unmobilized Guard units in 2007 was 75 percent of wartime equipment) would need considerable additional cross-leveling when it mobilized. And often the unit would only acquire most of the large items, such as vehicles, when it arrived in-theater, making it difficult to train soldiers with the limited amount of equipment usually present at the mobilization site. Likewise, creation of the agricultural development and provincial reconstruction teams resulted in equipment and personnel with the needed skills being drawn from standard units, which suffered a loss in readiness as a consequence.[28]

While the reserve component maintained a high tempo of operations in U.S. Central Command's area, new missions for citizen-soldiers arose at home. At the request of President Bush, the National Guard provided volunteers to serve along the U.S.-Mexico border to help stem illegal immigration, drug smuggling, and the threat of terrorists entering the country. For 25 months beginning in June 2006, up to 6,000 guardsmen at a time assisted the U.S. Border Patrol. While their service on Title 32 orders enabled them to enforce federal laws if needed, they were not there to engage in a direct law enforcement role. When Operation Jump Start ended in July 2008, some 30,000 guardsmen had served. From 2010 to 2011, up to 1,200 Guard volunteers at a time (again in Title 32 status) supported security measures along the border with Mexico in a similar role.[29]

In 2008 the Pentagon established a U.S. Northern Command-assigned task force to assist civil authorities in the event of a natural disaster or biological, chemical, or nuclear attack. While the initial organization consisted mainly of active component personnel, Secretary Gates approved a plan that called for the Guard to establish 10 homeland response force (HRF) teams, one for each Federal Emergency Management Agency region, placed no more than a few hundred miles from potential disaster areas. The first teams began forming in 2010, each with more than 500 soldiers and airmen, including more than 100 full-time personnel. In July 2011 the Ohio National Guard's 600-member HRF was the first to undergo validation, which it completed at the urban training center at Muscatatuck. The states continued to form the 22-person National Guard civil support teams designed specifically to respond to attacks involving weapons of mass destruction.[30]

In a related development, between 2008 and 2010 the National Guard established two domestic all-hazards response teams (DARTs), one covering the eastern United States and another for the west. The DARTs identified Guard units that had appropriate capabilities in areas such as engineering, logistics, and aviation to respond to specific emergencies, from hurricanes and wildfires to biological attacks. Using the existing emergency management assistance compacts between various states, in a crisis the DART would serve as a regional liaison, coordinating the response of assets from other states to deal with a

natural or man-made emergency. In a corollary initiative, the Air National Guard moved to fill a requirement identified following Hurricane Katrina, when officials realized there was no entity assigned the task of recovering bodies in a disaster area. With the support of the National Guard Bureau chief, Lt. Gen. Steve Blum, the ANG activated fatality search and recovery teams. By 2013 the Air Guard had 27 such units, which could deploy overseas if needed and were aligned with the ARNG's civil support teams. The experience after Katrina even led to development of a disaster relief mobile kitchen trailer that could be easily transported to provide cooked meals in place of the ubiquitous packaged MRE ration.[31]

The National Guard Bureau chief from 2003 to 2008, Lt. Gen. H. Steven Blum supported dropping the length of Guard mobilizations to 12 months in order to allow for periodic additional mobilizations following sufficient "dwell time" at home. (U.S. Army photo by Staff Sgt. Jim Greenhill)

In spring 2009 the new Northern Command deputy commander,

Lieutenant General Blum, made clear the Guard's vital role: "What the Guard does underpins and is the foundation of the military response of Northern Command." One major concern remained the proper delineation between state and federal authority in responses to domestic emergencies. While states were the first to respond to disasters, depending on the type and extent of damage, governors might require federal assistance. But unlike the large Northern Command task force, the advantage of the DARTs, HRFs, and other Guard assets was that they operated under state control.[32]

The 2005 Base Realignment and Closure Commission affected the reserve components to a greater degree than any previous round. For the Army Reserve, that mainly meant relocating the Office of the Chief of Army Reserve and the Army Reserve Command headquarters, along with closing or realigning 176 facilities and moving into 125 new armed forces reserve centers. The impact on the air components was much greater, as recalled by Craig R. McKinley, Air National Guard director from 2006 to 2008:

> I spent most of my time as Air Director trying to mitigate the effects of BRAC. We didn't close any units. . . . It would have been a different story if we had just said this unit is closing. . . . We "re-roled" them. BRAC said, "You just lose your flying mission." Well, [the] flying mission for a Guard unit or Reserve unit is pretty much the centerpiece. . . . You've got security forces, you've got medics, you've got civil engineers and everything, but that's all part of the wing . . . part of the maintenance and [operations].[33]

In some cases, active and reserve component leaders were able to mitigate the effects of the changes. The Virginia ANG's F–16 unit at Richmond—which lost its aircraft—relocated in 2007 to nearby Joint Base Langley-Eustis, where it transitioned to the F–22 Raptor as an associate unit, becoming the first Guard outfit to fly the Air Force's newest stealth fighter. The Hawaii ANG also entered into an associate program operating the F–22, but in a reversal of typical roles, the Guard owned the aircraft and the regulars were the associate unit. The Air Force Reserve also joined in F–22 operations in 2007, with the activation of the 477th Fighter Group in an associate role at Elmendorf AFB, Alaska. In the same year the Missouri ANG established an associate relationship with the 509th Bomb Wing at Whiteman AFB, Missouri, flying the stealthy B–2 Spirit bomber.[34]

The BRAC process brought another reversal of roles. While its primary purpose was "to reduce infrastructure," General McKinley noted that the Air Guard "actually gained square footage out of BRAC." He cited Willow Grove

A pilot from the Virginia Air National Guard's 192nd Fighter Wing during a 2015 training exercise. Following the 2005 Base Closure and Realignment Commission's decisions, the Virginia Air National Guard's 192nd Fighter Wing became the first Guard unit to fly the Air Force's newest stealth fighter, the F–22, as part of that service's total force integration program. (USAF photo by Staff Sgt. Jonathan Garcia)

in Philadelphia, a Navy Reserve base with a Guard A–10 tenant, the 111th Fighter Wing. The wing lost its aircraft, but the Navy Reserve moved out all its units, so in 2011 the Pennsylvania ANG assumed responsibility for the installation, which McKinley mentioned is "not our forte, by the way." The ANG traditionally operated with a "very small footprint" on facilities maintained by the regular components, thereby allowing the Guard to stay focused on its primary mission. In the case of Willow Grove, the outcome for the Guard was replacing its former A–10 mission with the MQ–9 Reaper, with the establishment in 2013 of a ground control station at the renamed Horsham Air Guard Base. Air Guard units in Houston, Texas, and Syracuse, New York, also lost manned aircraft but replaced them with remotely piloted aircraft. While not ideal, the move furthered active-reserve integration involving cutting-edge weapon systems.[35]

For the Air Force Reserve, BRAC 2005 resulted in 7 wing realignments, 1 base closed, and another 28 installations affected. Lt. Gen. John Bradley, commander of the Air Force Reserve Command, observed that the BRAC created "tremendous turmoil," particularly while they were supporting combat operations in Southwest Asia. The air reserve chief noted: "The seven realignments ended up affecting us like seven closures, because when the . . . [AFR] moves its airplanes out of a place, even though we don't own the base, we are shutting down that wing." He emphasized that, unlike regular component personnel who are reassigned after a unit closure, "we and the Air National Guard don't get to do this. A reservist . . . whose airplanes are going away, is sort of on his or her own." More than 8,000 Air Force reservists—11 percent of the AFR's selected reserve strength—were affected by the BRAC. The command helped personnel with new jobs, early retirements, or waivers; developed a web-based guide to assist members with career options; and requested and received temporary authority to fund travel for dislocated reservists to perform inactive-duty training. Even so, Bradley acknowledged, "there's a lot of pain in this." More turmoil came soon after when the Air Force directed a cut in AFR end strength of some 7,700 personnel between FYs 2008 and 2010, largely achieved by reducing individual mobilization augmentee billets.[36]

The National Guard Bureau chief from 2008 to 2012, General Craig R. McKinley became the first four-star guardsman in the nation's history and a member of the Joint Chiefs of Staff, a testament to the Guard's indispensable role. (U.S. Air Force photo)

In December 2010 NGB chief McKinley touted the favorable relationships between the ANG and U.S. Air Force forged during almost a decade of combat operations, but tight budgets could quickly strain those bonds. In 2010 the Air Force sought to remove up to 11 C–130s from several ANG bases and station them with an active wing at Little Rock AFB, Arkansas. Guard leaders objected to the plan, and the Nevada adjutant general, Brig. Gen. William R. Burks, considered it "a mere iron grab." As a result, Congress included in the FY 2011 National Defense Authorization Act (NDAA) a requirement for the Air Force secretary to provide Congress a written agreement between the parties detailing any plan "to transfer aircraft from one component to the other."[37]

Moving Forward and Backward on the Continuum of Service

In early 2008 the final report of the Commission on the National Guard and Reserves devoted considerable attention to the continuum of service, criticizing the Pentagon for failing to adopt a "concrete description of what might actually constitute such a continuum." In October, Secretary Gates issued a white paper on managing the reserve component as an operational force that rectified that deficiency. The document defined continuum of service as:

> management policies that provide variable and flexible service options and levels of participation that could make military service attractive to a broad population . . . consistent with DOD manpower requirements and an individual's ability to serve over . . . a lifetime. . . . The continuum . . . aims to facilitate . . . transparent movement of individuals between active military, reserve military, and civilian service. Such policies offer the Department greater flexibility in accessing the variety of skills required to meet . . . requirements—particularly highly technical and civilian-acquired skills that are difficult to sustain full time in the force.[38]

The reference to participation levels suggested what others, including the CNGR, had envisioned, the establishment of "variable participation reserve units" whose members agreed to serve significantly more than 39 days per year if needed but were not expected to become full-time active-duty personnel. Under Secretary David Chu summed up the advantage: "You didn't . . . have to be stuck with this either 365 or 39 days-of-training model."[39]

A critical part of implementing an effective continuum of service program remained an integrated personnel management system that would ease the movement of members between duty statuses. Throughout the post-9/11 period, many observed the need to improve personnel and pay systems to keep up with the frequent activations of reservists. Despite the Marine Corps being a leader in the area of integrated personnel management, reserve Col. Gregory Baur wrote in the *Marine Corps Gazette* in 2007 of the "pay and administrative horror stories . . . common among reservists" and noted that such incidents arose "especially when going from one status to another." The CNGR summarized the basic issue: "One of the chief complaints among the services is their inability to write an order to bring a reservist on active duty and then efficiently and effectively provide pay and benefits."[40]

The Pentagon had been touting its Defense Integrated Military Human Resources System (DIMHRS) as the answer to the services' pay and personnel management needs. Development of the system had gotten underway in 1998, but nine years later it was the subject of a negative review by the Government Accountability Office. Comptroller General David M. Walker stated that "DOD has yet to deploy DIMHRS, and the concerns it was intended to address persist." The Army was still publicizing the system in 2008 as a commercial solution to the challenges of handling the pay and personnel data across its three components (regular, ARNG, USAR). The department effectively cancelled DIMHRS by early 2009, though it did not fully die until 2010. Senior officials called DIMHRS "a very sad situation," a "money-pit," and "a dismal failure." CNGR chairman Maj. Gen. Arnold Punaro, however, felt that the problem resulted as much from a lack of commitment to implementing the continuum of service concept as from the system's technological challenges. During the commission's work between 2005 and 2008, he found the Pentagon had "not made any of the underlying changes in the laws, rules, regulations, policies, procedures, funding and equipment" to produce a legitimate, ready operational reserve. So the DIMHRS fiasco was only a microcosm of the larger issue, according to Punaro.[41]

There was considerable evidence to support Punaro's point of view. Despite the Pentagon's 2003 mandatory civilian employment tracking initiative, the CNGR found that "DOD has been unable to verify employer data for approximately 24 percent of its reservists reporting civilian employment." That increased the likelihood of conflicts between the need to deploy a reservist and the need to keep them in a critical civilian position. Comptroller General Walker expressed concern that the Department of Defense lacked "adequate transparency over total costs to compensate reservists." He noted those costs had increased about 47 percent from FYs 2000 to 2006, and stated, "Much of the total growth in compensation is driven by the costs for deferred compensation—that is, funds set aside today for future compensation such as retirement pay and health care." Walker questioned the efficiency of setting aside such funds when historically only one in four reservists became eligible for them. He further critiqued the expansion of various types of reservist compensation in recent years without considering the ramifications. "Because costs to compensate service members are found in multiple budgets both within and outside of DOD and are not compiled in a single source to provide total cost," decision makers in Congress and the Defense Department lacked transparency as well as a valid means to determine "affordability, cost effectiveness, and . . . sustainability." The GAO argued that if the nation expected its reservists to remain operational, "DOD will also need to develop an integrated set of policies, procedures, and business systems to more efficiently enable reservists to move from peacetime to operational status"—the crux of a continuum of service.[42]

Another management concern was the need for senior reserve component officers to obtain professional military education, including joint education, intended to improve their strategic thinking. The Goldwater-Nichols legislation of the 1980s had specified joint requirements for active component officers, but it neglected the reserves. Three decades later, education for senior officers remained a challenge in the Army Reserve (and other components as well) despite the increased involvement in combat operations since 2001. John F. Hargraves, the civilian deputy director of training at the Army Reserve headquarters, commented:

> If you look at the Army Reserve colonel . . . [Troop Program Unit, or TPU] cohort, you can become an Army Reserve colonel without ever completing the Army War College or Senior Service College. . . . [In 2010] less than 30 percent of the Army Reserve Colonels in TPUs were War College grads. Which is exactly the opposite of the active component force. . . . And so, if we're going to remain a viable federal reserve into the future we've got to have officers and senior leaders who have got that broad perspective.[43]

The need for education competed, of course, with the demands of an unusually high reserve operational tempo, as well as civilian employment and family considerations.[44]

For the most part, the continuum of service remained largely aspirational. The Navy Reserve chief, Vice Adm. Dirk J. Debbink, made the continuum one of his three strategic focus areas from 2010 through 2012. But most of the initiatives were limited in scope, such as promoting the theme of being a "Sailor for Life" and "the value of 'Staying Navy' through service in the Navy Reserve," counseling regular personnel on reserve options as they neared release from active duty, expanding professional development opportunities for reservists, reviewing family programs, and recognizing employers' support. In 2011 one new idea Debbink pursued was Variable Service, which offered part-time sailors a continuum of service option that fell between typical Volunteer Training Unit service requirements and the Individual Ready Reserve, but that only encompassed unpaid training at the very low end of the service spectrum. As Punaro had observed, it would take serious and thorough legislative change to make continuum of service a viable reality.[45]

In some cases reserve component leaders pushed back when faced with the consequences of closer integration with the regular component. In 2008 Army Reserve chief Lieutenant General Stultz reported that increasing numbers of his soldiers were seeking transfers into the regular Army. The following year he implemented a rule that discouraged the trend by requiring mobilized enlisted USAR personnel to wait until after demobilization to apply for a transfer. At the same time, he encouraged regular Army soldiers to join the reserve by offering them a $10,000 bonus plus a guarantee that they would not be mobilized for two full years. At the fall 2010 Corona meeting of Air Force senior leaders, the four-star generals decided to apply the service's policy of 179-day deployments to all airmen who served in an Air Expeditionary Force—which included air reservists (ANG/USAFR). The change apparently came without input from the air reserves, whose standard (and predictable) deployment under the Air Expeditionary Force construct had been 120 days. Historically, the shorter time frame favored volunteerism, and Nevada Adjutant Brig. Gen. William Burks complained that the new policy was "a severe, if not fatal, blow" to volunteerism in the air reserves, if not also to integration efforts between the air components. Burks linked the attempted C–130 "iron grab" with the newly imposed 179-day requirement as another Air Force plan "to slowly diminish the Air Guard fleet."[46]

Burks' concern raised the question of which of the two basic processes to favor when activating citizen-soldiers—mobilization or volunteerism? The air reserves tended to favor volunteerism—as had Defense Secretary Rumsfeld—arguing that it helped to relieve the burdens on those who otherwise would be mobilized involuntarily to meet requirements. Other senior leaders emphasized that the failure to employ the mobilization option threatened to undermine its legitimacy in the long term as an accepted tool for protecting the nation's security. Moreover, many reservists who desired to serve operationally—and repeatedly—sought the protection of a mobilization order to mollify family members and employers. Lt. Gen. Harry M. Wyatt III, the ANG director, remembered airmen who said to him: "Yeah, I don't mind going, but you really need to mobilize me this time. If I raise my hand one more time, my spouse is going to shoot me." If continuum of service only meant serving for shorter periods when it suited the citizen-soldier, it would never fill the role that Pentagon leaders hoped it would. At the end of 2010 General Craig McKinley, the NGB chief, admitted as much when he cited the potential end to existing partial mobilization authority and the long-term requirement for a "continuing ready access to the National Guard" that would alleviate the fears of active component leaders "that they won't be able to get us in a rapid-enough way to use us properly."[47]

Refining the Reserve Experience

Early in the Long War, short notice of mobilization constituted a challenge for countless reservists. Service members and their families had little time to prepare for extended absences, and it delayed civilian employers in finding and training replacements. In general the timelines improved by 2007–2011.

Following his 2009 deployment for Iraqi Freedom, Marine Corps Reserve Lt. Col. J. Eric Davis noted: "The notification and activation process is the single biggest improvement that I've seen since my last activation in 2003." The first time, although he had been aware for three months that he would be called, official notification came just two days prior to his actual departure. Six years later, much longer advance notification allowed Davis and his employer to work out a plan for his absence. Davis also felt that family readiness had "greatly improved in the last few years." The Pentagon's May 2008 announcement alerting four ARNG brigades for deployment to Iraq in spring 2009 and a fifth brigade to Afghanistan in spring 2010 represented a dramatic improvement in terms of notification timelines from earlier in the war.[48]

After a decade of increased military duty for so many citizen-soldiers, two Pentagon-sponsored studies of employer support indicated that policies in that realm were working reasonably well, perhaps bolstered by a continuing high level of public support for military service members. In a 2011 survey of 78,000 businesses, 86 percent of employers were "satisfied overall" with reserve employees, and only 2 percent were "not satisfied." Seventy-nine percent of employers said their reservists "are good team players" with only 3 percent in disagreement. The results of a 2012 survey of 112,000 reserve component personnel were not as positive, but still showed that only a minority experienced significant issues. Seventy-four percent reported employers to be supportive of their military obligations, and more than two-thirds indicated they did not experience employment problems such as demotion, loss of job, or hostility from coworkers or supervisors related to their military service.[49]

Another effort to make service more attractive and improve medical readiness was the three-tiered TRICARE Reserve Select program that became available in October 2006. It increased health-care options for many reservists ineligible under the original system, but there was room for further improvement. Responding to the National Guard Association's initiative, Congress revamped the system to make all Selected Reserve members eligible, starting in October 2007, for a single premium level of health insurance virtually identical to TRICARE Standard/Extra, the plan for active-duty personnel, and much less expensive than the former three tiers. Just one year later, TRICARE Reserve Select membership had doubled to some 80,000 personnel and their families; by September 2009 coverage increased to more than 100,000. Thus, step by step, the reserve component gained increased access to health-care coverage at the low rates enjoyed by their regular counterparts—another reminder that maintaining a truly ready operational reserve was expensive. Three years later the 2010 NDAA further enhanced the program. For the first time reservists who had retired but were awaiting retirement pay that would start at age 60 (known as gray area retirees) became eligible for TRICARE Standard coverage. The law also doubled eligibility for TRICARE coverage to reservists from the previous 90 to a full 180 days before mobilization, and provided that personnel could not be denied coverage due to preexisting conditions.[50]

The Commission on the National Guard and Reserves argued in 2008 that mobilization and demobilization must be seen as "steps in creating a seamless, integrated force, and the relevant policies and procedures must be adjusted accordingly." The Marine Corps' 2010 version of the *Total Force Mobilization, Activation, Integration, and Deactivation Plan* paid more attention to deactivation than its 2007 predecessor, with the emphasis expanding beyond units to the "rapid deactivation and administrative out-processing of IRR, IMA and retired Marines." The CNGR noted that demobilization should be treated as "the first opportunity to prepare a reservist for his or her next deployment." When Lieutenant General Stultz, the USAR chief, testified to the commission he pointed out the critical role of demobilization in one of his most challenging issues, medical readiness, of which dental was a major part: "We need to treat the soldier . . . just like we treat a piece of equipment. When we bring a piece of equipment back from theater and it's returned . . . it comes back to me [within] standards. It's the Army's responsibility to fix that piece of equipment before it comes back to me." He observed that the Army lacked a policy requiring it to "take care of dental needs at the demobilization site," even though a soldier's dental health could be expected to deteriorate during a deployment from "lack of dental care while in the desert, plus their diet."[51]

With new authority from Congress, in October 2008, the Army Select Reserve Dental Readiness System began providing dental examinations without regard to where their unit was in the rotation cycle. The new system joined two other programs, including Demobilization Dental Reset, in demonstrating an increased commitment to the long-term dental readiness of Army reservists. Stultz oversaw a significant increase in Army Reserve mobilization dental readiness from just above 50 percent to 74 percent by 2010 and 78 percent in 2011. Secretary of the Army Geren also emphasized the issue in various forums, proving that dental readiness was by no means too far down in the weeds for the Army's civilian boss. In 2011 David McGinnis noted that "all Components have met or exceeded the Dental Readiness goal of 75%" and were trending in the right direction.[52]

Another aspect of demobilization that received increasing emphasis was reintegration of the returning citizen-soldier with his family and community. As the conflict wore on, leaders recognized that in shortening drastically the transit and downtime for personnel leaving the combat theater, the opportunity to talk about their experiences with their comrades-in-arms, decompress,

As the needs of reservists became more widely understood, in FY 2008 Congress mandated the nationwide Guard-Reserve Yellow Ribbon program to address predeployment, deployment, postdeployment, and demobilization concerns of reservists and families. (U.S. Air National Guard photo by Tech. Sgt. Aaron Perkins)

and begin preparing for the transition to life at home had been lost or, at best, truncated. The growing appreciation of post-traumatic stress disorder's unseen dangers argued all the more for some sort of institutionalized program with more substance than a single item on a mandatory redeployment checklist that few took seriously. In the same fashion as dental readiness, focused efforts at the end of active duty could pay dividends in improving personal and family readiness for the next deployment. Two initiatives in this area, the Returning Warrior Workshop (RWW) and the Yellow Ribbon Reintegration Program, better known simply as Yellow Ribbon, gained prominence.[53]

The RWW program predated Yellow Ribbon by about a year and was later rolled into Yellow Ribbon. During 2007–2008 the Navy Reserve formalized RWW, which arguably became one of the reserve component's most successful transitional programs. Its origins stemmed from the Navy's Deployment Support Program, a post-9/11 development intended primarily to help individual augmentees. In 2006 the Navy's Southwest Reserve Component Command turned its attention to the reintegration needs of all its Selected Reserve personnel returning from combat zones, developing the RWW concept and testing it at a pilot event in Flagstaff, Arizona. Workshop planners sought "to inform, educate and honor the sailors and their families who supported them during their deployment." By 2008 the program involved an entire weekend, with the service member able to bring a spouse, parent, sibling, or friend to attend the event, and all lodging and meals covered. A manual stated the program's purpose: "disseminate information helpful to the demobilized sailor and their family, and recognize and honor the service member and spouse . . . provide a large amount of information in a short . . . time (a drill weekend) . . . to both the service member and the person who supported them most during their deployment." The format included presentations by health-care, insurance, marriage, and communications professionals, while small-group breakout sessions offered opportunities for personal interaction. Through 2008, most RWWs included about 100 service members.[54]

The program appeared well-received and worthwhile. One attendee revealed: "Since that weekend, we have [been] attending counseling on a regular basis and I am very happy to announce we are no longer considering a divorce. We were also able to get a great deal of support information that we never knew was even available." Vice Admiral Cotton considered RWW a great success and lauded his deputy chief, Rear Adm. Craig O. McDonald, and his team for taking the program from its beginnings in the Southwest region and developing and institutionalizing it throughout the Navy. The RWW program eventually shared certain resources with the subsequent Yellow Ribbon program, including vendors, locations, materials, and partial funding.[55]

As the operational tempo continued at a high level, leaders in Congress, at the Pentagon, and in statehouses nationwide recognized the need to broaden and improve support for citizen-soldiers returning from deployment and their families. The 2004 suicide of a New Hampshire air guardsman just 24 hours after his return home from Iraq generated early attention toward the issue. In response, the state's adjutant general began a postdemobilization initiative for guardsmen. The Minnesota Guard's adjutant general, Larry W. Shellito, a Vietnam veteran, wanted something better for returning warriors than what his generation had experienced. In 2005 he tapped his state's deputy chaplain, John Morris, who threw himself into the effort, initially known as "Beyond the Yellow Ribbon."[56]

Chaplain Morris needed no convincing to take part: he had just returned from Fallujah, Iraq, and was well aware of the stresses of combat. He developed a program that included weekend reintegration events held 30, 60, and 90 days following a unit's demobilization. Each gathering emphasized particular topics. At the 30-day mark, it was "parenting and marital relationships," plus a job fair and explanations of benefits. At 60 days, health issues took center stage, to include "substance and gambling abuse and anger management." At the 90-day point—by which time previously undiagnosed neurological issues might be expected to appear (although this took longer in some cases)—personnel underwent a comprehensive health assessment. At first, the 30-day event posed a problem because policy forbade any mandatory formation for a Guard unit within 60 days of release from active duty, but the defense secretary granted a waiver.[57]

Observing the Minnesota program's favorable results, Representative John Kline (R–MN) led the House to include language in the FY 2008 Defense authorization bill directing the defense secretary to create the nationwide Guard-Reserve Yellow Ribbon Reintegration Program. The program encompassed predeployment, deployment, demobilization, and postdeployment concerns of reservists and their families. The legislation tasked the under secretary of defense for personnel and readiness office to "administer all reintegration programs in coordination with State National Guard organizations" as well as with reserve component family and support programs. The law called for an advisory board comprised mainly of the directors and chiefs of the six DoD reserve components plus the ASD(RA). With President George W. Bush's signature on the 2008 defense act, the Minnesota program went nationwide, expanding rapidly. About one-quarter million citizen-soldiers and family members had attended a Yellow Ribbon event by the end of 2009. In FY 2009 alone, the Guard reported holding more than 1,000 events, while the Army Reserve hosted some 250 gatherings. The following year, the USAR reported 525 Yellow Ribbon events serving 26,000 soldiers and 28,000 family members. The Coast Guard was not covered under the Defense Department's legislation, and when David McGinnis realized that service wasn't receiving funding for Yellow Ribbon through the Department of Homeland Security, he brought them into the ASD(RA)'s program. In fall 2010 the Coast Guard held its first event for returning deployers and their families.[58]

The diffuse nature of the reserves, with six different Defense Department components, played out in differing approaches to the implementation of Yellow Ribbon. While the law provided that "State National Guard and Reserve organizations shall hold reintegration activities at the 30-day, 60-day, and 90-day interval following demobilization," the services followed different timelines. The Army Reserve typically held the three events 30, 60, and 90 days after the date of demobilization. But some organizations interpreted it to mean that the second event should be held 60 days after the first event, and the third event 90 days after the second event, thus spreading them out over 180 days. In addition, the services differed on how they chose a location and participants. An Army Guard or Army Reserve event, for example, might be held locally, attended by a single unit's members and spouses or guests; a Navy Reserve or Air Force Reserve event might be a regional affair attended by reservists from various units, as well as individual augmentees. The NGB's Janet S. Salotti, chief of the reintegration/transition office, noted that some states were more creative than others, citing a 2010 Oregon Guard-sponsored event held at Clackamus Community College, with attendees staying in dormitories and local vendors providing the meals. She called Oregon "a robust state" for Yellow Ribbon.[59]

In July 2011 acting ASD(RA) McGinnis hailed Yellow Ribbon's goal of fostering resiliency among service members and families. Research increasingly linked the level of resiliency—the ability to deal with a setback—with the likelihood of PTSD. In recognition of the program's importance, the USD(P&R) nearly doubled Yellow Ribbon's funding from $12.9 million in FY 2010 to $23.5 million the next year. McGinnis noted that the program "is not a 'war time only' requirement, but must remain an enduring mission." In 2013 the House Armed Services Committee reaffirmed its support for Yellow Ribbon to be maintained as a "current, flexible, and viable" program because it believed there would continue to be a requirement for mobilizing the reserves in support of contingency operations for some years to come.[60]

In 2008 there were about 700 military family centers nationwide (400 operated by the Guard), but some citizen-soldiers still lacked easy access due to distance. Laura Stultz, wife of the Army Reserve chief, initiated what became known as family program virtual installations. Situated in areas distant from military bases, they would offer to reservists and their families the type of assistance normally found on a base. By 2010 there were three such sites, located in Rochester, New York; Brevard, North Carolina; and Coraopolis, Pennsylvania.[61]

Another major issue, which applied equally to citizen-soldiers and regulars, involved the care of combat wounded. The nation had not engaged in extended warfare since Vietnam, so there was a lack of recent experience in handling a large number of wounded personnel. The prevalence of severe injuries resulting from improvised explosive devices further strained the military and veteran medical systems. The matter came to the fore in early 2007 with media attention to problems at the Walter Reed Army Medical Center in Washington, DC. Congress responded with passage of the Wounded Warrior provisions in the FY 2008 NDAA. The law called for improvements in the housing of combat wounded, greater emphasis on understanding and treating traumatic brain injury (TBI), reform of the physical disability evaluation system, greater coordination between DoD and the Department of Veterans Affairs, better electronic medical records, and enhanced support for the families of the wounded.[62]

To better focus on the needs of wounded personnel and their families, in April 2007 the Marine Corps established the Wounded Warrior Regiment (WWR) at Quantico, Virginia. Maj. Christopher J. Iazzetta, the operations officer for the regiment's Marine for Life program from 2008 to 2012, noted the vast majority of personnel assigned to staff the organization were mobilized reservists. Also significant was the stand-up of a wounded warrior call center at Quantico in 2007, providing 24/7 toll-free service that enabled the wounded or a family member to request assistance with any nonmedical issue from a trained case manager over the phone. A reserve medical entitlements determination section at the WWR tracked and managed reserve Marines' care, both medical and nonmedical. In 2010 the incoming Marine Corps commandant, General James F. Amos, called the WWR "probably one of the greatest success stories coming out of this war." The other services took similar steps to ensure better care for their wounded warriors. One important issue was whether to keep personnel on active duty while they went through the disability evaluation process. Contrary to the Army's preference, McGinnis believed soldiers should remain on active duty until a disability finding was determined, citing research that four-fifths of the disability evaluation cases in the Army were located in only 11 Army hospitals.[63]

One ominous aspect of the situation was exemplified in the Air Guard. As of April 2013, more than half of its 314 wounded warriors had been diagnosed with PTSD. The invisible wounds of PTSD and TBI not only could be severe; they were the ones many were reticent to acknowledge and the ones often missed. In 2014 David McGinnis candidly voiced his opinion that, in general, the military's operational commands had been more aggressive in pursuing advances in PTSD and TBI treatment than the government's medical community. McGinnis noted the interest in learning about the approach of NASCAR and the NFL to cutting-edge TBI technology—the result of realizing that a race driver's brain injury from a crash at Bristol may not be much different than a HMMWV driver's from an improvised explosive device at Balad. A Michigan Army Guard senior officer described TBI as "the signature injury of the conflicts in Iraq and Afghanistan."[64]

—— Conclusion ——

Between 2007 and 2011 the Army National Guard and Army Reserve gradually moved toward the goal of 12-month mobilizations that Secretary Gates had directed in his far-reaching 19 January 2007 memorandum. While the desired BOG-to-dwell ratio was far from reality for many ground units, at least reservists and their families and employers had the assurance that a predictable and equitable rotation system was in the works. The reserve component also pioneered new missions and organizations, such as the agricultural development team program for counterinsurgency operations, and the homeland response force teams and domestic all-hazards response teams for homeland security. In each of these cases, the unique capabilities of citizen-soldiers filled a niche that would be difficult and expensive, if not impossible, for the regular component to replicate.

In 2008 the Commission on the National Guard and Reserves produced a comprehensive final report that reaffirmed the importance of many areas the services had already identified for improvements, especially in the pay, personnel, and career management of reserve component members. The DIMHRS failure hindered the services (excepting the Marine Corps and Coast Guard, which had their own integrated systems) in their attempts to solve the pay and personnel challenges at the core of the continuum of service concept. The continued expansion of programs to accommodate the demands of an operational reserve, from increased access to TRICARE Reserve Select to the highly acclaimed Yellow Ribbon Reintegration effort, were making it possible to rely heavily on the reserve component over the long haul, but at an ever-increasing cost.[65]

As the United States considered its post-Iraq/Afghanistan force structure and whether the decade-long model of an operational reserve would survive, some leaders warned that "the progress made in the last few years is not irreversible and that old tensions between active and reserve components could renew." Nearing retirement in 2010, Lieutenant General Blum, the deputy commander of Northern Command, put it plainly: "There are people out there who would like to put the toothpaste back in the tube." Defense Secretary Gates surmised just prior to his departure from the Pentagon in 2011 that the Guard and reserve would continue to have an operational role, but it would be years before that particular "known unknown"—an apt phrase from his predecessor—could be definitively answered.[66]

CHAPTER 8

Conclusion

I n January 2008 retired Maj. Gen. Arnold Punaro, the chairman of the Commission on the National Guard and Reserves, wrote that an "explicit recognition" had dawned on Pentagon leaders and planners, Congress, families, and employers across the country regarding "the evolution of the reserve components from a purely strategic force, with lengthy mobilization times designed to meet Cold War threats from large nation-states, to an operational force." Many civilians probably did not understand the nuances between strategic and operational, but they knew that family members, friends, neighbors, and coworkers had begun spending more time on military duty and had even deployed overseas, perhaps multiple times.[1]

A Militia Nation Returns to Its Roots

The initial objective of this study was to chronicle that evolution of the reserve component beginning in the 1990s from a strategic role (rarely called upon and only in time of major conflict) to an operational one (routinely and frequently employed in situations short of full-scale war). But in looking at the long arc of the history of American reserve policy, it becomes clear that this is not so much a new paradigm, as it is an echo of the original mission of the reserve component at the dawn of the United States. The founding fathers viewed a standing army as too expensive, too threatening, and largely unnecessary, and therefore placed the main weight of national defense on the nation's citizen-soldiers. Thus the militia carried a large share of the burden in early campaigns against American Indians, insurrectionists, and even the British in the War of 1812. That heavy reliance upon the militia to support a miniscule regular army in numerous small operations and a major war rivaled, and in many respects exceeded, the role of the reserve component during the 1990s and up through today.

Similar to the early years of the republic, today the United States is neither willing nor able to pay the cost of maintaining a regular force large enough to deal with all the missions undertaken in the name of national security. And while the American public generally no longer sees a standing military as a serious threat to democracy, after the Vietnam War the regulars themselves were wary of embarking on operations without strong public support and thus reemphasized a reliance on citizen-soldiers as a means to ensure that popular backing would be present. As a result of those two impetuses, although the repeated forays in the Balkans, Somalia, Haiti, and elsewhere in the 1990s were not much more frequent than campaigns in the first couple of decades of U.S. history, the role of the reserves was roughly equally critical in both eras.

The common thread across nearly 250 years of history is that the demands placed on the reserve component have increased tremendously as a result of the changing nature of U.S. national security requirements and of war itself. In the latter realm, in the late 1700s it was possible to expect nearly every eligible male to provide his own musket, powder horn, and cartridge box, and to periodically devote a few hours to practicing the rudiments of drill. A well-led militia force, by itself or in support of a small cadre of regulars, could protect the new nation against most of the threats it faced. The expanse of the oceans and the limitations of transportation meant the fledgling country did not have to face the full brunt of invasion by a large professional army. Merchant sailors and their ships also could readily supplement the Navy in times of conflict. As war grew increasingly complex, in technology and in tactics, it outstripped the ability of citizens to arm themselves properly and to train on a part-time basis at a level that would enable them to engage in combat on short notice, both as individuals and as members of a unit. A hundred neighbors cannot go to the village green these days and practice combined-arms warfare, and the country cannot readily convert commercial ships and aircraft to combat platforms.

From the end of the War of 1812 until the beginning of World War II, the nation maintained a small regular force, but it was sufficient to handle most operations short of major war, such as the Indian campaigns throughout the 1800s and the Banana Wars in the Caribbean between the World Wars. When necessary, volunteers and draftees joined with the Guard and reserve to reinforce regulars for large-scale conflicts, and often vastly outnumbered their full-time compatriots. As the United States grew into a superpower and took on the task of aiding allies overseas and maintaining international order, the scale of military operations, even ones short of major war, grew much larger, more challenging, and more expensive. Projecting power rapidly over long distances and maintaining large forces stationed far from home cost a great deal more than simply defending one's borders. Since the end of the Cold War, our allies have devoted a decreasing share of their resources to national security, thus increasing the relative burden on the United States. At the same time, the global economic dominance that the United States enjoyed in the post–World War II era has slowly receded, leaving the country with reduced capacity for military spending in comparison with the rest of the world. Likewise, growing requirements for social spending have competed for scarce budget dollars. That increasing disconnect between a greater use of American military power and the willingness and ability of the nation to pay for it led policymakers to reemphasize the role of citizen-soldiers in providing a less-expensive supplement to full-time active-duty forces.

Those transformations in warfare, defense policy, and economics, in turn, have driven dramatic alterations in reserve policy over the past two-plus centuries in an effort to maintain citizen-soldiers as a relevant part of national defense. The recurring theme, however, has been that efforts to fix the shortcomings in the system revealed by the most recent resort to reserve forces have never proven sufficient when the next mobilization occurred. In almost every case, the reserve component has been less ready than needed, but not due to any deficiency in the willingness of citizen-soldiers to serve their country. Instead, nearly every problem can be traced to flaws in the laws and policies governing the reserves. To cite one example, the long-running issue of poor dental readiness in the reserve component did not arise because reservists and guardsmen are less careful about their teeth than their active-duty counterparts, but simply because policies never provided them the same access to free dental care.

On the Horns of Our Own Dilemma

Sometimes the inadequate state of reserve component capability and readiness has been due to the aforementioned changes in the nature of war and national security requirements. Like the old saying that the military always prepares for the last war, our national leaders (civilian and military) have rarely dealt with emerging challenges to the reserve system until an adverse impact occurred as a result of mobilization. Often, however, the difficulty has stemmed less from a failure to foresee problems than from the inability to find a solution that leaders could agree upon before negative consequences forced their hand. Even then, the reforms usually have fallen short of what was truly required. In many cases, this was not a failure of leadership per se. Rather it has been a function of the challenge of identifying and implementing good alternatives, arising from a host of reasons generally beyond the control of those making policy.

A major hurdle to finding common ground to improve our reserve system is built into the very nature of the U.S. Constitution, with a representative government and federalism. Members of both houses of Congress must carry out the will of their respective citizens while working for the common good, and the states are not mere regional subsets of the national government but have certain realms of authority in their own right. Like Emory Upton or the Gray Board, one might wish to simplify matters with a federal-only reserve component, but short of a dramatic and unimaginable change in our Constitution or public opinion, for the foreseeable future we will have a system that includes a state-based National Guard and must operate within that framework.

Other issues arise from contradictions that are inherent and thus unavoidable. In the same fashion that maneuver warfare theory seeks to put an enemy on the horns of a dilemma where there are no obviously good choices, leaders are faced with many serious quandaries in formulating reserve policy. One simple example involves personnel who have critical civilian occupations. There have been efforts over the years to identify such individuals, so that they are not mobilized when doing so would create unwanted disruption, whether it be keeping police on duty to deal with terrorism or machinists at work producing weapons. While these attempts have obvious merit, they also come at a significant cost. Not mobilizing some members of a unit results in a loss of cohesion at the very moment when that organization is going off to war. And in many cases, the skills that make them valuable at home are the same ones that the reserve system is counting on them to provide, such as civilian police, firefighters, medical personnel, and so forth. Policy could dictate that no one in critical occupations be permitted to join the reserve component, but that would both limit the pool of people who could enlist and cut off a source of valuable expertise. A reserve combat medic who works full time as an emergency medical technician is inherently better trained and prepared than one who holds a nonmedical civilian occupation.

One dilemma that developed over time and is unlikely to be remedied is the mismatch between the types of units in the Guard and the nature of state-centered missions. It would make sense if many service and support functions resided primarily in the Guard, since governors have a need for military police, engineering, transportation, water processing, and other capabilities that can help with handling domestic emergencies. Instead, the Guard has a disproportionate percentage of combat units, even though armored brigades and jet fighter squadrons have little utility at the state level. The Guard had to choose between the not-inconsiderable value of tradition, which can be a strong motivator to soldiers, and the more practical benefit of particular capabilities to state missions. It opted to maintain its strong historic connection with its original combat regiments and divisions, while the regular Army used the 1993 Offsite Agreement to focus more of its federal Army Reserve on service and support functions needed to get its own divisions and corps into combat on short notice. In 1947 the Air Force inherited the Guard's aviation units and found it politically impossible to relegate the new ANG to a nonflying role.

Another feature of our reserve system that creates built-in dilemmas is its geographic basis in both the state and federal components. While this contributes to unit cohesion (people from the same community or region serve together) and is efficient in some respects (personnel can get to drill weekends with minimal travel), it also presents major challenges. One is the concentration of loss in a single locality when a reserve unit suffers heavy casualties. Another and more universal problem arises from the frequent mismatch of individual skills to unit requirements, which routinely arises in several ways. A person enlists and acquires a skill for his local unit, only to move later to another area where no organization requires that specialty. A service member leaves active duty and takes up residence in an area where available units do not need her skill. Or a service repurposes a unit, rendering many or all of its personnel unqualified. In each of these cases, much of the experience gained by individuals through past training is rendered irrelevant, and they must undergo costly and time-consuming retraining. And for some considerable period they fill a billet for which they are unqualified, rendering the unit less ready and leading to a loss of unit cohesion during mobilization, since they will have to be replaced from some other source. The geographic system also makes it more difficult for individuals to advance into appropriate billets for their rank and thus gain the experience they need as their career progresses. Finally, and perhaps most significant, it leads to constant churn in units as individuals move due to their civilian schooling, job changes, or other considerations. (There is turnover in active-duty units as well, but it generally involves routine end-of-tour departures that include scheduled arrival of trained replacements.) Geographic organization thus decreases unit cohesion, in direct negation of the benefit from having neighbors serve together.

As the skills required by modern warfare have grown more complex and the requirement for rapid employment after mobilization has grown more urgent, the need has risen for more and better premobilization training. The day is long gone when an individual could enlist in his local unit and learn on the job, or when units could muster for a couple of hours one evening in the drill hall and conduct useful training. And the trend continues toward even greater demands on the time of citizen-soldiers. The Army Force Generation process, for instance, has required units to conduct more than the usual 48 drills and two weeks of active duty in the years immediately preceding mobilization. The continuum of service option is predicated on some reservists devoting more than the usual amount of time to active service. But those demands for more time run counter to the need for citizen-soldiers to maintain and advance their civilian careers, and may also impact the willingness of employers and families to accept participation in the reserve component. If reserve service makes it too difficult to be successful in many civilian career fields, that will necessarily reduce the pool of people willing to serve. On the other hand, emerging trends such as the decline of standard nine-to-five, 40-hour-week positions and the rise of the gig economy may make greater reserve service possible and more attractive.

This issue of time devoted to reserve service is especially salient as the nation's involvement in conflicts draws down from the levels experienced since 2001. Several leaders have advocated for the United States to preserve the high state of readiness and the wealth of combat experience in the operationalized reserve by continuing to routinely deploy it on a rotating basis. In 2011, Marine Corps Lt. Col. Morgan Mann recommended mobilizing "at least one Reserve infantry battalion per year in support of our global operational commitments" to maintain the reserve component's relevance to the active component, "inject fresh operational experiences into the units, and ensure that our Reserve regiments and division stay proficient." Dennis McCarthy, then the assistant secretary of defense for reserve affairs, offered a similar rationale for continuing to operationally employ the reserve force. First, when the reserve component is not visible "as a part of the everyday force . . . it becomes a resource competitor with the Active Component"; second, "if you don't use the Reserve Component, it atrophies"; and, third, if it goes unused, "the best people don't want to waste their time with it." McCarthy's successor, David McGinnis, testified before a House subcommittee that prudence dictated the reserve component continue its "expanded role" as part of the operational total force: "To lose the training, experience and integration of the Reserve components by relegating them to a strategic reserve would squander a resource we can't afford to waste." David Chu, the long-serving under secretary of defense for personnel and readiness, observed in 2007: "Most Guardsmen and Reservists have already decided whether they want to join, remain in or leave the military based on the expectations of an operational reserve." Arnold Punaro, chairman of the Commission on the National Guard and Reserve, opined that those joining the reserves at that time were "not getting in there to hide out, and if we get to the point where we are not using the Guard and Reserve, it's going to significantly deteriorate in terms of the quality of people that go in it." Maj. Gen. Raymond Carpenter, the Army National Guard's acting director from 2009 to 2011, said bluntly: "The National Guard needs to stay in combat." In 2011, the Kansas adjutant general, Maj. Gen. Lee Tafanelli, stated: "[Today's guardsmen] want to be decisively engaged. They want to be challenged. Or they don't want to be there." That same year the Joint Chiefs of Staff vice chairman, Admiral James A. Winnefeld Jr., flatly asserted: "Returning the reserve component, especially the National Guard, in particular, to [a] strictly strategic reserve role is a nonstarter."[2]

These recent opinions harken back to the Gray Board's 1948 recommendation to strengthen the reserve component "by rotating reserve force personnel and units on active duty for substantial periods of time." Shifting to a system of periodic mobilization of slices of the reserve raises a number of issues. Secretary Gates decreed the model of one year in six to balance the need to support the active force in war while not unduly burdening the reserve component. Would that be the best ratio to maintain reserve readiness in peacetime? Certainly a great deal of the benefit of a year on active duty would dissipate by the third or fourth year, as the temporary benefits of active duty training steadily eroded and as personnel departed the unit. Perhaps more important, what would be the impact on the size of the active component force? Over time, would the nation and Congress decide that the regulars could be cut by one-sixth due to the ongoing contribution of the reserve component? Or would the mobilizations be cut as an unnecessary expense in peacetime?[3]

Routine mobilization also would be a major departure from historic norms of part-time service. While personnel may want to serve on active duty during a conflict, it is difficult to predict if that will hold true during periods of relative peace, when the apparent need is less urgent and the rewards (such as combat pay, veterans status, and fulfilling a patriotic duty) are much reduced or nonexistent. Employers and families who accepted the sacrifice of repeated mobilization during war also may not be as accommodating when the purpose is something much more nebulous like maintaining readiness. The mobilization for the Berlin Crisis in 1961 resulted in some resentment, but activations for frequent operations in the 1990s generally did not (though they involved real world requirements, not routine deployments to enhance readiness).

Routine mobilization of units also would have a major impact on the Individual Ready Reserve, since experience has shown that a significant number of individual replacements are always needed. That percentage might be smaller for noncombat mobilizations, as unqualified individuals in a unit would not necessarily need to be replaced, but more unit personnel might also find reasons to opt out of peacetime active duty. Since IRRs by definition are not generally interested in serving with a unit, the likelihood of routine mobilization might drive down IRR membership to only those who have a required commitment at the end of their initial active-duty contract. Only experience over time will reveal whether the benefits of a peacetime operational reserve can be obtained without imposing an unacceptable cost in reduced willingness to participate.

The Challenge of Increasing Integration

Another longstanding issue is friction between the active and reserve components, which predates the nation itself. Throughout most of this long history, relations generally have been chilly at best, and often downright hostile. Assistant Secretary of Defense for Reserve Affairs Thomas Hall put it plainly: "Cultural differences are a euphemism . . . [for] 'why doesn't the active duty *like* the Reserves?'" In the aftermath of Desert Shield and Desert Storm, Col. David E. Shaver, an Army War College faculty member who had served in all three Army components, addressed "the root causes of AC/RC problems. . . . For an RC officer, the AC officer seems to possess an *arrogance toward*, and an *ignorance of*, the RC." Although he admitted that feeling of dislike often went both ways, he was convinced that "elimination of the perception of AC arrogance, more than anything else, save resolving the AC lack of knowledge about the RC, is vital to the harmonization of the components." Secretary McCarthy focused on knowledge in disparaging an all-too-common mindset in the AC:

> If you had a Marine Corps battalion commander stand up in front of his boss and say, "Well, I don't know much about fire support, but I got a little guy [on] my staff that takes care of that for me," that would be his last word as a battalion commander. But if he said, "I don't know much about the Marine Corps Reserve, but I got a little guy on my staff who takes care of that," well, that's great....This [Reserve] is a supporting arm, and I would suggest that if you don't know how to employ this supporting arm at whatever level you happen to be at, then you're not a "full-up round."

A perfect example of regulars lacking respect for citizen-soldiers came in 2007 as the Army Guard sought to shorten postmobilization training for its combat units in order to maximize their deployed time. The ARNG director, Lt. Gen. Clyde Vaughn, viewed the matter of regulars insisting on revalidating training as one of "trust between the components."[4]

Secretary of Defense William Cohen's landmark 1997 memorandum highlighted the inseparable links between intercomponent relations, integration, and combat readiness. He called on the Pentagon "to eliminate 'all residual barriers structural and cultural' to effective integration of the Reserve and

Active components into a 'seamless Total Force.'" He defined integration as the "conditions of readiness and trust needed for the leadership of all levels to have well-justified confidence that Reserve component units are trained and equipped to serve as an effective part of the joint and combined force within whatever timelines are set for the unit—in peace and war." McCarthy, Vice Adm. John Cotton, and other senior leaders believed the decade of combat operations after 9/11 produced an unprecedented degree of understanding and a corresponding reduction of friction between the active and reserve components. But they also warned that familiarity and trust are highly perishable commodities that might dissipate when combat operations wind down, reserve units cease to deploy periodically, and defense budgets shrink.[5]

Greater integration of the active and reserve components would reduce friction between them, but poses its own dilemmas. The Coast Guard led the way in integration in the 1990s, to the point of disestablishing reserve units and merging the personnel into active commands. After 9/11 the service realized it had to emphasize the special administrative needs of reservists to ensure that their critical requirements did not get overlooked. The Marine Corps, from very early in the life of its reserve component, employed a different approach, establishing the Inspector-Instructor system, with active duty Marines bringing needed expertise to reserve training and returning to the regular side with firsthand knowledge of reserve capabilities. The Army, which has a regular-to-Selected Reserve/Guard ratio of less than one to one (as opposed to the Marine Corps' more than four to one), might find it much more difficult to implement a similar system.

Secretary of Defense Robert Gates acknowledged another potential drawback in 2008 when he directed the service secretaries: "Integrate AC and RC organizations to the greatest extent practicable, including the use of cross-component assignments, both AC to RC and RC to AC. Such assignments should be considered as career enhancing and not detrimental to a Service member's career progression." If carried out to the extent necessary to have widespread effect, exchange tours could create new problems. A regular serving as an operations officer in a reserve infantry battalion, for instance, would acquire much less practical experience than doing so in an active unit. Even if a promotion board did not hold that against the officer, the fact would remain that the officer would be less prepared for more senior billets than a counterpart who performed the same function in an active-duty battalion. Likewise, frequent activations of reserve component personnel to serve in regular units might prove too disruptive to civilian careers and family life, especially if these tours were in addition to routine unit mobilizations. Perhaps one solution could involve swapping reserve personnel from mobilized units with regulars, which would achieve cross-pollination without depriving a regular of full-time experience or requiring additional active-duty time of a citizen-soldier. Gates' policy of cross-component assignments never took hold, but the real impact of such a program would only come to light after it was in place for an extended period.[6]

The final unavoidable dilemma—and perhaps the most significant one—is that the more the nation does to raise the readiness of the reserve component to perform an operational role, the greater the cost, thus undercutting one of the primary rationales for relying on citizen-soldiers as a supplement to regulars. As the years since 9/11 have shown, recruiting a force that will be actively employed is more difficult and more expensive. Incentives in the form of benefits (such as medical insurance and care) also must increase, to the point that they essentially match those available to an individual in the active force. More duty time not only increases immediate personnel costs, it also will lead to more individuals receiving bigger retirement checks. Over the 11-year period from fiscal year 2005 through FY 2015, the number of retired reservists increased by 41 percent, while total reserve retired pay increased by 83 percent. The reserve component now requires the same up-to-date weapons and equipment found in the active force, and will wear it out nearly as rapidly. Increased readiness requires greater numbers of full-time personnel, sometimes exceeding more than 30 percent of a unit's strength in the Air National Guard. Though the point has been debated, taking care of reserve families spread out in the civilian world may be more expensive than supporting regular families located on or around a home base. As the cost differential shrinks between the regular and reserve components, the remaining savings due to part-time service must be compared to factors such as the cost in time and money of mobilizing a unit and transporting it to a base, the loss of unit cohesion as fillers replace unqualified personnel, the reduced flexibility of employing a unit that has a built-in countdown to demobilization, and similar utilitarian dynamics. And in many cases, the reserve component force also will be less effective, simply because it will have undergone less training and generally have less-experienced personnel (though sometimes reservists can be more experienced, because they have remained in the same unit doing the same thing for many years, or due to their civilian skills that apply directly to their military billet).[7]

In the early days of our republic, the nation chose to rely upon an operational reserve component because it saved money and met the national security needs of the time. For roughly two centuries after that, the reserves were rarely used, essentially kept in a case labeled: "Break glass in time of major war." Beginning with the adoption of Total Force policy in the early 1970s, the paradigm has shifted back toward an operational reserve, in large measure to "obtain maximum defense capabilities from the limited resources available," as Secretary of Defense Melvin Laird put it. That change gained seemingly irreversible momentum following 9/11. The reserve component met and overcame a host of severe challenges over the course of a long and still ongoing conflict, for the most part performing extremely well in the crucible of combat. Now, as the nation's overseas engagements dial back from a boil to a simmer, civilian and military leaders will have to determine whether the reserve component continues to mobilize, as Secretary McCarthy expressed, "on a judicious but regular basis," or not. There are no easy answers to that question, but this study illuminates the issues that policymakers will have to take into account as they develop the answer.[8]

Appendix 1
End Strengths of Reserve Components by Year

TABLE 1.
Authorized End Strengths for Selected Reserve

	FY 2002	FY 2008	FY 2011	FY 2012
ARNG	350,000	351,300	358,200	358,200
USAR	205,000	205,000	205,000	205,000
USNR	87,000	67,800	65,500	66,200
USMCR	39,558	39,600	39,600	39,600
ANG	108,400	106,700	106,700	106,700
USAFR	74,700	67,500	71,200	71,400
USCGR	8,000	10,000	10,000	10,000

Source: National Defense Authorization Act (FYs 2002, 2008, 2011, 2012).

TABLE 2.
Selected Reserve, Actual End Strength as of
30 September 1997–2011

	1997	1998	1999	2000	2001	2002	2003	2004	2005	2006	2007	2008	2009	2010	2011
ARNG	370,044	362,444	357,469	353,045	351,829	351,078	351,089	342,918	333,177	346,288	352,707	360,351	358,391	362,015	361,561
USAR	212,850	204,968	206,836	206,892	205,628	206,682	211,890	204,131	189,005	189,975	189,882	197,024	205,297	205,281	204,803
USNR	95,317	93,171	89,172	86,933	87,913	87,958	88,156	82,558	76,466	70,500	69,933	68,136	66,508	65,006	64,792
USMCR	41,997	40,842	39,953	39,667	39,810	39,905	41,046	39,644	39,938	39,489	38,557	37,523	38,510	39,222	39,772
ANG	110,022	108,096	105,715	106,365	108,485	112,071	108,137	106,822	106,430	105,658	106,254	107,679	109,196	107,676	105,685
USAFR	71,986	71,970	71,772	72,340	73,757	76,632	74,754	75,322	75,802	74,075	71,146	67,565	67,986	70,119	71,321
DoD Total	902,216	881,491	870,917	865,242	867,422	874,326	875,072	851,395	820,818	825,985	828,479	838,278	845,888	849,319	847,934
USCGR	7,524	7,587	8,110	7,965	5,199	7,816	7,720	8,011	8,187	7,945	7,777	7,970	7,693	7,942	7,933

Source: Reserve Forces Almanac, 1998–2010; Reserve Forces Policy Board Annual Report, FY 1998–2005. Note the RFPB end strengths as of 30 September 2001 for USAFR and USCGR differed from those contained in Reserve Forces Almanac. We elected to use the Almanac's numbers in the table; all other component end strengths were in agreement between both sources (2001). Note the RFPB annual reports for FY 2010 and FY 2011 did not include component end strengths; data for FY 2010 and FY 2011 was provided to the authors by OASD(RA), 9 July 2015.

TABLE 3.
Individual Ready Reserve/Inactive National Guard, Actual End Strength
as of 30 September 1997–2011

	1997	1998	1999	2000	2001	2002	2003	2004	2005	2006	2007	2008	2009	2010	2011
ARNG*	4,729	4,714	4,590	4,212	4,049	3,142	2,138	1,428	1,504	1,795	2,285	2,677	4,734	4,891	3,608
USAR	273,298	226,479	183,900	161,622	151,745	138,646	117,405	114,732	112,668	93,798	76,548	66,840	76,972	78,911	83,890
USNR	134,498	113,138	103,462	97,147	80,541	71,140	64,699	66,085	64,355	61,302	58,488	55,023	42,763	37,343	38,223
USMCR	56,741	58,276	59,050	60,188	59,567	58,039	57,822	61,799	59,882	61,033	62,230	58,225	56,689	57,865	60,681
ANG	0	0	0	0	0	0	0	0	0	0	0	0	0	0	0
USAFR	66,240	56,459	54,271	50,304	47,940	41,095	37,004	37,015	41,319	44,904	49,406	49,301	43,182	40,555	35,493
DoD Total	535,506	459,066	405,273	373,473	343,842	312,062	279,068	281,059	279,728	262,832	248,957	232,066	224,340	219,565	221,895
USCGR	5,728	5,284	4,544	4,772	7,658	5,117	5,241	4,570	4,693	4,803	3,374	2,303	1,706	1,795	1,593

Source: Reserve Forces Almanac, 1998–2010.

Technically, the ARNG does not include IRR personnel. This is because a guardsman must be assigned to a unit in order to be considered part of the National Guard. An IRR member, however, is by definition not part of a unit. In any case, the ARNG maintains the capability to call IRR personnel, former guardsmen, to active service as guardsmen, an option that was employed beginning in 2004 (see chapter 6). Although the ARNG does not have an IRR, it has an Inactive National Guard; their numbers are included above. Data for FYs 2008, FY 2010, and FY 2011 provided by OASD(RA), 9 July 2015.

Appendix 2
Terminology Issues in the Reserve Component

Any in-depth work addressing the issues, organizations, policies, and programs of the armed forces of the United States at some point faces the challenges of consistent terminology. A work focused on the seven reserve components, however, faces an even more daunting task because the reserve component is much less monolithic than the active component, consisting as it does of reservist categories, programs, statuses, and even histories and cultures. In some cases these vary not merely between the services, but, in the case of the National Guard, between no fewer than 54 entities (states, territories, and the District of Columbia). Ultimately, the fact that a reservist maintains a dual identity—as a civilian and as a military member—probably makes such complexities unavoidable. This appendix attempts to highlight a few of the more difficult terms that warrant a lengthier explanation.

Probably the most confusing term is "mobilization." While many individuals, families, employers, and even government and military organizations and publications refer to *mobilization* (or some variant of the word *mobilize*) in a broad sense, the present work attempts to limit the use of this term in the text to those situations involving *involuntary* active duty in response to a mobilization authority implemented by the president or Congress. This is in accord with the relevant statutes. On the other hand, *voluntary* active duty by a reserve component member in support of a named operation or contingency is generally referred to in the text as *activation*. Probably the main reason for the overuse of *mobilization* in lieu of *activation* in American society is that the former term is perceived as providing a degree of protection for a reservist/guardsman whose spouse, children, and/or civilian employer might be less supportive of the member's time away from home and job if the reason for the absence is something that sounds less than mandatory.[1]

Another particularly troublesome distinction resides in the discussion of full-time support and Full-Time Support (FTS) programs and personnel. Many documents and publications, official and unofficial, use the terms indiscriminately, but the present study adopts the view that a conceptual distinction should be made between those active and reserve component programs and personnel that support reserve component units on a full-time basis and those strictly from the reserve component that support reserve component units full-time. The present study uses "full-time support" (lower case) to refer to either active component or reserve component personnel that support reserve units full-time, whereas the abbreviation FTS (Full-Time Support, upper case) refers specifically to reserve component personnel (and omits active component personnel) who support the reserves full time. In the present study, FTS consists mainly of Active Guard and Reserve (AGR) and Military Technician program (MT) personnel (and this emphasis reflects the reality of the programs/personnel in the reserve components). Note the distinction between full-time support and FTS does not exist in the National Guard; when the Guard refers to full-time support, it is identical to FTS.[2]

The Marine Corps' programs provide a case in which the above distinction is especially helpful. The Marines' Inspector-Instructor (I-I) program was (and remains) a "full-time support" program. But because the I-I program consists strictly of active component personnel that support Marine Selected Reserve units full-time, I-I is not an "FTS" program. The Marines' Active Reserve program, however, constitutes the service's FTS program (full-time support by strictly reserve component members).[3]

Abbreviations

ADOS	Active Duty for Operational Support
ADT	Agricultural Development Team
AFB	Air Force Base
AFHRA	Air Force Historical Research Agency
AFR	Air Force Reserve (After 1997. See also AFRES.)
AFRC	Air Force Reserve Command
AFRC/HO	Air Force Reserve Command History Office
AFRES	Air Force Reserve (Up to 1997. See also AFR.)
AGR	Active Guard-Reserve
ANG	Air National Guard
AR	Active Reserve (used by USMC)
AREF	Army Reserve Expeditionary Force
ARFORGEN	Army Force Generation
ARNG	Army National Guard
ASD	Assistant Secretary of Defense
ASD(RA)	Assistant Secretary of Defense for Reserve Affairs
BCT	Brigade Combat Team
BOG	Boots-on-the-Ground
BRAC	Base Realignment and Closure
BUR	Bottom-Up Review
CCC	Civilian Conservation Corps
CNGR	Commission on the National Guard and Reserves
CS	Combat Support
CSS	Combat Service Support
DART	Domestic All-Hazards Response Team
DIMHRS	Defense Integrated Military Human Resources System
DoD	Department of Defense
ESGR	Employer Support of the Guard and Reserve
FTS	Full-Time Support (Differs from "full time support." See Appendix 2.)

FY	Fiscal Year
GAO	Government Accountability Office (General Accounting Office before 2004)
GPO	Government Printing (now "Publishing") Office
HCAS	House Committee on Armed Services
HD/LD	High-Demand/Low-Density
H.R.	House of Representatives
HRF	Homeland Response Force Team
I-I	Inspector-Instructor
IMA	Individual Mobilization Augmentee
IRR	Individual Ready Reserve
JCS	Joint Chiefs of Staff
MarForRes	Marine Forces Reserve
MRE	Meal-Ready-to-Eat
MT	Military Technician
NATO	North Atlantic Treaty Organization
NCO	Noncommissioned Officer
NDAA	National Defense Authorization Act
NECC	Navy Expeditionary Combat Command
NGAUS	National Guard Association of the United States (or, NGA)
NGB	National Guard Bureau
NROTC	Naval Reserve Officers' Training Corps
OASD(RA)	Office of the Assistant Secretary of Defense for Reserve Affairs
OEF	Operation Enduring Freedom
OIF	Operation Iraqi Freedom
ORC	Officers' Reserve Corps
OSD/HO	Historical Office, Office of the Secretary of Defense
P&R	Personnel and Readiness
PRC	Presidential Reserve Call-Up
PSRC	Presidential Selected Reserve Call-Up
PSU	Port Security Unit
PTSD	Post-Traumatic Stress Disorder

Pub. L	Public Law
QDR	Quadrennial Defense Review
RA	Reserve Affairs
Ret.	Retired
RFPB	Reserve Forces Policy Board
ROTC	Reserve Officers' Training Corps
ROWS	Reserve Order Writing System
RTC	Regional Training Center
RWW	Returning Warrior Workshop
SEAL	Sea-Air-Land
SecDef	Secretary of Defense
TAR	Training and Administration of the Reserves
TBI	Traumatic Brain Injury
TPU	Troop Program Unit
TRS	TRICARE Reserve Select
UMT	Universal Military Training
USAF	U.S. Air Force
USAR	U.S. Army Reserve
USARC	U.S. Army Reserve Command
U.S.C.	United States Code
USCG	U.S. Coast Guard
USCGR	U.S. Coast Guard Reserve
USD	Under Secretary of Defense
USERRA	Uniformed Services Employment and Reemployment Rights Act of 1994
USMC	U.S. Marine Corps
USMCR	U.S. Marine Corps Reserve
USN	U.S. Navy
USNR	U.S. Naval Reserve (Navy Reserve after April 2005)
WWR	Wounded Warrior Regiment

Endnotes

Preface

1. Ronald R. Fogleman, "Fundamental to Military Tradition: America, Militia Nation," remarks delivered on 7 Sep 1995, U. S. Department of Defense, Office of the Assistant Secretary of Defense (Public Affairs), including quotes, <http://www.defense.gov/Speeches/Speech.aspx?SpeechID=967>, accessed 6 Jun 2015.

2. Fogleman, "Fundamental to Military Tradition," including quotes.

3. Ron Fogleman, "Militia Model Could Cut U.S. Expenditures," *Defense News*, 16 Jan 2012, including quotes, at <http://archive.defensenews.com/article/20120116/DEFFEAT05/301160015/Going-Back-Future>, accessed 6 Jun 2015.

4. Fogleman, "Militia Model," including quote.

Chapter 1

1. Eilene Galloway, *A Brief History of United States Military Policy on Reserve Forces, 1775–1951*, appendix to *Hearings before a Subcommittee of the Committee on Armed Services United States Senate on H.R. 5426* (Washington, DC: GPO, 1952), 317; David Chandler, ed., *The Oxford Illustrated History of the British* Army (New York: Oxford University Press, 1994), 26; Russell F. Weigley, *History of the United States Army* (1967; repr., Bloomington: Indiana University Press, 1984), 3–4; John K. Mahon, *History of the Militia and the National Guard* (New York and London: Macmillan, 1983), 6–15, including quote, training manual quoted by Mahon.

2. Allan R. Millett and Peter Maslowski, *For the Common Defense: A Military History of the United States of America* (New York and London: Free Press, 1984), 30–35; Mahon, *History of the Militia and the National Guard*, 26–27; Michael D. Doubler, *Civilian in Peace, Soldier in War: The Army National Guard, 1636–2000* (Lawrence: University Press of Kansas, 2003), 21–22.

3. Weigley, *History of the United States Army*, 6–8; Mahon, *History of the Militia and the National Guard*, 31–32; Doubler, *Civilian in Peace, Soldier in War*, 16.

4. Marvin A. Kreidberg and Merton G. Henry, *History of Military Mobilization in the United States Army, 1775–1945* (Washington, DC: Department of the Army, 1955), 7–8, including quote; Weigley, *History of the United States Army*, 18–20; Doubler, *Civilian in Peace, Soldier in War*, 25–26.

5. David McCullough, *1776* (New York and London: Simon & Schuster, 2005), 210–213, including quotes; Weigley, *History of the United States Army*, 36–41, 67–68; Mahon, *History of the Militia and the National Guard*, 40, 44; Doubler, *Civilian in Peace, Soldier in War*, 42, 51–60. Various sources use "Kips Bay" or "Kip's Bay."

6. Weigley, *History of the United States Army*, chapter 5; Doubler, *Civilian in Peace, Soldier in War*, 61–63; U.S. Const., art. I, sec. 8, including quote; Millett and Maslowski, *For*

the Common Defense, 88–89; Kreidberg and Henry, *History of Military Mobilization in the United States Army*, 25–26.

7. U.S. Const., art. I, sec. 8, including quotes (emphasis added); Millett and Maslowski, *For the Common Defense*, 88; Mahon, *History of the Militia and the National Guard*, 48–49.

8. U.S. Const., art. I, sec. 8, including quote; Millett and Maslowski, *For the Common Defense*, 89–90; Mahon, *History of the Militia and the National Guard*, 53; Doubler, *Civilian in Peace, Soldier in War*, 68.

9. The Militia Act of 1792 is also referred to as the Uniform Militia Act of 1792; see Millett and Maslowski, *For the Common Defense*, 89–90. Doubler, *Civilian in Peace, Soldier in War*, 67–68, including quote 1; Weigley, *History of the United States Army*, 93–94, including quote 2; Millett and Maslowski, *For the Common Defense*, 89–90; Mahon, *History of the Militia and the National Guard*, 52–53; Kreidberg and Henry, *History of Military Mobilization in the United States Army*, 30–31, including quote 2; U.S. Congress, 3rd Cong., 2nd sess., "An Act to provide for calling forth the Militia to execute the laws of the Union, suppress insurrections, and repel invasions; and to repeal the Act now in force for those purposes" (1 Stat. 424), 28 Feb 1795, including quote 3. The three-months-per-year limitation was established by the Calling Forth Act (2 May 1792) and clarified by the 1795 act.

10. Millett and Maslowski, *For the Common Defense*, 99; Mahon, *History of the Militia and the National Guard*, 63–69, including quote; Weigley, *History of the United States Army*, 104–115, 120; Doubler, *Civilian in Peace, Soldier in War*, 80–83; Kreidberg and Henry, *History of Military Mobilization in the United States Army*, 36–40.

11. U.S. Congress, "Bill for Establishing Naval Militia," Dec 1805, manuscript/mixed material, Series 1: General Correspondence, 1651–1827, microfilm reel 035, Thomas Jefferson Papers, Library of Congress, Washington, DC, <https://www.loc.gov/item/mtjbib015471>, accessed 6 Jun 2017, including quote.

12. Millett and Maslowski, *For the Common Defense*, 107–114, including quote; Weigley, *History of the United States Army*, 122–132, 154–57; Mahon, *History of the Militia and the National Guard*, 69–77; Doubler, *Civilian in Peace, Soldier in War*, 83–86.

13. Weigley, *History of the United States Army*, 140–143; Mahon, *History of the Militia and the National Guard*, 79; Doubler, *Civilian in Peace, Soldier in War*, 86–87, 90–91; Kreidberg and Henry, *History of Military Mobilization in the United States Army*, 61. The permanent volunteer militia system that increased in numbers and matured in the 19th century was another iteration on a broader scale, with differing motives and legal basis, of the volunteer units chartered mostly between 1774 and 1786 (Doubler).

14. Weigley, *History of the United States Army*, 157; Millett and Maslowski, *For the Common Defense*, 129–130; Mahon, *History of the Militia and the National Guard*, 83–86; Doubler, *Civilian in Peace, Soldier in War*, 90–96.

15. Doubler, *Civilian in Peace, Soldier in War*, 86–87, including quote 1; Weigley, *History of the United States Army*, 140–43, including quote 2; Millett and Maslowski, *For the Common Defense*, 121–122, including quote 3; Mahon, *History of the Militia and the National Guard*, 82–83; Kreidberg and Henry, *History of Military Mobilization in the United States Army*, 61.

16. Weigley, *History of the United States Army*, 182–183; Millett and Maslowski, *For the Common Defense*, 141; Mahon, *History of the Militia and the National Guard*, 90–91; Doubler, *Civilian in Peace, Soldier in War*, 90, 96–98; Kreidberg and Henry, *History of Military Mobilization in the United States Army*, 62–66. Between May 1846 and February 1847 (depending on source), the one-year limitation for enlistees was changed to the duration of the war (Weigley).

17. Weigley, *History of the United States Army*, 173–174, 183–189, including quote, quoted by Weigley; Mahon, *History of the Militia and the National Guard*, 91–94; Doubler, *Civilian in Peace, Soldier in War*, 96–98; Kreidberg and Henry, *History of Military Mobilization in the United States Army*, 66–81; 155th Armored Brigade Combat Team, <http://ms.ng.mil/aboutus/units/155abct/Pages/default.aspx>, accessed 10 Jul 2014; Millett and Maslowski, *For the Common Defense*, 137, 142–143.

18. Millett and Maslowski, *For the Common Defense*, 130, including quote.

19. Weigley, *History of the United States Army*, 198–201, 216; Millett and Maslowski, *For the Common Defense*, 165–166; Mahon, *History of the Militia and the National Guard*, 97–99; Doubler, *Civilian in Peace, Soldier in War*, 101–103; Kreidberg and Henry, *History of Military Mobilization in the United States Army*, 85, 88, 92–95, 134. Several authors mistakenly refer to the Militia Act of 1792 as the basis for Lincoln's call for militia in April 1861; Doubler correctly cites the Calling Forth Act. In March 1861 the Confederacy's provisional congress also authorized the raising of a regular army consisting of 10,600 men.

20. Weigley, *History of the United States Army*, 198–199, 216; Millett and Maslowski, *For the Common Defense*, 167–169; Doubler, *Civilian in Peace, Soldier in War*, 103, 106; Kreidberg and Henry, *History of Military Mobilization in the United States Army*, 94–95, 120. The Battle of Wilson's Creek in August 1861 was another large engagement fought early in the war mainly by existing militia/volunteers, and, perhaps, quickly raised volunteer units; see Mahon, *History of the Militia and the National Guard*, 98–102. Mahon states 40 percent of the 93,000 militiamen who responded to Lincoln's call in April 1861 were from old volunteer units. In any case, Kreidberg and Henry note that as the war evolved, "Militia quotas and three-year Volunteer quotas became inextricably confused. Many regiments mobilized under the Militia call later volunteered for three years thereby upsetting administrative accounting" (100). For the 69th regiment, see <http://www.69thnewyork.co.uk/69history1861.htm>, accessed 10 Jul 2014.

21. Weigley, *History of the United States Army*, 205–208; Millett and Maslowski, *For the Common Defense*, 196–198; Mahon, *History of the Militia and the National Guard*, 100–103; Doubler, *Civilian in Peace, Soldier in War*, 109; Kreidberg and Henry, *History of Military Mobilization in the United States Army*, 103–104.

22. Millett and Maslowski, *For the Common Defense*, 198–201; Weigley, *History of the United States Army*, 208–210; Mahon, *History of the Militia and the National Guard*, 100; Doubler, *Civilian in Peace, Soldier in War*, 109; Kreidberg and Henry, *History of Military Mobilization in the United States Army*, 108–109.

23. Joseph P. Reidy, "Black Men in Navy Blue During the Civil War," *Prologue* 33, no. 3 (Fall 2003); Enrollment Act of 1864, 38th Cong., 1st sess. 1, 13 Stat. 6 (1864), <http://legisworks.org/sal/13/stats/STATUTE-13-Pg6.pdf>, accessed 6 Jun 2017; Michael J. Bennett, *Union Jacks: Yankee Sailors in the Civil War* (Chapel Hill: University of North Carolina Press, 2011), 5–9.

24. Weigley, *History of the United States Army*, 265–267; Millett and Maslowski, *For the Common Defense*, 236–241; Mahon, *History of the Militia and the National Guard*, 110.

25. Wingate's dual role with the National Rifle Association and the National Guard Association, and his emphasis on marksmanship in the Guard, led to a close association between the NRA and military marksmanship that endures to this day. Mahon, *History of the Militia and the National Guard*, 118–119, including quote; Doubler, *Civilian in Peace, Soldier in War*, 111–114, 118; Forrest C. Pogue, *George C. Marshall: Education of a General, 1880–1939* (New York: Viking Press, 1963), 280–282.

26. Doubler, *Civilian in Peace, Soldier in War*, 119, including quote; Mahon, *History of the Militia and the National Guard*, 111. For the 28th Infantry Division, Pennsylvania Army National Guard, see <http://pa.ng.mil/ARNG/28ID/Pages/default.aspx>, accessed 10 Jul 2014.

27. Weigley, *History of the United States Army*, 275–281, 335–337, including quote; Millett and Maslowski, *For the Common Defense*, 256–258; Mahon, *History of the Militia and the National Guard*, 120–21; Doubler, *Civilian in Peace, Soldier in War*, 138–141.

28. Weigley, *History of the United States Army*, 295–297; Millett and Maslowski, *For the Common Defense*, 268–273; Mahon, *History of the Militia and the National Guard*, 126–127; Doubler, *Civilian in Peace, Soldier in War*, 129; Kreidberg and Henry, *History of Military Mobilization in the United States Army*, 150–156; Brian McAllister Linn, *The Philippine War, 1899–1902* (Lawrence: University Press of Kansas, 2000), 10.

29. Weigley, *History of the United States Army*, 297–298, 307–308; Mahon, *History of the Militia and the National Guard*, 126–127, 136; Doubler, *Civilian in Peace, Soldier in War*, 129; Kreidberg and Henry, *History of Military Mobilization in the United States Army*, 157–159.

30. Weigley, *History of the United States Army*, 306–308, including quote 1, quoted by Weigley; Millett and Maslowski, *For the Common Defense*, 290; Linn, *Philippine War*, 63, including quote 2.

31. Weigley, *History of the United States Army*, 313–327; Millett and Maslowski, *For the Common Defense*, 309–313; Mahon, *History of the Militia and the National Guard*, 138–141; Doubler, *Civilian in Peace, Soldier in War*, 136–141; Kreidberg and Henry, *History of Military Mobilization in the United States Army*, 176–179.

32. Weigley, *History of the United States Army*, 320–323, 345; Millett and Maslowski, *For the Common Defense*, 312–313; Mahon, *History of the Militia and the National Guard*, 139–141; Doubler, *Civilian in Peace, Soldier in War*, 143–145. The current volume can in no way address the complexities of the Dick Act. For example, National Guard historians seem to differ on whether the act permitted the integrity of Guard units that might be called into federal service. Without such a guarantee, the Guard could become merely a manpower pool of partially trained volunteers with consequent loss of unit identification, morale, and hometown support. Mahon states, "No portion of the Dick Act guaranteed the integrity of National Guard units when in federal service" (140); Mahon did not address whether the law *permitted* unit integrity. In contrast, Doubler writes, "Charles Dick and the NGA included important provisions that *allowed* NG [National Guard] troops to be called up for as long as nine months *while remaining together as distinct units under the leadership of Guard officers*" (144, emphasis added), but he did not address the lack of a *guarantee* that units remained intact. Millett and Maslowski state the 1908 modifications to the Dick Act contained "a provision that Guardsmen would go to war

as units, not individual replacements for Army regiments" (313). To relieve such concerns on the part of Guard leaders, the 1908 law also established the National Guard Bureau. The bureau chief reported directly to the secretary of war rather than to the general staff (314). Also, note that since the 1880s some Guard units participated informally in maneuvers with the regular Army, but the Dick Act ensured guardsmen would receive federal pay and subsistence for such duty (Weigley, 322).

33. Weigley, *History of the United States Army*, 324–325, including quote, quoted by Weigley. The constitutionality of the law, upon which depended no small part of the Uptonians' opposition to any federal reliance upon state-affiliated militia, remained in doubt until the National Defense Act of 1916 settled the issue; see Millett and Maslowski, *For the Common Defense*, 313–314, 324–325; Mahon, *History of the Militia and the National Guard*, 142, 148–149; Doubler, *Civilian in Peace, Soldier in War*, 144–152, 154–158.

34. Weigley, *History of the United States Army*, 335–346; Millett and Maslowski, *For the Common Defense*, 322–324; Mahon, *History of the Militia and the National Guard*, 152–153; Doubler, *Civilian in Peace, Soldier in War*, 154–156. Weigley refers to "the Uptonians of the Army insisting that at least two years was necessary to the making of a soldier, and even that was not really enough" (337).

35. Millett and Maslowski, *For the Common Defense*, 324–325; Weigley, *History of the United States Army*, 347–348; Mahon, *History of the Militia and the National Guard*, 148–149; Doubler, *Civilian in Peace, Soldier in War*, 156–159.

36. Weigley, *History of the United States Army*, 348–350; Millett and Maslowski, *For the Common Defense*, 324–325; Mahon, *History of the Militia and the National Guard*, 148–149; Doubler, *Civilian in Peace, Soldier in War*, 156–159.

37. Rick Bigelow, Mel Chaloupka, and Andy Rockett, "United States Naval Reserve: Chronology 1992," Naval Reserve Project, 1 Oct 1992, Navy Department Library Special Collections, Washington Navy Yard, Washington, DC, 9, 13–16, 18–19.

38. Four years earlier (1908), Congress passed legislation that established the (Army) Medical Reserve Corps. That act has been considered the birth date of the U.S. Army Reserve. As a result of the creation of the Officers' Reserve Corps under the provisions of the National Defense Act of 1916, however, the Medical Reserve Corps ceased to exist, its officers being absorbed into the new, larger reserve entity; see Richard B. Crossland and James T. Currie, *Twice the Citizen: A History of the United States Army Reserve, 1908–1983* (Washington, DC: Office of the Chief, Army Reserve, 1984), 17–19; Bigelow, Chaloupka, and Rockett, "Naval Reserve: Chronology," 20–21, 24–26, 29–31; Daniel F. Goergen, "The Impetus Behind the Creation of the United States Naval Reserve" (MA thesis, U.S. Army Command and General Staff College, 2005), 65; Millett and Maslowski, *For the Common Defense*, 322; Marine Corps Division of Reserve, *The Marine Corps Reserve: A History* (Washington, DC: Division of Reserve, Headquarters, U.S. Marine Corps, 1966), 4–5; Naval Service Appropriation Act, Pub. L. No. 271, 83 Stat. 629 (2015), <https://www.loc.gov/law/help/statutes-at-large/63rd-congress/session-3/c63s3ch83.pdf>, accessed 6 Jun 2017.

39. Bigelow, Chaloupka, and Rockett, "Naval Reserve: Chronology," 25, 29.

40. Crossland and Currie, *Twice the Citizen*, 17–20.

41. Weigley, *History of the United States Army*, 352–357; Millett and Maslowski, *For the Common Defense*, 331–332; Mahon, *History of the Militia and the National Guard*, 155–156; Doubler, *Civilian in Peace, Soldier in War*, 169–171; Kreidberg and Henry, *History of Military Mobilization in the United States Army*, 241–251. Doubler writes of the Selective Service Act, "With a stroke of the president's pen, the techniques used since colonial times for creating volunteer armies based on State quotas died a quiet death. The Selective Service Act of 1917 was the first effort at gearing all of the manpower of the United States not already serving in the Regular Army, the National Guard, and the Organized Reserves into a coordinated pool of obligated manpower directed toward a single, national purpose" (169).

42. Weigley, *History of the United States Army*, 356–358, 372; Millett and Maslowski, *For the Common Defense*, 332; Mahon, *History of the Militia and the National Guard*, 155–156; Doubler, *Civilian in Peace, Soldier in War*, 169; Kreidberg and Henry, *History of Military Mobilization in the United States Army*, 253, 277–279. Millett and Maslowski state that 90 percent of draftees were unmarried men (332).

43. Pogue, *Education of a General*, 150, 157, including quote; Weigley, *History of the United States Army*, 385, 393; Mahon, *History of the Militia and the National Guard*, 167; Doubler, *Civilian in Peace, Soldier in War*, 182; Kreidberg and Henry, *History of Military Mobilization in the United States Army*, 246, 277, 307, 375; Peyton C. March, *The Nation at War* (New York: Doubleday, Doran, 1932), 310. Note that the numbers of personnel reported at certain times in the war varied by source; we have followed Kreidberg and Henry, the authors of the Army's official mobilization study, clearly the most authoritative source. Charles Joseph Gross, *The Air National Guard and the American Military Tradition: Militiaman, Volunteer, and Professional* (Washington, DC: Historical Services Division, National Guard Bureau, 1995), 30–35. An Air Force Reserve history argues "its formal origins" dates from the 1916 defense act. For the sake of simplicity, we elected to begin coverage of the Air Force Reserve only in the post-World War II period during which the U.S. Air Force separated from the Army (1947). The first "U.S. Air Force Reserve" units were formed shortly thereafter (see chapter 2); see Gerald T. Cantwell, *Citizen Airmen: A History of the Air Force Reserve, 1946–1994* (Washington, DC: Air Force History and Museums Program, 1997), 1–2.

44. Bigelow, Chaloupka, and Rockett, "Naval Reserve: Chronology," 32, 35–36, 40; Weigley, *History of the United States Army*, 387; Mahon, *History of the Militia and the National Guard*, 161; Doubler, *Civilian in Peace, Soldier in War*, 179; USMC Division of Reserve, *Marine Corps Reserve: A History*, 9–11.

45. Nathaniel Patch, "The Story of the Female Yeoman during the First World War," *Prologue* 38, no. 3 (Fall 2006), <https://www.archives.gov/publications/prologue/2006/fall/yeoman-f.html>, accessed 6 Jun 2017; Capt. Linda L. Hewitt, *Women Marines in World War I* (Washington, DC: U.S. Marine Corps, 1974), 3–4, 25.

46. Crossland and Currie, *Twice the Citizen*, 21, including quote, quoted by authors; Weigley, *History of the United States Army*, 360; Doubler, *Civilian in Peace, Soldier in War*, 184–186. Millett and Maslowski write, "Manpower mobilization had always fascinated military policymakers, but the experience of World War I showed that industrial mobilization plans equaled manpower policies in importance"; see Millett and Maslowski, *For the Common Defense*, 367.

47. Doubler, *Civilian in Peace, Soldier in War*, 149, 180–181, 187, including quote, quoted by Doubler; Weigley, *History of the United States Army*, 389. Forrest C. Pogue writes

that in 1940 General Marshall was "haunted by recollections of the droves of unfit commanders" that Pershing reassigned to noncombat roles. In 1940 General Marshall told the House Military Affairs Committee, "Leadership in the field depends to an important extent on one's legs, and stomach, and nervous system, and on one's ability to withstand hardships, and lack of sleep, and still be disposed energetically and aggressively to command men, to dominate men on the battlefield"; see Forrest C. Pogue, *George C. Marshall: Ordeal and Hope, 1939–1942* (New York: Viking Press, 1966), 91–97.

48. See paragraph for note 34 above. Wood's six-month minimum was based largely not on raw recruits but, rather, on guardsmen who had undergone some training. Presumably, raw recruits required more than six months.

49. Weigley, *History of the United States Army*, 384–385, 392–393, including quotes, Baker quoted by Weigley. For a useful biography of Baker, see C. H. Cramer, *Newton D. Baker, A Biography* (New York: World Publishing, 1960).

50. Pogue, *Education of a General*, 147, 150–154, including quote 1; Weigley, *History of the United States Army*, 392–394, including quote 2, Pershing quoted by Weigley; "Legislation, Personnel and Pay," *Marine Corps Gazette* 19, no. 1 (May 1934): 19, including quote 3 of Hunter Liggett; Mahon, *History of the Militia and the National Guard*, 152–153; George C. Marshall, *Memoirs of My Services in the World War, 1917–1918* (Boston: Houghton Mifflin, 1976), 15, 19, 36.

51. *The Statutes at Large of the United States of America from December, 1915, to March, 1917*, vol. 39, pt. 1 (Washington, DC: GPO, 1917), 166; Weigley, *History of the United States Army*, 348–349. For the 1916 and 1920 defense laws, see chapter 2, present work.

Chapter 2

1. Kreidberg and Henry, *History of Military Mobilization in the United States Army*, 377–379, including quote 1; Weigley, *History of the United States Army*, 396–401, including quote 2, Palmer quoted by Weigley; Millett and Maslowski, *For the Common Defense*, 365–366; Mahon, *History of the Militia and the National Guard*, 169–170; Doubler, *Civilian in Peace, Soldier in War*, 185–187.

2. Kreidberg and Henry, *History of Military Mobilization*, 378, including quote, statute quoted by authors; *The Statutes at Large of the United States of America*, vol. 39, *December, 1915, to March, 1917* (Washington, DC: GPO, 1917), 166; Millett and Maslowski, *For the Common Defense*, 365–367; Mahon, *History of the Militia and the National Guard*, 171–172; Doubler, *Civilian in Peace, Soldier in War*, 188; Crossland and Currie, *Twice the Citizen*, 34, 52. The phrasing, "the National Guard while in the service of the United States," referred to the federalization of the Guard under the Constitution's militia clauses; Lt. Col. Les' A. Melnyk, ARNG, conversation with Marion, 30 Apr 2012. We are indebted to Lieutenant Colonel Melnyk, the public affairs advisor to the director, ARNG, for his insightful comments on this and several other paragraphs; see also Les' Andrii Melnyk, "A True National Guard: The Development of the National Guard and Its Influence on Defense Legislation, 1915–1933" (PhD diss., The City University of New York, 2004).

3. Weigley, *History of the United States Army*, 399–401; Millett and Maslowski, *For the Common Defense*, 366–367. Although the law referred to the "organized Reserves," most sources used "Organized Reserve." We have followed the latter practice in this chapter.

4. Weigley, *History of the United States Army*, 399; Mahon, *History of the Militia and the National Guard*, 171; Doubler, *Civilian in Peace, Soldier in War*, 188.

5. Melnyk, "A True National Guard," 458–461, including quotes, quote 3 quoted by Melnyk from 1933 law; Lt. Col. Les' A. Melnyk, ARNG, email message to Marion, 13 Jun 2012; Mahon, *History of the Militia and the National Guard*, 174–175. Millett and Maslowski were mistaken in stating, "In 1933 additional legislation ensured that mobilized Guard units would not be broken up" (378).

6. Crossland and Currie, *Twice the Citizen*, 40–45, 48–49, including quotes, quoted by authors; Doubler, *Civilian in Peace, Soldier in War*, 196; Pogue, *Education of a General*, 274–280. Due largely to the 1916 defense act, there were many cases in which guardsmen received pay for inactive duty training while federal-only reservists went unpaid; see also Mahon, *History of the Militia and the National Guard*, 175; USMC Division of Reserve, *Marine Corps Reserve: A History*, 35.

7. Weigley, *History of the United States Army*, 400–403, 406; Millett and Maslowski, *For the Common Defense*, 366–367, 378; Mahon, *History of the Militia and the National Guard*, 173–174; Doubler, *Civilian in Peace, Soldier in War*, 189. Presumably, the original intent was that a regular Army division's training detachment would train the citizen-soldier officers and enlisted men of the three Organized Reserve divisions within a given corps area, and they, in turn, would train the reserve division draftees inducted in an emergency.

8. USMC Division of Reserve, *Marine Corps Reserve: A History*, 23, including quote, 1925 law quoted by authors; Bigelow, Chaloupka, and Rockett, "Naval Reserve: Chronology," 43–44, 53, 56. In 1925 the Naval Reserve regulations defined the requirements of a "drill" period for reservists: a preplanned assembly consisting of at least 1.5 hours of practical work "in duties pertaining to the Navy"; only one drill per week was authorized; see Bigelow, Chaloupka, and Rockett (56).

9. USMC Division of Reserve, *Marine Corps Reserve: A History*, 40, 45, 48, 57, including quotes, Partridge quoted by authors (both quotes); *Statutes at Large of the United States of America*, vol. 47, *December 1931 to March 1933* (Washington, DC: GPO, 1933), 684–685; Dr. Fred Allison, Marine Corps Historical Division, email to Marion, 13 Apr 2012. In 2008 the Commission on the National Guard and Reserves observed that the Inspector-Instructor program, still fulfilling its original purpose, contributed to the success of the Marine Corps Reserve; Commission on the National Guard and Reserves, *Transforming the National Guard and Reserves into a 21st-Century Operational Force: Final Report to Congress and the Secretary of Defense* (Arlington, VA: CNGR, 31 Jan 2008), <http://cgsc.cdmhost.com/cdm/singleitem/collection/p4013coll11/id/1655/rec/12#img_view_container>, accessed 24 Jul 2014, 204.

10. Gross, *Air National Guard and the American Military Tradition*, 37–46.

11. Bigelow, Chaloupka, and Rockett, "Naval Reserve: Chronology," 69–71; USMC Division of Reserve, *Marine Corps Reserve: A History*, 57; Nathaniel Patch, National Archives, email message to Marion, 10 Apr 2012; Robert Cressman, Naval History and Heritage Command, email message to Marion, 11 Apr 2012.

12. Weigley, *History of the United States Army*, 423–424, including quote; Millett and

Maslowski, *For the Common Defense*, 395; Doubler, *Civilian in Peace, Soldier in War*, 196–197; Crossland and Currie, *Twice the Citizen*, 63–67; Kreidberg and Henry, *History of Military Mobilization in the United States Army*, 379.

13. Weigley, *History of the United States Army*, 426–427, 434; Mahon, *History of the Militia and the National Guard*, 179–180; Doubler, *Civilian in Peace, Soldier in War*, 197–198; Pogue, *Ordeal and Hope*, 145–155. Other units, mainly coast artillery, were mobilized along with the four Guard divisions (Mahon, 180).

14. Weigley, *History of the United States Army*, 428–431, including quote, Marshall quoted by Weigley; Millett and Maslowski, *For the Common Defense*, 396; Mahon, *History of the Militia and the National Guard*, 180–183; Pogue, *Ordeal and Hope*, 82–83, 164–165. Some sources considered the Guard to have contributed a 19th division, the Americal Division (Doubler, 203–204, 209).

15. Pogue, *Ordeal and Hope*, 91–100, including quotes; Doubler, *Civilian in Peace, Soldier in War*, 199–200, 207, 213; Mahon, *History of the Militia and the National Guard*, 186–187; Cornelius Ryan, *The Last Battle* (New York: Simon and Schuster, 1966), 293.

16. Mahon, *History of the Militia and the National Guard*, 181, including quote 1; Weigley, *History of the United States Army*, 428, including quote 2.

17. Mahon, *History of the Militia and the National Guard*, 183, 188–194, including quote; Doubler, *Civilian in Peace, Soldier in War*, 203–204; Jon T. Hoffman, *Chesty: The Story of Lieutenant General Lewis B. Puller, USMC* (New York: Random House, 2001), 194.

18. Holland M. Smith and Percy Finch, *Coral and Brass* (1949; repr., Nashville, TN: Battery Press, 1989), 168–169, including quote; Mahon, *History of the Militia and the National Guard*, 189; Robert Sherrod, *On to Westward: War in the Central Pacific* (New York: Duell, Sloan, and Pearce, 1945), 88–93, 150. Mahon viewed the 27th Division as unfairly treated. Sherrod, who was on the island of Saipan during the battle, took a more impartial view while accepting the basic version of events favorable to the Marines, particularly concerning the events of 7 July 1944. Note General Marshall, according to his biographer, considered the 27th "a well-trained division in Hawaii with excellent leaders"; see Forrest C. Pogue, *George C. Marshall: Organizer of Victory, 1943–1945* (New York: Viking Press, 1973), 254.

19. Smith and Finch, *Coral and Brass*, 168–619, 173, including quotes.

20. USMC Division of Reserve, *Marine Corps Reserve: A History*, 59–61, 98–99, including quotes (quote 1, Partridge quoted by authors).

21. Bigelow, Chaloupka, and Rockett, "Naval Reserve: Chronology," 86–95, including quotes, Navy Secretary Frank Knox and DuBose Board quoted by authors. Similar to the Coast Guard and the Navy, the Marines in early 1943 established a women's component; see USMC Division of Reserve, *Marine Corps Reserve: A History*, 77–82. Because most of the reservists referred to in the above quote had been "procured and trained" since the war began, they may be viewed in a somewhat different context than those reservists that had served as citizen-sailors for some years prior to the war's outbreak. To varying degrees, the same distinction could be made in the other services as well. Essentially, the above reservists were little different from sailors who enlisted or were inducted since the start of the war; see also *Marine Corps Reserve: A History*, 72.

22. John L. Parkhurst, "Ringing In Our 50th Year!" *Coast Guard Reservist*, Feb–Mar 1991, 4–5, including quote.

23. "Women Marines," *Life*, 27 Mar 1944, 81, including quote, General Holcomb quoted by authors.

24. Harry S. Truman, *Memoirs,* vol. 1, *Year of Decisions* (Garden City, NY: Doubleday, 1955), 506–509, including quotes; Doubler, *Civilian in Peace, Soldier in War*, 225.

25. Truman, *Memoirs*, 510–511, including quotes; Harry S. Truman Library and Museum, "Harry S. Truman Biographical Sketch," <http://www.trumanlibrary.org/hst-bio.htm>, accessed 16 Jul 2014.

26. Truman, *Memoirs*, 510–511, including quote 1; Weigley, *History of the United States Army*, 497–500, including quote 2, Palmer-Marshall policy quoted by Weigley; Cantwell, *Citizen Airmen*, 24–27.

27. Weigley, *History of the United States Army*, 428; Pogue, *Ordeal and Hope*, 99–101; Gross, *Air National Guard and the American Military Tradition*, 57.

28. Weigley, *History of the United States Army*, 486, 497–500, including quote 1, Marshall quoted by Weigley; Doubler, *Civilian in Peace, Soldier in War*, 220–224, including quote 2, War Department directive quoted by Doubler; Mahon, *History of the Militia and the National Guard*, 206; Gross, *Air National Guard and the American Military Tradition*, 60–61; Cantwell, *Citizen Airmen*, 27, 33.

29. Cantwell, *Citizen Airmen*, 23, including Partridge quote, 28–37, 45–50, 53–55; Mahon, *History of the Militia and the National Guard*, 203–204; Doubler, *Civilian in Peace, Soldier in War*, 226; Gross, *Air National Guard and the American Military Tradition*, 60, 61, 65–70. Gross stated 58,000 as the projected strength of the ANG; Cantwell indicated about 44,000. The difference might have been one of timing, which was not specified in the text. The point was that the Air Reserve (in 1947, Air Force Reserve) was larger than the ANG in terms of active reserve personnel but Air Reserve personnel were intended strictly as replacements to Army Air Forces (in 1947, the U.S. Air Force) and ANG units. The approved air reserve program called for 87,500 active reservists compared with no more than 58,000 air guardsmen.

30. Cantwell, *Citizen Airmen*, 34–35, 45–46, 97–98; Gross, *Air National Guard and the American Military Tradition*, 77–79. Drilling requirements during this period were not always standardized. For example, Organized Reserve Corps (after 1952, U.S. Army Reserve) personnel performed varying numbers of paid drills, some as few as 12, in addition to the 15-day annual training; see Kathryn Roe Coker, *United States Army Reserve Mobilization for the Korean War* (Fort Bragg, NC: Office of Army Reserve History, 2013), 36, <http://permanent.access.gpo.gov/gpo38677/Korean%20War%20Pub_Revised%20June%2012-2013.pdf>, accessed 14 Oct 2014.

31. Selective Service Act of 1948, Pub. L. No. 80-759, 62 Stat. 604 (1948); Weigley, *History of the United States Army*, 486, 501; Mahon, *History of the Militia and the National Guard*, 198–199, 200; Doubler, *Civilian in Peace, Soldier in War*, 228; Crossland and Currie, *Twice the Citizen*, 94; Cantwell, *Citizen Airmen*, 58. The 1948 Gray Board complained that the deferment program precluded a period of active duty deemed sufficient for the training of those reservists that enlisted under the selective service law. The reserves needed "a continuous flow

of pretrained officer and enlisted personnel," which the deferment option failed to provide. Department of Defense, Committee on Civilian Components, *Reserve Forces for National Security: Report to the Secretary of Defense* (Washington, DC: GPO, 1948), 4. The 1948 law offered other options as well, but the main ones are those discussed above.

32. Crossland and Currie, *Twice the Citizen*, 86–89; Cantwell, *Citizen Airmen*, 28. Note that the former Organized Reserve Corps had also used the ORC abbreviation. Mahon, *History of the Militia and the National Guard*, 199–200; Doubler, *Civilian in Peace, Soldier in War*, 231. The law was the Army and Air Force Vitalization and Retirement Equalization Act of 1948 (Pub. L. No. 80-810, 62 Stat. 1081).

33. Ltr, Forrestal to Truman, 2 Aug 1948, box 1051, Subject Files, OSD/HO. Original in Truman Library, including quotes 1–2; Committee on Civilian Components, *Reserve Forces for National Security*, 1, including quote 3, quoted by authors.

34. Committee on Civilian Components, *Reserve Forces for National Security*, 9, 16, including quotes; Mahon, *History of the Militia and the National Guard*, 203; Cantwell, *Citizen Airmen*, 59–61; memo, Gordon Gray for James V. Forrestal, 2 Jul 1948, subj: Synopsis of major recommendations of the Gray Board, original at Harry S. Truman Library, Papers of Harry S. Truman, President's Secretary's Files, Gray Board, box 156, copy at Air Force Reserve Command History Office, Robins AFB, GA. The Gray Report devoted 10 pages to the conclusion that each service should have one federal reserve force, more attention than that accorded any other issue. Also, the Gray Board recommended adopting the term "reserve forces" in lieu of "Civilian Components," which it deemed "inappropriate for those organizations which provided most of the wartime military establishment."

35. Committee on Civilian Components, *Reserve Forces for National Security*, 2, 4, 5, 7, 10, including quotes.

36. Ibid., 10, 87–89, including quotes, Palmer quoted by authors; Gross, *Air National Guard and the American Military Tradition*, 66.

37. Committee on Civilian Components, *Reserve Forces for National Security*, 2, 4, 7, including quotes (emphasis in original).

38. Ibid., 16, including quotes.

39. Ltr, Truman to Forrestal, 12 Aug 1948, box 1051, Subject Files, OSD/HO, including quote; Mahon, *History of the Militia and the National Guard*, 201–202; Weigley, *History of the United States Army*, 501–504; Millett and Maslowski, *For the Common Defense*, 477; Crossland and Currie, *Twice the Citizen*, 94–95; Keith D. McFarland and David L. Roll, *Louis Johnson and the Arming of America* (Bloomington and Indianapolis: Indiana University Press, 2005), 190–204. Not until August 1949 was the designation Department of Defense adopted; see McFarland and Roll (154) and Weigley (495).

40. Exec. Order No. 10007, Organization of the Reserve Units of the Armed Forces, 15 Oct 1948, box 1051, Subject Files, OSD/HO, including quotes 1–3 (also available at <http://trumanlibrary.org/executiveorders/index.php?pid=878>, accessed 3 May 2016); Secretary of Defense, *Semiannual Report of the Secretary of Defense, January 1 to June 30 1950* (Washington, DC: GPO, 1950), 21–22; Armed Forces Reserve Act of 1952, Pub. L. No. 476, 66 Stat. 497 (1952) Section 257; DoD Press Releases, No. A-202-49, 22 Aug 1949, and No.

207-49, 20 Sep 1949, box 1051, Subject Files, OSD/HO; Civilian Components Policy Board, Monthly Progress Report of Staff Actions, Oct 1949–Mar 1951, box 1051, Subject Files, OSD/ HO; Final Report to the Secretary of Defense of Mr. William T. Faricy Upon Relinquishing the Office of Chairman Civilian Components Policy Board, 4 May 1950, including quote 4, box 1051, Subject Files, OSD/HO.

41. Max Hastings, *The Korean War* (New York and London: Simon & Schuster, 1987), 52–53, 58, 63; Weigley, *History of the United States Army*, 505–509; Millett and Maslowski, *For the Common Defense*, 484–487; Mahon, *History of the Militia and the National Guard*, 208–209; Doubler, *Civilian in Peace, Soldier in War*, 231–238; Coker, *Mobilization for the Korean War*, 39.

42. Max Hastings, *The Korean War*, 106–114, chapter 9; Weigley, *History of the United States Army*, 513–516; Millett and Maslowski, *For the Common Defense*, 487–488, 492; Doubler, *Civilian in Peace, Soldier in War*, 232–235.

43. Crossland and Currie, *Twice the Citizen*, 95–100, including quote, Rear Adm. I. M. McQuiston quoted by authors; Weigley, *History of the United States Army*, 508; Coker, *Mobilization for the Korean War*, 43. Crossland and Currie acknowledge the number of Organized Reserve Corps members that served in Korea was unknown, although 240,000 organized reservists "were called to active duty" (99). Similar to today's Ready Reserve, in 1950 the Army's Organized Reserve included reservists in drill-for-pay status (unit reservists) or unpaid status (individual reservists). As defense secretary in 1950–1951, George Marshall promoted the name change from Civilian Components Policy Board to Reserve Forces Policy Board. During Korea there was no federally backed entity for employer support to the Guard and Reserve. In 1994 the Uniformed Services Employment and Reemployment Rights Act addressed such issues.

44. Bigelow, Chaloupka, and Rockett, "Naval Reserve: Chronology," 117–125, including quote, quoted by authors; USMC Division of Reserve, *Marine Corps Reserve: A History*, 165–173, 179–180. A valuable account of a single Marine Corps Reserve rifle company mobilized for Korea is Randy K. Mills and Roxanne Mills, *Unexpected Journey: A Marine Corps Reserve Company in the Korean War* (Annapolis, MD: Naval Institute Press, 2000).

45. Secretary of Defense, *Semiannual Report, January 1 to June 30, 1951*, 12, including Marshall quote; Weigley, *History of the United States Army*, 508–510; Mahon, *History of the Militia and the National Guard*, 208–210; Doubler, *Civilian in Peace, Soldier in War*, 233; Crossland and Currie, *Twice the Citizen*, 97. Weigley and Doubler agreed the Army National Guard contributed two of the seven (or eight) divisions sent to Korea. Weigley and Mahon stated the total number of Army soldiers who served on active duty in connection with Korea was 2,834,000.

46. Gross, *Air National Guard and the American Military Tradition*, 66, 70, 77, 79, 83, 86, 101–102, including quotes 1–2; quote 1 of Lt. Col. Thomas G. Lanphier Jr. as quoted by Gross; quote 2 of Lt. Gen. Ennis C. Whitehead as quoted by Gross; Mahon, *History of the Militia and the National Guard*, 209; "Guard Change Held Essential by Marshall," news clipping, 25 Oct 1950, box 1051, Subject Files, OSD/HO, including quote 3 ("cannibalizing") of Walsh quoted in news clipping.

47. Cantwell, *Citizen Airmen*, 87, 92–95, 98–99, 104–105, 115–117.

48. DoD Press Releases, No. 1310-50, 23 Oct 1950, and No. 1334-50, 27 Oct 1950, including quotes, box 1051, Subject Files, OSD/HO.

49. Universal Military Training and Service Act of 1951, Pub. L. No. 82–51, 65 Stat. 75 (1951); Weigley, *History of the United States Army*, 509; Mahon, *History of the Militia and the National Guard*, 206–208; Cantwell, *Citizen Airmen*, 122–124.

50. Secretary of Defense, *Semiannual Report, January 1 to June 30 1951*, 3, including Marshall quote; Weigley, *History of the United States Army*, 508–511; memo, National Security Training Commission for Gen. Dwight D. Eisenhower, subj: "National Security Training," 31 Dec 1952, 1–3, copies at OSD/HO and AFHRA, Maxwell AFB, AL.

51. Senate Armed Services Committee, *Statement of Maj. Gen. Ellard A. Walsh, President, National Guard Association of the United States, Armed Forces Reserve Act of 1952: Hearings on H.R. 5426, Before a Subcommittee of the Committee on Armed Services*, 82nd Cong., 1st sess. (Washington, DC: GPO, 1952), 105–108; *Report to Accompany H.R. 5426*, 27 Sep 1951, 82nd Cong., 1st sess., 1, including quote; Mahon, *History of the Militia and the National Guard*, 211–212; Crossland and Currie, *Twice the Citizen*, 100–101; Cantwell, *Citizen Airmen*, 124–126.

52. Crossland and Currie, *Twice the Citizen*, 100; Armed Forces Reserve Act of 1952, Pub. L. No. 476, 66 Stat. (1952). Reproduced in Air Force Bulletin No. 16, "Armed Forces Reserve Act of 1952" (Washington, DC, 18 Jul 1952), 11–13, including quotes; Doubler, *Civilian in Peace, Soldier in War*, 238; Cantwell, *Citizen Airmen*, 124–125.

53. Cantwell, *Citizen Airmen*, 126, including quote 1; Gross, *Air National Guard and the American Military Tradition*, 84, including quote, quoted by Gross; Air Force Bulletin No. 16, "Armed Forces Reserve Act of 1952," 4–5.

54. Walsh and Rosenberg Testimony, *Armed Forces Reserve Act of 1952: Hearings on H.R. 5426*, 109, 237, including quotes 1 and 3; Statement of Assistant Secretary Anna M. Rosenberg Before the Brooks Subcommittee on Reserve Policies, 18 Apr 1951, box 1051, Subject Files, OSD/HO, quote 2; Cantwell, *Citizen Airmen*, 123–125.

55. Armed Forces Reserve Act of 1952, reproduced in Air Force Bulletin No. 16, 2, including quotes; Mahon, *History of the Militia and the National Guard*, 211–112; Crossland and Currie, *Twice the Citizen*, 100–101; Rosenberg testimony concerning H.R. 5426.

Chapter 3

1. USMC Division of Reserve, *Marine Corps Reserve: A History*, 182, including quote, Wilson quoted by authors; Richard M. Leighton, *Strategy, Money, and the New Look, 1953–1956* (Washington, DC: OSD Historical Office, 2001), 38–39; Millett and Maslowski, *For the Common Defense*, 511–512, 528–529; Crossland and Currie, *Twice the Citizen*, 115–116; Mahon, *History of the Militia and the National Guard*, 214–215; Charles Joseph Gross, *Prelude to the Total Force: The Air National Guard, 1943–1969* (Washington, DC: Office of Air Force History, 1985), 100–101.

2. House Committee on Armed Services (HCAS), *National Reserve Plan: House of Representatives Report No. 457* [to accompany H.R. 5297] (Washington, DC: GPO, 1955), 10, including quote 1; HCAS, *First Interim Report of Subcommittee No. 1, Committee on Armed Services, House of Representatives, on Implementation of the Reserve Forces Act of 1955*

(Washington, DC: GPO, 1956), 5299–5300, including quote 2; Millett and Maslowski, *For the Common Defense*, 528; memo, Col. Joseph H. West, USAF, deputy chief of staff-personnel, HQ Fourth Air Force, for [various offices], 28 Nov 1955, subj: Reserve Forces Act of 1955, Air Force Reserve Command History Office, Robins AFB, GA; Crossland and Currie, *Twice the Citizen*, 125. Somewhat different numbers (percentage of drilling reservists was the same) were provided by Millett and Maslowski, who stated that prior to the 1955 act, 700,000 reservists, out of some 2.5 million, drilled with units; see their 1994 edition (551).

3. Memo, Arthur S. Flemming, Director of Office of Defense Mobilization, for Dwight D. Eisenhower, 6 Jan 1954, AFRC/HO, including quotes; Galloway, *History of United States Military Policy on Reserve Forces*, 476; Cantwell, *Citizen Airmen*, 127–128. Recall that the UMT feature of the 1951 law was in name only; UMT was never implemented.

4. Task Force on Reserve Mobilization Requirements, *A Report to the Secretary of Defense* (Washington, DC: Office of the Assistant Secretary of Defense for Manpower & Personnel, 1954), 38–41, including quotes; memo, Flemming for Eisenhower, 6 Jan 1954; Cantwell, *Citizen Airmen*, 128–130. Dwight D. Eisenhower, Special Message to Congress on National Security Requirements, 13 Jan 1955, <http://www.presidency.ucsb.edu/ws/?pid=10254>; Congressional Quarterly, "Military Reserves Strengthened," *CQ Almanac 1955*, 11th ed. (Washington, DC: Congressional Quarterly, 1956), 334–343.

5. Eisenhower, Special Message to Congress on National Security Requirements, including quotes 1–3; HCAS, Subcommittee No. 1, *Implementation of the Reserve Forces Act of 1955*, 5299–5301, 5306; Galloway, *History of United States Military Policy on Reserve Forces*, 479–481; memo, West for various offices, 28 Nov 1955; Crossland and Currie, *Twice the Citizen*, 120–124; John H. Thompson, "Await Rush of GIs Under Reserve Act," *Chicago Tribune*, 29 Aug 1955, 16. The Army and the Marine Corps were the first two services to implement the six-month program.

6. Memo, West for various offices, 28 Nov 1955; Eisenhower, Statement by the President upon Signing the Reserve Forces Act of 1955, 9 Aug 1955, including quote; Mahon, *History of the Militia and the National Guard*, 216–219; Congressional Quarterly, "Military Reserves Strengthened," 334–343.

7. Mahon, *History of the Militia and the National Guard*, 216–219; Cantwell, *Citizen Airmen*, 132–133; HCAS, *National Reserve Plan*, 6; Galloway, *History of United States Military Policy on Reserve Forces*, 486; "Compromise Program Ends Guard Controversy," *Cornell Daily Sun*, 27 Feb 1957, 8, including Wilson quote.

8. Mahon, *History of the Militia and the National Guard*, 220–221; Doubler, *Civilian in Peace, Soldier in War*, 249–250; Bigelow, Chaloupka, and Rockett, "Naval Reserve: Chronology," 132; Crossland and Currie, *Twice the Citizen*, 116–120, including quote; Cantwell, *Citizen Airmen*, 135; memo, West for various offices, 28 Nov 1955. Original job protection for reservists came in the joint resolution authorizing mobilization in 1940, as amended in the law authorizing the draft soon after. S. J. Res. 286, 76th Cong., 3d sess. (1940), Sec 3. (b), <http://legisworks.org/congress/76/pubres-96.pdf>; Selective Training and Service Act of 1940, Pub. L. No. 76-783, 54 Stat. 885 (1940), Sec 8 (f), <http://www.legisworks.org/congress/76/publaw-783.pdf>. Congress extended coverage to state and local governments in 1974. Detailed information on what is now known as the Uniformed Services Employment and Reemployment Rights Act (Pub. L. 103-353, 108 Stat. 3149, now codified at 38 U.S.C. 4301-4335) is available at <http://www.roa.org/lawcenter>.

9. Crossland and Currie, *Twice the Citizen*, 128–129, 217; Bigelow, Chaloupka, and Rockett, "Naval Reserve: Chronology," 130; Cantwell, *Citizen Airmen*, 159–164; Continental Air Command News Release 58–50, "Air Reserve Technician Program," 15 May 1958, AFRC/HO; Office of the Assistant Secretary of Defense (Manpower, Reserve Affairs and Logistics), *Report on Full-Time Training and Administration of the Selected Reserve*, Jun 1978 (hereafter Gerard Study), see John P. White memorandum of 24 May 1978, reproduced on pages 1–4, and subsequent chapter 1, page I-8. The aforementioned report, also known as the Gerard Study, explained other differences between the technician programs of the various services. Medical disqualification and mandatory retirement age were the two most common reasons for loss of military status through no fault of the reservist. The Air Force Reserve's Air Reserve Technician program was the federal-only air reserve counterpart to the Army's Military Technician program; see Cantwell, *Citizen Airmen*, 301. Note that "full-time support" (lower case) programs included both active component and reserve component personnel who served in support of reserve units full-time, whereas the abbreviation FTS and the capitalized spelling of "Full-Time Support" referred specifically to reserve component personnel and did not include active component personnel. Various sources conflate these two categories, however. In the absence of a need to use "FTS" in a given sentence, we have chosen to use "full-time support" to spare the reader an abbreviation.

10. Gross, *Prelude to the Total Force*, chap. 4, including quote 1; Thomas D. White, "New Accent on the Air Reserve Forces," *Air Force Magazine* 43, no. 7 (Jul 1960): 103, including quote 2 (emphasis added); U.S. Army, "The Army Reserve as Part of the Operational Force," *STAND-TO!* (blog), 20 Dec 2010, <https://www.army.mil/standto/archive/2010/12/20/>, accessed 9 May 2016; John J. Kruzel, "Army Reserve Now Part of Operational Force, General Says," *American Forces Press Service*, 25 Jun 2007, <https://www.army.mil/article/3797/Army_Reserve_Now_Part_of_Operational_Force__General_Says>, accessed 9 May 2016; HCAS, Subcommittee No. 1, *Implementation of the Reserve Forces Act of 1955*, 5303. Note General White's use of the term "total force." This is the earliest official use of the term we have discovered. In 1963 the next Air Force chief of staff, General Curtis E. LeMay, employed similar language when he referred to the ANG and AFRES performing "their tasks in the total Air Force mission"; Gen. Curtis E. LeMay, CSAF, "Policy on Using Reserve Forces," *Air Force Information Policy Letter for Commanders* 18, no. 12 (15 Jun 1963).

11. HCAS, Subcommittee No. 1, *Implementation of the Reserve Forces Act of 1955*, 5300; "RFA '55, 3 Years Later," *Army Reservist*, Sep 1958; Millett and Maslowski, *For the Common Defense*, 528–529. Millett and Maslowski indicated a total of 937,000 drill-pay reservists of all services in 1961–1962, a number close to the one million stated for 1960 (537). Army Reserve strength increased from 99,000 to 223,000 drilling members.

12. Millett and Maslowski, *For the Common Defense*, 530–532, 537; Director of Information, Office of the Secretary of the Air Force, *Air Force Information Policy Letter for Commanders* supplement, Jan 1962, 2, 4, including quote, Kennedy quoted by authors; Frederick J. Shaw, ed., *Locating Air Force Base Sites: History's Legacy* (Washington, DC: Air Force History and Museums Program, 2004), 101–102, 105–107.

13. *Air Force Information Policy Letter for Commanders* supplement, Jan 1962, including quotes 1–2, Kennedy quoted by authors; Weigley, *History of the United States Army*, 531; Cantwell, *Citizen Airmen*, 177–179; Gross, *Prelude to the Total Force*, 126–127. HCAS, *Military Reserve Posture, Report of Subcommittee No. 3 on Military Reserve Posture* (Washington, DC:

GPO, 17 Aug 1962), 6654–6656, including quote 3; Gross, *Prelude to the Total Force*, 128, 133, 136; Cantwell, *Citizen Airmen*, 179–184. The recall of reservists was authorized (1 Aug 1961) by a joint resolution of Congress (Pub. L. 87-117, at http://www.gpo.gov/fdsys/pkg/STATUTE-75/pdf/STATUTE-75-Pg242.pdf). The partial mobilization law was not employed in 1961; rather, the Kennedy administration carried out the mobilization on the basis of the 31 July 1961 joint resolution that authorized the recall of 250,000 reservists for 12 months. A major problem experienced by the ANG was that pilots trained for nuclear, not conventional, missions, and had to undergo "a crash program of intensive advanced flight training."

14. Weigley, *History of the United States Army*, 531; Doubler, *Civilian in Peace, Soldier in War*, 251–253; Mahon, *History of the Militia and the National Guard*, 228–229; Office of the Secretary of the Air Force, *Air Force Information Policy Letter Supplement for Commanders*, including quote 1, quoted by authors; memo, Secretary of Defense McNamara for President Kennedy, ca. 28 Feb 1962, subj: Release of Reservists Involuntarily Recalled to Active Duty, Mandatory Review Case NLK-86-30, Document 2, JFK Library (copy at AFRC/HO), including quote 2; Crossland and Currie, *Twice the Citizen*, 136–147; HCAS, *Military Reserve Posture*, 6657; Gross, *Prelude to the Total Force*, 139; Cantwell, *Citizen Airmen*, 187–191.

15. HCAS, *Military Reserve Posture*, 6657–6659, 6661–6662, 6667, including quotes; Crossland and Currie, *Twice the Citizen*, 138–140, 146–148. Of the 700,000 drill-pay Army reservists, 400,000 were National Guard; 300,000 Army Reserve.

16. Capt. Jon T. Hoffman, "Reforming the Reserves," *Marine Corps Gazette* 73, no. 4 (Apr 1989): 49–50.

17. Crossland and Currie, *Twice the Citizen*, 164–173; Doubler, *Civilian in Peace, Soldier in War*, 255–256.

18. Doubler, *Civilian in Peace, Soldier in War*, 257–258; Crossland and Currie, *Twice the Citizen*, 173–174; Gross, *Prelude to the Total Force*, 143–146, 150–151. In 1967 McNamara reconciled his views with those of Congress by proposing end strengths of 400,000 for the Army Guard and 260,000 for the Army Reserve. From that time on, the Army National Guard maintained the majority of combat units while the Army Reserve maintained primarily combat support and combat service support units (Crossland and Currie, 176–178).

19. James T. Currie, "The Army Reserve and Vietnam," *Parameters* 14, no. 3, 77, including quote; Cantwell, *Citizen Airmen*, 209–211; Cantwell, *The Air Force Reserve in the Vietnam Decade: 1965–1975* (Robins Air Force Base, GA: Directorate of Historical Services, Headquarters Air Force Reserve, Nov 1979), 1–8, 57–58. The nonmobilized aircrews conducted the airlift missions either on inactive-duty-for-training, active-duty training (also known as the "annual tour"), or military personnel appropriation (MPA) orders; see *Air Force Reserve in the Vietnam Decade*, 2–3.

20. Crossland and Currie, *Twice the Citizen*, 173–174, 197–201, 207, 211; Weigley, *History of the United States Army*, 561; Millett and Maslowski, *For the Common Defense*, 559–560; Doubler, *Civilian in Peace, Soldier in War*, 257–261; Gross, *Prelude to the Total Force*, 145–146, 152, 156–165; Cantwell, *Citizen Airmen*, 205–207, 209–210, 214–217, 220–223; Cantwell, *Air Force Reserve in the Vietnam Decade*, 1–8, 46–47, 57–58. Although the January 1968 mobilization was in response to the *Pueblo*'s seizure by North Korea, some units later deployed to Vietnam (Gross, *Prelude to the Total Force,* 158). The May 1968 mobilization

was more in response to stresses on the U.S. force in Vietnam than in Korea, yet those recalled deployed to Vietnam, Japan, and Korea, while others remained stateside (Cantwell, *Citizen Airmen*, 221).

21. Reserve Forces Bill of Rights and Vitalization Act, Pub. L. No. 90-168, 81 Stat. (1967), <http://www.gpo.gov/fdsys/pkg/STATUTE-81/pdf/STATUTE-81-Pg521.pdf>; Crossland and Currie, *Twice the Citizen*, 181–183; Gross, *Prelude to the Total Force*, 155.

22. Gross, *Prelude to the Total Force*, 155; Library of Congress, Federal Research Division, *Historical Attempts to Reorganize the Reserve Components* (Washington, DC: Library of Congress, Oct 2007), 13–14; Kathryn Roe Coker, *The Indispensable Force: The Post–Cold War Operational Army Reserve, 1990–2010* (Fort Bragg, NC: Office of Army Reserve History, 2013), 40; John A. Boyd, USARC, Office of Army Reserve Historian, email message to Marion, 14 Nov 2014; Cantwell, *Citizen Airmen*, 238–246; Crossland and Currie, *Twice the Citizen*, 179–183.

23. William R. Kreh, *Citizen Sailors: The U.S. Naval Reserve in War and Peace* (New York: David McKay Co., 1969), 6–9, 64; USMC Division of Reserve, *Marine Corps Reserve: A History*, 234, 241, 269; "Reserve Training Reviewed," *Coast Guard Reservist* 15, no. 1 (Nov 1967); "Individual Reservists May Be Called To Active Duty If Not Fulfilling Their Reserve Obligation," *Coast Guard Reservist* 15, no. 1 (Nov 1967); "Reservists Have Been Involuntarily Ordered To Active Duty," *Coast Guard Reservist* 15, no. 7 (May 1968); John D. McCubbin, "The Admiral's Corner," *Coast Guard Reservist* 15, no. 12 (Oct 1968); "Involuntary Call-Up Defended," *Coast Guard Reservist* 15, no. 12 (Oct 1968). This issue was misprinted as "Sept. 1968"; "The Coast Guard in Vietnam," *Coast Guard Reservist* 16, no. 9 (Jul 1969). As of late 1967, about 7,500 Army reservists and a total of 400 reservists from the Air Force, Navy, and Marine Corps had been recalled to active duty due to unsatisfactory performance in the reserve; see Bigelow, Chaloupka, and Rockett, "Naval Reserve: Chronology," 153; Military Selective Service Act of 1967, Public Law 90-40; see http://www.gpo.gov/fdsys/pkg/STATUTE-81/pdf/STATUTE-81-Pg100.pdf; see also Crossland and Currie, *Twice the Citizen*, 197–198; Cantwell, *Citizen Airmen*, 207; "Nonparticipating Reservists Face Active Duty Call-Up," *Coast Guard Reservist* 14, no. 10 (Oct 1967).

24. Weigley, *History of the United States Army*, 567, including quote 1; Richard Hunt, draft manuscript biography of Melvin Laird (Nov 2014), chapter 14, pages 11–14, 17–18, 20, 30, 33–34, including quote 2, Gates Commission quoted by Hunt (manuscript provided to authors by OSD/HO); Millett and Maslowski, *For the Common Defense*, 561–562, 569–570.

25. Lewis Sorley, *Thunderbolt: General Creighton Abrams and the Army of His Times* (New York: Simon & Schuster, 1992), 364, including quote, Abrams quoted by General John W. Vessey Jr.; Coker, *Indispensable Force*, 4, 19, 463. The so-called Abrams Doctrine has been disputed by others who argue there is no contemporary documentation confirming this was Abrams' rationale, though some suspect it "might have been seen as a positive collateral spinoff" of active-reserve mix established for other policy reasons. Conrad Crane and Gian Gentile, "Understanding the Abrams Doctrine: Myth Versus Reality," War on the Rocks, 9 Dec 2015, <https://warontherocks.com/2015/12/understanding-the-abrams-doctrine-myth-versus-reality> accessed 30 May 2017. In any case, by 1993 it was accepted wisdom in many quarters that "the Army, in particular, should be structured to make active and reserve units so interdependent that a president could not send military forces to combat without activating the reserves." National

Defense Research Institute, *Assessing the Structure and Mix of Future Active and Reserve Forces: Final Report to the Secretary of Defense Executive Summary* (Washington, DC: 1993), 2.

26. Millett and Maslowski, *For the Common Defense*, 566; Crossland and Currie, *Twice the Citizen*, 263; Doubler, *Civilian in Peace, Soldier in War*, 284; Cantwell, *Citizen Airmen*, 338–339. We have used the term "call" and avoided the term "mobilize" in connection with the 1976 law and its amendments because the option could be used for peacetime purposes rather than solely for armed conflict; moreover, for that reason ASD(RA) Stephen M. Duncan preferred not to refer to the law as authorizing a "mobilization." Later, PRC authority was also known as Title 10, U.S.C. 12304 (referring to the U.S. Code section number), or simply as 12304.

27. "'Total Force' Concept Revamps Readiness Policy," *Coast Guard Reservist* 20, no. 2 (Nov 1972), including quote 1, Laird quoted by authors; Melvin R. Laird, *National Security Strategy of Realistic Deterrence: Secretary of Defense Melvin R. Laird's Annual Defense Department Report, FY 1973* ([Washington, DC: 1972]), 24, including quote 2 (Laird testimony on 17 Feb 1972); Mahon, *History of the Militia and the National Guard*, 248–249, 265; Doubler, *Civilian in Peace, Soldier in War*, 273–274, 277–278; Crossland and Currie, *Twice the Citizen*, 214–215, 253; Gross, *Air National Guard and the American Military Tradition*, 114–115, including quote 3, Schlesinger quoted by Gross. An overlooked aspect of Laird's Total Force concept was that it included the role of U.S. allies, as in his statement, "The conceptual thrust of Total Force is toward the efficient integration of *all relevant Free World* resources to provide more security for all of us"; see Laird, *National Security Strategy of Realistic Deterrence*, 24 (emphasis added).

28. Crossland and Currie, *Twice the Citizen*, 254–256; Doubler, *Civilian in Peace, Soldier in War*, 279–284. By the late 1970s the Roundout program enabled the Army to increase from 13 to 16 active combat divisions; Abbott A. Brayton, "American Mobilisation Policies for the 1980s," *Journal of the Royal United Services Institute for Defense Studies* 126, no. 1 (Mar 1981): 26–33; Center of Military History, *Department of the Army Historical Summary Fiscal Year 1979* (Washington, DC: Center of Military History, 1982), 129.

29. Cantwell, *Citizen Airmen*, 333–334, including quote 1, National Defense University study quoted by Cantwell; Gross, *Air National Guard and the American Military Tradition*, 126, including quote 2.

30. Gross, *Air National Guard and the American Military Tradition*, 115–117; Cantwell, *Citizen Airmen*, 329; Brig. Gen. Richard R. Severson, USAF, interview by Betty R. Kennedy, Jul 2008, Robins Air Force Base, GA, AFRC/HO, 17.

31. Reserve Forces Policy Board, *Annual Report of the Reserve Forces Policy Board, Fiscal Year 1980* (Washington, DC: Office of the Secretary of Defense, 1981), 4. Hereafter these reports will be cited as, e.g., RFPB, *Annual Report, Fiscal Year 1980*, 4; *Reserve Readiness and Proficiency*, ECP 15-8 (Quantico, VA: Education Center, Marine Corps Development and Education Command, 1980), 3–4; Brayton, "American Mobilisation Policies," 26–33; J. E. Johansen, "The Admiral's Corner," *Coast Guard Reservist* 21, no. 3 (Dec 1973); J. W. Moreau, "The Admiral's Corner," *Coast Guard Reservist* 20, no. 1 (Oct 1972); "Coast Guard Reservists Activated for First Time to Aid in Containing Flood-Swollen Rivers in Second District," *Coast Guard Reservist* 20, no. 8 (May 1973); Rear Adm. Sidney B. Vaughn, "Admiral's Corner," *Coast Guard Reservist* (Nov-Dec 1980); Vaughn, "Admiral's Corner," *Coast Guard Reservist* (May-Jun 1981).

32. Brayton, "American Mobilisation Policies," 26–33.

33. Ibid.," 26–33, including quotes 1, 4; Department of Defense, *Annual Report of the Secretary of Defense on Reserve Forces, Fiscal Year 1977* (Washington, DC: DoD, n.d.), Introduction, 12, including quote 2; Crossland and Currie, *Twice the Citizen*, 259–262, including quote 3. Regarding the 1978 mobility exercise, Army Reserve historians Crossland and Currie concluded that "[t]he entire mobilization at [Camp] Shelby would have been a disaster" (260).

34. Weigley, *History of the United States Army*, 568–569, 572; Doubler, *Civilian in Peace, Soldier in War*, 273–276; Crossland and Currie, *Twice the Citizen*, 231–232, 239, including quote 1; annual reports of the secretary of defense on reserve forces, 1970–1979; RFPB, *Annual Report, Fiscal Year 1980*, 18, including quote 2. There were no IRR personnel in the Army National Guard or Air National Guard.

35. See White Memorandum, reproduced on pages 1–4 of the Gerard Study and the study's "Major Conclusions", including quote 1–2; Crossland and Currie, *Twice the Citizen*, 218–222; Cantwell, *Citizen Airmen*, 301. In 1980 the chief of Army Reserve, testified before the Senate Armed Services Committee that the "assignment of full-time military to positions in Army Reserve units has the greatest potential for improving unit readiness," and he sought funding for 5,400 positions (Crossland and Currie, 222); Thomas Frank England, "The Active Guard/Reserve Program: A New Military Personnel Status," *Military Law Review* 106 (Fall 1984): 8–9; Gerald Cantwell provided an extended discussion of the Air Reserve Technician controversy in the 1970s; see his *Citizen Airmen*, 298–307. The so-called "status quo" issue in which air reserve technicians who lost their military status through no fault of their own continued as civil service technicians was a very minor issue for the Air Force Reserve.

36. Weigley, *History of the United States Army*, 567–568; Bigelow, Chaloupka, and Rockett, "Naval Reserve: Chronology," 204–205; "The Admiral's Corner," *Coast Guard Reservist* 21, no. 8 (May 1974); RFPB, *Annual Report, Fiscal Year 1981*, 21, including quote; Crossland and Currie, *Twice the Citizen*, 237–238.

37. Millett and Maslowski, *For the Common Defense*, 583–584, including quote 1, Reagan quoted by authors; William F. Ward Jr., "Total Force Finds Rare Skills in Army Reserve," *Army* [Green Book], Oct 1987, 181. Although the Carter presidency was associated with the "hollow force" of the late 1970s, the 1980s' defense buildup under Reagan actually began to a limited degree during Carter's last year in office following seizure of the U.S. Embassy in Tehran and the Soviet invasion of Afghanistan (November–December 1979). The buildup included establishing, in 1980, the Rapid Deployment Joint Task Force, forerunner to the U.S. Central Command created three years later; *Cong. Rec.*, 15 Jul 1983, 19466, including quote 2; DoD News Release 43-86, "Remarks Prepared for Delivery by The Honorable Caspar W. Weinberger" [to Reserve Officers Association], 27 Jan 1986, *Public Statements of Secretary of Defense Caspar W. Weinberger* (Washington, DC: OSD/HO, 1986), 117, including quote 3; Department of Defense Authorization Act, Pub. L. No. 98-94, 97 Stat. 614, 24 Sep 1983, Sec. 1212; DoD News Release 274-84, "First Assistant Secretary of Defense for Reserve Affairs Sworn In," 23 May 1984, OSD/HO; United States Congress, *Biographical Directory of the United States Congress 1774–Present*, online ed. (Washington, DC: U.S. Congress, 1998–), "James H. Webb," <http://bioguide.congress.gov/scripts/biodisplay.pl?index=w000803>, accessed 7 Nov 2014; RFPB, *Annual Report, Fiscal Year 1983*, 3.

38. RFPB, *Annual Report, Fiscal Year 1983*, 14, including quote 1, Weinberger quoted by RFPB; *Cong. Rec.*, 15 Jul 1983, 19466, including quote 2, quote of Senator John C. Stennis;

RFPB, *Annual Report, Fiscal Year 1986*, 54–55; RFPB, *Annual Report, Fiscal Year 1985*, 6–8, 29–30, including quotes 3–4; RFPB, *Reserve Component Programs, Fiscal Year 1988*, 23, 84, 110, 173 (table 38), including quote 5 (p. 110); RFPB, *Reserve Component Programs, Fiscal Year 1989*, 12, 33 (table 11), 90; Doubler, *Civilian in Peace, Soldier in War*, 289–295; Gross, *Air National Guard and the American Military Tradition*, 120–121; Susan Rosenfeld and Charles J. Gross, *Air National Guard at 60: A History* (Arlington, VA: Air National Guard, 2007), 14; Bigelow, Chaloupka, and Rockett, "Naval Reserve: Chronology," 212–213, 218.

39. RFPB, *Annual Report, Fiscal Year 1983*, 3; General Accounting Office, *Military Downsizing: Balancing Accessions and Losses Is Key to Shaping the Future Force* (Washington, DC: GAO, 1993), 44; Doubler, *Civilian in Peace, Soldier in War*, 276; Center of Military History, *Department of the Army Historical Summary FY 1988* (Washington, DC: Center of Military History, 1993), 12–13.

40. England, "The Active Guard/Reserve Program: A New Military Personnel Status," 9–11; RFPB, *Annual Report, Fiscal Year 1983*, 20, including quote 1; RFPB, *Reserve Component Programs, Fiscal Year 1989*, 33, 49; Gross, *Air National Guard and the American Military Tradition*, 126. The FY 1983 full-time support ratio in the reserve component was 13 percent *authorized* strength, which probably differed from *actual* strength. The Army Reserve was authorized only 8 percent full-time support personnel, the lowest among reserve components. For the remainder of the 1980s, the Army Reserve's full-time support ratios fluctuated between 8 and 10 percent of its Selected Reserve.

41. Doubler, *Civilian in Peace, Soldier in War*, 289–295; Anne Nelson, "National Guard Now Used as Auxiliary Fighting Force," *Los Angeles Times*, 10 Aug 1986, 1; "Training Authority and the National Guard: Statement by ASD(RA) James H. Webb Jr., to Senate Armed Services Committee," *Defense Issues* 1, no. 51 (15 Jul 1986): 1–3, 6; RFPB, *Reserve Component Programs, Fiscal Year 1987*, 103–104 (table 34); David S. Broder, "Hands Off National Guard, Governors Say," *Washington Post*, 27 Aug 1986, 5; James H. Webb Jr., Letter to the Editor, *New York Times*, 7 Oct 1986; William V. Kennedy, "Conflict Brews over Training of National Guard Units," *Christian Science Monitor*, 6 Aug 1987, 5. In 1989–1990 a U.S. Circuit Court of Appeals, and then the U.S. Supreme Court, ruled in favor of the federal government against the governors; see "States Lose Battle over Control of Guard," *Washington Times*, 29 Jun 1989, 4. For the "Status Act," see Les' Andrii Melnyk, "A True National Guard," 458–461.

42. Cantwell, *Citizen Airmen*, 359; Crossland and Currie, *Twice the Citizen*, 261–265, including quote 1, Lt. Gen. Robert C. Kingston quoted by authors; William R. Berkman, "Today's Total Army Commits Its Reserve," *Army* [Green Book], Oct 1986, 161; RFPB, *Annual Report, Fiscal Year 1986*, 3 (table 2); William R. Berkman, "Reserve Readiness Shows Steady Rise," *Army* [Green Book], Oct 1985, 189; Ward, "Total Force Finds Rare Skills in Army Reserve," 183. By FY 1983, the Army Reserve had no combat divisions (RFPB, *Annual report, Fiscal Year 1983*, 4, table 2); RFPB, *Annual Report, Fiscal Year 1983*, 19, including quote 2; H.R. Rep. No. 107, 98th Cong., 1st sess. 202 (1983), including quote 3; Doubler, *Civilian in Peace, Soldier in War*, 276 (table 7), 289–291, 298; RFPB, *Reserve Component Programs, Fiscal Year 1988*, 6 (table 2); DoD News Release 114-82, "Army National Guard Exceeds 400,000 in Strength," 19 Mar 1982, OSD/HO.

43. James H. Webb Jr., interview by Alfred Goldberg and Roger Trask, 3 and 15 Jun 1998, Arlington, VA, OSD/HO, including quote 1; Dennis J. Rockstroh, "5,000 Former Soldiers Recalled in Test of U.S. Military Strength," *Philadelphia Inquirer*, 1 Jan 1986, 8, 10, including

quote 2, Pete Shugert quoted by Rockstroh; "Military Aide Asks New Reserve Plan," *New York Times*, 5 Nov 1985, 29; "US Military to Call Up All Inactive Reservists for One Day a Year," *Boston Globe*, 21 Nov 1985, 48; RFPB, *Annual Report, Fiscal Year 1985*, 11; RFPB, *Annual Report, Fiscal Year 1986*, 22. One of many indicators of the increasing importance of the RC and its Total Force role was in the transition of the main body of the RFPB annual report from roughly 30 pages in 1983 to 110 pages in 1986, and to 140 pages in 1989. From FYs 1981 to 1985 the Selected Reserve increased from 899,000 to 1.1 million.

44. Stephen M. Duncan, *Citizen Warriors: America's National Guard and Reserve Forces & the Politics of National Security* (Novato, CA: Presidio Press, 1997), 11, 16, including quotes 1, 3 (emphasis in original); Stephen M. Duncan, "Selected Reserve Passes Call-Up Test," *Defense Issues* 3, no. 2 (22 Dec 1987), including quote 2; "20,000 Called Up in Test of Reserves, National Guard," *Washington Post*, 25 Oct 1987, 20; "Most Weekend Warriors Heed Call as Emergency Readiness Is Tested," *Washington Times*, 23 Nov 1987, 4; RFPB, *Annual Report, Fiscal Year 1986*, 62–63.

45. RFPB, *Annual Report, Fiscal Year 1986*, 64–65, 75, including quote 1; RFPB, *Reserve Component Programs, Fiscal Year 1989*, 54–56, including quote 2; RFPB, *Annual Report, Fiscal Year 1985*, vi; RFPB, *Reserve Component Programs, Fiscal Year 1987*, 59–60; DoD News Release 280-88, "Department of Defense Conducts Survey of Reserve Component Spouses," 2 Jun 1988, OSD/HO.

46. "Reserve Forces of the United States: Prepared Statement by ASD(RA) Stephen M. Duncan," *Defense Issues* 4, no. 12 (6 Apr 1989), including quote; RFPB, *Annual Report, Fiscal Year 1985*, vi; RFPB, *Annual Report, Fiscal Year 1986*, 27; RFPB, *Reserve Component Programs, Fiscal Year 1988*, 67–68; RFPB, *Reserve Component Programs, Fiscal Year 1989*, 60–61.

47. Gerard Study, I-2, including quote 1 (emphasis in original); Duncan, "Reserve Forces of the United States," including quote 2; RFPB, *Reserve Component Programs, Fiscal Year 1989*, 5 (table 2). The 1.18 million Selected Reserve strength was as of 30 September 1989.

48. Alford, O'Ferrall, Rehberg, and Riedler, "The Transformation of Reserve Component (RC) Modernization," Weinberger quoted by authors; USMC Division of Reserve, *Marine Corps Reserve: A History*, 182, including quote, Wilson quoted by authors.

Chapter 4

1. H. Norman Schwarzkopf and Peter Petre, *It Doesn't Take a Hero: The Autobiography of General H. Norman Schwarzkopf* (New York and Toronto: Linda Grey Bantam Books, 1992), 295–308.

2. Dan Balz and Rick Atkinson, "Bush Orders Mobilization of Military Reserves," *Washington Post*, 23 Aug 1990, 1, including quote, quoted by authors; George H. W. Bush, "Executive Order 12727: Ordering the Selected Reserve of the Armed Forces to Active Duty," 22 Aug 1990, The American Presidency Project, <http://www.presidency.ucsb.edu/ws/?pid=23568>, accessed 20 Nov 2014; Marygail Brauner, Harry Thie, and Roger Brown, *Assessing the Structure and Mix of Future Active and Reserve Forces: Effectiveness of Total Force Policy During the Persian Gulf Conflict* (Santa Monica, CA: RAND, 1992), xiv–xvi, <http://www.rand.org/content/dam/rand/pubs/monograph_reports/2006/MR132.sum.pdf>, accessed 20 Nov 2014; Doubler, *Civilian in Peace, Soldier in War*, 306–307.

3. Frank N. Schubert and Theresa L. Krause, eds., *Thé Whirlwind War* (Washington, DC: Center of Military History, 1995), 72–73; Gross, *Air National Guard and the American Military Tradition*, 149–154, 161, including quote; Cantwell, *Citizen Airmen,* 370–371; Bush, "Executive Order 12727"; George H. W. Bush, "Executive Order 12722–Blocking Iraqi Government Property and Prohibiting Transactions with Iraq," 2 Aug 1990, The American Presidency Project, <http://www.presidency.ucsb.edu/ws/index.php?pid=23563>, accessed 23 Jun 2016. EO 12722 officially declared a "national emergency," but initiated only economic sanctions against Iraq in response to its "unusual and extraordinary threat to the national security and foreign policy of the United States." Oddly, EO 12727 did not refer to that state of national emergency, or use it to grant explicit authority to mobilize reservists for up to two years. Instead it found only that reserves were "necessary to augment the active armed forces of the United States for the effective conduct of operational missions in and around the Arabian Peninsula."

4. George H. W. Bush, Exec. Order No. 12733, Authorizing the Extension of the Period of Active Duty of Personnel of the Selected Reserve of the Armed Forces, 13 Nov 1990, <http://www.presidency.ucsb.edu/ws/index.php?pid=23572>, accessed 4 Apr 2017. Regarding 673b authority, Congress had replaced 90 days in both places with 180 days, for a total of 360 days of activation. Duncan, *Citizen Warriors*, 66–67, 69, 76.

5. Duncan, *Citizen Warriors*, 66–72, 76, 84–85, 89; Schubert and Krause, *The Whirlwind War*, 126; Doubler, *Civilian in Peace, Soldier in War*, 313–317; George H. W. Bush, "Executive Order 12733—Authorizing the Extension of the Period of Active Duty of Personnel of the Selected Reserve of the Armed Forces," 13 Nov 1990, <http://www.presidency.ucsb.edu/ws/index.php?pid=23572>, accessed 10 Dec 2014; Stephen M. Duncan, "Capabilities and Future Needs of the Reserve Components," *Defense Issues* 7, no. 32 (1 May 1992): 2, 5; Coker, *Indispensable Force*, 182–183, 215.

For further discussion of IRR, see chapter 3, present work. Following the FY 1998 law, the term "presidential selected reserve call-up" (PSRC) authority was changed to "presidential reserve call-up" (PRC) to indicate the reality that the call-up authority was no longer limited to the *Selected* Reserve (IRR members are part of the Ready Reserve, not the Selected Reserve). Cases in point were in August 1990 and September 1994: implementation of 673b authority (another term for PSRC) by Presidents Bush and Clinton did not affect the IRR. Prior to the mid-1990s, "PSRC authority" was often referred to as "673b authority." Bush's executive order in August 1990 did not mention PSRC or any similar term; see his Executive Order 12727. The same was true in September 1994 regarding Clinton's Executive Order 12927 (see William J. Clinton, "Executive Order 12927—Ordering the Selected Reserve of the Armed Forces to Active Duty," <http://www.archives.gov/federal-register/executive-orders/pdf/12927.pdf>, accessed 9 Dec 2014. Both presidents referred to 673b authority rather than to PSRC. In December 1995, however, the term "Presidential Selected Reserve" appeared in reference to the reserve call-up for the Balkans; see "President Clinton Authorizes Reserve Call-up," American Forces Press Service, 13 Dec 1995, <http://archive.defense.gov/news/newsarticle.aspx?id=40501>, accessed 9 Dec 2014. In April 1999, the term "PSRC" was applied *retroactively* to refer to the 1990 and 1994 call-ups, which *at the time were referred to strictly as 673b authority*; see DoD News Release 197-99, "Secretary Cohen Announces Presidential Selected Reserve Call-Up," 27 Apr 1999, <http://archive.defense.gov/Releases/Release.aspx?ReleaseID=2066>, accessed 24 May 2016.

6. Gross, *Air National Guard and the American Military Tradition*, 141–142, chapter 6; Cantwell, *Citizen Airmen*, 364–367; Department of Defense, *Conduct of the Persian Gulf*

Conflict: An Interim Report to Congress (Washington, DC: Department of Defense, 1991), chapter 11, page 1. Guard personnel serving in an overseas contingency or supporting it from stateside must be federalized. The following three groups were federalized: volunteer reservists activated for Desert Shield and Desert Storm, reservists activated involuntarily under 673b authority (22 Aug 1990), and reservists mobilized involuntarily under partial mobilization authority (18 Jan 1991); David P. Anderson (Air National Guard/National Guard Bureau History Office) email messages to Marion, 5 Nov 2012 and 11 Dec 2012. For the full text of the president's partial mobilization order, see George H. W. Bush, Executive Order 12743: Ordering the Ready Reserve of the Armed Forces to Active Duty, 18 Jan 1991, <http://www.presidency.ucsb.edu/ws/?pid=23582>, accessed 24 Jul 2014.

7. Gross, *Air National Guard and the American Military Tradition*, 148–149, 157; Cantwell, *Citizen Airmen*, 366–367.

8. Duncan, *Citizen Warriors*, 94–97; Cantwell, *Citizen Airmen*, 368.

9. Duncan, *Citizen Warriors*, 84, 99–101, 232, including quote; Bigelow, Chaloupka, and Rockett, "Naval Reserve: Chronology," 236, 243–249; Department of the Navy, *The United States Navy in "Desert Shield"/"Desert Storm"* (Washington, DC: Department of the Navy, Office of the Chief of Naval Operations, 15 May 1991), <http://www.history.navy.mil/research/library/online-reading-room/title-list-alphabetically/u/us-navy-in-desert-shield-desert-storm.html>, accessed 17 Jun 2016.

10. Mark F. Cancian, "Marine Corps Reserve Forces in Southwest Asia," *Marine Corps Gazette*, Sep 1991, 35–37; F. G. Hoffman, "Reversing Course on Total Force?" *Marine Corps Gazette*, Sep 1991, 38–39; Mark F. Cancian, "Depend on the Marine Reserve," *Marine Corps Gazette*, Mar 1994, 18–19, including quote; Lt. Col. Dennis P. Mroczkowski, *With the 2d Marine Division in Desert Shield and Desert Storm* (Washington, DC: History and Museums Division, U.S. Marine Corps, 1993), 4; Department of Defense, *Conduct of the Persian Gulf Conflict*, 11–13.

11. Cancian, "Marine Corps Reserve Forces in Southwest Asia," 35–36, including quote (emphasis in original). Under the I-I program, selected regular Marines served tours with Selected Reserve units to facilitate their combat readiness; such tours were considered to enhance rather than harm the regular's career.

12. Mike Price, "PSUs: A Lightning-Quick Response to 'The Call,'" *Reservist*, Nov 1990, 4, 6–7; "Rest of PSUs 303 and 301 follow closely behind first 15 to arrive," *Reservist*, Apr 1991, 7; "What We Do…" *The Coast Guard Reserve, Fac Pac 90*, 3, 6–7. The Coast Guard Reserve was established in 1941, thus 1990 was its fiftieth year; see chapter 1, present work. By 1996, PSUs included active component personnel; see Edward J. Kruska, "CG Reservists help train active duty PSU in Ohio," *Coast Guard Reservist*, Jan 1996, 8; "PSU 303 decommissioning," *Coast Guard Reservist*, Jan 1997, 4. Between 1995 and December 1998, the Coast Guard activated five "official" (not notional) PSUs, for a total of six PSUs by 1999; see Rear Adm. Steven E. Day, USCGR, interview by Forrest L. Marion, 6 Mar 2012, Arlington, VA, OSD/HO; Thomas J. Vitullo and Robert A. Stohlman, "PSU Update," *Coast Guard Reservist*, Nov 1995, 5–7; "Welcome PSU 313," *Coast Guard Reservist*, Feb 1999; Jeffrey D. Smith, USCGR (ret.), email messages to Marion, Oct 2012. By the late 1990s, PSUs included a small number of active component personnel.

13. Coker, *Indispensable Force*, 33, 36–37, including quote.

14. Coker, *Indispensable Force*, 19–20, 27; John A. Boyd, USARC, Office of the Army Reserve Historian, comment on draft to authors, 10 Oct 2014. Coker stated some 79,000 Army Reserve soldiers were activated for Desert Shield and Desert Storm, but about 84,000 probably is a more accurate number based on the following: First, the Reserve Forces Policy Board reported that 63,398 Army Guard personnel were activated for the Persian Gulf; see RFPB, *Annual Report, Fiscal Year 1991*, 11–12, <http://www.dtic.mil/dtic/tr/fulltext/u2/a249015. pdf>, accessed 10 Dec 2014. Second, a GAO study referenced 147,000 activated reservists from the Army Reserve and Army National Guard (147,000 minus 63,000 Army Guard equals 84,000 Army Reserve); see GAO, *National Guard: Peacetime Training Did Not Adequately Prepare Combat Brigades for Gulf War* (Washington, DC: GAO, 1991), <http://www.gao.gov/ assets/160/151085.pdf>, accessed 22 Nov 2014, 8; third, the estimate of 84,000 Army Reserve soldiers activated also appeared in an Army Reserve annual history; see Kathryn Roe Coker, *The 2001 Army Reserve Historical Summary (*Fort McPherson, GA: Office of Army Reserve History, 2003), xxiii.

15. Duncan, *Citizen Warriors*, 35–37; Stephen M. Duncan, "Gulf War Was a Test of Reserve Components and They Passed," in *Desert Shield/Desert Storm Employment of Reserve Component: Extracts of Lessons Learned* (Washington, DC: U.S. Naval War College, n.d.), <http://dtic.mil/doctrine/doctrine/research/p162.pdf>, accessed 9 Dec 2014, 21, 25, 30; Department of Defense, *Conduct of the Persian Gulf Conflict*, 11–14; Doubler, *Civilian in Peace, Soldier in War*, 302–303, 306–307, 329; RFPB, *Reserve Component Programs, Fiscal Year 1991*, 11–12; F. G. Hoffman, "Reversing Course on Total Force?" *Marine Corps Gazette*, Sep 1991, 38–39. Hoffman stated that as of 1 March 1991 about 101,600 of 225,600 activated reservists (45 percent) had deployed overseas. We have chosen to use the term "activation" rather than "mobilization" in order to distinguish between the authorities available to the president. Because initially President Bush did not employ statutory mobilization authority, "activation" is the best term. (Later, in January 1991 the president employed partial mobilization authority, also known as Section 673.) Former ASD(RA) Stephen Duncan argued that, technically, an augmentation based on Section 673b was not a *mobilization* because the Section 673b authority could be used for peacetime operational purposes; see Duncan, *Citizen Warriors*, 16, 49; and chapter 3, present work.

16. Schubert and Krause, *The Whirlwind War*, 57–58.

17. Duncan, *Citizen Warriors*, 37–38, including quotes 1–2; Schwarzkopf, *It Doesn't Take a Hero*, 323, including quotes 3–4.

18. Doubler, *Civilian in Peace, Soldier in War*, 331, including quote 1; Duncan, *Citizen Warriors*, 49–50, 63–64, including quote 2, Montgomery quoted by Duncan; Schubert and Krause, *The Whirlwind War*, 72.

19. Doubler, *Civilian in Peace, Soldier in War*, 331, including quote 1; Robert L. Goldich, "The Army's Roundout Concept after the Persian Gulf War" (Washington, DC: Congressional Research Service, Library of Congress, 22 Oct 1991), ii, including quote 2; Duncan, *Citizen Warriors*, 49–50, 63–64. In the Army's official account of the Gulf War, leading Army warrior-scholar Brig. Gen. (later, Maj. Gen.) Robert H. Scales Jr., wrote that the 48th Infantry Brigade was "a late-deploying unit in order to allow time for postmobilization training to prepare for combat"; see his *Certain Victory: United States Army in the Gulf War* (Washington, DC: Office of the Chief of Staff, U.S. Army, 1993), 52. His statement should put to rest once and for all any notions that roundout brigades were intended to deploy almost immediately upon mobilization,

assuming their parent organizations did so. A detailed biography of Scales is at <http://www.deanza.edu/faculty/swensson/article_scales.html>, accessed 20 Nov 2014.

20. Goldich, "Army's Roundout Concept After the Persian Gulf War," including quote; Schubert and Krause, *The Whirlwind War*, 73; Duncan, *Citizen Warriors*, 36; Doubler, *Civilian in Peace, Soldier in War*, 312.

21. GAO, *Peacetime Training Did Not Adequately Prepare Combat Brigades*, 3, 12–13, 16–20, including quotes; Barton Gellman, "Cheney Says Guard Units May Need Reorganizing," *Washington Post*, 15 Mar 1991, 34; Doubler, *Civilian in Peace, Soldier in War*, 316. For Roundout brigade program, see chapter 3, present work. The ARNG history office noted that at least in the program's inception, Roundout also served as a means for the Army to preserve the maximum number of divisional flags.

22. GAO, *Peacetime Training Did Not Adequately Prepare Combat Brigades*, 20–21, including quote.

23. Thomas P. Christie and Richard A. Fejfar, *Desert Shield/Desert Storm After Action Report* (Alexandria, VA: Institute for Defense Analyses, 1992), 77, 94–95; GAO, *Peacetime Guard Did Not Adequately Prepare Combat Brigades* (Washington, DC: GAO, 1991), 13–14; Les' Melnyk, *Mobilizing for the Storm: The Army National Guard in Operations Desert Shield and Desert Storm* (Washington, DC: National Guard Bureau, 2001), 23.

24. Melissa Healy, "Cheney Would Reduce Reserve Combat Role," *Los Angeles Times*, 14 Mar 1991, 1, <http://articles.latimes.com/1991-03-14/news/mn-149_1_u-s-central-command>, accessed 19 May 2016, including quote 1, Cheney quoted by Healy; Goldich, "Army's Roundout Concept after the Persian Gulf War," ii, including quote 2; "Sullivan to Congress: It Takes 90 Days To Train Brigades, Year To Train Divisions," *Inside the Army*, 2 Mar 1992, 2; Duncan, *Citizen Warriors*, 82–84; Doubler, *Civilian in Peace, Soldier in War*, 330–331. For predeployment training regimens between 2007 and 2011, see chapter 7, present work. Dennis P. Chapman, *Planning for Employment of the Reserve Components: Army Practice, Past and Present*, Land Warfare Paper No. 69 (Washington, DC: Association of the United States Army, Sep 2008), 10, including quote 3.

25. Truman, *Memoirs*, 506; HCAS, Military Personnel and Compensation Subcommittee, *Redeployment of Reserves From Operation Desert Storm: Hearing, April 18, 1991* (Washington, DC: GPO, 1992), 2, 25, 41; HCAS, *Reserve Demobilization Problems: Hearing, 30 December 1991* (Washington, DC: GPO, 1992), 38; Duncan, *Citizen Warriors*, 118–121.

26. Duncan, *Citizen Warriors*, 33, 121–130, including quote; Senate Committee on Armed Services, Subcommittee on Manpower and Personnel, *Department of Defense Procedures for Return and Release from Active Duty of National Guardsmen and Reservists Called Up for Operation Desert Shield/Desert Storm: Hearing, June 11, 1991* (Washington, DC: GPO, 1991), 5–8, 13; Gross, *Air National Guard and the American Military Tradition*, 158–159.

27. Senate Armed Services Committee, *Procedures for Return and Release from Active Duty*, 60, including quote 1; Duncan, *Citizen Warriors*, 124, including quote 2. By late August 1991, all but 4 percent of mobilized RC personnel had been demobilized. The last unit to remain on active duty involuntarily was the Army Reserve's 1184th Transportation Terminal Unit, released on 19 November 1991; see Duncan, 130.

28. RFPB, *Reserve Component Programs, Fiscal Year 1991*, xv, 52–54, including quotes. Prior to 1990, the Naval Reserve lacked an institutional family support system (53); Doubler, *Civilian in Peace, Soldier in War*, 330; Cantwell, *Citizen Airmen*, 372–373.

29. RFPB, *Reserve Component Programs—FY 1992* (Washington, DC: Office of the Secretary of Defense, 1993), 48–49; RFPB, *Annual Report, Fiscal Year 1991*, 53; Coker, *Indispensable Force*, 137, 232–233, including quote; Cantwell, *Citizen Airmen*, 372–374. The date of the National Guard's lead-agent designation was unspecified, but it appeared to be *post*-Desert Shield/Storm. Air National Guard family programs were "administered in conjunction with the Army National Guard through each State Headquarters with oversight responsibilities in the National Guard Bureau." Quote in RFPB, *Reserve Component Programs—FY 1992*, 49.

30. Duncan, *Citizen Warriors*, 111–115.

31. RFPB, *Reserve Component Programs, Fiscal Year 1991*, 50–52; Cantwell, *Citizen Airmen*, 374–375; Duncan, "Capabilities and Future Needs of the Reserve Components," 3; Duncan, *Citizen Warriors*, 111–115. The committee was eventually located within the Office of the Assistant Secretary of Defense for Reserve Affairs; Cantwell, *Citizen Airmen*, 374–375, including quote.

32. Lorna S. Jaffe, *The Development of the Base Force, 1989–1992* (Washington, DC: The Joint History Office, 1993), 2–4; Colin L. Powell, *My American Journey*, with Joseph E. Persico (New York: Random House, 1995), 451, including quotes 1–2 (emphasis in original); Duncan, "Capabilities and Future Needs of the Reserve Components," 8–9, including quotes 3–4, quoted by Duncan; Duncan, *Citizen Warriors*, 168–170; Doubler, *Civilian in Peace, Soldier in War*, 334–335, 343–344; Coker, *Indispensable Force*, 47; Jaffe, *Development of the Base Force*, 44. The official dissolution of the Soviet Union took place in December 1991.

33. Duncan, "Capabilities and Future Needs of the Reserve Components," 8, including quote, Bush quoted by Duncan; Melissa Healy, "U.S. Role in Mideast Helped to Put a Lid on Defense Cuts, Strategists Say," *Los Angeles Times*, 2 Oct 1990, 18, <http://articles.latimes.com/1990-10-02/news/mn-1750_1_operation-desert-shield>, accessed 9 Apr 2015; Duncan, "Capabilities and Future Needs of the Reserve Components," 8; "The Disarmed Services Budget," *Washington Times*, 1 Oct 1990, G-2.

34. Duncan, *Citizen Warriors*, 199, including quote, Aspin quoted by Duncan.

35. Duncan, *Citizen Warriors*, 199–203; Richard B. Cheney and Colin Powell, "Drawing Down the Guard and Reserve," press briefing, *Defense Issues,* 26 Mar 1992, 1–3, 6, including quote; Duncan, "Capabilities and Future Needs of the Reserve Components," 5. The term "the base force," used throughout this briefing, referred to the smaller, refocused, post–Cold War U.S. armed forces. The term dated from 1990 and referred to the minimum force structure required "to retain superpower status," which Duncan considered "an awfully fuzzy standard"; see his *Citizen Warriors*, 167–170, "superpower" quote of Powell and Paul Wolfowitz, under secretary of defense for policy, quoted by Duncan.

36. Cheney and Powell, "Drawing Down the Guard and Reserve," 3, including quote.

37. Cheney and Powell, "Drawing Down the Guard and Reserve," 3, 4–5, including quotes; Duncan, *Citizen Warriors*, 202; Doubler, *Civilian in Peace, Soldier in War*, 344.

38. Duncan, "Capabilities and Future Needs of the Reserve Components," 6, 9, including quotes; Duncan, *Citizen Warriors*, 205–207.

39. Duncan, "Capabilities and Future Needs of the Reserve Components," 10, including quote.

40. Lt. Col. Thomas C. Stredwick, *Title XI: An Underfunded Initiative* (Carlisle Barracks, PA: Army War College, 15 Apr 1996), <http://www.dtic.mil/cgi-bin/GetTRDoc?Location=U2&doc=GetTRDoc.pdf&AD=ADA309074>, accessed 13 Jun 2017.

41. Les Aspin, *Report on the Bottom-Up Review* (Washington, DC: U.S. Department of Defense, 1993), iii, 1, 7, 19, 92–93, 94, including quotes, <http://www.dod.mil/pubs/foi/administration_and_Management/other/515.pdf>, accessed 2 Dec 2014; Duncan, *Citizen Warriors*, 212–213; Doubler, *Civilian in Peace, Soldier in War*, 349–350; Andrew F. Krepinevich, *The Bottom-Up Review: An Assessment* (Washington, DC: Defense Budget Project, Feb 1994), i–iv, 1, 12, 17–19, 21–26, 55, 61; Coker, *Indispensable Force*, 50–51; Cheney and Powell, "Drawing Down the Guard and Reserve," 4. While the defense secretary announced the BUR on 1 September 1993, the date that appeared on the published BUR was October 1993; the online PDF version (accessed by the above link) appears to have several copies of the BUR packaged together.

42. Aspin, *Bottom-Up Review*, 22, 91–94, including quotes (quote 2 emphasis added); Eric V. Larson, David T. Orletsky, and Kristin J. Leuschner, *Defense Planning in a Decade of Change: Lessons from the Base Force, Bottom-Up Review, and Quadrennial Defense Review* (Santa Monica, CA: RAND Corporation, 2001), <http://www.rand.org/pubs/monograph_reports/MR1387.html>, accessed 24 May 2016, chapter 3, 49, 64; Doubler, *Civilian in Peace, Soldier in War*, 350, 362, 384; Coker, *Indispensable Force*, 51.

43. Coker, *Indispensable Force*, 52–53, 148, 468; John A. Boyd, USARC, Office of the Army Reserve Historian, comments on draft and email messages to authors, 10 Oct 2014 and 3 Dec 2014.

44. Aspin, *Bottom-Up Review*, 95; Duncan, *Citizen Warriors*, 205, 211–212, 294; Coker, *Indispensable Force*, 215; William Matthews, "Call-Up Power Remains with the President," *Army Times*, 22 Aug 1994, 22. The new length of activation (270 days) was stated in President Clinton's announcement of PSRC for Operation Joint Endeavor (13 December 1995); see the DoD news article at <http://archive.defense.gov/news/newsarticle.aspx?id=40501>, accessed 5 Apr 2017.

45. Cheryl Y. Marcum, Robert M. Emmerichs, Jennifer Sloan McCombs, and Harry J. Thie, *Methods and Actions for Improving Performance of the Department of Defense Disability Evaluation System* (Santa Monica, CA: RAND Corporation, 2002), Appendix A, 151, including quote, <http://www.rand.org/content/dam/rand/pubs/monograph_reports/MR1228/MR1228.appa.pdf>, accessed 7 Apr 2015; *National Defense Authorization Act for Fiscal Year 1994*, Pub. L. No. 103-160, 107 Stat. 1727 (1993), <https://www.congress.gov/bill/103rd-congress/house-bill/2401>, accessed 30 Jul 2016.

46. Uniformed Services Employment and Reemployment Rights Act, Pub. L. 103-353, 105 Stat. 55 (1994), including quote 1; Staub v. Proctor Hospital, 562 U.S. 1186 (2011).

47. Commission on Roles and Missions of the Armed Forces, *Directions for Defense: Report of the Commission* (Washington, DC: GPO, 1995), ES-1, ES-5, 1–2, 2–24, Conclusion, including quote, <http://edocs.nps.edu/dodpubs/topic/general/ADA295228.pdf>, accessed 24 May 2016.

48. Doubler, *Civilian in Peace, Soldier in War*, 362–364, including quote; Coker, *Indispensable Force*, 54–55. The other two broad areas addressed by the commission were civilian management/support to DoD and planning/programming/budgeting processes (1–4). Commission on Roles and Missions, *Directions for Defense*, 2–24; Aspin, *Bottom-Up Review*, 94; Doubler, *Civilian in Peace, Soldier in War*, 363–364; CNGR, *Transforming the National Guard and Reserves*, 204–208. In 2008, the Commission on the National Guard and Reserves addressed both FTS (Full-Time Support) and full-time support personnel. While "FTS" was concerned strictly with reserve component members supporting reserve units fulltime, "full-time support" personnel could be either active component (e.g., "active duty advisors") or regular component (e.g. usually, Active Guard and Reserve, or AGR; or Military Technician, or MT) members. The distinction was often blurred and confused even in official reports.

49. Commission on Roles and Missions, *Directions for Defense*, 2–23 through 2–25, including quotes 1–2; Dennis J. Reimer, *Army Vision 2010* (Washington, DC: Headquarters Dept. of the Army, 1996), 9, including quote 3; Coker, *Indispensable Force*, 55.

50. Department of Defense, *The Report of the Quadrennial Defense Review* (Washington, DC: Department of Defense, 1997), iii–x, 7–18, including quote 1, <http://history.defense.gov/Portals/70/Documents/quadrennial/QDR1997.pdf>, accessed 5 Dec 2014; Charles C. Krulak, "Quadrennial Defense Review Implementation," *Marine Corps Gazette*, Jun 1997, 22–23, including quote; Commission on Roles and Missions, *Directions for Defense*, 4–9; Doubler, *Civilian in Peace, Soldier in War*, 364–365; Coker, *Indispensable Force*, 168–169, 175.

51. House Committee on National Security, Military Personnel Subcommittee, *Reserve Component Issues from the Quadrennial Defense Review: Hearing, 29 Jul 1997* (Washington, DC: GPO, 1998), 1, 3, 5–6, 12, 16–17, including quote, <http://babel.hathitrust.org/cgi/pt?id=p st.000032141221#view=1up;seq=5>, accessed 5 Dec 2014; Department of Defense, *Report of the Quadrennial Defense Review*, 29–34; Doubler, *Civilian in Peace, Soldier in War*, 364–366; Coker, *Indispensable Force*, 172; *Report of the Quadrennial Defense Review*, 29–34, 39–52; Max Baratz, "A Reorganized Army Reserve: Relevant and Ready," supplement, *Army*, Oct 1997, 93–94; DoD News Release 635-97, "FY 1998 Reserve Component Inactivations Closed Out [from BUR]," 26 Nov 1997, <http://archive.defense.gov/Releases/Release.aspx?ReleaseID=1512>, accessed 5 Dec 2014. The QDR concluded that the Army National Guard division redesign program, directed in 1996 by Secretary of the Army Togo D. West Jr., "will relieve an important warfighting shortfall by converting lower priority combat brigades into higher priority CS/CSS forces"; see Department of Defense, *Report of the Quadrennial Defense Review*, 47. The QDR accelerated this conversion; see also Bernard F. Veronee Jr., *Army National Guard Division Redesign*, 1, <http://www.almc.army.mil/alog/issues/JulAug99/MS466.htm>, accessed 5 Dec 2014; Philip Gold, "The Army vs. the National Guard," *Washington Times*, 5 Jun 1997, 21, <http://www.discovery.org/a/243>, accessed 5 Dec 2014.

52. House Committee on National Security, Military Personnel Subcommittee, *Hearing on Reserve Component Issues from the Quadrennial Defense Review, Jul 29, 1997*, 5, including quote; Rosenfeld and Gross, *Air National Guard at 60*, 27–31; Cantwell, *Citizen Airmen*, 379–381.

53. Rosenfeld and Gross, *Air National Guard at 60*, 18–31; Charles J. Gross, *Adapting the Force: Evolution of the Air National Guard's Air Mobility Mission* (Washington, DC: National Guard Bureau Historical Services Division, 1999), 48–51; "Air National Guard," *Air Force Magazine*, May 1993, 104; "Major Commands," *Air Force Magazine*, May 1994, 59; "Major

Commands," *Air Force Magazine*, May 1995, 72; "Major Commands," *Air Force Magazine*, May 1996, 78; "Major Commands," *Air Force Magazine*, May 1997, 81; Cantwell, *Citizen Airmen*, 378. In 1996, the ANG activated its first space mission unit, the 137th Space Warning Squadron, Colorado Air National Guard; see Rosenfeld and Gross, *Air National Guard at 60*, 19–20.

54. Duncan, *Citizen Warriors*, 211; Mary I. Nolan, "'Vision 2000': The Future of the Naval Reserve," *Sea Power*, Oct 1995, 37–40; Rear Adm. Thomas F. Hall, USN, ret., interview by Forrest L. Marion, 23 Sep 2013, including quotes; RFPB, *Reserve Component Programs— FY 1992*, 35; Nolan, "'Vision 2000'" 37–40; Jon R. Anderson, "Good news: Bad News Is Over," *Handbook for the Guard & Reserve*, 1995, 55.

55. James E. Livingston and Eric L. Chase, "Marine Reserve Force: Critical Back-Up Muscle for America's Post–Cold War Force-in-Readiness," *Marine Corps Gazette*, Mar 1994, 14–17, including quotes; Mark F. Cancian, "Depend on the Marine Reserve," *Marine Corps Gazette*, Mar 1994, 18; CNGR, *Transforming the National Guard and Reserves*, 331. By 1995, Marine Corps active duty strength reached 174,000, the first service to reach the active- duty manpower level mandated by the Bottom-Up Review; see "'We Just Changed the Whole Philosophy', Interview with Lt. Gen. George R. Christmas," *Sea Power*, Jul 1995, 11. In 2008, the CNGR echoed the recommendation to eliminate the "R" for all reservists, a small matter administratively but one possessing significant cultural weight.

56. Livingston and Chase, "Marine Reserve Force: Critical Back-Up Muscle," 14–17, including quote 1; James E. Livingston, "Reserve Vision Revisited," *Marine Corps Gazette*, Jun 1995, 47; Ronald D. Richard, "Seamless Integration at Work," *Marine Corps Gazette*, Jan 1996, 43–44, including quote 2; Allen E. Weh, "The Marines and Total Force: 1997," *Marine Corps Gazette*, Mar 1994, 22.

57. "Integration," *Coast Guard Reservist*, May–Jul 1993, 7–11; Stephen Wehrenberg, "Restructuring, Right People, Right Places," *Coast Guard Reservist*, Aug–Sep 1993, 5–8; Ivette A. Quarles, "Reserve Downsizing Plan," *Coast Guard Reservist*, Jan 1994, 15; Richard M. Larrabee, "A View from the Bridge," *Coast Guard Reservist*, Apr 1995, 4; Richard W. Schneider, "A View from the Bridge," *Coast Guard Reservist*, Jan 1996, 5; Richard W. Schneider, "A View from the Bridge," *Coast Guard Reservist*, May 1996, 4; Day interview, 6 Mar 2012.

58. Robert E. Kramek, "A View from the Bridge," *Coast Guard Reservist*, Oct 1994, 3, including quotes 1–2; Day interview, 6 Mar 2012, 4–5, including quote 3; Schneider, "A View from the Bridge," *Coast Guard Reservist*, May 1996, 4, including quote 4; Robert E. Sloncen, "A View from the Bridge," *Coast Guard Reservist* Jun 1994, 5; "An Interview With Our Commandant," *Coast Guard Reservist*, Aug 1997, 5–11; *1998 Team Coast Guard Customer and Reserve Member Appraisals* (N.p., ca. 1998), 3, 6; CNGR, *Transforming the National Guard and Reserves*, 132–136, 329. The CNGR called for the same option—termed "continuum of service"—throughout the reserve component while also crediting the Coast Guard with being the first maritime service to implement integration of active and reserve components. Day, who participated later in a reserve strategic assessment, felt it was after 2003 when full integration occurred.

59. Carlton Moore, "Relevant and Ready . . . Today and Tomorrow," *Coast Guard Reservist*, Nov 1999, 6, including quote. Moore's full title was deputy for mobilization and reserve component affairs, Pacific area.

60. DoD, News Release 472-97, "Secretary Cohen Signs Memorandum Emphasizing Increased Reliance on the Reserve Components," 11 Sep 1997, including quotes, <http://archive. defense.gov/Releases/Release.aspx?ReleaseID=1390>, accessed 24 May 2016; Deborah Lee-James, secretary of the Air Force, interview by Marion via video teleconference, 12 Sep 2014; Coker, *Indispensable Force*, 175–176; Nolan, "'Vision 2000'," 40; Terrence M. O'Connell, *Report of the Chairman of the Reserve Forces Policy Board* [Fiscal Year 1998] (Washington, DC: Office of the Secretary of Defense, 1998), <http://fas.org/man/docs/adr_00/rfpbstat.htm>, accessed 7 Apr 2015.

61. Doubler, *Civilian in Peace, Soldier in War*, 355–357; Coker, *Indispensable Force*, 161, 164, 215–218, 221; Baratz, "A Reorganized Army Reserve," 96-100; "President Clinton Authorizes Reserve Call-Up," American Forces Press Service, 13 Dec 1995, <http://archive. defense.gov/news/newsarticle.aspx?id=40501>, accessed 8 Dec 2014; "Operation Joint Endeavor" GlobalSecurity.org, <http://www.globalsecurity.org/military/ops/joint_endeavor. htm>, accessed 8 Dec 2014; DoD News Release 271-96, "Reserve Units Begin Mobilization for Rotation to Support Operation Joint Endeavor," 10 May 1996, <http://archive.defense. gov/Releases/Release.aspx?ReleaseID=878>, accessed 4 Apr 2017; "Operation Joint Guard," GlobalSecurity.org, <http://www.globalsecurity.org/military/ops/joint_guard.htm>, accessed 8 Dec 2014; DoD News Release 197-99, 27 Apr 1999, accessed 1 Jul 2016; "Operation Allied Force" GlobalSecurity.org, <http://www.globalsecurity.org/military/ops/allied_force.htm> accessed 8 Dec 2014; R. Cody Phillips, *Operation Joint Guardian: The U.S. Army in Kosovo* (Washington, DC: U.S. Army Center of Military History, 2007), 6, 52, <http://www.history. army.mil/brochures/Kosovo/Kosovo.pdf>, accessed 8 Dec 2014. Note that by 2001, the Army Guard and Army Reserve were "fully integrated" into the Army's five-year deployment cycle for the Balkans, and the Air Force Reserve and Air Guard participated "in the maturing Air Force's Air Expeditionary Warfare initiative"; see Marty Kauchak, "Reserves In Transformation," *Armed Forces Journal International*, Aug 2001, 11. In 2001, Michèle A. Flournoy's pre-QDR study acknowledged the Guard's "growing role in rotational deployments in support of peace, humanitarian, and other operations"; see Michèle A. Flournoy, ed., *QDR 2001, Strategy-Driven Choices for America's Security* (Washington, DC: National Defense University Press, 2001), 98.

62. Rosenfeld and Gross, *Air National Guard at 60*, 25–27; DoD News Release 197–199, 27 Apr 1999.

Chapter 5

1. Sue Cathcart, "Defining Homeland Defense," *National Guard*, Jun 2001, 30–32, including quote, quoted by Cathcart; Flournoy, ed., *QDR 2001*. Flournoy served as principal deputy assistant secretary of defense for strategy and threat reduction.

2. Air Force Bulletin No. 16, "Armed Forces Reserve Act of 1952" (Washington, DC, 18 Jul 1952), 2; Flournoy, *QDR 2001,* 97, 102, 230–231, including quotes 1–2; Kristin Patterson, "Emerging Threats," *National Guard*, Jul 2001, 24–25, including quote 3, quoted by Patterson; *Quadrennial Defense Review Report* (Department of Defense, 30 Sep 2001), 19, including quote 4; "Rumsfeld: Review Will Offer 'No Dramatic Changes,'" *National Guard*, Jun 2001, 16; David S. Chu, email message to Jon Hoffman, 28 Mar 2017. The same paragraph in the QDR report that called for the definitions also addressed the terror attacks on the World Trade Center and the Pentagon and thus must have been prepared or modified *after* the attacks.

3. The chief, U.S. Coast Guard Reserve, remained a rear admiral (two-star rank); Dr. Robert M. Browning, USCG historian, email message to Marion, 1 Apr 2013. Although the FY 2000 NDAA, signed into law by President Clinton, contained "provisions allowing Reserve component chiefs to be promoted," no such promotions actually took place until 2001; see RFPB, *Annual Report, Fiscal Year 1999*, xxviii–xxix. Lt. Gen. Thomas J. Plewes, USAR, interview by Kathryn R. Coker, 15 Nov 2010, Office of Army Reserve History, including quotes 1–2; Vice Adm. John B. Totushek, USNR, interview by Capt. Kevin Gillis, USNR, et al., 14 Oct 2003, 28, Arlington, VA, printed by Naval Historical Center, 2003, including quote 3; Vice Adm. John G. Cotton, USN, ret., interview by Forrest L. Marion, 6 Jun 2013, OSD/HO, copy at AFHRA, including quote 4; "'We're Going to Make Sure We Have *a Footprint in Future Missions,'* A Conversation with Lt. Gen. Daniel James III," *National Guard*, Sep 2002, 67–70, including quote 5. The promotion of the ARNG director, Roger C. Schultz, was confirmed by the U.S. Senate at the same time as Lt. Gen. Plewes; see Coker, *Indispensable Force*, 318–319; Coker, *2001 Army Reserve Historical Summary*, 46.

4. Michael D. Doubler, *The National Guard and the War on Terror: The Attacks of 9/11 and Homeland Security* (Washington, DC: National Guard Bureau, Office of Public Affairs, May 2006), 32, 40–46; National Guard Bureau, *Annual Review of the Chief, Fiscal Year 2002* (Arlington, VA: National Guard Bureau, [2002]), 26; "Update: Total Force Integration," *Naval Reserve Association News*, Apr 2002, 7; Rosenfeld and Gross, *Air National Guard at 60*, 40.

5. Coker, *Indispensable Force*, 266–267. The president issued Executive Order 13223 on 14 September 2001. In the order, he did not cite the partial mobilization authority by name (Title 10, U.S. Code, Section 12302), but he quoted from it, invoking that authority to order units and members of the Ready Reserve "to active duty for not more than 24 consecutive months"; see American Presidency Project, Executive Order 13223, 14 Sep 2001, <http://www.presidency. ucsb.edu/ws/?pid=61504>, accessed 11 Jul 2016.

6. P. J. Capelotti, *Rogue Wave: The U.S. Coast Guard on and after 9/11* (Washington, DC: U.S. Coast Guard Historians Office, n.d.), 72, 86, 89–90, 94, 97, 131, 154–160; Dana L. Smith, ed., *2002 Reserve Forces Almanac* (Falls Church, VA: Uniformed Services Almanac, Inc., 2002), 97; Master Chief Petty Officer Jeffrey D. Smith, USCGR, ret., interview by Forrest L. Marion, 5 Mar 2012, Washington, DC, OSD/HO; Rear Adm. Steven E. Day, USCGR, interview by Forrest L. Marion, 6 Mar 2012, Washington, DC, OSD/HO.

7. Betty R. Kennedy, Donald C. Boyd, et al., *Turning Point 9.11, Air Force Reserve in the 21st Century, 2001–2011* (Robins AFB, GA: Headquarters Air Force Reserve Command, Sep 2012), 79–80; Rosenfeld and Gross, *Air National Guard at 60*, 41–42; National Guard Bureau, *Annual Review of the Chief, Fiscal Year 2002*, 26; Charles J. Gross, comp., "A Chronological History of the Air National Guard and Its Antecedents, 1908–2007," 2 Apr 2007, 119–120, copy provided to Forrest Marion by Gross, the ANG command historian. On 11 September, Navy fighter and E–2 surveillance aircraft helped patrol the airspace in the vicinity of New York City and Washington (*Air National Guard at 60*, 40). Three-fourths of USAF's mortuary affairs support capability resided in the AFR.

8. Rosenfeld and Gross, *Air National Guard at 60*, 43–44. The U.S. Northern Command was activated on 1 October 2002 with the mission of homeland defense; see "NorthCom Setup Becomes Clearer," *National Guard*, Sep 2002, 33; "Newly Activated Homeland Command Includes Guard," *National Guard*, Nov 2002, 12–14.

9. Under "homeland security" were the categories of homeland defense, civil support, and emergency preparedness; see Under Secretary of Defense (P&R), "Comprehensive Review of Active/Reserve Force Mix," briefing (in-progress review), 18 Apr 2002, slide 5, copy at AFHRA; "Homeland Security is '*a* Mission, but Not *the* Mission for the Guard,'" *National Guard*, Feb 2002, 16–19, including quote (emphasis in original); Sue Cathcart, "Pentagon Makes Homeland Security Mission One," *National Guard*, Oct 2001, 14; "29th Infantry Division Takes Over Bosnia Duty," *National Guard*, Nov 2001, 17; Doubler, *National Guard and the War on Terror: The Attacks of 9/11 and Homeland Security*, 15.

10. The new Transportation Security Agency assumed the airport passenger-screening mission at the end of May 2002. Between September 2001 and May 2002, several hundred air guardsmen performed airport security duty. Col. Charles P. Baldwin, Iowa National Guard, ret., interview by Forrest L. Marion, 11 Jun 2013, OSD/HO, copy at AFHRA, including quote; National Guard Bureau, *Annual Review of the Chief, Fiscal Year 2002*, 26; Christopher Prawdzik, "Turned Heads," *National Guard*, Jun 2002, 30–31; Gross, "Chronological History of the Air National Guard," 121; Bob Haskell, "Golden Performance," *National Guard*, Mar–Apr 2002, 92–94. In March 2015 a document at OASD(RA) (Readiness, Training, and Mobilization) indicated that a total of 10,807 guardsmen participated in the airport security mission by 31 May 2002, of which 975 were ANG; see O-drive/RT&M/RTMQA-Airport Security.

11. Sue Cathcart, "State vs. Federal," *National Guard*, Nov 2001, 26; Kristin Patterson, "President Urged to Keep Guardsmen Under State Control," *National Guard*, Mar/Apr 2002, 14, including quote, Kane quoted by Patterson; "'We're Looking at What *Best Fits* this Nation for the *Long Haul*,'" interview with ASD(RA) Thomas F. Hall, *National Guard*, Dec 2002/Jan 2003, 28–31. Note that the action of *federalizing* reserve component members only applied to ARNG and ANG personnel, because the members of the other reserve components were always in federal status.

12. Patterson, "President Urged to Keep Guardsmen," *National Guard*, Mar/Apr 2002, 14; "President Approves 23 More Civil Support Teams," *National Guard*, Dec 2002/Jan 2003, 17–19; Christopher Prawdzik, "Next Battle," *National Guard*, May 2003, 28; "A Conversation with Lt. Gen. H. Steven Blum, National Guard Bureau Chief," *National Guard*, Jul 2003, 22. California maintained two teams; every other state and territory, plus the District of Columbia, had one.

13. Capelotti, *Rogue Wave*, 72, 79, 86, 89–90, 97, 154–155, 179; Smith interview, 5 Mar 2012; Smith, *2002 Reserve Forces Almanac*, 97; Dana L. Smith, ed., *2003 Reserve Forces Almanac* (Falls Church, VA: Uniformed Services Almanac, Inc., 2003), 100.

14. DoD News Release 426-01, "Partial Mobilization of National Guard, Reserve Authorized," 14 Sep 2001, <http://archive.defense.gov/Releases/Release.aspx?ReleaseID=3040>, accessed 14 Jan 2015; Coker, *2001 Army Reserve Historical Summary*, 200–201, 246. The cap for each service reflected Rumsfeld's intent for a light footprint in Afghanistan, emphasizing the employment of airpower and special operations personnel in lieu of a large ground force. "Involuntary Reserve Activations for U.S. Military Operations Since World War II," <http://congressionalresearch.com/RL30637/document.php>, accessed 14 Jan 2015; GAO, *Bosnia: Military Services Providing Needed Capabilities but a Few Challenges Emerging,* (Washington, DC: GAO, Apr 1998), 12–13; National Guard Bureau, *Annual Review of the Chief, Fiscal Year 2002*, 24. In FY 1999, Congress modified the name of the augmentation authority from presidential selected reserve call-up (PSRC) to presidential reserve call-up

(PRC), reflecting the recent change in law that authorized the call-up of Individual Ready Reserve personnel under that authority (IRR members were not part of the *Selected* Reserve); see RFPB, *Annual Report, Fiscal Year 1998*, 5, which refers to FY 1998 NDAA that "provided for the involuntary call-up of up to 30,000 members from the Individual Ready Reserve under a PSRC." RFPB, *Reserve Component Programs . . . Fiscal Year 1999*, 5, refers to the president's authority to "order up to 200,000 members of the Reserve components to Active Duty for up to 270 days under the presidential reserve call-up (formerly known as the presidential selected reserve call-up), as prescribed in Title 10, United States Code."

15. Michael D. Doubler, *The National Guard and the War on Terror: Operation Enduring Freedom and Defense Transformation* (Washington, DC: National Guard Bureau, Office of Public Affairs, Mar 2008), 15–17, 20–21, 31–32; National Guard Bureau, *Annual Review of the Chief, Fiscal Year 2002*, 25. During 2002 a succession of elements from the 23rd Marines also provided security at Guantanamo Bay; see Dennis M. McCarthy, "Congratulations and Thanks," *Continental Marine*, Fall 2002, 3.

16. Kennedy, et al., *Turning Point 9.11*, 75–78, 87–88, 99–100; Gross, "Chronological History of the Air National Guard," 121–124, 126; Rosenfeld and Gross, *Air National Guard at 60*, 46–51; Lt. Gen. John A. Bradley, AFRC commander, interview by Betty R. Kennedy, Apr–May 2008, 66–68, 71, 100, AFRC Hist Office, copy at AFHRA; "Selected Demobilization Begins for Air Force," *National Guard*, Jul 2002, 18–19; Lisa Daniel, "In Harm's Way," *National Guard*, Aug 2002, 22–23; "Air Force Extends Guard Call-Up," *National Guard*, Sep 2002, 32; "Air Force Wants Guard and Reserve Airmen Home," *National Guard*, Sep 2003, 22. Note that the AFRC F–16s, which carried the LITENING II targeting pod and associated datalink, were the most capable F–16s in the theater (Bradley, 69, 101).

17. Michael D. Doubler, *The National Guard and the War on Terror: Operation Iraqi Freedom* (Washington, DC: National Guard Bureau, Office of Public Affairs, Nov 2008), 10, 15, 20–23, 27–31; "Guard in Largest Call-Up Since Korean War," *National Guard*, Apr 2003, 18. Linguistic support came again from the 142nd Military Intelligence Battalion (Utah), previously mobilized for Operation Enduring Freedom. At the start of OIF, the Pentagon reported a total of more than 212,000 reserve and Guard personnel on active duty including units and individual augmentees; see DoD, News Release 127-03, "National Guard and Reserve Mobilized As Of March 19, 2003," 19 Mar 2003, <http://archive.defense.gov/releases/release.aspx?releaseid=3664>, accessed 15 Jan 2015. By comparison, seven weeks earlier the total was 94,000 reserve component members mobilized; see DoD News Release 039-03, 29 Jan 2003, "National Guard and Reserve Mobilized As Of Jan. 29, 2003," <http://archive.defense.gov/releases/release.aspx?releaseid=3611>, accessed 15 Jan 2015.

18. Coker, *Indispensable Force*, 289–291.

19. Rosenfeld and Gross, *Air National Guard at 60*, 52–55; Christopher Prawdzik, "Smooth Landing," *National Guard*, Jul 2002, 22–24; Gross, "Chronological History of the Air National Guard," 124. The 116th transitioned to the JSTARS (Joint Surveillance Target Attack Radar System) mission.

20. Kennedy, et al., *Turning Point 9.11*, 138–140, 143–144, 162, 167–168.

21. Totushek interview, 14 Oct 2003, 25–26, including quote. For data on the VFA–201, see "Carrier Air Wing EIGHT History," <http://www.public.navy.mil/airfor/cvw8/Documents/history.htm>, accessed 15 Jan 2015.

22. Dennis M. McCarthy, "Still Ready, Willing and Able," *Continental Marine*, Winter 2002, 3, including quote; Ryan J. Skaggs, "Leading Leatherneck Motivates MarForRes," *Continental Marine*, Fall 2003, 17; Thomas W. Crecca, *United States Marine Corps Reserve Operations: 11 September 2001 to November 2003* (New Orleans: U.S. Marine Corps Reserve, 2005), 12; Amy Forsythe, "Civil Affairs: Only in the Reserves," *Continental Marine*, Fall/ Winter 2001, 18–19; Phil Mehringer, "Civil Affairs Group's Mission In Kosovo Continues," *Continental Marine*, Fall 2002, 8; Zachary A. Bathon, "From the Ground Up," *Continental Marine*, Fall 2003, 8.

23. John Neal, "N.Y. Marines Return Home after Year-Long Deployment," *Continental Marine*, Winter 2002, 8; Crecca, *Marine Corps Reserve Operations*, 9, 49–51, 53, 55–57, 83. In 2002, the 4th Marine Division (i.e., reserves) reported nearly 22,800 marines and sailors in 106 locations; see Jeff Hawk, "New Commanding General Takes the Helm at 4th Marine Division," *Continental Marine*, Fall 2002, 5.

24. Kennedy, et al., *Turning Point 9.11*, 126; Dennis M. McCarthy, "MarForRes: Always Ready, Willing, Able," *Continental Marine*, Fall/Winter 2001, 3–4, including quote; Clay T. McCutchan, Donald N. Cullen, and Forrest L. Marion, "Answering the Call: Contributions of the Air Force Individual Mobilization Augmentee to the Global War on Terrorism, 11 September 2001 through 11 September 2003" (unpublished manuscript, 8 Feb 2005), copy at AFHRA, 5–6, 30–31, 68; "Seapower/Reserves," *Almanac of Seapower*, Jan 2003, 22; "Mobilization History" (chart) provided by Capt. John J. McCracken III, USN, in email to Marion, 3 May 2013; Elizabeth A. Jones, "A New Year and New Mission," *Naval Reserve Association News*, Jan 2002, 30. In September 2002, 6,000 naval reservists were still mobilized; see "An Interview with VADM John B. Totushek, USNR, Director of Naval Reserve," *Naval Reserve Association News*, Oct 2002, 15, <http://www.ausn.org/Portals/0/Services_pdfs/OCTNRAN-02.pdf>, accessed 20 Jan 2015. It is possible that the term "mobilized" was used incorrectly in one or more of the above sources, as "volunteers" may have been included in the numbers cited.

25. Dr. David S. C. Chu, interview by Forrest L. Marion, 22 Apr 2013, OSD/HO, copy at AFHRA, including quote (emphasis in original); MarForRes officials Col. James E. Bacchus, Tom Nelson, Glenn Davis, in discussion with Marion, 10 Jul 2013; Col. J. J. Garcia, MarForRes/G-1, in discussion with Marion, 10 Jul 2013. Individual augmentees included IRR, IMA, and any personnel that filled an unstructured billet; Lt. Col. Shawn P. Wonderlich, USMCR, email message to Marion, 29 Jul 2013.

26. Lt. Gen. Thomas L. Plewes, interview by Capt. Suzanne L. Summers, USAR, 29 Apr 2002, 15, Fort Bragg, NC, Office of Army Reserve History, including quotes; "Army Extends Stop-Loss to Army Guard, Reserve," *National Guard*, Jan 2002, 13. A very small number of inactive National Guard personnel were included with the IRR under the Ready Reserve. Aside from fulfilling the military obligation of many members, IRR status allowed some members, seeking a reserve retirement but wanting a temporary break from the more demanding unit or IMA categories, to remain in the reserves and still earn points toward retirement (but not pay).

27. RFPB, *Annual Report, Fiscal Year 2003*, 18, including quotes. PRC was also known as Title 10, U.S.C. [Section] 12304.

28. GAO, *DOD Actions Needed to Improve the Efficiency of Mobilizations for Reserve Forces*, (Washington, DC: GAO, Aug 2003), <http://www.gao.gov/assets/240/239291.html>, accessed 13 Jan 2015; Remarks to the Reserve Officers Association, 20 Jan 2003, *Rumsfeld*

Public Statements 2003, 5:78, including quote; Donald Rumsfeld, *Known and Unknown: A Memoir* (New York: Sentinel, 2011), 443; Mark Thompson and Michael Duffy, "Pentagon Warlord," *Time*, 27 Jan 2003; "GAO: One-Fourth of Guard, Reserves Not Ready After 9/11," *National Guard*, Sep 2003, 20. A detailed discussion of Rumsfeld's involvement in mobilization decisions and the havoc it caused for planning and carrying out OIF is contained in a draft manuscript on the Combined Forces Land Component Command in Operation Iraqi Freedom, by W. Shane Story, U.S. Army Center of Military History.

29. McCutchan, Cullen, and Marion, "Answering the Call," 26–28; Chad Warren, "MilPDS Upgrade: Stay Ahead of the Curve," Barksdale Airforce Base website, 18 Oct 2012, <http://www.barksdale.af.mil/News/Article/320618/milpds-upgrade-stay-ahead-of-the-curve>, accessed 21 Jan 2015; Kenneth J. Albrecht (HQ AFRC/A1M) and Earnest W. Sowell (HQ AFRC/A1K), interview by Forrest L. Marion, 21 Aug 2013, OSD/HO, copy at AFHRA. Warren stated there had not been an upgrade to the Military Personnel Database System since its implementation in 2001.

30. Robin C. Porche, email message to Marion, 18 Jul 2013, including quote 1; Totushek interview, 14 Oct 2003, 7, including quote 2; Marine Corps Reserve Combat Assessment Team, *Marine Corps Reserve Forces In Operation Iraqi Freedom: Lessons Learned* (Quantico, VA: Marine Corps Combat Development Center, Jan 2004), 85, 90, 102, <http://www.globalsecurity.org/military/library/report/2004/usmcr-oif-ll_efcat_5-20-2004.pdf>, accessed 10 Mar 2015; Paul E. Pratt, MarForRes/Acting G-3/5, interview by Forrest L. Marion, 11 Jul 2013, OSD/HO, copy at AFHRA; Katherine Roe Coker, *The 2003 Army Reserve Historical Summary* (Fort McPherson, GA: Office of Army Reserve History, 2006), 98; see also Lauren Malone, et al., *An Analysis of Marine Corps Reserve Mobilization Processes and Policies* ([Washington, DC]: Center for Naval Analyses, Oct 2009), 36, <https://www.mccll.usmc.mil/index.cfm?disp=myIdolSearch_XML.cfm>, accessed 15 Jan 2015. Probably in 2005—when the *Naval* Reserve was redesignated the *Navy* Reserve—the name changed from *Naval* Reserve Order Writing System to *Navy* Reserve Order Writing System (see chapter 6, present work). According to the Totushek interview in *Naval Reserve Association News*, the 2002 version was known as the "New Order Writing System." According to the Commission on the National Guard and Reserves, it was in 2004 that the Navy implemented the "Naval Reserve Order Writing System" in an attempt to improve an unsatisfactory, manual, centralized system then in use by reservists when requesting orders; see CNGR, *Transforming the National Guard and Reserves.* The above references may have erred regarding the years and/or the designations for each order-writing system. From an interview with Vice Admiral Cotton, it appeared that the two different names of the order-writing system actually referred to the same system. As Cotton changed the name by deleting the word "Reserve," the authors assumed that early in his tenure the name used was "Naval Reserve Order Writing System" which he altered to "Naval Order Writing System." It was Cotton's initiative that led to the change in 2005, in an executive order signed by President Bush, from the "U.S. *Naval* Reserve" to the "U.S. *Navy* Reserve," which led to the revised designation of the order-writing system as the "*Navy* Reserve Order Writing System."

31. Kathryn Roe Coker, *The 2002 Army Reserve Historical Summary* (Fort McPherson, GA: Office of Army Reserve History, 2004), xxxi–xxxii, 40, 74, 83–84, 119–120, 196, 203; Coker, *Indispensable Force*, 351; Lt. Gen. James R. Helmly, USAR, interview by Kathryn Roe Coker, 2 Sep 2010, Office of Army Reserve History; Robert V. Taylor, "Correcting Future Call-Ups," *National Guard*, Apr 2003, 30–31; CNGR, *Transforming the National Guard and*

Reserves, 189; National Guard Bureau, *Annual Review of the Chief, Fiscal Year 2002,* 37; National Guard Bureau, *Annual Review of the Chief, Fiscal Year 2003* (Arlington, VA: National Guard Bureau, [2003]), 43; Baldwin interview, 11 Jun 2013. In October 2003 a transient account pilot program went into effect at the 81st Regional Readiness Command. Some information on the Defense Integrated Manpower Human Resources System was taken from the following: Wanda R. Langley (GS-15, ANG/A1 associate director), interview by Forrest L. Marion, 22 Mar 2013, OSD/HO, copy at AFHRA. The system was never employed and was finally terminated in 2010 after about 12 years of expense and effort.

32. Totushek interview, 14 Oct 2003, 2, 6, 20, 26–27, including quotes; L. Edgar Prina, "Seapower/Reserves," *Almanac of Seapower,* Jan 2002, 270. It was about 2004 when the "ship-based" version of the Navy Standard Integrated Personnel System was implemented; Capt. Scott A. Langley, USN, CNRFC N6, telephone conversation with Marion, 24 May 2013; Scott A. Langley, email messages to Marion, 29–30 Jul 2013. Although termed the Navy Standard Integrated *Personnel* System, perhaps the earliest version did not standardize active-reserve personnel matters but only the pay transactions; see "Mr. Harvey C. Barnum Jr., Deputy Assistant Secretary of the Navy for Reserve Affairs Answers Our Questions," *Naval Reserve Association News,* Jun 2003, 14, 17, <http://www.ausn.org/Portals/0/Services_pdfs/JUN03-NRAN.pdf>, accessed 21 Jan 2015. In any case, in 2003 Barnum acknowledged the Navy operated "two separate personnel systems," one for the active component and one for the reserve component.

33. Baldwin interview, 11 Jun 2013, including quotes; CNGR, *Transforming the National Guard and Reserves,* 28, 85, 186; National Guard Bureau, *Annual Review of the Chief, Fiscal Year 2003,* 46; GAO, *Reserve Forces: Actions Needed to Better Prepare the National Guard for Future Overseas and Domestic Missions* (Washington, DC: Government Accountability Office, 2004), 12, 14–15.

34. CNGR, *Transforming the National Guard and Reserves,* 85, including quote 1; Pratt interview, 11 Jul 2013, including quote 2; Col. Dennis P. Chapman, Michigan National Guard, interview by Forrest L. Marion, 14 Jun 2013, Arlington, VA, OSD/HO, copy at AFHRA, including quote 3; Baldwin interview, 11 Jun 2013; "Stop-Loss Freezes Mobilized Reserves," *National Guard,* Dec 2002/Jan 2003, 20.

35. Brig. Gen. Richard R. Severson, AFRC/Asst. Vice Cmdr., end of tour interview by Betty R. Kennedy, Jul 2008, 50, 63–64, AFRC History Office, copy at AFHRA, including quote 1; Bradley interview, Apr–May 2008, 97–99, 107, 109–110, 127, including quotes 2–3; "Brigadier General Richard 'Ric' Severson," U.S. Air Force website, <http://www.af.mil/AboutUs/Biographies/Display/tabid/225/Article/107912/brigadier-general-richard-ric-severson.aspx>, accessed 15 Jan 2015; "Lieutenant General John A. Bradley," U.S. Air Force website, <http://www.af.mil/AboutUs/Biographies/Display/tabid/225/Article/104723/lieutenant-general-john-a-bradley.aspx>, accessed 15 Jan 2015. In short, the advantages of mobilization over volunteerism are better benefits, "dwell time" protection, and civilian employer protection—that is, in the *minds* of both the employee and employer despite the law's equal protection regardless of volunteer/nonvolunteer status. The civilian employment issue also probably helped explain the tendency of many to overuse the term "mobilization" in lieu of "activation."

36. Totushek interview, 14 Oct 2003, 21–23, including quotes (emphasis added); memo, OPNAVINST 1001.24, 5 Jul 2000, subj: Individual augmentation policy and procedures, 2, enclosure (2). OPNAV–N3/N5 also validated requests for unit forces from USNR (see

OPNAVINST 1001.24, enclosure 4). On 13 February 2003, Secretary Rumsfeld delegated mobilization authority to the service secretaries; Mobilization Briefing, slide labeled "Mobilization Policy/Memo's 1 of 4," provided to Marion by Steven E. Owens, ANG/A3XW, 17 Apr 2013.

37. Totushek interview, 14 Oct 2003, 22–23, including quotes. Beginning in 2006 the Navy implemented an "open architecture" known as Navy Reserve Homeport (Sharepoint); James C. Grover, Office of the Chief of the Navy Reserve, email message to Marion, 30 Jul 2013; Capt. Scott A. Langley, commander, Navy Reserve Forces Command, email message to Marion, 30 Jul 2013; RFPB, *Mobilization Reform: A Compilation of Significant Issues, Lessons Learned and Studies Developed Since September 11, 2001* (Washington, DC: Reserve Forces Policy Board, 2003), 5, including quote 5, Rumsfeld quoted by authors.

38. Chu interview, 22 Apr 2013, including quote; Coker, *2002 Army Reserve Historical Summary*, 270; Taylor, "Correcting Future Call-Ups," 30–31; Marygail K. Brauner, Timothy Jackson, and Elizabeth K. Gayton, *Medical Readiness of the Reserve Component* (Santa Monica, CA: RAND Center for Military Health Policy Research, 2012), 16; Frank M. Hudgins, "Activation/Partial Mobilization of the US Army Reserves and Associated Personnel Management System Problems" (Carlisle Barracks, PA: Army War College, 27 Mar 1992), 7–8. For more on dental unreadiness in 1990–1991, see chapter 4, present work.

39. Taylor, "Correcting Future Call-Ups," 30–31, including quote 1; Baldwin interview, 11 Jun 2013, including quote 2; "Barnum . . . Answers Our Questions," 14; CNGR, *Transforming the National Guard and Reserves*, 29, 43–44, 193–195.

40. Brauner, Jackson, and Gayton, *Medical Readiness of the Reserve Component*, 15–16, 33, 41, including quote, quoted by authors; Chu interview, 22 Apr 2013; CNGR, *Transforming the National Guard and Reserves*, 193–195, 241.

41. McCutchan, Cullen, and Marion, "Answering the Call," 56; Chris Prawdzik, "GAO: Guardsmen, Reservists Need More TRICARE Education," *National Guard*, Nov 2002, 12; "Post-Deployment Medical Assessments Bolstered," *National Guard*, Jun 2003, 18; "Demobilized Reservists Get Improved Transitional Health Care Benefits," *Naval Reserve Association News*, Oct 2002, 10, <http://www.ausn.org/Portals/0/Services_pdfs/OCTNRAN-02.pdf>, accessed 20 Jan 2015.

42. Coker, *2001 Army Reserve Historical Summary*, 204–208.

43. Bradford Booth, et al., *What We Know About Army Families: 2007 Update* (N.p.: ICF International, [2007]), 49, 53–57, 63, including quote 1, <http://tapartnership.org/enterprise/docs/RESOURCE%20BANK/RB-FAMILY-DRIVEN%20APPROACHES/General%20Resources/What_We_Know_about_Army_Families_2007.pdf>, accessed 20 Jan 2015; Baldwin interview, 11 Jun 2013, including quote 2.

44. National Guard Bureau, *Annual Review of the Chief*, 2002, 21–22, 38, including quotes 1–2; Booth, *What We Know about Army Families*, 57, including quote 3.

45. Sue Cathcart, "Help For Those Left Behind," *National Guard*, Jan 2002, 24–25, including quotes, quoted by Cathcart; National Guard Bureau, *Annual Review of the Chief, Fiscal Year 2002*, 21–22, 38; National Guard Bureau, *Annual Review of the Chief, Fiscal Year 2003*, 25, 51; Booth, *What We Know About Army Families*, 58; Senate Committee on Armed Services,

Subcommittee on Personnel, *Hearings and Joint Hearings: Issues Affecting Families of Soldiers, Sailors, Airmen, and Marines,* 2 Jun and 7 Oct 2003, 24 Jun and 11 Dec 2003 (Washington, DC: GPO, 2005), 187–188, 209, <https://archive.org/stream/issuesaffectingf00unit#page/208/mode/1up>, accessed 21 Jan 2015; Associated Press, "U.S. Expands R&R Program for Iraq Troops," 31 Oct 2003, <http://www.foxnews.com/story/2003/10/31/us-expands-rr-program-for-iraq-troops>, accessed 21 Jan 2015.

46. Coker, *2001 Army Reserve Historical Summary*, 9; Coker, *2002 Army Reserve Historical Summary*, 201–206, 266, 309, 351; Coker, *2003 Army Reserve Historical Summary*, 214–215; Maj. Gen. Herbert L. Altshuler, US Army, interview by Capt. Suzanne L. Summers, USAR, 29 Jan 2002, 24, Fort Bragg, NC, Office of Army Reserve History. The courses were held in late 2003.

47. Thomas W. Mobley, "The Role of Family Readiness in Mission Readiness," *Naval Reserve Association News*, Apr 2003, 13–15 <http://www.ausn.org/Portals/0/Services_pdfs/APR03-NRAN.pdf>, accessed 21 Jan 2015; "Barnum . . . Answers Our Questions," 14–15, including quote. In December 2003, John D. Winkler, deputy assistant secretary of defense for reserve affairs (manpower/personnel), testified before a Senate subcommittee that "mission readiness and family readiness are extremely intertwined"; see *Issues Affecting Families of Soldiers, Sailors, Airmen, and Marines*, 190–191. The MarForRes commander, Lieutenant General McCarthy, emphasized his component's family readiness program, specifically the key volunteer network and the LINKS program; see his "It Is Not Over," *Continental Marine*, Summer 2002, 3.

48. *Issues Affecting Families of Soldiers, Sailors, Airmen, and Marines*, 191, 212–213, 221, including quote 1; C. C. Dysart, "MCCS One Source...Anytime, Anyplace, Anywhere," *Continental Marine*, Winter 2002, 6, including quote 2.

49. *Issues Affecting Families of Soldiers, Sailors, Airmen, and Marines*, 197–201, including quotes; "Who Is ESGR," Employer Support of the Guard and Reserve website, <http://www.esgr.mil/About-ESGR/Who-is-ESGR/What-is-ESGR.aspx>, accessed 14 Jan 2015; Matthew J. Apprendi, "Reserve Marines Receive Employer Support from ESGR," *Continental Marine*, Summer 2002, 36; "Overview of USERRA," Department of Labor website, <http://www.dol.gov/elaws/vets/userra/userra.asp>, accessed 14 Jan 2015.

50 "Frequently Asked Questions," Employer Support of the Guard and Reserve website, <http://www.esgr.mil/USERRA/Frequently-Asked-Questions.aspx>, accessed 14 Apr 2015; Robin C. Porche, MarForRes/G-1 assistant operations officer, interviews by Forrest L. Marion, 10 and 12 Jul 2013, Arlington, VA, OSD/HO, copy at AFHRA.

51. David S. C. Chu, "Testimony to the Senate Armed Services Committee, February 13, 2002," *Naval Reserve Association News*, Apr 2002, 7, including quotes 1–2; CNGR, *Transforming the National Guard and Reserves*, 70, including quote 3, Cotton quoted by authors; "'Unsung Patriotic American Heroes': Interview with Deputy Assistant Secretary of the Navy (Reserve Affairs) Harvey C. Barnum, Jr.," by James D. Hessman, *Sea Power*, Feb 2002, 10–11; RFPB, *Annual Report, Fiscal Year 2000*, 53.

52. Doubler, *National Guard and the War on Terror: Operation Enduring Freedom*, 32; Crecca, *Marine Corps Reserve Operations*, 9, 83; "Eclectic Colonel Who Lost Case vs. P. Diddy Hunts Iraqi Treasures," *USA Today*, 17 May 2003, <http://usatoday30.usatoday.com/news/world/iraq/2003-05-17-unusual-marine_x.htm>, accessed 14 Jan 2015; CNGR, *Transforming*

the National Guard and Reserves, 70. The CNGR spelled the surname "Bagdanos"; *USA Today* used "Bogdanos"; we elected to follow the CNGR.

53. Bob Haskell, "Reserve Component Civilian Employment Information Program Begins," *DoD News*, 31 Mar 2004, <http://archive.defense.gov/news/newsarticle. aspx?id=26978>, accessed 14 Jan 2015; GAO, *Military Personnel: Additional Actions Needed to Improve Oversight of Reserve Employment Issues* (Washington, DC: GAO, Feb 2007), 5, 15, < http://www.gao.gov/new.items/d07259.pdf>, accessed 14 Jan 2015; Government Accountability Office, *Military Personnel: DOD Needs Data to Determine If Active Duty Service Has an Impact on the Ability of Guard and Reservists to Maintain Their Civilian Professional Licenses or Certificates* (Washington, DC: GAO, May 2008), <http://www.gao.gov/assets/100/95490. html>, accessed 14 Jan 2015; CNGR, *Transforming the National Guard and Reserves*, 149–150.

54. "Selected Demobilization Begins for Air Force," *National Guard*, Jul 2002, 18, including quotes 1–2, Jumper quoted by *National Guard*; "'. . . A Footprint in Future Missions.' A Conversation with Lt. Gen. Daniel James III," *National Guard*, Sep 2002, 68–69, including quotes 3–5.

55. Memo (Staff Summary Sheet), Major Mathis, AF/REPX (Action Officer), "Request for Exception to Policy to DOD Directive 1327.5 Regarding Special Pass for Deployed Air Force Reserve Members in Support of Current Contingency Operations," 18 Apr 2002 (unsigned copy provided to Marion by Lt. Col. George A. Kirkpatrick, HQ AFRC/JA, copy at AFHRA), including quotes, quote 2 (emphasis added); memo (unsigned draft), AF/RE for ASD (FMP), no date, "Request for Exception to Policy to DOD Directive 1327.5, *Leave and Liberty*, Regarding Special Pass for Deployed Air Force Reserve (AFR) Members Supporting Current Contingency Operations," copy at AFHRA; Daniel N. Powell (HQ AFRC/A5XW), Gerald J. Mekosh (HQ AFRC/A5XW), and Columbus Brown (HQ AFRC/A1RR), interview by Forrest L. Marion, 22 Aug 2013, OSD/HO, copy at AFHRA. This issue is also addressed in chapters 6 and 7, present work.

56. Christopher Prawdzik, "Sketching A New Paradigm," *National Guard*, Oct 2002, 24–26, including quote 1, Chu quoted by Prawdzik; Coker, *2003 Army Reserve Historical Summary*, 33; James R. Helmly, "Statement by LTG James R. Helmly, Chief, Army Reserve . . . Before the Subcommittee on Total Force, Committee on Armed Services, United States House of Representatives," Record Version, 31 Mar 2004, 12, including quote 2; Prawdzik, "Next Battle," 28. In 2008, the CNGR devoted an entire chapter, about one-sixth of its final report, to "Creating a Continuum of Service: Personnel Management for an Integrated Total Force"; see CNGR, *Transforming the National Guard and Reserves*, 113–175.

57. John B. Totushek, "The Naval Reserve in Sea Power 21, Leveraging to Win: Drawing Agility from the Naval Reserve," *Naval Reserve Association News*, Apr 2003, 27–29, including quote 1, <http://www.ausn.org/Portals/0/Services_pdfs/APR03-NRAN.pdf>, accessed 20 Jan 2015; Cotton interview, 6 Jun 2013, including quotes 2–3.

58. Coker, *2001 Army Reserve Historical Summary*, 217–218, including quotes 1–2; Coker, *2003 Army Reserve Historical Summary*, 207–208, including quote 3.

59. Porche interviews, 10 and 12 Jul 2013, including quote from 10 Jul interview. The two smallest military services, the Coast Guard and Marine Corps, took significant steps toward active-reserve integration as early as the mid-1990s.

60. Totushek interview, 14 Oct 2003, 5, including quote 1; "21st Century Vision for a Fully Integrated Active and Reserve Naval Force" (unpublished paper, [4 Dec 2002], unknown author), 1–3, including quotes 2–4, document provided by James C. Grover, Office of the Chief, Navy Reserve, in email message to Marion, 6 Mar 2012; slides (draft), "VCNO Brief 18 Apr 1 Ver16.ppt," slide 3 of 15, [2003], including quote 5, document provided by Grover in email message to Marion, 6 Mar 2012 (document was labeled predecisional but Grover assessed it to be very close to the final version); Scott C. Truver, "To Dissuade, Deter, and Defeat: U.S. Naval Power in the 21st Century," *Sea Power*, Feb 2003, 31, 34; "Barnum . . . Answers Our Questions," 16–18; memo, VCNO (Adm. William J. Fallon), subj: Fully integrated active and naval reserve force, document provided by James C. Grover in email message to Marion, 6 Mar 2012; "Biographies in Naval History, Admiral Vernon Clark," U.S. Navy website, <http://www.navy.mil/navydata/bios/navybio.asp?bioID=5>, accessed 15 Jan 2015.

61. Smith interview, 5 Mar 2012, including quotes 1–3; John C. Acton, "Becoming a More Effective and Efficient Reserve Force," *Reservist*, Jan 2005, 6–7, <http://www.uscg.mil/reservist/issues/2005/01/issue.pdf>, accessed 5 Feb 2015; John C. Acton, "Is There a Leader Inside of You?," *Reservist*, issue 5-05, ca. Aug 2005, 14, including quote 4.

62. Day interview, 6 Mar 2012, including quote 1. For more on active component-reserve component integration, see chapter 4, present work. Rear Admiral Day was a two-star (USCG uses the rank of rear admiral, with differing abbreviations, for both one- and two-stars). Robert J. Papp Jr., "Fair Winds, Shipmates," *Reservist*, Apr 2004, 6, including quote 2; Robert J. Papp, "Reserve Force Update," *Reservist*, May–Jun 2003, 6; James C. Van Sice, "See You in New London!," *The Reservist*, issue 4-05, ca. Jun 2005, 14, <http://www.uscg.mil/reservist/issues/2005/04/issue.pdf>, accessed 5 Feb 15; Sally Brice-O'Hara, "A Note From The New Director," *Reservist*, issue 6-05, ca. Sep 2005, 14; Duncan C. Smith III, "Values or Metrics?," *USCG Reservist*, issue 4-06, ca. Jun 2006, 14. Note the periodical's name change in 2006. As the reserve and training director, Papp was a one-star; Acton served as a two-star.

63. Coker, *2001 Army Reserve Historical Summary*, xxv, 82, including quote; Coker, *2002 Army Reserve Historical Summary*, 213–214, 266. We do not know how many of the 950 authorizations were funded. Full-time support programs included all active component and reserve component personnel that supported reserve units on a full-time basis. Full-Time Support (FTS) programs included *only reserve component members* who supported reserve units full time, mainly AGRs and MTs. The distinction was often blurred even in official documentation. For example, the Marines' Inspector-Instructor (I-I) program was (and remains) a "full-time support" program. But because the I-I program consisted of active component personnel, I-I was not an "FTS" program. Note the aforementioned distinction between full-time support and FTS did not exist in the National Guard; when the Guard referred to full-time support, it was identical to FTS.

64. National Guard Bureau, *Annual Review of the Chief, Fiscal Year 2002*, 35–36, including quote 1; Gus L. Hargett, "Our Important Dual Focus," *National Guard*, Apr 2003, 10; National Guard Bureau, *Annual Review of the Chief, Fiscal Year 2003*, 47; Baldwin interview, 11 Jun 2013.

65. History, Headquarters Air Force Reserve Command, 1 Oct 1999–30 Sep 2002, v. 1, 142–143, including quotes, call no. K419.01, copy at AFHRA.

66. Pratt interview, 11 Jul 2013, including quotes 1–2; U.S. Marine Corps Reserve Combat Assessment Team, *Marine Corps Reserve Forces in Operation Iraqi Freedom*, 25, including quote 3.

67. Col. James P. McGuire, USMC, discussion with Marion, 11 Jul 2013; Robin C. Porche, email message to Marion, 14 Jan 2015.

68. GAO, *DOD Actions Needed*, 1–2; USD(P&R), Department of Defense Directive 1235.10: Activation, Mobilization, and Demobilization of the Ready Reserve, 23 Sep 2004.

Chapter 6

1. Kathryn Roe Coker, *The 2004/2005 Biannual Army Reserve Historical Summary* (Fort McPherson, GA: Office of Army Reserve History, 2007), 19, 56, including quote, quoted by Coker. In FY 2004, USAR "missed its retention and end strength objectives," but in FY 2005 it "exceeded its retention goal"; see memo, Secretary of the Army Francis J. Harvey for Secretary of Defense Donald Rumsfeld, 25 Feb 2005, subj: U.S. Army Reserve availability, Rumsfeld Papers, <http://papers.rumsfeld.com/library>, accessed 2 Feb 2015.

2. Seth Cline, "The Other Symbol of George W. Bush's Legacy," *U.S. News & World Report*, 1 May 2013, <http://www.usnews.com/news/blogs/press-past/2013/05/01/the-other-symbol-of-george-w-bushs-legacy>, accessed 9 Jun 2017, including quotes 1–2, quoted by Cline; George W. Bush, Remarks by the President from the USS *Abraham Lincoln*, press release, Office of the Press Secretary, 1 May 2003, <http://georgewbush-whitehouse.archives.gov/news/releases/2003/05/20030501-15.html>, accessed 9 Jun 2017, including quote 3; DoD Personnel Reports, https://www.dmdc.osd.mil/appj/dwp/dwp_reports.jsp.

3. Robert H. Smiley, interview by Forrest L. Marion, 24 Sep 2013, OSD/HO, copy at AFHRA, including quote; Chapter 1209: Active Duty, 10 U.S.C. § 12302, <http://www.gpo.gov/fdsys/pkg/USCODE-2011-title10/html/USCODE-2011-title10-subtitleE-partII-chap1209-sec12302.htm>, accessed 4 Feb 2015. From his retirement as an Army Reserve colonel in the ASD(RA)'s office in 2003, Smiley served until 2009 as assistant deputy for training, readiness, and mobilization in the Office of the Secretary of the Army. He then returned to OASD(RA).

4. Coker, *2004/2005 Biannual Army Reserve Historical Summary*, 8–10, including quote 1, Schoomaker quoted by Coker; Coker, *Indispensable Force*, 293, including quote 2, Helmly quoted by Coker. For the rationale behind using the term, "mobilized/activated" and discussion of this terminology issue, see notes 18, 31–33 below.

5. Coker, *2004/2005 Biannual Army Reserve Historical Summary*, 8–10; Office of the Deputy Assistant Secretary of Defense for Reserve Affairs [ODASD(RA)], *Rebalancing Forces: Easing the Stress on the Guard and Reserve* (Washington, DC: Office of Deputy Assistant Secretary of Defense for Reserve Affairs, 15 Jan 2004), 7.

6. Secretary of Defense, *Rebalancing Forces* (9 Jul 2003), including quotes 1–3; ODASD(RA), *Rebalancing Forces*, v, 1, 4 including quotes 4–5, Rumsfeld quoted by, Chu quoted by; Coker, *2004/2005 Biannual Army Reserve Historical Summary*, 15; Coker, *Indispensable Force*, 325. In July 2003 Secretary Rumsfeld forwarded to General Schoomaker a thought-provoking paper by General Gorman, U.S. Army, titled "Army Culture and Transformation"; see memo, Rumsfeld for Schoomaker, 18 Jul 2003, subj: Army culture and transformation, Rumsfeld Papers, <http://papers.rumsfeld.com/library>.

7. ODASD(RA), *Rebalancing Forces,* 4–5, 8–11; Coker, *Indispensable Force,* 326.

8. Coker, *2004/2005 Biannual Army Reserve Historical Summary,* 8–10, 32, including quotes 1–2, Schoomaker (quote 1) quoted by Coker.

9. Coker, *2004/2005 Biannual Army Reserve Historical Summary,* 30–33; "A Conversation with Francis J. Harvey, Secretary of the Army," *National Guard,* Nov 2005, 30–33; Sara Wood, "Unit Rebalance Will Make Guard More Effective, Army Secretary Says," *DoD News,* American Forces Press Service, 18 Jan 2006, <http://archive.defense.gov/news/newsarticle.aspx?id=14585>, accessed 15 Apr 2015; John Goheen, "Opposition Mounts to Proposal to Cut Army Guard," *National Guard,* Feb 2006, 14; ODASD-RA, *Rebalancing Forces,* 13–14; Doubler, *National Guard and the War on Terror: Operation Iraqi Freedom,* 48; Coker, *The 2006/2007 Biannual Army Reserve Historical Summary* (Fort McPherson, GA: Office of Army Reserve History, 2008), 11, 28. At the same time as it was rebalancing its forces, the Army Reserve responded to the 2005 BRAC by closing or realigning many facilities (including its headquarters), a process it completed in 2011. Note the USAR had the highest percentage of BRAC-affected facilities among the services; see Jack C. Stultz, "Army Reserve: 'Integral Component of the World's Best Army,'" *Army* [*Green Book*] 56, no. 10 (Oct 2006): 130–132; United States Army, *Statement on the Posture of the United States Army,* 2007, 12. For a thorough study of modularity, see William M. Donnelly, *Transforming an Army at War: Designing the Modular Force, 1991–2005* (Washington, DC: U.S. Army Center of Military History, 2007).

10. "Some Army Guard Iraq Tours Extended 90 Days," *National Guard,* May 2004, 17–18.

11. Chapter 1209: Active Duty, 10 U.S.C. § 12302, including quote; Dennis P. Chapman, *Manning Reserve Component Units for Mobilization: Army and Air Force Practice* (Institute of Land Warfare, Sep 2009), <http://www.ausa.org/publications/ilw/ilw_pubs/landwarfarepapers/Documents/LWP74.pdf>, accessed 4 Feb 2015, 1. Note that in the executive order of 14 September 2001, President Bush invoked partial mobilization authority and quoted directly from the above paragraph, yet without citing Title 10, U.S. Code, Section 12302.

12. Larry M. Eig, *Statutory Interpretation: General Principles and Recent Trends* (Washington, DC: Congressional Research Service, 2011), 13.

13. Memo, Under Secretary of Defense for Personnel & Readiness, 20 Sep 2001, subj: Mobilization/demobilization personnel and pay policy for reserve component members ordered to active duty in response to the World Trade Center and Pentagon attacks, authors' files, OSD/HO, including quote 1; Chapman interview, 14 Jun 2013, including quote 2; National Guard Bureau, *Annual Review, 2004* (Arlington, VA: National Guard Bureau, 2004), 41. The first ARNG brigade called up for Iraq was North Carolina's 30th Brigade, alerted in Jul 2003; see Doubler, *The National Guard and the War on Terror: Operation Iraqi Freedom,* 41–43, 47, 55–56.

14. Will Dunham, "U.S. Army Asking Guardsmen to Stay Longer in Iraq," 21 Jul 2004, <http://www.rense.com/general54/sstay.htm>, accessed 8 Jul 2017, including quotes 1–2; memo, Rumsfeld for undisclosed recipients, 22 Jul 2004, subj: Extending troops, Rumsfeld Papers,<http://papers.rumsfeld.com/library>, including quotes 3–4.

15. Senate Committee on Armed Services, *The Armed Forces Reserve Act of 1952, Report to Accompany H.R. 5426,* 19 Jun 1952, 9, including quote 1; Ready Reserve, 10 U.S.C. § 12302

(Jul 1952), including quote of paragraph (b); David S. C. Chu, email message to Hoffman, 31 Mar 2017.

16. Chapman interview, 14 Jun 2013, including quote; DoD News Release 073-04, 4 Feb 2004, "National Guard and Reserve Mobilized as of Feb. 4, 2004," <http://archive.defense.gov/ Releases/Release.aspx?ReleaseID=7052>, accessed 4 Feb 2015. The 39th Brigade redeployed in December 2004; see National Guard Bureau, *Annual Review, Fiscal Year 2005* (Arlington, VA: National Guard Bureau, 2005), 48.

17. Steven Lee Myers, "Bush Warns Against 'Overdeployment,'" *New York Times,* 15 Feb 2001, <http://www.nytimes.com/2001/02/15/us/bush-warns-against-overdeployment.html>, including quote 1; Eric Schmitt, "Pentagon Is Set to Activate Thousands More Reservists," *New York Times*, 5 Dec 2002, A1, including quote 2, Hollingsworth quoted by Schmitt; Remarks to the Reserve Officers Association, 20 Jan 2003, *Rumsfeld Public Statements 2003,* 1:80, including quote 3.

18. "DoD: No Plans to Extend Reservists," *National Guard*, Aug 2004, 18, including quote, Rumsfeld quoted by *National Guard* (emphasis added); "Mobilization Rules Still in Place, Official Says," *National Guard*, Dec 2006, 20. *National Guard* quoted the secretary as follows: "My understanding is that there may be a law or a regulation or a policy that talks about 24 consecutive months and then there has been a practice that addresses the 24—not from consecutive months, but from cumulative months, which is obviously a lesser threshold." Note the term "mobilization" refers to a reservist who is called involuntarily to active duty under a mobilization authority (in this case, the partial mobilization authority); a volunteer, however, is not mobilized but is "activated" under a different authority.

19. Thomas F. Hall, interview by Forrest L. Marion, 23 Sep 2013, OSD/HO, copy at AFHRA, including quote 1; Dennis M. McCarthy, interview by Forrest L. Marion, 17 Sep 2013, OSD/HO, copy at AFHRA; Dennis McCarthy, email message to Marion, 29 Jan 2015; Rumsfeld, *Known and Unknown,* 456; H. Steven Blum, interview by Forrest L. Marion, 17 Mar 2015, OSD/HO, copy at AFHRA, including quotes 2–3; Chu to Hoffman, email, 31 Mar 2017, copy in authors' files, OSAD Historical Office. After 1994 the ASD(RA) reported to the USD(P&R) rather than directly to the secretary of defense, altering the ASD(RA)'s access to the secretary of defense depending on personalities and relationships within the Pentagon.

20. Chapman interview, 14 Jun 2013, including quote 1; Barbara Y. Lee, telephone conversation with Marion, 28 Aug 2013, including quote 2.

21. Coker, Indispensable Force, 299, including quote 1, Helmly quoted by Coker; Coker, *2004/2005 Biannual Army Reserve Historical Summary*, 19–21, including quote 2, Helmly quoted by Coker; memo, James R. Helmly for Chief of Staff U.S. Army Schoomaker, 20 Dec 2004, subj: Readiness of the United States Army Reserve, including quotes 3–6. In July 2005, GAO Report 05-660 supported Helmly's concerns; see GAO, *Reserve Forces: An Integrated Plan Is Needed to Address Army Reserve Personnel and Equipment Shortages* (Washington, DC: GAO, 2005), <http://www.gao.gov/assets/250/247044.pdf>.

22. Helmly for Schoomaker, 20 Dec 2004, including quotes; Doubler, *National Guard and the War on Terror: Operation Iraqi Freedom*, 79; Coker, *2004/2005 Biannual Army Reserve Historical Summary*, 22, 63; Christopher Prawdzik, "Fractured Inventory: States Scramble as Many Army National Guard Units Are Forced to Leave Equipment in Iraq," *National Guard*, Apr 2005, 30–33. As of 31 December 2004, the USAR had filled a total of 115,333

mobilization billets since 9/11, including those soldiers who served multiple mobilizations (probably including voluntary activations); see memo, Vice Chairman of the Joint Chiefs of Staff Peter Pace for Rumsfeld, 11 Apr 2005, subj: Mobilization and deployment of forces since 9/11, Rumsfeld Papers, <http://papers.rumsfeld.com/library>. The scope of the present study did not allow a detailed examination of Helmly's various concerns. The two-page memo was followed by six pages of enclosures. By the end of 2005, some 144,000 USAR soldiers had been "mobilized"; see Coker, *2004/2005 Biannual Army Reserve Historical Summary*, 10. Again, voluntary activations probably were included in the total. Although the Joint Staff's document used the term "mobilized," its authors appeared to include (voluntary) activations/deployments in addition to (involuntary) mobilizations, a common error in terminology. If such a high number of soldiers had, in fact, been mobilized (involuntarily) by the end of 2004, Helmly would not have felt the need to complain, in the memo cited above, that "demands to use only 'volunteers' from the Reserve Components threaten to distort the very nature of service in the [reserve component]."

23. Memo, Secretary of the Army Francis J. Harvey for Rumsfeld, 25 Feb 2005, subj: U.S. Army Reserve availability, Rumsfeld Papers, <http://papers.rumsfeld.com/library>, accessed 9 Jun 2017, including quote. Coker, *2004/2005 Biannual Army Reserve Historical Summary*, 22; Raymond W. Carpenter, interview by Les' Melnyk, 7 Mar 2012, part 2: 3–4, NGB Public Affairs. OIF-4 deploying units rotated into Iraq in mid- to late-2005 and OIF-5 deploying units in mid- to late-2006; see "US Forces Order of Battle," GlobalSecurity.org, <http://www.globalsecurity. org/military/ops/iraq_orbat.htm>, accessed 2 Feb 2015. In early 2005, USD(P&R) David Chu was quoted: "There are no plans to expand the mobilization period to a policy of 24 consecutive months"; see Mark Mazzetti, "Pentagon Won't Extend Reservists' Deployment," *Los Angeles Times*, 3 Feb 2005, <http://articles.latimes.com/2005/feb/03/nation/na-troops3>, accessed 10 Feb 2015.

24. Coker, *2004/2005 Biannual Army Reserve Historical Summary*, 22, including quote 1; Coker, *2006/2007 Biannual Army Reserve Historical Summary*, 31, including quotes 2–3, Schoomaker quoted by Coker. At least one battalion commander agreed with Schoomaker that cross-leveling was "evil"; see CNGR, *Transforming the National Guard and Reserves*, 186; Department of Defense Directive 1235.10, 1 Jul 1995, subj: Activation, mobilization, and demobilization of the Ready Reserve, 5, including quote 4.

25. Doubler, *National Guard and the War on Terror: Operation Iraqi Freedom*, 79, including quote; National Guard Bureau, *Annual Review 2005*, 7, 43. GAO, *Reserve Forces: Actions Needed to Better Prepare the National Guard for Future Overseas and Domestic Missions* (Washington, DC: GAO, Nov 2004), 3; GAO, *Reserve Forces: Plans Needed to Improve Army National Guard Equipment* (Washington, DC: GAO, Oct 2005), 4; First Army slide deck, "2007 Observations", n.d., and slide deck, "45th IBCT M-RSOI After-Action Review," author files for manuscript, *History of Guard Mobilization*, Center of Military History; John R. Maass, *Department of the Army Historical Summary, Fiscal Year 2007* (Washington, DC: U.S. Army, 2013), 35.

The monthly *National Guard* magazine reported the following losses of deployed ARNG soldiers: 10 in October 2004, 11 in November 2004, 15 in December 2004, 21 in January 2005, 12 in February 2005, 17 in March 2005, 7 in April 2005, 15 in May 2005, 16 in June 2005, 14 in July 2005, 23 in August 2005, 28 in September 2005, 18 in October 2005, 8 in November 2005, and 11 in December 2005. The worst consecutive months were August to October 2005.

26. Carpenter interview, 7 Mar 2012, part 1:11–12, including quotes; Carpenter interview, 7 Mar 2012, part 2:15; "Reserve Forces," draft PowerPoint slide, ASD(RA), working papers, ca. Aug 2005, copy at AFHRA. Prior to the Gates' memo of January 2007, Carpenter felt "we were on a path to destroy the Reserve Component" because the ARNG and USAR were "not going to be able to meet their mobilization responsibilities," Carpenter interview, 7 Mar 2012, part 1:12; Carpenter interview, 7 Mar 2012, part 2:4.

27. CNGR, *Transforming the National Guard and Reserves*, 184, 196–209, 200, including quote 1–2; National Guard Bureau, *Annual Review, 2004*, 58–59; National Guard Bureau, *Annual Review, Fiscal Year 2005*, 82. AGRs were RC members serving on active duty, mainly with reserve units/organizations. Military technicians were federal civilians most of whom maintained dual status as members of the Selected Reserve assigned to the same units they served as civilians. The Marines used the term "Active Reserve" to refer to reservists on full-time active duty tours; while most were assigned to RC units, some were assigned to active component units. The CNGR noted concerns with active component Army members assigned to RC units in that many were close to retirement and their promotion rates were significantly lower than for active component-assigned personnel of the same grade. CNGR, *Transforming the National Guard and Reserves*, 203. Such was part of the cultural divide between active and reserve components.

28. Coker, *2006/2007 Biannual Army Reserve Historical Summary*, 51–52, including quote 1; CNGR, *Transforming the National Guard and Reserves,* 85, including quote 2; James R. Helmly, *A Statement on the Posture of the United States Army Reserve 2006: Posture Statement Presented to the 109th Congress, 2nd Session* (Washington, DC: Department of the Army, 2006), P21; Jack C. Stultz, *A Statement on the Posture of the United States Army Reserve 2007: Posture Statement Presented to the 110th Congress, 1st Session* (Washington, DC: Department of the Army, 2007), 27. In 2005, the USAR began eliminating some billets in nondeployable units.

29. National Guard Bureau, *Annual Review, 2004*, 10, including quote 1; Charles P. Baldwin, interview by Forrest L. Marion, 11 Jun 2013, OSD/HO, copy at AFHRA, including quote 2; "Full-Time Support Crucial," *National Guard*, May 2006, 14, including quote 3, Vaughn quoted by *National Guard*; Smiley interview, 24 Sep 2013, including quote 4; Coker, *2004/2005 Biannual Army Reserve Historical Summary*, 19, including quote 5, Helmly quoted by Coker; CNGR, *Transforming the National Guard and Reserves,* 198; "Full-Time Manning," *National Guard*, Apr 2008, 62. The FY 2005 NDAA authorized the ARNG some 26,600 AGR and 26,600 MT personnel; see National Guard Bureau, *Annual Review, 2005*, 82.

30. In this context the term "remobilization" was confusing at best, because a *voluntary* mobilization or remobilization was a misnomer; if a volunteer, the reservist was *activated*. Lee telephone conversation, 28 Aug 2013, including quote 1; Chapman interview, 14 Jun 2013, including quote 2; Charles Abell, interview by Thomas Christiansen and Anthony Crain, 16 Sep 2014, 33, OSD/HO. In December 2006, *National Guard* stated the 24-cumulative-months policy remained in effect, or, perhaps more accurately, that the policy was once again the primary determining factor in the selection of units and individual reservists for mobilization. "Mobilization Rules Still In Place, Official Says," *National Guard*, Dec 2006, 20. One joint staff briefing in September 2006 made a distinction between the *policy* of 24 cumulative months and the *practice* of "no involuntary remobilization" (regardless of how many months remained in the 24-month "gas tank"). Note that a mobilization was, by definition, an involuntary service of active duty; a voluntary service of active duty was an activation.

31. Coker, *2004/2005 Biannual Army Reserve Historical Summary*, 19, including quote 1, Helmly quoted by Coker; memo, Helmly for Schoomaker, 20 Dec 2004, including quotes 2–5; McCarthy interview, 17 Sep 2013, including quote 6. McCarthy felt "that Secretary Rumsfeld and his senior team very much mismanaged the mobilization of the Reserve Component and did so to the detriment of the mobilization process." An address in September 2003 was indicative of Rumsfeld's concerns regarding the reserves: "You've got to be very sensitive about the risk of back to back deployment for active service, you've got to be very careful about short call up periods for the reserve, you've got to give them as much certainty as possible, you have to use volunteers to the greatest extent possible and you have to undertake a project to rebalance the Guard and the Reserve with the Active force"; ODASD(RA), *Rebalancing Forces*, 1, Rumsfeld quoted by authors. Legally, those individuals brought onto active duty under the partial mobilization authority (Title 10, U.S. Code, Section 12302[a]) are *mobilized*; those that serve under the volunteerism authority (Section 12301[d]) are not mobilized, but rather, *activated*. Helmly felt that the informal and incorrect use of the term "mobilized" tended to downplay the voluntary nature of one's service and thus potentially avoided negative reactions from employers and/or family members to a reservist volunteering for active duty.

32. Lt. Gen. John A. Bradley, interview by Betty R. Kennedy, Apr-May 2008, 97–98, 107, 110, 127, AFRC Historical Services, copy at AFHRA, including quotes.

33. Rumsfeld, *Known and Unknown*, 692–699, including quote 1; Carpenter interview, 7 Mar 2012, part 2:3–4, including quote 2; "Won't Rely on the Guard as Much," *National Guard*, Feb 2006, 12; "Coming Home, The Minnesota National Guard's 1st Brigade Combat Team, 34th Infantry Division, Have Earned Their Welcome Home," *Grand Forks Herald*, 22 Jul 2007, 1D, accessed via <http://nl.newsbank.com>, accessed 2 Feb 2015; "Reserve Forces," draft PowerPoint slide, ca. Aug 2005, ASD(RA) working papers, copy at AFHRA; "Total Force Sourcing for the Long War," PowerPoint briefing slides, version 28, modification 74, 31 Aug 2006, Joint Staff J-3, copy at AFHRA; CNGR, *Strengthening America's Defense in the New Security Environment: Second Report to Congress*, 1 Mar 2007, 21; Hall interview, 23 Sep 2013, including quote 3; Coker, *2004/2005 Biannual Army Reserve Historical Summary*, 22–23, 34–35. "Predictability" or "predictable" occurred no less than seven times in the cited pages. The USAR chief from 2006 to 2012, Lt. Gen. Jack C. Stultz, stated in congressional testimony, "What our Soldiers tell me they want is predictability in their lives." Quoted in Coker, *2006/2007 Biannual Army Reserve Historical Summary*, 23. The Air Force Reserve Command commander from 2004 to 2008, Lt. Gen. John A. Bradley, also emphasized the importance of predictability; see Bradley interview, Apr–May 2008, 113.

34. Carpenter interview, 7 Mar 2012, part 1:13–15, including quote. Perhaps in some cases the duplicative effort was a matter of soldiers' records not keeping up with the soldiers themselves as they moved around, as had happened in Korea. A valuable account of a single Marine Corps Reserve rifle company mobilized for Korea is: Randy Keith Mills and Roxanne Mills, *Unexpected Journey: A Marine Corps Reserve Company in the Korean War* (Annapolis, MD: Naval Institute Press, 2000).

35. Carpenter interview, 7 Mar 2012, part 1:13, including quote 1, Blum quoted by Carpenter; Clyde A. Vaughn, interview by Forrest L. Marion, 25 Mar 2015, OSD/HO, copy at AFHRA, including quote 2.

36. John Goheen, "Off Base," *National Guard*, Jun 2005, 22–25, including quote 1; William B. Lynch, "State of the Air National Guard: Out of the Shadows," *National Guard*,

Apr 2006, 42–44; Bradley interview, 78–79, including quote 2; Daniel L. Haulman, "Base Realignment and Closure Commission, 2005," in *Locating Air Force Base Sites*, ed. Frederick J. Shaw, 211–212, 217, 224, <http://www.afhso.af.mil/shared/media/document/AFD-100928-010.pdf>, accessed 4 Feb 2015. The cut was known as Program Budget Decision 720, also referred to as Program Budget *Directive* 720 depending on source.

37. Jack C. Stultz, telephone interview by Kathryn Roe Coker, 28, 6 Jul 2012, USAR History Office, Fort Bragg, NC, including quotes; "Army Guard Boosts Enlistment Age Limit," *National Guard*, Apr 2005, 23, <http://www.highbeam.com/doc/1P3-828941381.html>, accessed 4 Feb 2015; "Military—US Army End Strength," GlobalSecurity.org, <http://www.globalsecurity.org/military/agency/end-strength.htm>, accessed 4 Feb 2015.

38. Coker, *2004/2005 Biannual Army Reserve Historical Summary*, 34–36, including quote, Helmly quoted by Coker; Coker, *2006/2007 Biannual Army Reserve Historical Summary*, 24–25; Coker, *Indispensable Force*, 339–340. The USAR headquarters' G-7, a colonel, stated, "AREF is just the way we organize the units to support ARFORGEN; to rotate." Coker, *2006/2007 Biannual Army Reserve Historical Summary*, 24, quoted by Coker.

39. Coker, *2004/2005 Biannual Army Reserve Historical Summary*, 36–37; Coker, *2006/2007 Biannual Army Reserve Historical Summary*, 23–25; Stultz, "Army Reserve: 'Integral Component,'" *Army*, Oct 2006, 134. Note in the *2006/2007 Biannual Army Reserve Historical Summary*, page 25, there appeared to be some confusion over the level of training (i.e., platoon should precede company) conducted during each year of the five-year cycle. A contributing factor, no doubt, was that in some cases, depending on the source, AREF years were numbered chronologically 5 through 1, but in other cases they were numbered 1 through 5. Sources varied on the percentage of mobilized forces supplied by AREF in FY 2006. Two sources stated "approximately 77 percent of the Army Reserve's mobilized units were from the ARFORGEN model"; see Jack C. Stultz, "The Army Reserve: No Longer a Strategic Reserve," *Army*, Oct 2007, 142; Jack C. Stultz, *A Statement on the Posture of the United States Army Reserve 2007*, <http://handle.dtic.mil/100.2/ADA471367>, 9. The Army Reserve history office's publication for FY 2006/2007 stated that AREF packages 1 and 2 provided 53 percent of mobilized units for FY 2006; see Coker, *2006/2007 Biannual Army Reserve Historical Summary*, 25. It was possible that both percentages were correct. Although AREF packages 1 and 2 (from year one, the *available* pool) were those expected to provide mobilizing units, perhaps units from other packages, from year two for example (the *ready* pool), were mobilized although they may not have been validated/certified for allocation in the *available* pool. Or perhaps there was an error. In any case, we elected to use the more conservative rate supplied by the component's history office.

40. Coker, *2004/2005 Biannual Army Reserve Historical Summary*, 32–36, including quote; Stultz, *Posture of the United States Army Reserve 2007*, 27; Coker, *2006/2007 Biannual Army Reserve Historical Summary*, 21–25, 28; Coker, *Indispensable Force*, 335, 339–340.

41. Chapman interview, 14 Jun 2013, including quotes; "Army to Mobilize 5,600 IRR Soldiers," *National Guard*, Jul 2004, 22–23; memo, Gen. Peter J. Schoomaker for Deputy Secretary of Defense Wolfowitz, 11 Dec 2003, subj: "Access to the Individual Ready Reserve (IRR)," copy at AFHRA; Jeffrey C. Larrabee, email message to Marion, 1 Aug 2016; Inactive Army National Guard, National Guard Regulation 614–1, 18 Mar 2010. Chapman recommended the Army Guard formalize the practice of requisitioning a set number of IRRs automatically for every mobilizing brigade. He viewed IRRs as a better solution than cross-leveling, which

tended to deplete units of certain specialties and could contribute to "cascading un-readiness." He favored the IRR Affiliation Program whereby each IRR was connected loosely with an Army Guard or Army Reserve unit. The intent was to provide a human point of contact for issues that arose for the IRR soldier. A corollary benefit was that the soldier might decide to join the unit and enter active (Selected Reserve) status. In 2006 the Army initiated a transition of the IRR to "Individual Warriors" in an attempt to increase soldier readiness and weed out those personnel lacking "further potential for useful military service"; see "Army Officials to Transform IRR," *National Guard*, May 2006, 21.

42. Memo, Gen. W. L. Nyland to Secretary of Defense Rumsfeld, 20 Aug 2004, subj: Keeping in touch with the Individual Ready Reserve (IRR), Rumsfeld Papers, including quote 1; McCarthy interview, 17 Sep 2013, including quotes 2–4; RFPB, *Annual Report, Fiscal Year 2003*, 18. From 1993 to 1995, then-Brig. Gen. Dennis M. McCarthy, commanding general of Marine Corps Reserve Support Command (later named Mobilization Command), held one-day IRR musters as part of the command's active management of the IRR. Apparently, by 2001 the practice had been forgotten, as evidenced by the "postcard" system. McCarthy interview, 17 Sep 2013.

43. Col. James E. Bacchus, Tom Nelson, and Glenn Davis (all MarForRes officials), conversation with Marion, 10 Jul 2013, including quote 1; John G. Cotton, interview by Forrest L. Marion, 6 Jun 2013, OSD/HO, copy at AFHRA, including quote 2. Tom Nelson, email message to Marion, 9 Aug 2016. Prior to 2011, the present-day Marine Corps Individual Reserve Support Activity's designation was "Mobilization Command (MOBCOM)."

44. ODASD(RA), *Rebalancing Forces*, 21, 28, including quotes; David S. C. Chu, interview by Forrest L. Marion, 22 Apr 2013, OSD/HO, copy at AFHRA; "Army Guard Seeks Native Speakers in 20 Languages," *National Guard*, Sep 2005, 27, <http://www.highbeam.com/doc/1P3-904072721.html>, accessed 5 Feb 2015; Lauren Bigge, "Native Tongues," *National Guard*, Oct 2006, 28–29. The Arabic linguist program was also known as "09-Lima."

45. Daniel B. Denning, "Building and Sustaining America's Army," *Army*, Oct 2006, 50–52; Helmly, *Posture of the United States Army Reserve 2007*, P11; Coker, *2004/2005 Biannual Army Reserve Historical Summary*, 14, 30–32; Coker, *2006/2007 Biannual Army Reserve Historical Summary*, 11, 21.

46. John G. Cotton, telephone conversation with Marion, 4 Nov 2013; Michael Evans, "Provincial Reconstruction Team in Afghanistan Commanded by a Naval Reservist (FTS)," *Naval Reserve Association News*, Jun 2005, 30, <http://www.ausn.org/Portals/0/Services_pdfs/JUN-05-NRAN.pdf>, accessed 5 Feb 2015; Cotton interview, 6 Jun 2013; John A. "Andy" Mueller, telephone conversation with Marion , 25 Oct 2013.

47. "DoD Offers Health Care as Deployment Reward," *National Guard*, Apr 2005, 22–23; "Guard Can Seek Medical, Dental Claims," *National Guard*, Aug 2004, 17–18; "Deadline Looms for Tricare Reserve Select," *National Guard*, Sep 2005, 26.

48. Stephen M. Koper, "Behind the Fanfare," *National Guard*, May 2005, 10, including quotes 1–2; Coker, *2006/2007 Biannual Army Reserve Historical Summary*, 54–55, including quote 3, Stultz quoted by Coker; memo, Deputy Director, TRICARE Management Activity for ASD(HA), 6 Apr 2006, subj: Final rule; transitional assistance management program: early eligibility for TRICARE for certain reserve component members, AFHRA; memo with

attachment, Jody Donehoo (TRICARE program analyst), ca. May 2006, subj: Interim final rule, TRICARE reserve select for certain members of the Selected Reserve, AFHRA; memo (draft), Deputy Director, TRICARE Management Activity, to ASD(HA), 31 May 2006, subj: Policy guidance for TRICARE reserve select (TRS), AFHRA; "Guardsmen Still Eligible for Tricare Dental Plan," *National Guard*, May 2006, 18–19; "New Three-Tier Tricare Coverage Plan Begins," *National Guard*, Aug 2006, 18. The Army Reserve history stated 1 October 2007 as the TRICARE eligibility date for Selected Reserve members rather than 1 October 2006, the correct date. Tier 1 required the member to pay 28 percent of total premium while Tier 2 required 50 percent and Tier 3, 85 percent; see "TRICARE Reserve Select" flyer, ca. mid-2006; "New Three-Tier Tricare Coverage Plan Begins," *National Guard*, Aug 2006, 18.

49. CNGR, *Transforming the National Guard and Reserves*, 281–288, including quotes, quote 3 testimony quoted by CNGR.

50. Carpenter interview, 7 Mar 2012, part 1:13–14, including quotes.

51. Craig Collins, "National Guard Family Programs: Holding the Pieces Together for the Families of Deployed Service Members," in *The Modern National Guard: Fighting the War on Terrorism* (Tampa, FL: Faircount LLC, 2005), 102–109, including quotes; Coker, *2004/2005 Biannual Army Reserve Historical Summary*, 49–52; Coker, *2006/2007 Biannual Army Reserve Historical Summary*, 57; Coker, *Indispensable Force*, 430–432.

52. Ike Skelton and Jim Cooper, "You're Not from around Here, Are You?" *Joint Force Quarterly*, Dec 2004, 13, including quote 1; Hall interview, 23 Sep 2013, including quote 2; McCarthy interview, including quote 3.

53. Richard R. Burgess, "Navy Cracking Glass Wall Between Reserve, Active Forces," *Sea Power*, Jul 2004, 10, including quotes 1, 3, Cotton quoted by Burgess (emphasis added), <http://www.military.com/NewContent/0,13190,NL_Reserve_072604,00.html>, accessed 10 Jun 2017; Mike Kramer, "Be Ready—Chief of Navy Reserve," *Naval Reserve Association News*, Feb 2005, 30, including quote 2, Cotton quoted by Kramer; Cotton interview, 6 Jun 2013. Cotton also notes that an integral part of the Navy's evolution was VCNO Admiral William J. Fallon's "zero-based review" of the USNR.

54. Cotton interview, 6 Jun 2013, including quotes; John J. McCracken III and Joyce Z. Randle, interview by Forrest L. Marion, 25 Apr 2013, OSD/HO, copy at AFHRA; Dennis M. McCarthy, "The Continuum of Reserve Service," *Joint Force Quarterly*, Dec 2004, 34, <https://www.questia.com/magazine/1G1-131164211/the-continuum-of-reserve-service>, accessed 5 Feb 2015; see "The Condition of the Strategic Operational Navy Reserve," *Association of the United States Navy*, 1 Mar 2006, <http://www.ausn.org/NewsPublications/NavyMagazine/MagazineArticles/tabid/2170/ID/11937/The-Condition-of-the-Strategic-Operational-Navy-Reserve.aspx>, accessed 5 Feb 2015. The above article linked integration with culture change. memo, George W. Bush for Rumsfeld, 29 Apr 2005, subj: Redesignation of the United States Naval Reserve to the United States Navy Reserve, the American Presidency Project, <http://www.presidency.ucsb.edu/ws/index.php?pid=63724&st=&st1=#axzz2j1cmIP2r>, accessed 5 Feb 2015; Vice Adm. John G. Cotton, telephone conversation with Marion, 4 Nov 2013. Vice Admiral Cotton readily attributed the "RE-serve" concept to his friend, Charles L. Cragin, the Acting ASD(RA) from April 1998 to May 2001.

55. John D. Winkler and Barbara A. Bicksler, eds., *The New Guard and Reserve* (San Ramon, CA: Falcon Books, 2008), 223; ODASD(RA), *Rebalancing Forces*, 18–19. Of the 32 pages comprising the body of *Rebalancing Forces*, nearly 20 percent (18–23) were devoted to the continuum of service. The continuum included not only ready reservists but military retirees and even civilians who wanted to contribute. Advocates referred to the successful Civil Air Patrol and Coast Guard Auxiliary as examples of civilian entities that shared the military's culture and core values and that were capable of performing valuable service.

56. John D. Winkler, et al., "A 'Continuum of Service' for the All-Volunteer Force," in *The All-Volunteer Force: Thirty Years of Service,* eds. Barbara A. Bicksler, Curtis L. Gilroy, and John T. Warner (Washington, DC: Brassey's, 2004), 298–303, including quotes. Note we are using 38 days as the traditional number of required, paid duty days per year. Some sources used 39 days as the standard, possibly due to differing travel day policies for the annual tour. In any case, 38 or 39 days was the standard annual requirement.

57. McCarthy, "The Continuum of Reserve Service," 31–34, including quotes. McCarthy felt most of the barriers to continuum of service were rooted in service policy rather than in the law; see McCarthy interview, 17 Sep 2013.

58. CNGR, *Transforming the National Guard and Reserves,* 24–25, 164–165, 168–169, 203, including quote (which constituted CNGR's Recommendation, page 25). Note the ADOS category did not affect Active Guard and Reserve (AGR) personnel; AGRs had a separate strength authorization. This authorization was also known as 10 U.S.C. 12301(d), or volunteerism.

59. Department of Defense, *Quadrennial Defense Review Report* (Washington, DC: OSD, 2006), 76–77, including quote 1, <http://www.defense.gov/qdr/report/Report20060203.pdf>, accessed 9 Feb 2015; Stultz interview, 6 Jul 2012, 35–36, including quote 2; John Warner National Defense Authorization Act for Fiscal Year 2007, Pub. L. No. 109-364, 120 Stat. 2192, Sec. 522, Revisions To Reserve Call-Up Authority (2006); Stultz, *Posture of the United States Army Reserve 2007*, 12.

60. Coker, *2006/2007 Biannual Army Reserve Historical Summary*, 54–55; "Online Resources Assist Families During Deployment," *National Guard*, Nov 2004, 16; "Mental Health Screening Now Available Online," *National Guard*, May 2006, 19–20; "Pentagon Mental Health Task Force Established," *National Guard*, Jul 2006, 22–23; "Post-Deployment Health Reassessment (PDHRA) Program (Department of Defense Form 2900)," DoD Deployment Health Clinical Center, <http://www.pdhealth.mil/dcs/pdhra.asp>, accessed 9 Feb 2015. The history of the National Center for PTSD is at <http://www.ptsd.va.gov/about/mission/history_of_the_national_center_for_ptsd.asp>, last accessed 9 Feb 2015.

61. Erika N. Cotton, "Psychological Casualties: States Adapt to Address Post Traumatic Stress Disorder in Guardsmen Returning from Combat," *National Guard*, Jul 2005, 24–27, including quote 1; Cotton interview, 6 Jun 2013, including quotes 2–4. Vice Admiral Cotton attributed the idea expressed above to Assistant Secretary of the Navy (Manpower and Reserve Affairs) William A. Navas Jr. Navas' official Navy bio is at <http://www.navy.mil/navydata/bios/navybio.asp?bioID=16>, accessed 9 Feb 2015. Erika Cotton's article stated guardsmen were relieved of duty for 90 days following demobilization, but official documentation indicated the policy was 60 days for involuntary duty such as inactive-duty-for-training or Annual Tour; see memo, David S. C. Chu for Secretary of the Army, Secretary of the Navy, and Secretary of the Air Force, 15 Mar 2007, subj: "Revised mobilization/demobilization personnel and pay

policy for reserve component members ordered to active duty in response to the World Trade Center and Pentagon attacks—Section 1," 4. A copy of the memo can be found at the AFHRA.

62. Cotton, "Psychological Casualties," 27, including quote 1, quoted by Cotton; Smiley interview, including quote 2; Anthony Lanuzo and Louis Proper, interview by Forrest L. Marion, 26 Mar 2013, OSD/HO, including quote 3. A copy of the transcript can be found at the Air Force Historical Research Agency. Coker, *2006/2007 Biannual Army Reserve Historical Summary*, 54. In November 2005, the Army's Disabled Soldier Support System was redesignated the U.S. Army Wounded Warrior Program (Army W2); see *Army Reserve Posture Statement 2006*, P23.

63. Marcus Luttrell, *Lone Survivor: The Eyewitness Account of Operation Redwing and the Lost Heroes of SEAL Team 10,* with Patrick Robinson (New York and Boston: Little, Brown, 2007), 348–356; Betty R. Kennedy, et al., *Turning Point 9.11*, 191–193; Daniel Cooney, "In Afghan Crash, Deadly Chain of Events for U.S.," *Philadelphia Inquirer*, 7 Jul 2005; Bradley interview, 107. In June 2007, a *Washington Post* article published at the time of release of Luttrell's book briefly mentioned the Air Force Reserve identities of the rescue helicopter crew; see Laura Blumenfeld, "The Sole Survivor," *Washington Post,* 11 Jun, 2007, <http://www. washingtonpost.com/wp-dyn/content/article/2007/06/10/AR2007061001492.html>, accessed 9 Feb 2015. This was two years after the rescue took place, however. For additional detail of the Luttrell rescue and dissemination of the story, see chapter 8, present work. Contrast the omission of reserve component identification in Luttrell's rescue and the Katrina relief effort with the Abu Ghraib prisoner abuse scandal. The Army Reserve identity of those soldiers responsible for misconduct at Abu Ghraib was clearly identified in numerous reports, such as Jonathan Eig, "Inside Abu Ghraib: Missed Red Flags, Team Under Stress," *Wall Street Journal*, 23 Nov 2004; John W. Gonzalez, "Judge Refuses to Recuse Himself in Court-Martial of Pfc. England," *Houston Chronicle*, 8 Jul 2005; T. R. Reid, "England to Plead Not Guilty in Second Trial," *Washington Post*, 8 Jul 2005; John W. Gonzalez, "Judge Rules Out Use of Comments by Pfc. England to Interrogators," *Houston Chronicle*, 9 Jul 2005. The latter three articles identified England as a reservist.

64. William B. Boehm, Renee Hylton, and Thomas W. Mehl, *In Katrina's Wake: The National Guard on the Gulf Coast, 2005* (Arlington, VA: National Guard Bureau, [2010]), 7–8, 24, 31–32, 35; David P. Anderson, *Storm Surge: The Role of the Air National Guard in Hurricane Katrina Relief Operations* ([Arlington, VA]: National Guard Bureau, 2011), 4, 11; Rosenfeld and Gross, *Air National Guard at 60*, 59–63; Les Melnyk, "Katrina Lessons Learned," *Soldiers*, Jun 2006, 29; Christopher Prawdzik, "East of Big Easy," *National Guard*, Sep 2006, 48–52, <http:// www.highbeam.com/doc/1P3-1140699241.html >, 9 Feb 2015; Coker, *Indispensable Force*, 364, 366, 416; William G. Morris, "Reserve Response to Search and Rescue Operations Following Hurricane Katrina," *Disaster Recovery Journal*, 6 Jul 2010, <http://www.drj.com/articles/online-exclusive/reserve-response-to-search-and-rescue-operations-following-hurricane-katrina.html>, accessed 4 Nov 2015. Boehm's study indicated that unverified reports of crime in New Orleans were rampant and "had a negative effect on relief operations" (21–22). Anderson stated that "in less than 36 hours after Army and Air National Guard security forces arrived, the [civil law and order] situation dramatically improved" in New Orleans (*Storm Surge*, 46–47). The loss estimate caused by Katrina was $125 billion. The figure of 80,000 deployed soldiers probably included those whose units were returning stateside at the time. Lt. Col. Jon S. Middaugh (U.S. Army, Center of Military History), email message to Marion, 23 Sep 2015. Note that Melnyk listed 79,000 guardsmen then in "federal service in the war on terrorism."

65. Boehm, Hylton, and Mehl, *In Katrina's Wake*, 10, 26–27, 35, including quote 1; Anderson, *Storm Surge*, 47, 55–56, including quote 2. In the first and second weeks of the relief operation, guardsmen served on "state active duty" (SAD), but on 7 September acting Deputy Secretary of Defense Gordon England approved the use of federal funds to place guardsmen in Title 32 status (federally funded, under state control). The move was primarily for the purpose of ensuring medical benefits to guardsmen who were working in hazardous conditions, including potentially toxic waters, especially in New Orleans. Anderson, *Storm Surge*, 56.

66. Boehm, Hylton, and Mehl, *In Katrina's Wake*, 29; Melnyk, "Katrina Lessons Learned," 32–33, including quote. For an article featuring Lieutenant General Honoré's role, published on the one-year anniversary of Katrina, see "Army General Recalls Katrina Aftermath," *Washington Post,* 7 Sep, 2006, <http://www.washingtonpost.com/wp-dyn/content/article/2006/09/07/AR2006090700163_2.html>, accessed 9 Feb, 2015. Inexplicably, the article failed to mention the National Guard. The Guard sought to correct the record in its own periodical; see John Maietta, "Katrina: Myths and Reality," *National Guard*, Jan 2006, 48.

67. "Bush: Time for New Pentagon Leadership," *National Guard*, Dec 2006, 18, including quote; White House News Release, 8 Nov 2006, "President Nominates Dr. Robert M. Gates to be Secretary of Defense," <http://georgewbush-whitehouse.archives.gov/news/releases/2006/11/20061108-4.html>, accessed 9 Feb 2015; Doubler, *National Guard and the War on Terror: Operation Iraqi Freedom* 75–76, 83, 106. According to Doubler (75–76), Houma, in a parish of 32,000, suffered the loss of six guardsmen in a single incident in Iraq; Paris, a town of 9,000, lost five Guard members in Iraq.

Chapter 7

1. Ready Reserve, 10 U.S.C. § 12302a (1952), <http://www.gpo.gov/fdsys/pkg/USCODE-2011-title10/html/USCODE-2011-title10-subtitleE-partII-chap1209-sec12302.htm>, accessed 23 Feb 2015.

2. Joint Staff J-3, "Total Force Sourcing for the Long War," version 28, mod 74 (briefing slides, 31 Aug 2006), copy at AFHRA, 6–7, including quotes; Robert H. Smiley, OASD(RA), email message to Marion, 30 Mar 2015, copy at AFHRA; David S. Chu, email message to Marion, 2 Jun 2017, copy in authors' files at OSD.

3. Robert H. Smiley, OASD(RA), interview by Forrest L. Marion, 24 Sep 2013, OSD/HO, including quotes, copy at AFHRA. Lieutenant General Blum served as chief, National Guard Bureau, from 2003 to 2008. Lieutenant General Vaughn served as ARNG director from 2005 to 2009; Lt. Gen. H. Steven Blum, US Army, ret., interview by Forrest L. Marion, 17 Mar 2015, OSD/HO, copy at AFHRA.

4. Memo, Secretary of Defense for Secretaries of the Military Departments, Chairman of the Joint Chiefs of Staff, Under Secretaries of Defense, 19 Jan 2007, subj: Utilization of the total force, including quotes (Gates Utilization memo hereinafter). Also in January 2007, Congress authorized a temporary increase of 74,200 soldiers: 65,000 (Army), 8,200 (ARNG), and 1,000 (USAR); see Coker, *The Indispensable Force*, 345. In 2009 Gates approved an additional temporary increase in Army end strength of 22,000 soldiers.

5. Gen. Clyde A. Vaughn, "We've Got the Youngest Force We've Ever Had," interview, *National Guard*, Aug 2007, 42–44, including quote (emphasis added); see data on Lieutenant General Vaughn at https://www.cna.org/reports/economy/board>, accessed 3 Mar 2015; another online biographical sketch, more easily accessible and from a quasi-official source, listed erroneously his years as ARNG director, see <http://www.ausa.org/MEETINGS/ NATIONALAWARDSAUSA/Pages/2010-LieutenantGeneralClydeAVaughn.aspx>, accessed 23 Feb 2015.

6. Ron Jensen, "Precious Commodity," *National Guard*, Dec. 2007, 29, including quote, Germain quoted by Jensen; OASD(RA), "Changes to Total Force Policy: Briefing to Defense Senior Leader Conference" (briefing slides, 23 Jan 2007), slide 6 "Manage Mobilizations on a Unit Basis," copy at AFHRA; Gates Utilization memo, including quote 2; Peter Pace, *Posture Statement of General Peter Pace, USMC, Chairman of the Joint Chiefs of Staff, before the 110th Congress, Senate Armed Services Committee*, 6 Feb 2007, 12, including quote 3, <http:// www.au.af.mil/au/awc/awcgate/dod/posture_6feb07pace.pdf>, accessed 20 Apr 2015; Robert M. Gates, "Strategic Perspective," *National Guard*, Sep 2008, 16. The 1:5 boots-on-the-ground-to-dwell rate has been referred to in various documents as the "dwell rate" or "dwell ratio." Despite the clear wording in the memorandum, apparently there has been confusion in some cases over whether the "5" equated to the last year of dwell or the next year of mobilization eligibility. Part of the answer may relate to the fact that under ARFORGEN, a unit in its year of mobilization eligibility might be mobilized in its first month or—nearly a year later—in its twelfth month. The reset clock did not start until the redeploying unit demobilized. Additionally, the Army Reserve used a five-year ARFORGEN cycle (1:4) whereas the ARNG may in some cases have used a 1:5 cycle; eEmail, Thomas E. Welke, Deputy G-33, USAR, to Kathryn R. Coker, historian, USAR, 21 Apr 2014, subj: FW: ARFORGEN question, copy at AFHRA.

Col. James E. Porter, the ALARNG chief of staff since 2009, felt the 1:4 versus 1:5 issue was a "compromise" of sorts. Col. James E. Porter, conversation with Marion, 23 Apr 2014. In 2007 the USCGR sought "more predictability about when and where reservists will mobilize"; see John C. Acton, "Readiness to Mobilize: It's What We're All About!" *USCG Reservist* 54, no. 6 (2007): 4. By 2010, the USCG sought a 1:5 mobilization rate; see Daniel R. May, "View from The Bridge," *USCG Reservist*, 57, no. 1 (2010): 4; Rear Adm. Steven E. Day, USCGR, interview by Forrest L. Marion, 6 Mar 2012, 9–10, OSD/HO, copy at AFHRA. Paul E. Pratt, the MarForRes deputy G-3/5 at Marine Corps Support Facility New Orleans, stated the Marine Corps Reserve's BOG-to-dwell rate "is more of a one to four" with infantry battalions typically having 48 months of dwell. Paul E. Pratt, interview by Forrest L. Marion, 11 Jul 2013, OSD/HO, copy at AFHRA; see also note 13 below.

7. Kathryn Roe Coker, *The Indispensable Force*, 345. The department offered compensation when it failed to meet the objective of "one day of "administrative absence" a month for every month beyond 12 they are mobilized in a 72-month period"; see "DoD to Offer Days Off For Extra Deployments," *National Guard*, May 2007, 16.

8. Preston M. "Pete" Geren, interview by Forrest L. Marion, 2 Apr 2014, OSD/HO, copy at AFHRA, including quote; Ron Jensen, "Beyond the Yellow Ribbon," *National Guard*, Jan 2008, 22–23; Richard M. Green, "A Continuous Process," *National Guard*, Nov 2007, 12; Robert H. Smiley, email message to Marion, 24 Feb 2014. Green's article listed a 22-month mobilization. The *30-day* reintegration event for 1/34 was held on 15–16 September 2007; see

Richard Kemp, "30 Day Reintegration Event," NorthStar Guard Online, 17 Sep 2007, <http://www.minnesotanationalguard.org/press_room/e-zine/articles/index.php?item=1046>, accessed 25 Feb 2015. Thus 1/34's 22-month mobilization must have ended by August 2007. Note a news article dated 22 July 2007 reported the 1/34's return home that very week (at least the lead elements); see "Coming Home, The Minnesota National Guard's 1st Brigade Combat Team, 34th Infantry Division, Have Earned Their Welcome Home," *Grand Forks Herald*, 22 Jul 2007.

    9. Smiley interview, 24 Sep 2013, including quotes 1–2 (emphasis added); Robert H. Smiley, email message to Marion, 24 Feb 2014; Col. James E. Porter, chief of staff, Alabama ARNG, interview by Forrest L. Marion, 10 Dec 2013, OSD/HO, copy at AFHRA, including quote 3; Green, "A Continuous Process," 12; House Committee on Veterans' Affairs, *Witness Testimony of Major General Larry W. Shellito, 18 Oct 2007*, <http://veterans.house.gov/witness-testimony/major-general-larry-w-shellito>, accessed 25 Feb 2015; Green, "A Continuous Process," 12; Smiley email message, 24 Feb 2014. Some 700 soldiers from other states were affected as well.

    10. Kathryn Roe Coker, *The 2008/2009 Biannual Army Reserve Historical Summary* (Fort Bragg, NC: Office of Army Reserve History, 2013), appendix pages 1, 16, 27, including quotes 1–2, Casey quoted by Coker; Porter interview, 10 Dec 2013, including quote 3; James E. Porter in discussion with Marion, 23 Apr 2014; Kathryn Roe Coker, *United States Army Reserve 2011 Annual Historical Summary* (Fort Bragg, NC: Office of Army Reserve History, 2013), 13, 98. Porter became chief of staff of the Alabama ARNG in August 2009 and continued in that capacity as of this writing. Porter agreed with Colonel Chapman (see chapter 6, present work) that the IRR programs (including IRR affiliation which ARNG began by 2005, perhaps in "pilot" status) worked well in Alabama, and some IRRs actually joined units as a result of affiliation. The Army Reserve began its own IRR Affiliation Program as a one-year pilot in December 2010; see Coker, *Army Reserve 2011 Annual Summary*, 25. The Army formally began IRR affiliation in July 2011; see Army Reserve Communications, "Army Reserve, Army National Guard to launch IRR Affiliation Program," U.S. Army website, 1 Jul 2011, <http://www.army.mil/article/60932/Army_Reserve__Army_National_Guard_to_launch_IRR_Affiliation_Program>, accessed 16 Sep 2015.

    Some confusion was unavoidable due to the following: first, the ARFORGEN model called for a 1:4 (BOG-to-dwell) cycle; and, second, the Gates mobilization directive called for a goal of 1:5 (BOG to dwell). The reality, of course, was that for several years neither 1:4 nor 1:5 was a realistic option for a number of ground combat or CS/CSS units. A number of sources referred to either a 1:4 or 1:5 cycle without mentioning the other model or the reason for the difference; see also note 6 above.

    In his interview, Porter discussed how the RC has gained "by accident . . . a level of operational savvy" not seen during Vietnam, and not since then—the result of 12 years of war. "We can't buy this kind of experience" or readiness, he stated. "We can't take them all the way back" to being a strategic force. Acknowledging that the Guard can't put a brigade out the door in only 30 days, he noted that except for "the ready-brigades at Fort Bragg . . . [and other special operations units], you can't spin an active duty armor brigade that's not sitting in the theater of operations out the door in 30 days either." But the Guard "*can* put brigades out the door in *39* days, because that's what we've done" (emphasis added).

    11. Lt. Gen. Jack C. Stultz, interview by Kathryn R. Coker, 3 Aug 2010, USAR History Office, copy at AFHRA, including quote; Coker, *2008/2009 Biannual Army Reserve Historical*

Summary, 15–16, 27; Coker, *Indispensable Force*, 335; Kathryn Roe Coker, *Army Reserve 2011 Annual Historical Summary*, 6, 12; "Five Guard Brigades Alerted for Deployment," *National Guard*, Jun 2008, 20, including quote 2. For the May 2008 announcement of upcoming Army Guard deployments, see Donna Miles, "Upcoming Iraq, Afghanistan Rotations Announced," *DoD News*, 19 May 2008, at <http://www.defense.gov/news/newsarticle.aspx?id=49926>, accessed 23 Feb 2015.

12. Stultz interview, 3 Aug 2010, including quotes; Gates Utilization memo; Preston M. Geren interview, 2 Apr 2014; Coker, *2008/2009 Biannual Army Reserve Historical Summary*, 19. Geren served as under secretary of the Army from February 2006 to March 2007 when he was named acting secretary of the Army. He was confirmed as the secretary of the Army in July 2007; see Army News Service, "Senate Names Pete Geren 20th Secretary of the Army," U.S. Army website, 13 Jul 2007, <http://www.army.mil/article/4042/senate-names-pete-geren-20th-secretary-of-the-army>, accessed 23 Feb 2015. The article mistakenly stated he served as the under secretary "until Feb. 21, 2006." Rather, he *became* the under secretary on that date. By the start of 2012, most Army Guard units transitioned to nine-month boots-on-ground deployments in support of "named operations outside the continental United States"; see Coker, *Army Reserve 2011 Annual Summary*, 98.

13. Coker, *The Indispensable Force*, 378–382; Coker, *2008/2009 Biannual Army Reserve Historical Summary*, 26–29; email, Lt. Col. Nicky G. Medley, Mobilization Readiness Officer, Alabama ARNG, to Col. James E. Porter Jr., chief of staff, Alabama ARNG, 23 Apr 2014, subj: Mob plan, copy in Marion's possession; Lt. Col Nicky G. Medley, in discussion with Marion, 14 Aug 2014. By 2012 Camp Shelby and Forts Lewis and Benning were no longer needed as mobilization platforms.

Clarifying that the RTC provided a *pre*mobilization capability, Maj. Paul Nichols of the USARC G-7 office stated: "RTC is the final catch-all, ensuring individual tasks are accomplished *prior to units and soldiers being mobilized* in the execution of the train-alert-deploy construct" (Coker, *Indispensable Force*, 381, emphasis added). Fort McCoy was one of five Army Reserve installations; the others were Forts Buchanan (PR), Devens (MA), Hunter Liggett (CA), and Camp Parks (CA); see Coker, *Army Reserve 2011 Annual Summary*, 104. The USAR RTCs may have been used for postmobilization as well as pre-mob training, but their primary purpose was pre-mob (possible other sites used for post-mobilization training, including the ARNG's mobilization platforms; USAR historian J. Boyd agreed with this assessment).

14. Coker, *2008/2009 Biannual Army Reserve Historical Summary*, 26–29, including quotes 1–2, Stultz quoted by Coker; "Five Guard Brigades Alerted for Deployment," *National Guard*, Jun 2008, 20, including quote 3.

15. Smiley interview, 24 Sep 2013, including quotes; Robert H. Smiley, email message to Marion, 14 Aug 2014; memo, Lt. Gen. Clyde A. Vaughn, Director, Army National Guard, for The Adjutants General of all States, Puerto Rico, the US Virgin Islands, Guam, and the Commanding General of the District of Columbia, 4 Apr 2007, subj: Premobilization training certification, copy at AFHRA, provided to Marion by Col. James E. Porter, Alabama ARNG; memo, SecDef to Secretaries of the Military Departments, Chairman of the Joint Chiefs of Staff, Under Secretaries of Defense, General Counsel of the Department of Defense, 14 Mar 2011, subj: Reserve component contiguous training, copy at AFHRA; Lt. Gen. Clyde A. Vaughn, interview by Forrest L. Marion, 25 Mar 2015, OSD/HO, copy at AFHRA; memo, 14 Mar 2011,

subj: Reserve component contiguous training, Historian files, Guard mobilization manuscript, Center of Military History. A subsequent memorandum issued by Lt. Gen. Vaughn called for the establishment of a premobilization training assistance element in each joint force headquarters to assist the adjutants general in "certification of premobilization training"; see memo, Lt. Gen. Clyde A. Vaughn, Director, Army National Guard, for The Adjutants General of all States, Puerto Rico, the US Virgin Islands, Guam, and the Commanding General of the District of Columbia, 7 Sep 2007, subj: Change to the premobilization training memo, copy at AFHRA, provided to Marion by Col. James E. Porter, Alabama ARNG.

16. David L. McGinnis, interview by Forrest L. Marion, 7 Mar 2014, OSD/HO, copy at AFHRA, including quote.

17. Coker, *2006/2007 Biannual Army Reserve Historical Summary*, 11–13; Coker, *Indispensable Force*, 333–334, 359; Coker, *2008/2009 Biannual Army Reserve Historical Summary*, 81–84, including quote, quoted by Coker; Coker, *Indispensable Force*, 356–358; email, Thomas E. Welke to Kathryn Roe Coker, 20 May 14, subj: RE: Our History—Official Site of the U.S. Army Reserve, copy in Marion's possession.

18. "Army Guard Hits End-Strength Goal Early, Readiness High," *National Guard*, Oct 2009, 16–17, including quote; Morgan Mann, "The Operational Reserve," *Marine Corps Gazette*, Feb 2011, 41–42. Note that Mann cited a Manpower Plans and Policy Division report, "Reserve Company Grade Officer Shortfalls" (Washington, DC: 10 Apr 2010). For ARNG's establishment of Transients-Trainees-Holdees-Students, see chapter 5, present work.

19. Office of the Assistant Secretary of Defense for Reserve Affairs, Deputy Assistant Secretary for Readiness, Training & Mobilization, "Full-Time Support to the Reserve Components" (briefing slides, 22 May 2007), copy at AFHRA, slide 2, including quote 1; CNGR, *Transforming the National Guard and Reserves*, 200–203, 206, including quote 2 (emphasis added). The section on full-time support was found between pages 196 and 209. The CNGR's study found the same problem that a RAND study in 2000 had uncovered: only one in four "full-time support" (apparently used interchangeably therein with "FTS") billets of the Army reserves (both ARNG and USAR) was located at the company level or below; see CNGR, *Transforming the National Guard and Reserves*, 85, 202. A debate in Navy circles concerned whether Navy FTS personnel "should be assigned to operational tours"; see Matt Dubois, "Navy Reserve Full-Time Support," *Naval Reserve Association News*, Apr 2007, 22–23.

In 2011 the NGB explicitly rejected "a return to the Cold War strategic reserve model"; see "National Guard Bureau Implementing the Army Force Generation Model in the Army National Guard, A Formula for Operational Capacity, White Paper," Army National Guard Directorate, G5: SPZ, 1 Aug 2011, version 3, page 1, <https://g1arng.army.pentagon.mil/Featured%20News/Attachments/ARFORGEN_Whitepaper_1AUG11.pdf >, accessed 20 Apr 2015. "Full-Time Manning," *National Guard*, Apr 2007, 61; William Matthews, "Good News Bad News," *National Guard*, Apr 2007, 26–29, including quotes 3–4; Ron Jensen, "Still Short," *National Guard*, Jun 2009, 24–26, including quote 5; "A Boost For Full-Time Manning," *National Guard*, Nov 2008, 12. Maine's adjutant general, Maj. Gen. John W. Libby, stated the increase enabled his state to bump up to 223 military technicians—of 432 required. Maine's AGRs ramped up to 201, but the state required 312.

20. R. Martin Umbarger, "Silver Bullet," *National Guard*, May 2008, 10, including quote 1; Jensen, "Still Short," 26, including quote 2. Major General Umbarger served as the adjutant general of Indiana. He stated many company-size units required five or six full-time positions

but, given the current funding, they could fill no more than two. In 2013 Colonel Porter stated the Alabama ARNG stood at 67 percent of authorized full-time strength; see Porter interview, 10 Dec 2013.

21. Daniel R. May, "View From The Bridge: Modernizing the Reserve Force," *USCG Reservist* 56, no. 3 (2009): 14; Admiral Thad W. Allen, interview, *USCG Reservist*, special issue, 2008, 13; Michael R. Seward, "Post 9-11 Training Challenges," *USCG Reservist* 56, no. 4 (2009): 10; Andrea L. Contratto, "The View," *USCG Reservist* 58, no. 3 (2011): 6; Admiral Robert J. Papp Jr., USCG, interview by Forrest L. Marion, 9 Mar 2012, OSD/HO, copy at AFHRA; Master Chief Petty Off. Jeffrey D. Smith, USCGR, ret., interview by Forrest L. Marion, 5 Mar 2012, OSD/HO, copy at AFHRA. The FTS initiative was one part of the Reserve Force Readiness System; see Daniel R. May, "View from the Bridge: New Director Outlines Three Major Initiatives," *USCG Reservist* 55, no. 3 (2008): 14. May was a one-star, Day, a two-star; both ranks are termed "rear admiral" in the Coast Guard, although with different abbreviations (not used in the present work to avoid confusion).

22. "News Call: Violence Escalates in Afghanistan," *Army*, Aug 2008, 8; "Reserve Component Mobilizations," *Naval Reserve Association News*, Dec 2008, 11; Barak Obama, "Remarks by the President on a New Strategy for Afghanistan and Pakistan," Washington, DC, 27 Mar 2009, <http://www.nytimes.com/2009/03/27/us/politics/27obama-text.html>, accessed 10 Jul 2017, including quote; DoD Personnel Reports, <https://www.dmdc.osd.mil/appj/dwp/dwp_reports.jsp>, accessed 11 Jul 2016. For the force increases (totaling 21,000) announced by March 2009, see Peter Baker and Thom Shanker, "Obama Sets New Afghan Strategy," *New York Times*, 26 Mar 2009, <http://www.nytimes.com/2009/03/27/washington/27prexy.html>, accessed 23 Feb 2015. The surge announced in December 2009 was for 30,000 troops; see Barak Obama, "Remarks by the President in Address to the Nation on the Way Forward in Afghanistan and Pakistan," 1 Dec 2009, White House Press Office Archive, <https://obamawhitehouse.archives.gov//the-press-office/remarks-president-address-nation-way-forward-afghanistan-and-pakistan>, accessed 23 Feb 2015.

23. Andrew Waldman, "Unique Guard Program Helps Afghan Farmers Rebuild," *National Guard*, Mar 2009, 20, including quote; on Kansas guard, Melissa Raney, "Guard Agribusinessmen Help Afghan Farmers Plant Saffron," *National Guard*, Nov 2009, 44–45; Vaughn interview, 25 Mar 2015; "Afghan farmers continue to struggle," *Show Me* 11, no. 3 (May/Jun 2007): 15–16. The Missouri National Guard established the first ADT in 2007; see "Army Guard Handles President's Afghan Agricultural Initiative," *National Guard*, Jan 2010, 14. In 2009, Kansas, Kentucky, Indiana, and Tennessee were scheduled for ADTs. The term "agri*business* development team" was also used; see Jon Soucy, "Missouri Guard's Agricultural Mission Grows in Afghanistan," *DoD News*, 23 Dec 2008, <http://www.defense.gov/News/newsarticle.aspx?id=52447>, accessed 17 Feb 2015. Another nontraditional mission for Army guardsmen was that of security forces/theater security (SECFOR/TSEC) from which, by 2007, Guard leaders sought relief. Lieutenant General Blum, Lieutenant General Vaughn, and Maj. Gen. R. Martin Umbarger objected to the Army's use of guardsmen in "security-force companies" in a piecemeal fashion and not according to doctrine; see Lt. Gen. Steve Blum, "We Have a Diminished Capability to Respond," interview, *National Guard*, May 2007, 27; [R. Martin Umbarger] "Here We Go Again," *National Guard*, Jun 2007, 10.

24. On Indiana, Tennessee, Texas: "Sowing Seeds of Hope: Teams Give Boost to Afghan Farmers," *National Guard*, Feb 2010, 46–47; Ron Jensen, "Seeding Hope," *National Guard*, May 2010, 24–27; on Iowa: "Guard Ag Team Helps Afghans Battle Deadly Rabies Outbreak,"

National Guard, Oct 2010, 55; on Iowa: "Agriculture Team Conducts Class for Afghan Veterinarians," *National Guard*, Jan 2011, 42; on Texas: Laura Childs, "Greening Afghanistan: Guard Farmers Help Reforest Ghazni," *National Guard*, May 2011, 52–53; Ron Jensen, "Citizen Warrior," *National Guard*, Aug 2011, 32–35. By spring 2010 more than 1,000 guardsmen had participated with ADTs in Afghanistan. In an earlier version of U.S. agricultural support for Afghanistan, in 1962 an Oklahoma ANG C–97 transport airlifted a dozen cows and two bulls as a diplomatic gift for King Mohammed Zahir Shah with intent to improve the quality of beef in the country; see Ron Jensen, "'Bull Shippers,'" *National Guard*, Jul 2011, 34–36.

25. Morgan Mann, "The Operational Reserve," *Marine Corps Gazette*, Feb 2011, 41–42, including quotes, commandant quoted by Mann.

26. Jennifer Smith, "Executing the Navy's Maritime Strategy in an Expanded Battlespace," *Naval Reserve Association News*, Apr 2008, 15–21, <http://www.navy-reserve.org/Portals/0/NRA%20News/APR-08/NRAN-APR-08.pdf>, 23 Feb 2015; Vice Adm. John G. Cotton, USN, ret., interview by Forrest L. Marion, 6 Jun 2013, OSD/HO, copy at AFHRA including quote; Casey Coane, "The Seascape as It Appears To Me—Part 3," *Naval Reserve Association News*, May 2008, 16; "Navy Adds Civil Affairs Unit," *Naval Reserve Association News*, May 2007, 21.

27. McGinnis interview, 7 Mar 2014, including quotes; Coker, *2008/2009 Biannual Army Reserve Historical Summary*, 89; Coker, *Indispensable Force*, 354.

28. Mobilization and Readiness Division, Army National Guard G-3 National Guard Bureau, slide deck, "ARNG BCT Mob History," 8 Dec 2014; "TX ADT-02 Mobilization AAR Comments," 22 Feb 2009, 1–2; "39th Infantry Brigade Combat Team: Mobilization and Deployment Journal," 21–23; all three documents in Historian files, Guard Mobilization manuscript, Center of Military History; Maass, *Department of the Army Historical Summary, Fiscal Year 2007*, 35.

29. Michael D. Doubler, *Operation Jump Start: The National Guard on the Southwest Border, 2006–2008* (Washington, DC: NGB Office of Public Affairs, 24 Oct 2008), 15, 23–27, 32–33, 42–43, 63, 72; "Officials: New Border Mission Similar to Operation Jump Start," *National Guard*, Jul 2010, 14; "Guard's New Border Mission Set to Begin Early This Month," *National Guard*, Aug 2010, 24; "National Guard Reaches 1,200 Troops on Border," *National Guard*, Oct 2010, 18, 20; "Back to the Border," *National Guard*, Oct 2010, 54–55; Andrew Waldman, "Southern Watch," *National Guard*, Nov 2010, 22–24; "Bargain on the SW Border: Efficient Guard May Extend," *National Guard*, Jan 2011, 16. Title 32 status meant federal funding, under state control (see chapter 6, present work). In 2010–2011 the guardsmen supported the U.S. Customs and Border Protection agency. For mention of the 1916 use of the National Guard along the border with Mexico, see chapter 1, present work.

30. "DoD Creates Task Force to Aid Domestic Response," *National Guard*, Jan 2009, 16; William Matthews, "Preparing for the Worst," *National Guard*, Jan 2011, 22–25; On Florida: Thomas Kielbasa, "Second Civil Support Team Passes Realistic Evaluation," *National Guard*, Feb 2011, 44; "National Guard Bolsters WMD Response Capabilities," *National Guard*, Nov 2010, 19–20. For the Ohio National Guard's HRT validation, see Matthew Scotten, "Ohio National Guard Homeland Response Force First to Undergo Mission-Capable Evaluation, Validation," Ohio National Guard News, <http://www.ong.ohio.gov/stories/2011/August/080811_muscatatuck.html>, accessed 25 Feb 2015. For the Ohio National Guard's annual report for FY 2012 including information on its HRF, Ohio National Guard, Ohio Adjutant

General's Department, *2012 Annual Report* (Columbus: Ohio Adjutant General's Department, [2013]), <http://www.ong.ohio.gov/annual_reports/2012ONG-AnnualReport.pdf?bid=181>, accessed 25 Feb 2015. In 2010 the Guard had 17 enhanced-response force packages capable of responding to an attack with a weapon of mass destruction.

31. Andrew Waldman, "Guard Adds, Streamlines Emergency Response Capabilities," *National Guard*, Jul 2010, 12; Lt. Col. Anthony Lanuzo, USAF, and Louis Proper, ANG, interview by Forrest L. Marion, 26 Mar 2013, OSD/HO, copy at AFHRA; Lanuzo and Proper interview, 26 Mar 2013; "Part of History," *National Guard*, Feb 2009, 36–37.

32. "Blum: Guard Vital to Northern Command," *National Guard*, Apr 2009, 25, including quote; Matthews, "Preparing for the Worst."

33. Coker, *Indispensable Force*, 436–439; Gen. Craig R. McKinley, Florida Air National Guard, ret., interview by Forrest L. Marion, 10 Mar 2014, OSD/HO, copy at AFHRA, including quote.

34. Lt. Gen. Craig R. McKinley, "What I'm Most Concerned about Is Our Air Combat Command Footprint," interview, *National Guard*, Aug 2007, 47–48; "F–22s at Langley Fully Operational," *National Guard*, Jan 2008, 20–21; Ron Jensen, "Flying Colors," *National Guard*, Feb 2009, 26–28; McKinley, "We're Going to Go through Leaner Times," 32; McKinley interview, 10 Mar 2014; Craig Carper, "Virginia Air Guard F–22 Pilot Soars Past 1,000 Hours," 192d Fighter Wing Public Affairs website, 13 Feb 2014, accessed 24 Feb 2015 (page discontinued); on Missouri: "B–2 Pilot Flies 1,000 Hours; Fourth in Wing to Hit Mark," *National Guard*, May 2010, 44. Associate units shared the same aircraft between USAF and ANG/USAFR pilots/aircrews. McKinley promoted the associate unit model; see his "We Are Adaptable, Accessible and Rapidly Deployable," interview, *National Guard*, Jul 2009, 24–29.

35. McKinley interview, 10 Mar 2014, including quotes; Richard M. Green, "A Process Gone Awry," *National Guard*, Jul 2008, 12. For the conversion of the A–10 to MQ–9 mission at Willow Grove, see "Air Force Selects Horsham's 111th Fighter Wing for New High-Tech Mission," 19 Mar 2013, <http://www.prnewswire.com/news-releases/air-force-selects-horshams-111th-fighter-wing-for-new-high-tech-mission-198980501.html>, accessed 24 Feb 2015. For the MQ–9 Reaper, see the USAF fact sheet of 18 Aug 2010, <http://www.af.mil/AboutUs/FactSheets/Display/tabid/224/Article/104470/mq-9-reaper.aspx>, accessed 24 Feb 2015. Both the 147th Reconnaissance Wing and 174th Attack Wing lost F–16s but transitioned to remotely piloted aircraft (the MQ–1B for 147th, the MQ–9 for 174th); see Andrew Waldman, "Eyes on Texas," *National Guard*, Jan 2010, 22–25. The Houston unit was the 147th Reconnaissance Wing; the Syracuse unit was the 174th Attack Wing.

36. Lt. Gen. John A. Bradley, USAF, interview by Betty R. Kennedy, Apr–May 2008, AFRC Historical Services, copy at AFHRA, 76, 78, including quotes 1–3. Bradley also served as chief, U.S. Air Force Reserve, and in that capacity was a member of the air staff. Bradley interview, Apr–May 2008, 77–79, including quote 4.

37. "Lawmakers Tell Air Force: Not So Fast on 'Plane Grabs,'" *National Guard*, Feb 2011, 16, including quotes, quote 1, quoted by *National Guard*; William R. Burks, "Total Force or Total Farce?" *National Guard*, Apr 2011, 34–36, including quote 1.

38. CNGR, *Transforming the National Guard and Reserves*, 113, including quote 1; *Managing the Reserve Components as an Operational Force* (Department of Defense white

paper), at <http://ra.defense.gov>, accessed 17 Apr 2014 (page discontinued), 9, including quote 2; see USD(P&R), Department of Defense Directive Number 1200.17, subj: Managing the reserve components as an operational force, 29 Oct 2008, <http://www.dtic.mil/whs/directives/corres/pdf/120017p.pdf>, accessed 24 Feb 2015.

39. CNGR, *Transforming the National Guard and Reserves*, 34–35, 149–150, 244–246, including quote 1; David S. C. Chu, interview by Forrest L. Marion, 22 Apr 2013, OSD/HO, copy at AFHRA, including quote 2; *Managing the Reserve Components as an Operational Force*, 9. Note that some sources referred to 38 training days as the standard in the Selected Reserve; others referred to 39 days. For civilian employment issues, see chapter 5, present work.

40. Gregory Baur, "Our Future Reserve," *Marine Corps Gazette*, Jan 2007, 44–45, including quotes 1–2; CNGR, *Transforming the National Guard and Reserves*, 153, including quote 3.

41. GAO, *Guard and Reserve Personnel: Fiscal, Security, and Human Capital Challenges Should Be Considered in Developing a Revised Business Model for the Reserve Component* (Washington, DC: GAO, 20 Jun 2007), 18, including quote 1 (Walker testimony), <http://www.gao.gov/assets/120/117036.pdf>, accessed 24 Feb 2015; Chu interview, 22 Apr 2013, including quote 2; Wanda R. Langley, interview by Forrest L. Marion, 22 Mar 2013, AFHRA, including quote 3; Maj. Gen. Arnold L. Punaro, USMC, ret., interview by Forrest L. Marion, 23 Sep 2013, OSD/HO, copy at AFHRA, including quote 4; "Panel Slams Pentagon Treatment of Guard," *National Guard*, Apr 2007, 20, including quote 5, Punaro quoted by *National Guard*; GAO, *DOD Systems Modernization: Management of Integrated Military Human Capital Program Needs Additional Improvements* (Washington, DC: GAO, Feb 2005), 26, <http://www.gao.gov/assets/250/245300.pdf>, accessed 24 Feb 2015; CNGR, *Transforming the National Guard and Reserves*, 136, 153–156; "Army to Launch New Pay, Personnel System," *National Guard*, Jan 2008, 17. USD(P&R) Chu gave three main reasons for the DIMHRS failure: 1) USD(P&R) was removed from the program's oversight; 2) the service with the data in the worst condition (the Army) went first; and, 3) the service with the data in the best condition (the Air Force), was not allowed to go first. Given the known problems with DIMHRS by 2008 if not before, why the program remained alive until 2010 is a valid question.

42. CNGR, *Transforming the National Guard and Reserves*, 34–35, 149–150, 244–246, including quote 1, quoted by CNGR; *Managing the Reserve Components as an Operational Force*, 9. The CNGR quoted GAO, *Military Personnel: Additional Actions Needed to Improve Oversight of Reserve Employment Issues*. Note that some sources referred to 38 training days as the standard in the Selected Reserve; others referred to 39 days. For civilian employment issues, see chapter 5, present work. GAO, *Guard and Reserve Personnel*, 4, 7, 16, 19, 21, 26, 28, including quotes 2–6.

43. John F. Hargraves, interview by U.S. Army Reserve Historical Office, 2 Apr 2013, copy at AFHRA, including quote. The CNGR addressed the needs of RC senior officers to attain joint education and qualification; see CNGR, *Transforming the National Guard and Reserves*, 138–149.

44. Hargraves interview, 2 Apr 2013.

45. Memo, Vice Adm. Dirk J. Debbink for USNR, n.d., subj: "Ready now": Navy Reserve strategic plan—2009, commander's intent," including quotes 1–2, copy provided to Marion by James C. Grover, Office of the Chief of Navy Reserve; memo, Debbink to USNR, n.d., subj :

"Ready now": Navy Reserve strategic plan—2010, commander's intent"; Debbink to USNR, 1 Oct 2011, subj: "Ready Now": the Navy Reserve strategic Plan—2012, commander's intent. We are indebted to Mr. Grover for his strong support of this study in various ways including his providing us with electronic copies of the above-cited USNR strategic plans and for assistance with Navy interview candidates.

46. Coker, *2008/2009 Biannual Army Reserve Historical Summary*, 4–5; "Lawmakers Tell Air Force: Not So Fast on 'Plane Grabs,'" *National Guard*, Feb 2011, 16; William R. Burks, "Total Force *or Total Farce?*" *National Guard*, Apr 2011, 34–36, including quotes; "McKinley: Relationship Strong Between Guard, Active Duty," *National Guard*, Jan 2011, 16, 18.

47. Lt. Gen. Harry M. Wyatt III, "'It's Lining Up Pretty Well for the Air National Guard,'" interview, *National Guard*, Aug 2011, 42–46, 48, including quote 1, quoted by Wyatt; Lt. Gen. Dennis M. McCarthy, USMC, ret., interview by Forrest L. Marion, 17 Sep 2013, OSD/HO, copy at AFHRA. Lieutenant General Bradley, the AFRC commander, favored volunteerism and viewed mobilization as a "last resort"; see Bradley interview, Apr–May 2008, 97–98, 110; Kennedy, et al., *Turning Point 9.11*, 227–228. Volunteerism was addressed under Title 10, U.S. Code, Section 12301(d). Legally, such members were *activated*, not *mobilized*, but incorrect terminology was often used probably in large part as a means of "protecting" the member from perceived or actual negative reactions to volunteerism on the part of employers and family members. Gen. Craig R. McKinley, "We're Going to Go Through Leaner Times," interview, *National Guard*, Dec 2010, 28–32, including quotes 2–3; Andrew Waldman, "Guardedly Optimistic," *National Guard*, Oct 2010, 40–41.

48. J. Eric Davis, "Building a Battalion from Scratch," *Marine Corps Gazette*, May 2011, 70–71, including quotes. The 2008 *National Defense Strategy* used the term, "Long War," to describe post-9/11 combat operations; see <http://archive.defense.gov/pubs/2008NationalDefenseStrategy.pdf>, accessed 23 Feb 2015. Because, for example, the 2010 National Security Strategy failed to provide an updated proper name for the conflicts described therein as "today's wars," "the war in Iraq," and "a war against al-Qaida," We elected to continue use of the simple, clear proper name, the Long War. Stultz interview, 3 Aug 2010; "Five Guard Brigades Alerted for Deployment," *National Guard*, Jun 2008, 20. For the May 2008 announcement of upcoming Army Guard deployments, see Donna Miles, "Upcoming Iraq, Afghanistan Rotations Announced," *DoD News*, 19 May 2008, <http://www.defense.gov/news/newsarticle.aspx?id=49926>, accessed 23 Feb 2015.

49. Defense Manpower Data Center, Human Resources Strategic Assessment Program, Survey Note, No. 2013-001, 15 Jan 2013, subj: 2011 Department of Defense National Survey of Employers and June 2012 Status of Forces Survey of Reserve Component Members: Employer Support for Reserve Component Members, copy provided to Marion by OASD(RA) at AFHRA, 1–3, including quotes. In 2008 Lieutenant General Stultz initiated the Employer Partnership Initiative, "a joint venture designed to give business leaders real world benefits for employing and sharing soldier-employees." The American Trucking Association and Inova Health Systems of Northern Virginia became the first two businesses to sign agreements with the Army Reserve. In 2009 the plan expanded from the USAR to "all seven reserve components, family members, wounded warriors, and veterans," and the name changed to the Employer Partnership of the Armed Forces. By 2010 more than 1,300 employers participated in the partnership; see Coker, *Indispensable Force*, 435–436, including endnote quotes; Chu interview, 22 Apr 2013.

50. "Affordable Health Care," *National Guard*, Sep 2007, 14; "DoD Offers Health Care as Deployment Reward," *National Guard*, Apr 2005, 22–23; "New Three-Tier Tricare Coverage Plan Begins," *National Guard*, Aug 2006, 18; "TRICARE Reserve Select Monthly Rates Reduced," *National Guard*, Feb 2009, 14; "TRICARE Reserve Numbers Increase," *National Guard*, Sep 2009, 37; Coker, *Indispensable Force*, 423; Punaro interview, 23 Sep 2013; "New TRICARE benefits provide retired reservists with earlier coverage," *Continental Marine*, Oct–Dec 2009, 10; "TRICARE Sought for Gray Area Retirees," *National Guard*, Jul 2008, 14. The Tricare eligibility of "gray area" retirees was delayed until October 2010 and, even then, rates were considerably higher than initially expected; see "TRICARE Benefit Delayed For 'Gray Area' Retirees," *National Guard*, Aug 2010, 24; "'Gray Area' TRICARE Benefit Includes Sky-High Premiums," *National Guard*, Sep 2010, 14; "TRICARE for Guard Retirees Available, But Expensive," *National Guard*, Oct 2010, 16.

51. CNGR, *Transforming the National Guard and Reserves*, 309, 311, including quotes 1 and 3, 4–6, Stultz quoted by CNGR; Marine Corps Order 3000.19A, 25 Aug 2010 subj: U.S. Marine Corps total force mobilization, activation, integration, and deactivation plan (short title: USMC MAID-P), 3–16, including quote 2. For the parallel paragraph in the 2007 version, see MAID-P, 6 Jul 2007, C-1-8. Although "demobilization" and "deactivation" were distinct terms, for the purpose of this paragraph it appeared the Marine Corps order's section on "deactivation" matched closely enough to "demobilization" for them to be used interchangeably. Indeed, some allowances must be made for any meaningful discussion of the several components because of different terminology between them. In some cases, differences exist even between similar components, such as the Air Force Reserve and Air National Guard, to whom, for example, a "transfer to active duty" does not mean the same thing; see Langley interview, 22 Mar 2013. Department of the Army, *Army Regulation 40-35, Dental Readiness and Community Oral Health Protection* (Washington, DC: Headquarters Department of the Army, 2 Aug 2004), i, <http://armypubs.army.mil/epubs/pdf/r40_35.pdf>, accessed 23 Feb 2015.

52. Coker, *Indispensable Force*, 412–413; Coker, *2008/2009 Biannual Army Reserve Historical Summary*, 34; *The United States Army Reserve 2010 Posture Statement*, iv; Coker, *Army Reserve 2011 Annual Summary*, 32; Geren interview, 2 Apr 2014. Note the term "Army Selected (not 'Select') Reserve Dental Readiness System" was used in USAR's 2008/2009 summary. Note that *Indispensable Force* specified "mobilization dental readiness" for the 74 percent statistic but did not use the word "mobilization" when stating the "52.5 percent dental readiness." We elected to assume that the percentages, used in consecutive paragraphs, did in fact compare apples to apples. *Army Regulation 40-35* did not employ the term, "mobilization dental readiness." In the FY 2008 NDAA, Congress extended from 90 to 180 days the period following separation from active duty (of 90 days or longer) during which a member was eligible to receive "onetime dental treatment" from the VA; see CNGR, *Transforming the National Guard and Reserves*, 314. Note the Army Reserve maintained paper medical and dental records until 2009 when it began implementation of digitized records under the Health Readiness Record system; see Coker, *2008/2009 Biannual Army Reserve Historical Summary*, 35. Sources varied on the USAR's dental readiness percentage in 2008, but slightly above 50 percent was a good estimate.

David L. McGinnis, Statement before the House Committee on Armed Services, Subcommittee on Personnel, 27 Jul 2011, including quotes, <http://www.dod.mil/dodgc/olc/docs/testMcGinnis07272011.pdf>, accessed 24 Feb 2015, webpage discontinued.

53. Casey Coane, "Seascape IV," *Naval Reserve Association News*, May 2009, 19.

54. Cotton interview, 6 Jun 2013; memo, Commander, Navy Reserve Forces Command, 17 Mar 2008, subj: Reunion and reintegration return warrior event, copy provided to Marion by Capt. John E. Cole, USN, ret., on 24 Oct 2013; Peter Weeks, OASD(RA), Director, Center of Excellence, Office for Reintegration Programs, email message to Marion, 6 Mar 2014. The original name was Returning Warrior *Weekend*, but in 2007 it was changed to *Workshop*. The policy of all redeploying personnel from Afghanistan spending several days at an intermediate station, Manas Air Base, Kyrgyzstan, provided a limited opportunity to "decompress" and begin the transition process; Marion's observations, Manas Air Base, Jun 2009, May 2011.

Returning Warrior Workshop Instruction Manual (N.p.: [Navy] Deployment Support Program, ca. mid-2007), conclusion, preface and overview, including quotes, copy emailed to Marion by Capt. John E. Cole, USN, ret., 24 Oct 2013, copy at AFHRA; Capt. Andrew J. Turnley, USN, ret., email message to Marion, 31 Jan and 3 Feb 2014. On acknowledgment of Turnley's key role: John E. Cole, email message to Marion, 24 Oct 2013. A Navy captain is an O-6; for reasons of standardization, the Navy's rank abbreviation was not used in the text. Of USNR's mobilized personnel, 90 percent served as individual augmentees; see *Returning Warrior Workshop Instruction Manual*. "Navy Reserve Returning Warrior Workshop," briefing, slide 5 of 8, provided to Marion by John E. Cole on 24 Oct 2013.

55. *Returning Warrior Workshop Manual*, conclusion, including quote; Capt. John E. Cole, USN, ret., email messages to Marion, 16 Apr 2014; Cotton interview, 6 Jun 2013; Coane, "Seascape IV," 19. In 1999 the Guard began a program known as "Building Strong and Ready Families," which evolved into the Army's "Strong Bonds Enrichment" program. The program was designed to "increase Soldier and family readiness through relationship education and skills training." Although not actually part of Yellow Ribbon, Strong Bonds also sought to improve marital and family relationships. The Army Reserve held more than 200 Strong Bonds events in FY 2008; and more than 300 events with some 12,500 participants three years later. In 2008 the Guard reported 8,000 soldiers and family members had attended Strong Bonds events. Similar in some respects to RWW, it also differed. For instance, Strong Bonds was chaplain-led whereas RWW was not (although chaplains were key participants). Also, Strong Bonds included some activities *prior to* a deployment; see "Army Strong Bonds Program," at http://www.strongbonds.org/skins/strongbonds/home.aspx, accessed 25 Feb 2015; Coker, *2008/2009 Biannual Army Reserve Historical Summary*, 65; Coker, *Indispensable Force*, 426; Coker, *Army Reserve 2011 Annual Summary*, 48–49; "Marriages Strengthened at 'Strong Bonds' Event," *National Guard*, Oct 2008, 25–26.

56. "Guardsman Called Upbeat Day before Suicide," *Associated Press*, 22 Aug 2004, <http://www.seacoastonline.com/article/20040822/News/308229983>, 20 Apr 2015; Janet S. Salotti, Chief of Reintegration and Transition Office for NGB, conversation with Marion, Arlington Hall, VA, 31 Mar 2015; Ron Jensen, "Beyond the Yellow Ribbon," *National Guard*, Jan 2008, 22–23.

57. Jensen, "Beyond the Yellow Ribbon," 23, including quotes. A waiver from the defense secretary was required for a National Guard unit to hold a mandatory formation within 60 days of the unit's redeployment. In April 2008 USD(P&R) Dr. Chu changed the policy to allow "reintegration training programs" to be held within 60 days of *demobilization*; see memo, USD(P&R) to Secretary of the Army, Secretary of the Navy, Secretary of the Air Force, 2 Apr 2008, subj: Change to current mobilization/demobilization personnel and pay policy, copy at AFHRA.

58. National Defense Authorization Act for Fiscal Year 2008, Pub. L. No. 110-181, 122 Stat. 123, § 582, Yellow Ribbon Reintegration Program, including quote, <http://www.gpo.gov/fdsys/pkg/PLAW-110publ181/pdf/PLAW-110publ181.pdf>, accessed 25 Feb 2015; "Reintegration Program Part of House Mark," *National Guard*, Jun 2007, 14; Saxby Chambliss, "Just Rewards," *National Guard*, Sep 2008, 18; Weeks, email message to Marion, 6 Mar 2014; on Alabama: Katrina Timmons, "Yellow Ribbon Program Debuts for Alabama Troops, Families," *National Guard*, Oct 2008, 57–58; "Yellow Ribbon Program: Big and Getting Bigger," *National Guard*, Nov 2009, 16–17; Coker, *2008/2009 Biannual Army Reserve Historical Summary*, 64–65, 111; Coker, *Indispensable Force*, 425–426; McGinnis interview, 7 Mar 2014; Cmdr. Robert M. Cooper, Yellow Ribbon Program Manager, USCG, email message to Marion, 12 Aug 2014.

59. National Defense Authorization Act for Fiscal Year 2008, 122 Stat. 125, including quote 1; Terry L. Stegemeyer, Chief, USARC Services and Support Division, Fort Bragg, NC, conversation with Marion, 14 Mar 2014; Coker, *Indispensable Force*, 425–426; Salotti conversation, 31 Mar 2015, including quote 2; "Yellow Ribbon Veteran's Career and Benefit Fair," Vimeo video, 29 Jun 2010, posted by WorkSource Oregon, <https://vimeo.com/12944683>, accessed 20 Apr 2015. In any case, two arguments favored the longer version of Yellow Ribbon: first, personnel suffering from PTSD/TBI did not necessarily manifest their injuries until several months after returning home; and, second, the law itself stated the "Reconstitution Phase shall constitute the period from arrival at home station until 180 days following demobilization" (125). The Army Reserve held both local and regional events, according to conversations with Stegemeyer and Salotti.

60. McGinnis, Statement, HCAS Subcommittee on Personnel, including quote 1; McGinnis interview, 7 Mar 2014; HCAS, *Report on H.R. 1960, National Defense Authorization Act for Fiscal Year 2014*, report 113-102 (Washington, DC: GPO, 7 Jun 2013), 152, including quote 2, <http://www.gpo.gov/fdsys/pkg/CRPT-113hrpt102/pdf/CRPT-113hrpt102.pdf>, accessed 25 Feb 2015. In FY 2011, Yellow Ribbon transferred to another office for administrative control but remained under the Pentagon's OASD(RA). Yellow Ribbon funding in FY 2012 was $23.7 million.

61. Coker, *Indispensable Force*, 426–429; "Family Readiness Groups Honored," *National Guard*, Mar 2008, 22.

62. Sarah A. Lister, Sidath Viranga Panangala, and Christine Scott, *"Wounded Warrior" and Veterans Provisions in the FY2008 National Defense Authorization Act: Report for Congress* (Washington, DC: Congressional Research Service, 13 Feb 2008), <https://www.fas.org/sgp/crs/misc/RL34371.pdf>, accessed 25 Feb 2015; Coker, *Indispensable Force*, 424.

63. Maj. Christopher J. Iazzetta, USMC, interview by Forrest L. Marion, 12 Jul 2013, OSD/HO, copy at AFHRA; Capt. Ryan M. Powell, email message to Marion, 8 Jan 2014; report, director, operations and plans directorate, Marine Corps Reserve, to commandant of the Marine Corps, 14 Mar 2008, subj: Annual command chronology [2007], Archives & Special Collections, Library of the Marine Corps, Quantico, VA; Aquita Brown, "Reserve Medical Entitlement Determination Program Aids Wounded Reserve Marines," *Continental Marines*, Fall 2011, 8, including quotes 1–2; Capt. Ryan M. Powell, USMC, telephone conversation with Marion, 8 Jan 14, including quote 3; Hope Hodge Seck, "No End in Sight for Marines' Wounded Warrior Regiment as War Winds Down," *Marine Corps Times*, 18 Jan 2014, including quote 4, Amos quoted by Seck, <http://www.marinecorpstimes.com/article/20140118/NEWS/301180003/No-end-sight-Marines-Wounded-Warrior-Regiment-war-winds-down>, accessed 25 Feb 2015, webpage discontinued; Iazzetta interview, 12 Jul 2013; Capt. Leticia Reyes, "Wounded Warrior

Regiment Dedicates Call Center to Fallen Marine," Headquarters Marine Corps news, 9 Dec 2008, <http://www.hqmc.marines.mil/News/News-Article-Display/Article/552805/wounded-warrior-regiment-dedicates-call-center-to-fallen-marine>, accessed 12 Aug 2014; McGinnis interview, 7 Mar 2014. Note that in 2009 an Army policy change allowed for wounded or ill ARNG and USAR soldiers to recover at warrior transition units or hospitals near their hometowns; see "Wounded Can Heal Closer to Home," *National Guard*, Jul 2009, 18–19.

64. LAPS Walk, "Ernie Irvan Returns to the Racetrack with Fellow NASCAR Celebrities for LAPS Walk," press release, 13 Aug 2007, <http://www.aaa.com/aaa/047/PDF/LAPSReleaseAug2007.pdf>, 25 Feb 2015, including quote; Mark W. Hamrick, interview by Forrest L. Marion, 16 Apr 2013, OSD/HO, copy at AFHRA; McGinnis interview, 7 Mar 2014.

65. Of the CNGR's 95 recommendations, Secretary Gates approved 82; see Coker, *2008/2009 Biannual Army Reserve Historical Summary*, xlvii. The Marines' pay/personnel system was known as the Marine Corps Total Force System. For details, see chapter 5, present work.

66. Ron Jensen, "Former Chief Retires," *National Guard*, Jun 2010, 14, including quotes, quote 2 quoted by Jensen.

Chapter 8

1. CNGR, *Transforming the National Guard and Reserves*, unnumbered page (accompanying letter, Arnold L. Punaro to Robert Gates, 31 Jan 2008), including quotes.

2. Morgan Mann, "The Operational Reserve," 43–45, including quotes 1–2; McCarthy interview, 17 Sep 2013, including quotes 3–5; McGinnis, Statement, HCAS Subcommittee on Personnel, including quotes 6–7; David S. C. Chu, "New Mobilization Reality," *National Guard*, Feb 2007, 12, including quote 8; Punaro interview, 23 Sep 2013, including quote 9; Carpenter interview, 7 Mar 2012, part 3, including quote 10; Ron Jensen, "Citizen Warrior," 33, including quote 11, Tafanelli quoted by Jensen; Ron Jensen, "Challenging Forecasts," *National Guard*, Oct 2011, 30–37, including quote 12 (page 37), Winnefeld quoted by Jensen.

3. Committee on Civilian Components, *Reserve Forces for National Security*, 4, including quote.

4. Hall interview, 23 Sep 2013, including quote 1 (emphasis added); David E. Shaver, "Closing Ranks: The Secret of Army Active and Reserve Component Harmony," U.S. Army War College paper (Carlisle Barracks, PA: Strategic Studies Institute, 1992), 3, including quotes 2–3 (emphasis in original); McCarthy interview, 17 Sep 2013, including quote 4; Vaughn interview, 25 Mar 2015, including quote 5.

5. DoD, News Release 472-97, 11 Sep 1997, including quotes 1–3; McCarthy interview, 17 Sep 2013; Cotton interview, 6 Jun 2013; Punaro interview, 23 Sep 2013.

6. Robert E. Kramek, "A View from the Bridge," 3; Day interview, 6 Mar 2012, 4–5; Department of Defense Directive 1200.17, 29 Oct 2008, 6, including quote 1; *Managing the Reserve Components as an Operational Force*.

7. Kristy N. Kamarck, *Military Retirement: Background and Recent Developments* (Washington, DC: Congressional Research Service, 2017), 2. During the same period, the number of regulars in retirement increased by only 2.2 percent, though their total compensation

increased 38.5 percent. Individually, regular retirement checks grew faster, but as a percentage of overall retirement pay, the reserve share grew from 10 to 13.5 percent.

8. Laird, *National Security Strategy of Realistic Deterrence*, 24, including quote 1; McCarthy interview, 17 Sep 2013, including quote 2.

Appendix 2

1. Former ASD(RA) Stephen M. Duncan preferred the term *augmentation* in lieu of *mobilization* with regard to activations under Title 10, U.S. Code, Section 673b authority; see his *Citizen Warriors*, 36–37, 62–63.

2. AGRs were reserve component members serving on active duty, mainly with reserve units/organizations. Military technicians were federal civilians, most of whom maintained "dual status" as members of the Selected Reserve assigned to the same units they served as civilians.

3. While most AR Marines served in support of RC units, some supported the active component.

Selected Bibliography

Document Collections

Air Force Historical Research Agency, Maxwell Air Force Base, Alabama.
Air Force Reserve Command History Office, Robins Air Force Base, Georgia.
American Presidency Project, <http://www.presidency.ucsb.edu>.
Office of the Secretary of Defense Historical Office, Arlington, Virginia.
Rumsfeld Papers, <http://papers.rumsfeld.com>.

Periodicals

Air Force Bulletin

Air Force Information Policy Letter for Commanders

Air Force Magazine

American Forces Press Service

Army (also known as the Green Book)

Army Reservist

Army Times

Biannual Army Reserve Historical Summary

Boston Globe

Chicago Tribune

Christian Science Monitor

Coast Guard Reservist

Continental Marine

Cornell Daily Sun

Defense Issues

Department of the Army Historical Summary

Grand Forks Herald

Joint Force Quarterly

Life

Los Angeles Times

Marine Corps Gazette

National Guard

Naval Reserve Association News

New York Times

Parameters

Philadelphia Inquirer

Reservist

Sea Power

Show Me

Soldiers

Time

U.S. News & World Report

USA Today

Washington Post

Washington Times

Interviews by Forrest L. Marion

Copies can be found at the Office of the Secretary of Defense Historical Office and the Air Force Historical Research Agency. An asterisk (*) indicates that the interview has not been transcribed.

Albrecht, Kenneth J., and Earnest W. Sowell. 21 Aug 2013.*

Baldwin, Col. Charles P. 11 Jun 2013.

Blum, Lt. Gen. Steven H. 17 Mar 2015.*

Chapman, Col. Dennis P. 14 Jun 2013.

Chu, David S.C. 22 Apr 2013.

Cotton, Vice Adm. John G. 6 Jun 2013.

Day, Rear Adm. Steven E. 6 Mar 2012.

Geren, Preston M. 2 Apr 2014.*

Hall, Rear Adm. Thomas F. 23 Sep 2013.

Hamrick, MSgt. Mark W. 16 Apr 2013.*

Iazzetta, Maj. Christopher J. 12 Jul 2013.

Langley, Wanda R. 22 Mar 2013.

Lanuzo, Lt. Col. Anthony, and Lt. Col. Louis Proper. 26 Mar 2013.

Lee-James, Deborah. 12 Sep 2014.*

McCarthy, Lt. Gen. Dennis M. 17 Sep 2013.

McCracken, Capt. John J., III, and Joyce Z. Randle. 25 Apr 2013.*

McGinnis, Brig. Gen. David L. 7 Mar 2014.

McKinley, General Craig R. 10 Mar 2014.

O'Connell, Charles F., Jr. 15 Aug 2013.*

Papp, Admiral Robert J., Jr. 9 Mar 2012.

Porche, Chief Warrant Officer 3 Robin C. 10 and 12 Jul 2013.

Porter, Col. James E. 10 Dec 2013.*

Powell, Daniel N., Gerald J. Mekosh, and Columbus Brown Jr. 22 Aug 2013.*

Pratt, Col. Paul E. 11 Jul 2013.

Punaro, Maj. Gen. Arnold L. 23 Sep 2013.

Smiley, Col. Robert H. 1 May 2012 and 24 Sep 2013.

Smith, Master Chief Petty Officer Jeffrey D. 5 Mar 2012.

Vaughn, Lt. Gen. Clyde A. 25 Mar 2015.*

Wightman, Maj. Gen. Richard O. W., Jr. 7 Mar 2014.

Additional Interviews

Abell, Charles. Interview by Thomas Christiansen and Anthony Crain, OSD Historical Office. 16 Sep 2014. OSD/HO, copy at AFHRA.

Altshuler, Maj. Gen. Herbert L. Interview by Suzanne L. Summers. 29 Jan 2002. Army Reserve History Office.

Bradley, Lt. Gen. John A. Interview by Betty R. Kennedy, AFRC History Office. Apr-May 2008. AFRC/HO, copy at AFHRA.

Carpenter, Maj. Gen. Raymond W. Interview by Les' Melnyk. 7 Mar 2012 (in 3 parts). ARNG Readiness Center, copy at AFHRA.

Hargraves, John F. Interview by Army Reserve Historical Office. 2 Apr 2013. Army Reserve History Office.

Plewes, Lt. Gen. Thomas J. Interview by Kathryn R. Coker, Army Reserve History Office. 15 Nov 2010. Army Reserve History Office.

Plewes, Lt. Gen. Thomas L. Interview by Suzanne L. Summers. 29 Apr 2002. Army Reserve History Office.

Severson, Brig. Gen. Richard R. Interview by Betty R. Kennedy, AFRC History Office. Jul 2008. AFRC/HO, copy at AFHRA.

Stultz, Lt. Gen. Jack C. Interview by Kathryn R. Coker, Army Reserve History Office. 3 Aug 2010. Army Reserve History Office.

Stultz, Lt. Gen. Jack C. Interview by Kathryn R. Coker, Army Reserve History Office. 6 Jul 2012. Army Reserve History Office.

Totushek, Vice Adm. John B. Interview by Capt. Kevin Gillis, USNR, et al. 14 Oct 2003. Navy Department Library, copy at AFHRA.

Webb, James H., Jr. Interview by Alfred Goldberg and Roger Trask, OSD Historical Office. 3 and 15 Jun 1998. OSD/HO.

Additional Sources

Anderson, David P. *Storm Surge: The Role of the Air National Guard in Hurricane Katrina Relief Operations*. [Arlington, VA]: National Guard Bureau, 2011.

Aspin, Les. *Report On The Bottom-Up Review*. Washington, DC: Department of Defense, 1993. <http://www.dod.mil/pubs/foi/administration_and_Management/other/515.pdf>, accessed 2 Dec 2014.

Bigelow, Rick, Mel Chaloupka, and Andy Rockett. "United States Naval Reserve: Chronology 1992." Naval Reserve Project, 1 Oct 1992. Navy Department Library Special Collections. Washington Navy Yard, Washington DC.

Boehm, William B., Renee Hylton, and Thomas W. Mehl. *In Katrina's Wake: The National Guard on the Gulf Coast, 2005*. Arlington, VA: National Guard Bureau, [2010]

Booth, Bradford, et al. *What We Know About Army Families: 2007 Update*. N.p.: ICF International, [2007] <http://tapartnership.org/enterprise/docs/RESOURCE%20BANK/RB-FAMILY-DRIVEN%20APPROACHES/General%20Resources/What_We_Know_about_Army_Families_2007.pdf>, accessed 11 Mar 2015.

Brauner, Marygail K., Timothy Jackson, and Elizabeth K. Gayton. *Medical Readiness of the Reserve Component*. Santa Monica, CA: RAND Center for Military Health Policy Research, 2012.

Bush, George H. W. Executive Order 12743: Ordering the Ready Reserve of the Armed Forces to Active Duty. 18 Jan 1991. <http://www.presidency.ucsb.edu/ws/?pid=23582>, accessed 24 Jul 2014.

Bush, George W. Executive Order 13223. 14 Sep 2001. <http://www.gpo.gov/fdsys/pkg/FR-2001-09-18/pdf/01-23359.pdf>, accessed 20 May 2015.

Cantwell, Gerald T. *The Air Force Reserve in the Vietnam Decade: 1965–1975*. Robins Air Force Base, GA: Directorate of Historical Services, Headquarters Air Force Reserve, November 1979.

————. *Citizen Airmen: A History of the Air Force Reserve, 1946–1994*. Washington, DC: Air Force History and Museums Program, 1997.

Capelotti, P. J. *Rogue Wave: The U.S. Coast Guard on and after 9/11*. Washington, DC: U.S. Coast Guard Historians Office, n.d.

Chapman, Dennis P. *Planning for Employment of the Reserve Components: Army Practice, Past and Present*. Land Warfare Paper No. 69. Washington, DC: Association of the United States Army, Sep 2008. <https://www.ausa.org/SiteCollectionDocuments/ILW%20Web-Ex-clusivePubs/Land%20Warfare%20Papers/LWP69.pdf>, accessed 22 Nov 2014.

————. *Manning Reserve Component Units for Mobilization: Army and Air Force Practice*. Institute of Land Warfare, Sep 2009. <http://www.ausa.org/publications/ilw/ilw_pubs/landwarfarepapers/Documents/LWP74.pdf>, accessed 4 Feb 2015.

Coker, Kathryn Roe. *The 2001 Army Reserve Historical Summary*. Fort McPherson, GA: Office of Army Reserve History, 2003.

————. *The 2002 Army Reserve Historical Summary*. Fort McPherson, GA: Office of Army Reserve History, 2004.

————. *The 2003 Army Reserve Historical Summary*. Fort McPherson, GA: Office of Army Reserve History, 2006.

————. *The 2004/2005 Biannual Army Reserve Historical Summary*. Fort McPherson, GA: Office of Army Reserve History, 2007.

————. *The 2006/2007 Biannual Army Reserve Historical Summary*. Fort McPherson, GA: Office of Army Reserve History, 2008.

————. *The 2008/2009 Biannual Army Reserve Historical Summary*. Fort Bragg, NC: Office of Army Reserve History, 2013.

————. *United States Army Reserve 2011 Annual Historical Summary*. Fort Bragg, NC: Office of Army Reserve History, 2013.

————. *The Indispensable Force: The Post-Cold War Operational Army Reserve, 1990–2010*. Fort Bragg, NC: Office of Army Reserve History, 2013.

————. *United States Army Reserve Mobilization for the Korean War*. Fort Bragg, NC: Office of Army Reserve History, 2013. <http://permanent.

access.gpo.gov/gpo38677/Korean%20War%20Pub_Revised%20
June%2012-2013.pdf>, accessed 14 Oct 2014.

Commission on Roles and Missions of the Armed Forces. *Directions for Defense: Report of the Commission.* Washington, DC: GPO, 1995. <http://www.dod.mil/pubs/foi/operation_and_plans/Other/734. pdf>, accessed 4 Dec 2014.

Commission on the National Guard and Reserves. *Transforming the National Guard and Reserves into a 21st-Century Operational Force.* Arlington, VA: CNGR, 31 Jan 2008.

Crecca, Thomas W. *United States Marine Corps Reserve Operations: 11 September 2001 to November 2003.* New Orleans: U.S. Marine Corps Reserve, 2005.

Crossland, Richard B., and James Currie. *Twice the Citizen: A History of the United States Army Reserve, 1908–1983.* Washington, DC: Office of the Chief, Army Reserve, 1984.

Department of Defense. *Annual Report of the Secretary of Defense on Reserve Affairs Fiscal Year 1977.* Washington, DC: DoD, n.d.

———. News Release, No. 127-03. "National Guard and Reserve Mobilized As Of March 19, 2003." 19 Mar 03. <http://www.defense.gov/releases/release.aspx?releaseid=3664>, accessed 15 Jan 2015.

———. News Release, Office of the Assistant Secretary of Defense for Public Affairs, No. 472-97. "Secretary Cohen Signs Memorandum Emphasizing Increased Reliance On The Reserve Components." 11 Sep 1997. <http://www.defense.gov/Releases/Release.aspx?ReleaseID=1390>, accessed 9 Mar 2015.

———. *Quadrennial Defense Review Report, 2006.* Washington, DC: 6 Feb 2006. <http://www.defense.gov/qdr/report/Report20060203.pdf>, accessed 9 Feb 2015.

———. *Quadrennial Defense Review Report, 2010.* [Washington, DC, 2010].

Department of Defense, Committee on Civilian Components. *Reserve Forces for National Security: Report to the Secretary of Defense.* Washington, DC: GPO, 1948.

Doubler, Michael D. *Civilian in Peace, Soldier in War: The Army National Guard, 1636–2000.* Lawrence: University Press of Kansas, 2003.

———. *The National Guard and the War on Terror: The Attacks of 9/11 and Homeland Security.* Washington, DC: National Guard Bureau, Office of Public Affairs, May 2006.

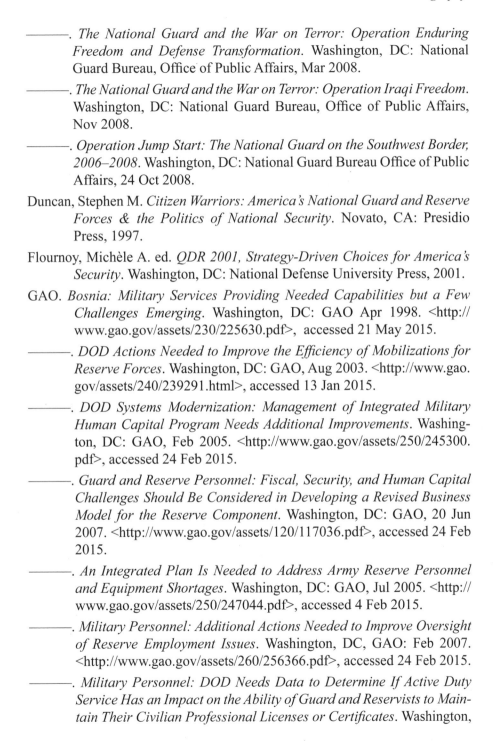

———. *The National Guard and the War on Terror: Operation Enduring Freedom and Defense Transformation.* Washington, DC: National Guard Bureau, Office of Public Affairs, Mar 2008.

———. *The National Guard and the War on Terror: Operation Iraqi Freedom.* Washington, DC: National Guard Bureau, Office of Public Affairs, Nov 2008.

———. *Operation Jump Start: The National Guard on the Southwest Border, 2006–2008.* Washington, DC: National Guard Bureau Office of Public Affairs, 24 Oct 2008.

Duncan, Stephen M. *Citizen Warriors: America's National Guard and Reserve Forces & the Politics of National Security.* Novato, CA: Presidio Press, 1997.

Flournoy, Michèle A. ed. *QDR 2001, Strategy-Driven Choices for America's Security.* Washington, DC: National Defense University Press, 2001.

GAO. *Bosnia: Military Services Providing Needed Capabilities but a Few Challenges Emerging.* Washington, DC: GAO Apr 1998. <http://www.gao.gov/assets/230/225630.pdf>, accessed 21 May 2015.

———. *DOD Actions Needed to Improve the Efficiency of Mobilizations for Reserve Forces.* Washington, DC: GAO, Aug 2003. <http://www.gao.gov/assets/240/239291.html>, accessed 13 Jan 2015.

———. *DOD Systems Modernization: Management of Integrated Military Human Capital Program Needs Additional Improvements.* Washington, DC: GAO, Feb 2005. <http://www.gao.gov/assets/250/245300.pdf>, accessed 24 Feb 2015.

———. *Guard and Reserve Personnel: Fiscal, Security, and Human Capital Challenges Should Be Considered in Developing a Revised Business Model for the Reserve Component.* Washington, DC: GAO, 20 Jun 2007. <http://www.gao.gov/assets/120/117036.pdf>, accessed 24 Feb 2015.

———. *An Integrated Plan Is Needed to Address Army Reserve Personnel and Equipment Shortages.* Washington, DC: GAO, Jul 2005. <http://www.gao.gov/assets/250/247044.pdf>, accessed 4 Feb 2015.

———. *Military Personnel: Additional Actions Needed to Improve Oversight of Reserve Employment Issues.* Washington, DC, GAO: Feb 2007. <http://www.gao.gov/assets/260/256366.pdf>, accessed 24 Feb 2015.

———. *Military Personnel: DOD Needs Data to Determine If Active Duty Service Has an Impact on the Ability of Guard and Reservists to Maintain Their Civilian Professional Licenses or Certificates.* Washington,

DC: GAO, 27 May 2008. <http://www.gao.gov/assets/100/95490. html>, accessed 14 Jan 2015.

———. *National Guard: Peacetime Training Did Not Adequately Prepare Combat Brigades for Gulf War*. Washington, DC: GAO, Sep 1991. <http://www.gao.gov/assets/160/151085.pdf>, accessed 10 Mar 2015.

Gross, Charles Joseph. *The Air National Guard and the American Military Tradition: Militiaman, Volunteer, and Professional*. Washington, DC: Historical Services Division, National Guard Bureau, 1995.

———. *Prelude to the Total Force: The Air National Guard, 1943–1969*. Washington, DC: Office of Air Force History, 1985.

House Committee on Armed Services. *First Interim Report of Subcommittee No. 1, Committee on Armed Services, House of Representatives, on Implementation of the Reserve Forces Act of 1955*. Washington, DC: GPO, 1956.

———. *Military Reserve Posture, Report of Subcommittee No. 3 on Military Reserve Posture*. Washington, DC: GPO, 17 Aug 1962.

———. *National Reserve Plan, House of Representatives, Report No. 457* [to accompany H.R. 5297]. Washington, DC: GPO, 1955.

House Committee on Armed Services, Military Personnel and Compensation Subcommittee. *Redeployment of Reserves From Operation Desert Storm, Hearing, April 18, 1991*. Washington, DC: GPO, 1992.

House Committee on National Security, Military Personnel Subcommittee, *Reserve Component Issues from the Quadrennial Defense Review: Hearing, July 29, 1997*. Washington, DC: GPO, 1998. <http://babel. hathitrust.org/cgi/pt?id=pst.000032141221#view=1up;seq=5>, accessed 5 Dec 2014.

House Committee on Veterans' Affairs. *Witness Testimony of Major General Larry W. Shellito, Minnesota National Guard, Adjutant General*. 18 Oct 2007. <http://veterans.house.gov/witness-testimony/major-general-larry-w-shellito>, accessed 25 Feb 2015.

Kennedy, Betty R., and Donald C. Boyd, et al. *Turning Point 9.11, Air Force Reserve in the 21st Century, 2001–2011*. Robins AFB, GA: Headquarters Air Force Reserve Command, 2012.

Kreidberg, Marvin A., and Merton G. Henry. *History of Military Mobilization in the United States Army, 1775–1945*. Washington, DC: Department of the Army, 1955.

Laird, Melvin R. *National Security Strategy of Realistic Deterrence: Secretary of Defense Melvin R. Laird's Annual Defense Department Report, FY 1973*. [Washington, DC, 1972].

Linn, Brian McAllister. *The Philippine War, 1899–1902.* Lawrence: University Press of Kansas, 2000.

Luttrell, Marcus. *Lone Survivor: The Eyewitness Account of Operation Redwing and the Lost Heroes of SEAL Team 10.* With Patrick Robinson. New York and Boston: Little, Brown, 2007.

Mahon, John K. *History of the Militia and the National Guard.* New York and London: Macmillan, 1983.

Malone, Lauren, et al. *An Analysis of Marine Corps Reserve Mobilization Processes and Policies.* [Washington, DC]: Center for Naval Analyses, 2009. <https://www.mccll.usmc.mil/index.cfm?disp=myIdolSearch_XML.cfm>, accessed 9 Mar 2015, via Marine Corps Center for Lessons Learned.

Marine Corps Division of Reserve. *The Marine Corps Reserve: A History.* Washington, DC: Division of Reserve, Headquarters, U.S. Marine Corps, 1966.

Marine Corps Reserve Combat Assessment Team. *Marine Corps Reserve Forces in Operation Iraqi Freedom: Lessons Learned.* Quantico, VA: Marine Corps Combat Development Center, Jan 2004. <http://www.globalsecurity.org/military/library/report/2004/usmcr-oif-ll_efcat_5-20-2004.pdf>, accessed 10 Mar 2015.

McGinnis, David L. Statement before the House Committee on Armed Services, Subcommittee on Personnel. 27 Jul 2011. <http://www.dod.mil/dodgc/olc/docs/testMcGinnis07272011.pdf>, accessed 24 Feb 2015. Webpage discontinued.

Millett, Allan R., and Peter Maslowski. *For the Common Defense: A Military History of the United States of America.* New York and London: Free Press, 1984.

National Guard Bureau. *Annual Review of the Chief, Fiscal Year 2002.* Arlington, VA: National Guard Bureau, [2002].

———. *Annual Review of the Chief, Fiscal Year 2003.* Arlington, VA: National Guard Bureau, [2003].

———. *Annual Review, 2004.* Arlington, VA, ca. 2004.

———. *Annual Review, Fiscal Year 2005.* N.p., ca. 2005.

Obama, Barak. "Remarks by the President in Address to the Nation on the Way Forward in Afghanistan and Pakistan." 1 Dec 2009. <http://www.nytimes.com/2009/03/27/us/politics/27obama-text.html>, accessed 23 Feb 2015.

[Office of the Assistant Secretary of Defense (Manpower, Reserve Affairs and Logistics)]. *Report on Full-Time Training and Administration of the Selected Reserve* [Gerard Study]. Jun 1978.

Pace, Peter. *Posture Statement of General Peter Pace, USMC, Chairman of the Joint Chiefs of Staff, Before the 110th Congress, Senate Armed Services Committee.* 6 Feb 2007. <http://www.au.af.mil/au/awc/awcgate/dod/posture_6feb07pace.pdf>, accessed 20 Apr 2015.

Pogue, Forrest C. *George C. Marshall: Education of a General, 1880–1939.* New York: Viking Press, 1963.

———. *George C. Marshall: Ordeal and Hope, 1939–1942.* New York: Viking Press, 1966.

———. *George C. Marshall: Organizer of Victory, 1943–1945.* New York: Viking Press, 1973.

Reserve Forces Policy Board. *Annual Report of the Reserve Forces Policy Board, Fiscal Year 1980.* Washington, DC: Office of the Secretary of Defense, 1981.

———. *Annual Report of the Reserve Forces Policy Board, Fiscal Year 1981.* Washington, DC, [1982].

———. *Annual Report of the Reserve Forces Policy Board, Fiscal Year 1986.* Washington, DC, [1987].

———. *Annual Report of the Reserve Forces Policy Board 2003.* Washington, DC, 2004.

———. *Fiscal Year 1985 Annual Report.* Washington, DC, [1986].

———. *Reserve Component Programs, Fiscal Year 1991, Report of the Reserve Forces Policy Board.* Washington, 1992. <http://www.dtic.mil/dtic/tr/fulltext/u2/a249015.pdf>, 10 Dec 2014.

———. *Reserve Component Programs: The Annual Report of the Reserve Forces Policy Board 2003.* Washington, DC, 2004.

———. *Reserve Forces Policy Board, Fiscal Year 1983 Annual Report.* Washington, [1984]. <http://www.dtic.mil/dtic/tr/fulltext/u2/a149815.pdf>, accessed 14 Nov 2014.

Rosenfeld, Susan, and Charles Gross. *Air National Guard at 60: A History.* Arlington, VA: Air National Guard, 2007.

Rumsfeld, Donald. *Known and Unknown: A Memoir.* New York: Sentinel, 2011.

Senate Committee on Armed Services, Subcommittee on Manpower and Personnel. *Department of Defense Procedures for Return and Release from Active Duty of National Guardsmen and Reservists Called Up for Operation Desert Shield/Desert Storm: Hearing, June 11, 1991.* Washington, DC: GPO, 1991.

Senate Committee on Armed Services, Subcommittee on Personnel. *Issues Affecting Families of Soldiers, Sailors, Airmen, and Marines: Hearings and Joint Hearings.* 2 Jun and 7 Oct 2003, 24 Jun and 11 Dec 2003. Washington, DC: GPO, 2005. <https://archive.org/stream/issuesaffectingf00unit#page/208/mode/1up>, accessed 21 Jan 2015.

Shaw, Frederick J., ed. *Locating Air Force Base Sites: History's Legacy.* Washington, DC: Air Force History and Museums Program, 2014.

Smith, Holland M., and Percy Finch. *Coral and Brass.* 1949. Reprint. Nashville, TN: Battery Press, 1989.

Task Force on Reserve Mobilization Requirements. *A Report to the Secretary of Defense.* Washington, DC: Office of the Assistant Secretary of Defense for Manpower & Personnel, 1954.

Truman, Harry S. *Memoirs.* Vol. 1, *Year of Decisions.* Garden City, NY: Doubleday, 1955.

Undersecretary of Defense (Personnel and Readiness). *Activation, Mobilization, and Demobilization of the Ready Reserve.* Department of Defense Directive (DoDD) 1235.10. 23 Sep 2004.

———. Department of Defense Directive 1200.17: Managing the Reserve Components as an Operational Force. 29 Oct 2008. <http://www.dtic.mil/whs/directives/corres/pdf/120017p.pdf>, accessed 9 Mar 2015.

U.S. Army. *Dental Readiness and Community Oral Health Protection.* Army Regulation 40-35. 2 Sep 2004. <http://armypubs.army.mil/epubs/pdf/r40_35.pdf>, accessed 11 Mar 2015.

Weigley, Russell F. *History of the United States Army.* 1967. Reprint. Bloomington: Indiana University Press, 1984.

Winkler, John D., and Barbara Bicksler, eds. *The New Guard and Reserve.* San Ramon, CA: Falcon Books, 2008.

Winkler, John D., et al. "A 'Continuum of Service' for the All-Volunteer Force." In *The All-Volunteer Force: Thirty Years of Service,* edited by Barbara A. Bicksler, Curtis L. Gilroy, and John T. Warner. Washington, DC: Brassey's, 2004.

Index

Illustrations are indicated by italicized page numbers and tables by "t" following page numbers.